FROMMER'S

COMPREHENSIVE TRAVEL GUIDE

SEATTLE & PORTLAND '92-'93

by Karl Samson

D1488201

PRENTICE HALL TRAVEL

NEW YORK • LONDON • TORONTO • SYDNEY • TOKYO • SIN

For my wife,
Jane

FROMMER BOOKS

Published by Prentice Hall General Reference
A division of Simon & Schuster Inc.
15 Columbus Circle
New York, NY 10023

Copyright © 1990, 1992 by Simon & Schuster Inc.

All rights reserved, including the right of reproduction in whole or in part
in any form.

PRENTICE HALL and colophon are registered trademarks of Simon &
Schuster Inc.

ISBN 0-13-333402-3
ISSN 1045-9308

Design by Robert Bull Design
Maps by Geografix Inc.

Manufactured in the United States of America

FROMMER'S SEATTLE & PORTLAND '92–'93
Editor-in-Chief: Marilyn Wood
Senior Editor: Judith de Rubini
Editors: Alice Fellows, Paige Hughes, Theodore Stavrou
Assistant Editors: Peter Katucki, Lisa Renaud
Managing Editor: Leanne Coupe

CONTENTS

LIST OF MAPS

INVITATION TO THE READERS

In researching this book, I have come across many wonderful establishments, the best of which I have included here. I am sure that many of you will also come across appealing hotels, inns, restaurants, guest houses, shops, and attractions. Please don't keep them to yourself. Share your experiences, especially if you want to comment on places that have been included in this edition that have changed for the worse. You can address your letters to:

Karl Samson
Frommer's Seattle & Portland '92–'93
c/o Prentice Hall Travel
15 Columbus Circle
New York, NY 10023

A DISCLAIMER

Readers are advised that prices fluctuate in the course of time and travel information changes under the impact of the varied and volatile factors that affect the travel industry. Neither the author nor the publisher can be held responsible for the experiences of readers while traveling. Readers are invited to write to the publisher with ideas, comments, and suggestions for future editions.

SAFETY ADVISORY

Whenever you're traveling in an unfamiliar city or country, stay alert. Be aware of your immediate surroundings. Wear a moneybelt and keep a close eye on your possessions. Be particularly careful with cameras, purses, and wallets, all favorite targets of thieves and pickpockets.

CHAPTER 1

INTRODUCING SEATTLE

It is the Emerald City of the Northwest—the jewel in the crown of a land of natural beauty. The sparkling waters of Elliott Bay, Lake Union, and Lake Washington surround this city of shimmering skyscrapers. Forests of evergreens crowd the city limits. Everywhere you look, another breathtaking vista unfolds. Once a sleepy backwoods town, Seattle has become one of the key cities of the Pacific Rim, forging new trading links with Japan and the rest of Asia. In many ways, the city is similar to San Francisco: It is surrounded by water, was built on hills, and has a Chinatown, a large gay comunity, and even a trolley. What makes Seattle different are its people and the pace of life.

Things move more slowly up here, and although Seattle is growing more cosmopolitan by the minute, it is the wildness of the Northwest that has attracted many of the city's residents. With endless boating opportunities and beaches and mountains within a few hours' drive, Seattle is ideally situated for the active lifestyle that is so much a part of life in the Northwest. The city's rainy weather may be infamous, but the people of Seattle have ways of forgetting about the clouds. They either put on their rain gear or retreat to the city's hundreds of excellent restaurants, its dozens of theaters and performance halls, and its outstanding museums. They never let the weather stand in the way of having a good time—and neither should you. Although summer is the best time to visit Seattle, the city offers year-round diversions and entertainment.

1. CULTURE, HISTORY & BACKGROUND

GEOGRAPHY/PEOPLE

Seattle is located on Puget Sound in northwestern Washington State. To the east is Lake Washington; to the north, Lake Union; and to the

WHAT'S SPECIAL ABOUT SEATTLE

Beaches
☐ Alki Beach stretches for 2½ miles down the west side of West Seattle.

Architectural Highlights
☐ The Space Needle is a futuristic-looking tower with observation deck and two restaurants.

Museums
☐ The Museum of Flight at Boeing Field is one of the best such museums in the world.
☐ At the Seattle Aquarium you can watch salmon returning to spawn if you happen to be here at the right time of year.

Events/Festivals
☐ Seafair, Seattle's summer extravaganza, features all manner of public spectacles, from starlight parades to powerboat races.

For the Kids
☐ Seattle Center, a little amusement park in the middle of Seattle, has rides, arcade games, and a children's museum.
☐ Ye Olde Curiosity Shop is part museum of the bizarre and part tacky gift shop.

Natural Spectacles
☐ Mount Rainier, only 90 miles away, is the highest mountain in the Northwest.
☐ Olympic National Park is home not only of the Olympic Mountains but of the only rain forest in the continental United States.

☐ The San Juan Islands make an idyllic summer getaway for urban Seattleites.

Regional Food & Drink
☐ Smoked seafood, salmon in particular, is a popular Seattle delicacy.
☐ Washington State wines are ranking high in international wine competitions.

Activities
☐ Sailing, sailboarding, and sea kayaking on any of the waters surrounding Seattle are favorites.

Shopping
☐ The Pike Place Market is filled with hundreds of shops and vendors selling everything from fresh produce to fine arts and crafts.

Great Neighborhoods
☐ The International District, which would be called Chinatown anywhere else, has lots of interesting shops and good restaurants.

Offbeat Oddities
☐ The Seattle Underground Tour takes the curious under the city's streets to see the remains of old Seattle, which burned to the ground in 1889.
☐ The Bus Tunnel, under downtown Seattle, provides electric bus service. All terminals have interesting works of art.

west, Puget Sound's Elliott Bay. These bodies of water were all formed by glaciers during the last ice age. When the glaciers receded, the valleys left behind were flooded. The Cascade Mountains, a volcanic range that includes Mount St. Helens (which last erupted in 1980), are 50 miles east; Mount Rainier, the highest peak in Washington and visible from Seattle on clear days, is about 90 miles southeast. The Olympic Mountains of the Olympic Peninsula are about 60 miles west. Beyond the Olympic Mountains is the Pacific coast, with its rugged headlands and long stretches of empty beaches.

Life in Seattle has been changing dramatically in the past few years. Not too long ago, it was considered the most livable city in America, with a cultural and natural diversity unrivaled in the U.S.A. However, so appealing a city was Seattle that tens of thousands of people moved here within a matter of a few years, causing a population boom and all its inherent problems. With this rapid population growth and the development of Seattle as the business hub of the Northwest, the population has changed a bit. Jeans and down jackets have been replaced by high fashion from Europe; and if you walk into a downtown bar, you are more likely to hear financial gossip than tales of mountain climbing. No longer is the populace as laid-back as it once was. However, Seattleites are still as proud of their cultural offerings as they are of "their" mountain (Mount Rainier). They are still an active lot, with water sports (sailing and sea kayaking) and skiing dominating their athletic agendas. This isn't surprising, considering how much water surrounds the city and how close the ski slopes are.

HISTORY/POLITICS
THE EARLY DAYS

Seattle got a late start in U.S. history, and to this day the city has been trying to make up for it. The first settlers didn't arrive until 1851, although explorers had visited the region much earlier. Captain George Vancouver of the British Royal Navy—who lent his name to both Vancouver, British Columbia, and Vancouver, Washington—had explored Puget Sound as early as 1792. However, there was little to attract anyone permanently to this remote region. Unlike Oregon to the south, Washington had little rich farmland, only acres and acres of forest. It was this seemingly endless supply of wood that finally enticed the first settlers.

The first settlement was on Alki Point, in the area now known as West Seattle. Because this location was exposed to storms, within a few years the settlers moved across Elliott Bay to a more protected spot, the present downtown Seattle. The new location for the village was a tiny island surrounded by mud flats. Although some of the early

DATELINE

- **1792** Captain George Vancouver of the British Royal Navy explores Puget Sound.
- **1841** Lieutenant Charles Wilkes surveys Puget Sound and names Elliott Bay.
- **1851** The first white settlers arrive in what will become West Seattle's Alki Point.
- **1852** These same settlers move to the east side of Elliott Bay from Alki Point, which is subject to storms.
- **1853** The Washington Territory is formed. *(continues)*

DATELINE

settlers wanted to name the town New York—even then Seattle had grand aspirations—the name Seattle was chosen as a tribute to Chief Sealth, a local Native American who had befriended the newcomers.

1864 The transcontinental telegraph reaches Seattle, connecting it with the rest of the country.

1866 Chief Sealth, for whom Seattle was named, dies and is buried across Puget Sound at Suquamish.

In the middle of town, on the waterfront, the first steam-powered lumber mill on Puget Sound was built by Henry Yesler. It stood at the foot of what is now Yesler Way—but what for many years was simply referred to as Skid Road, a reference to the way logs were skidded down from the slopes behind town to the sawmill. Over the years Skid Road developed a reputation for its bars and brothels. Some say that after an East Coast journalist incorrectly referred to it as Skid Row in his newspaper, the name stuck and was subsequently applied to derelict neighborhoods all over the country. But only Seattle can lay claim to the very first Skid Row. To this day, despite attempts to revamp the neighborhood, Yesler Way still attracts the sort of visitors one would expect, but it is also in the center of the Pioneer Historic District, one of Seattle's main tourist attractions.

1875 Regular steamship service begins between Seattle and San Francisco.

1889 The Great Seattle Fire levels most of downtown.

1893 The railroad first reaches Seattle.

1897 The steamer *Portland* arrives from Alaska carrying more than a ton of gold, thus starting the Yukon gold rush.

By 1889 the city had more than 25,000 inhabitants and was well on its way to becoming the most important city in the Northwest. On June 6 of that year, however, 25 blocks in the center of town burned to the ground. By that time the city—which had spread out to low-lying land reclaimed from the mud flats—had begun experiencing problems with mud and sewage disposal. The fire gave citizens the opportunity they needed to rebuild Seattle. The solution to the drainage and sewage problems was to regrade the steep slopes to the east of the town and raise the streets above their previous levels. Because the regrading lagged behind the rebuilding, the ground floors of many new buildings wound up below street level. Eventually these lower-level shops and entrances were abandoned when elevated sidewalks bridged the space between roadways and buildings. Today sections of several abandoned streets that are now underground can be toured (see Section 4 of Chapter 7 for details).

1907 Pike Place Market is founded.

1916 William Boeing launches his first airplane from Lake Union, beginning an industry that will become Seattle's lifeblood.

1940 The Mercer Island Floating Bridge opens.

1962 The Century 21 exposition is held in Seattle and the famous Space Needle is erected.

1977 Seattle is called the most livable city in America.

1982 Seattle *(continues)*

One of the most amazing engineering feats that took place after the fire was the regrading of Denny Hill. Seattle once had seven hills, but today has only six—nothing is left of Denny Hill. Hydraulic mining techniques, with high-powered water jets digging into hillsides, were used to level the hill, of which only a name remains—Denny Regrade, a neighborhood just south of Seattle Center.

DATELINE

ranked as the number one recreational city.

The new buildings went up quickly after the fire, and eight years later another event occurred that changed the city almost as much. The steamship *Portland* arrived in Seattle from Alaska, carrying a ton of gold from the recently discovered Klondike goldfields. Within the year Seattle's population swelled with prospectors ultimately headed north. Few of them ever struck it rich, but they all stopped in Seattle to purchase supplies and equipment, thus lining the pockets of Seattle merchants and spreading far and wide the name of this obscure Northwest city. When the prospectors came south again with their hard-earned gold, much of it never left Seattle, sidetracked by beerhalls and brothels.

20TH-CENTURY SEATTLE

A very important event in Seattle history took place on Lake Union in 1916. William Boeing and Clyde Esterveld launched their first airplane, a floatplane, with the intention of flying mail to Canada. Their enterprise eventually became the Boeing Company, which has since grown to become the single largest employer in the area. Unfortunately, until recently Seattle's fortunes were so inextricably bound to those of Boeing that hard times for the aircraft manufacturer meant hard times for the whole city. In the past few years, however, industry in Seattle has begun to diversify. Floatplanes still call Lake Union home, and if you should venture out on the lake by kayak, sailboard, or boat, be sure to watch out for air traffic.

Two years before the Boeing flight, in 1914, big changes had already begun in Seattle when the Smith Tower was erected. This 42-story building soared above the skyline and was for many years the tallest building west of the Mississippi. That same skyline today is crowded with dozens of skyscrapers that dwarf the Smith Tower. Foremost among these is the new 76-story Columbia Center, which is now the tallest building west of Houston.

IMPRESSIONS

The city has changed its look three times in the last thirty years, and half a dozen times in the last century.
—TIMOTHY EGAN, *THE GOOD RAIN*

Seattle is a comparatively new-looking city that covers an old frontier town like frosting on a cake.
—WINTHROP SARGEANT, IN *THE NEW YORKER*, 1978

Despite the significance of these two buildings, the most recognizable structure on the Seattle skyline is the Space Needle. Built in 1962 for Century 21, the Seattle World's Fair, the Space Needle was, and still is, a futuristic-looking structure. Situated just north of downtown—in the Seattle Center complex that was the site of the World's Fair—the Space Needle provides stupendous views of the city and all its surrounding natural beauty.

The 1962 World's Fair was far more than a fanciful vision of the future—it was truly prophetic for Seattle. The emergence of the Emerald City as an important Pacific Rim trading center is a step toward a bright 21st century. Seattle has witnessed extraordinary growth in recent years, with the migration of thousands of people in search of jobs, a higher quality of life, and a mild climate. To keep pace with its sudden prominence on the Pacific Rim, Seattle has also been rushing to transform itself from a sleepy Northwest city into a cosmopolitan metropolis. New restaurants, theaters, and museums are cropping up all over the place as new residents demand more cultural attractions. Visitors to Seattle will immediately sense the quickening pulse of this awakening city.

ART & ARCHITECTURE

ART

Seattle—and all of the Northwest for that matter—has a burgeoning art community. Outside of the fine-art glass produced at the Pilchuk School of Glass, though, Northwestern art has yet to develop a national following as has Southwestern art. Like the American Southwest, the Pacific Northwest has a Native American art heritage, which is evident in Seattle. There are several totem poles around the city, and Northwest Coast Native American designs show up everywhere, from T-shirts to restaurant decor. Several galleries exhibit and sell the works of Native American artists and artisans, and these works command high prices. Carved wooden masks generally start at around $2,000.

ARCHITECTURE

Aside from Seattle's Space Needle, which is one of the city's most immediately identifiable symbols, there is little particularly noteworthy about Seattle architecture. Most of the city burned to the ground in the fire of 1889, so its architectural heritage dates only to the period of rebuilding. Of interest is the fact that the city fathers chose to rebuild *on top of* the rubble. In order to raise the city above the mud flats upon which it was originally built, streets were filled in with any rubble that came to hand. To this day, there are still sections of the old city accessible beneath the streets of the Pioneer Square area. These dark recesses are the focus of the Seattle Underground Tour, a rather off-color look at the city's early years.

After the fire of 1889, Seattle rebuilt in brick and cast iron to prevent another such disaster. Today many of Pioneer Square's 100-year-old buildings, with their unusual cast-iron framed windows, have been restored. Also in this area are the Smith Tower and the much larger Columbia Seafirst Center.

2. RECOMMENDED BOOKS & FILMS

BOOKS

Timothy Egan's *The Good Rain* (1990) provides an enlightening overview of life in the Pacific Northwest, with a chapter devoted to Seattle and the many changes it has gone through in the past century.

If you are interested in learning more about the history of Seattle, there are two books that I'm sure you will find much more entertaining than a standard dry history: *Sons of the Profits* and *Doc Maynard, The Man Who Invented Seattle*. Both are by Bill Speidel, the man who conceived the Seattle Underground Tour. You can pick them up in Seattle or contact the Seattle Underground Tours gift shop, 610 First Ave. (tel. 682-1511).

FILMS

The Northwest has never been a popular film destination. Its unpredictable weather makes outdoor photography chancy. However, in recent years a few films have used this area as a backdrop. *An Officer and a Gentleman* (1982) was filmed at Fort Worden State Park in Port Townsend on the Olympic Peninsula. *Twice in a Lifetime* (1985), a domestic drama starring Gene Hackman and Ann-Margret, was shot in Seattle and its environs. *WarGames* (1983), the story of a teenage computer hacker who inadvertently almost initiates World War III, was also made in the Northwest. *Immediate Family* (1989), starring James Woods and Glenn Close, is another Seattle-based film, about a childless yuppie couple who buy a baby.

CHAPTER 2

PLANNING A TRIP TO SEATTLE

Seattle is becoming an increasingly popular destination for travelers, and as its popularity grows, so too does the need for previsit planning. Before leaving home, you should try to make hotel and car reservations. Not only will these reservations save you money, but you won't have to worry about finding accommodations when you arrive. Summer is the peak tourist season in Seattle and reservations are highly advisable, especially if you plan to visit during the Seafair festival in August, when every hotel in town can be booked up.

1. INFORMATION

SOURCES OF INFORMATION

The sources of information listed here can provide you with plenty of free brochures on Seattle, many with colorful photos to further tempt you into a visit.

If you still have questions about Seattle after reading this book, contact the **Seattle–King County Convention & Visitors Bureau,** 520 Pike St., Suite 1300, Seattle, WA 98101 (tel. 206/461-5840). They'll be happy to send you more information on the city and the surrounding areas. They're open Monday through Friday from 8:30am to 5pm. To find this information center, walk up Pike Street until it goes into a tunnel under the Convention Center. You'll see the information center on your left as you enter the tunnel.

These helpful people also operate the two **Visitor Information Centers** at Seattle-Tacoma (Sea-Tac) Airport (tel. 206/433-5218). You can't miss them—they're right beside the baggage-claim area (by carousels no. 1 and 9). They have brochures on many area attractions and can answer any last-minute questions.

For information on other parts of Washington, call the **Washington State Tourism Office** (tel. 206/586-2102 or, 206/586-2088, or toll free 800/544-1800).

If you decide that you'd like to take a trip to British Columbia while in the Northwest, you can contact **Tourism British Columbia,** 720 Olive Way, Suite 930, Seattle, WA 98101 (tel. 206/623-5937, or toll free 800/663-6000), open Monday through Friday from 8:30am to 4:30pm.

WHAT THINGS COST IN SEATTLE	U.S. $
Taxi from the airport to the city center	$20.00
Bus ride between any two downtown points	Free
Local telephone call	.25
Double at the Alexis Hotel (deluxe)	165.00
Double at the WestCoast Vance (moderate)	75.00
Double at the Travelodge Seattle Airport (budget)	50.00
Lunch for one at Café Hué (moderate)	12.00
Lunch for one at Macheezmo Mouse (budget)	5.00
Dinner for one, without wine, at The Georgian Room (deluxe)	45.00
Dinner for one, without wine, at Wild Ginger Asian Restaurant (moderate)	20.00
Dinner for one, without wine, at Gravity Bar (budget)	10.00
Pint of beer	3.00
Coca-Cola	.95
Cup of coffee	1.00
Roll of ASA 100 Kodacolor film, 36 exposures	5.50
Movie ticket	6.50
Theater ticket to the Seattle Repertory Theater	16.00

2. WHEN TO GO

CLIMATE

I'm sure you've heard about the climate in Seattle. Let's face it, the city's weather has a bad reputation. As they say out here, "The rain in Spain stays mainly in Seattle." Seattle can make London look like a desert. I wish I could tell you that it just ain't so, but I can't. It rains in Seattle—and rains and rains and rains. However, when December 31 rolls around each year, a funny thing happens: They total up the year's precipitation, and Seattle almost always comes out behind such cities as Washington, D.C., Boston, New York, and Atlanta. Most of the rain falls between September and April. If you visit during the summer, you might not see a drop of rain the entire time. But if July in Seattle is just too sunny for you, take a trip out to the Hoh Valley on the Olympic Peninsula. With more than 150 inches of rain a year, this is the wettest spot in the continental United States.

No matter what time of year you plan to visit Seattle, be sure to bring at least a sweater or light jacket. Summer nights can be quite cool, and daytime temperatures rarely reach above the low 80s. Winters are not as cold as in the East, but snow does fall in Seattle.

To make things perfectly clear, here's an annual weather chart:

Average Monthly Temperatures & Rainfall

	Jan	Feb	Mar	Apr	May	June	July	Aug	Sept	Oct	Nov	Dec
Temp. (°F)	46	50	53	58	65	69	75	74	69	60	52	47
Temp. (°C)	8	10	11	15	18	21	24	23	21	16	11	9
Days of Rain	19	16	17	14	10	9	5	7	9	14	18	20

THE FESTIVAL CITY

Seattleites will have a festival at the drop of a rainhat. Summers in the city seem to revolve around the myriad festivals that take place every week. Check the "Tempo Arts & Entertainment" section of the *Seattle Times* on Friday, or pick up a copy of *Seattle Weekly* to find out what special and free events will be taking place during your visit.

SEATTLE CALENDAR OF EVENTS

JANUARY

☐ **Chinese New Year.** International District. Date depends on lunar calendar (may even be in February).

FEBRUARY

☐ **Artstorm.** Downtown Seattle. A celebration of the arts. 3rd and 4th weeks of February.

MAY

☐ **Opening Day of Boating Season.** Lake Union and Lake Washington.

☐ **Seattle International Film Festival.** Theaters around town.

✪ *NORTHWEST FOLKLIFE FESTIVAL. This is the largest folklife festival in the country, with dozens of national and regional folk musicians performing on numerous stages. In addition, craftspeople from all over the Northwest show and sell. Lots of good food and dancing too.*
   ***Where:** Seattle Center.* ***When:** Memorial Day weekend.* ***How:** Free.*

☐ **Pike Place Market Festival.** Pike Place Market. A celebration of the market, with lots of free entertainment. Memorial Day weekend.

JUNE

☐ **Out to Lunch.** Parks throughout Seattle. Free lunchtime jazz and classical music concerts. Phone 206/623-0340 for a schedule. Beginning in late June.

JULY

☐ **Fourth of July fireworks.** Elliott Bay and Seattle waterfront. July 4.
☐ **Chinatown International District Summer Festival.** International District. Features the music, dancing, arts, and food of Seattle's Asian district. 2nd Sunday in July.
☐ **Bite of Seattle.** Seattle Center. Sample offerings from Seattle's best restaurants. Mid-July.
☐ **King County Fair.** King County Fairgrounds, Enumclaw, south of Seattle. Starts the 3rd Wednesday of the month.
☐ **Bellevue Jazz Festival.** Bellevue Downtown Park, Bellevue. Showcase for Northwest jazz musicians. 3rd weekend in July.

✪ *SEAFAIR This is the biggest event of the year, during which there are festivities every day: parades, hydroplane boat races, performances by the Navy's Blue Angels, a Torchlight Parade, ethnic festivals, sporting events, and open house on naval ships. This one really packs in the out-of-towners and sends Seattleites fleeing on summer vacations.*
   ***Where:** All over Seattle.* ***When:** 3rd weekend in July to the 1st weekend in August.* ***How:** Phone 206/728-0123 for details on events and tickets.*

☐ **Pacific Northwest Arts and Crafts Fair.** Bellevue Square, Bellevue. The largest arts and crafts fair in the Northwest. Last weekend in July.

AUGUST

☐ **Santa Fe Chamber Music Festival.** Meany Hall, University of Washington.

✪ *BUMBERSHOOT* *The city's second most popular festival derives its peculiar name from a British term for umbrella—an obvious reference to the rainy Seattle weather. Lots and lots of rock-and-roll music packs Seattle's younger set into Seattle Center. However, you'll find plenty of arts and crafts on display, too.*
   Where: Seattle Center. *When:* Labor Day weekend. *How:* Phone 206/684-7200 for schedule.

3. WHAT TO PACK

A raincoat, an umbrella, and a sweater or jacket are all absolutely essential any time of year. Other than that, you might want to bring skis (snow or water), hiking boots, boat shoes, running shoes, shorts, bicycling shorts, a bathing suit, and just about any other outdoor clothing or equipment you have on hand. The outdoors is a way of life in this part of the country.

4. TIPS FOR THE DISABLED, SENIORS, SINGLES, FAMILIES & STUDENTS

FOR THE DISABLED

Most hotels in Seattle offer handicapped-accessible accommodations, which are noted in the listings in this book.

FOR SENIORS

Be sure to ask about senior discounts when making hotel reservations. Also, museums, theaters, gardens, and tour companies usually offer senior-citizen discounts. These can add up to substantial savings, but you have to remember to ask for the discount.

FOR SINGLE TRAVELERS

One of the busiest singles bars in town is the **Pier 70 Restaurant and Chowder House,** at—you guessed it—Pier 70 on the waterfront.

FOR FAMILIES

Many of the less expensive hotels outside the city center allow kids to stay free in their parents' room. At mealtimes, keep in mind that many of the larger restaurants, especially those along the waterfront, offer children's menus. Finally, if you want to keep the kids entertained all day long, spend the day at **Seattle Center.**

FOR STUDENTS

See "For Students" in Section 3 at Chapter 4.

5. GETTING THERE

BY PLANE

Seattle-Tacoma International Airport (tel. 206/431-4444), known as **Sea-Tac** in the Seattle area, is located about 14 miles south of Seattle. It's connected to the city by I-5.

THE MAJOR AIRLINES

Sea-Tac Airport is served by more than 20 airlines, including the following:

Alaska Airlines (tel. 206/433-3100, or toll free 800/426-0333)
American Airlines (tel. toll free 800/433-7300)
America West (tel. 206/244-8021, or toll free 800/247-5692)
Continental (tel. toll free 800/525-0280)
Delta (tel. 206/625-0469, or toll free 800/221-1212)
Horizon Air (tel. toll free 800/547-9308)
Northwest (tel. 206/433-3500, or toll free 800/225-2525)
TWA (tel. toll free 800/221-2000)
United (tel. 206/441-3700, or toll free 800/241-6522)
USAir (tel. toll free 800/428-4322).

There are also a dozen foreign airlines offering flights to and from cities all over the world.

 FROMMER'S SMART TRAVELER: AIRFARES

1. Shop all the airlines that fly to your destination.
2. Always ask for the lowest-priced fare, not just for a discount.
3. Keep calling the airline—availability of cheap seats changes daily. Airline yield managers would rather sell a seat than have it fly empty. As the departure date nears, additional low-cost seats become available.
4. Watch the newspapers for special offers. You may be able to save several hundred dollars per ticket by changing your vacation plans to fit in with special low-fare offers.

In addition to air service at Sea-Tac Airport, there are several small airlines offering seaplane flights between Seattle and the San Juan Islands and British Columbia. These include **Lake Union Air Service** (tel. 206/284-0300, or toll free 800/826-1890) and **Kenmore Air** (tel. 206/486-8400 or 206/364-6990, or toll free 800/543-9595).

REGULAR AIRFARES AND SUPER APEX

At the time of this writing, round-trip **Super-APEX (Advance Purchase Excursion)** fares from the East Coast were about $360, though these were special summer fares. Shortly before the summer rates went into effect, fares had been running about $500 from the East Coast.

The round-trip full **coach** fare was $1,040, with **business class** costing about the same. The round-trip **first-class** fare was $1,364.

OTHER GOOD-VALUE CHOICES

You may be able to fly for less than the standard APEX fare by contacting a **ticket broker** (also known as a **bucket shop**). These companies advertise in the travel sections of major city newspapers with small boxed ads listing numerous destinations and ticket prices. You won't always be able to get the low price advertised (often it is available to students only), but you are likely to save a bit of money off the regular fare. Call a few and compare prices, making sure you find out about all the taxes and surcharges that may not be included in initial fare quote.

BY TRAIN

Amtrak trains arrive at and depart from the King Street Station, Third Ave. South and King St. (tel. 206/382-4128), near the Kingdome. Several trains run daily between Seattle and Portland, Oregon. The trip takes about 4 hours and costs $28 one way. These trains continue south to San Francisco and Los Angeles. There are also daily trains heading east by way of Spokane. For Amtrak reservations, call toll free 800/872-7245.

BY BUS

From the **Greyhound** bus station, Eighth Ave. and Stewart St. (tel. 206/624-3456), buses can connect you to almost any city in the continental United States.

BY CAR

I-5 is the main artery between Seattle and Portland and points south, stretching as far as the Mexican border. I-5 also continues north between Seattle and the Canadian border. **I-90** comes into Seattle from Spokane and from the east—all the way from Boston. **I-405** bypasses downtown Seattle on the east side of Lake Washington, passing through the city of Bellevue instead.

Here are some driving distances from selected cities (in miles):

Los Angeles	1,190
Portland	175
Salt Lake City	835
San Francisco	810
Spokane	285
Vancouver, B.C.	110

BY SHIP

Seattle is a major port. The city is served by the **Washington State Ferries** (tel. 206/464-6400, or toll free 800/84-FERRY in Washington State), the most extensive ferry system in the United States. Boats travel between Seattle and Vashon Island, Bainbridge Island, and the Olympic Peninsula. In addition, there is service north of Seattle between Anacortes and the San Juan Islands and between Edmonds and Kingston.

For high-speed passenger service between Seattle and Victoria, there is the *Victoria Clipper,* Pier 69, 2701 Alaskan Way, Seattle, WA 98121 (tel. 206/448-5000, or toll free 800/888-2535). The trip aboard this speedy catamaran takes only 2½ hours. Round-trip fare for adults is $67–$79; for seniors citizens and children ages 1 to 11, $57–$69. Round-trip tickets are substantially cheaper if purchased in advance.

IMPRESSIONS

The serenity of the climate, the innumerable pleasing landscapes, and the abundant fertility that unassisted nature puts forth, require only to be enriched by the industry of man with villages, mansions, cottages, and other buildings, to render it the most lovely country that can be imagined.
—Captain George Vancouver in 1792 on anchoring off what would one day become Seattle

CHAPTER 3

FOR FOREIGN VISITORS

1. PREPARING FOR YOUR TRIP
2. GETTING TO & AROUND THE U.S.A.
• FAST FACTS: FOR THE FOREIGN TRAVELER

Although American facts, fads, and fashions have spread across Europe and other parts of the world, so that America may seem like familiar territory before your arrival, there are still many peculiarities and uniquely American situations that any foreign visitor will encounter.

1. PREPARING FOR YOUR TRIP

TOURIST INFORMATION

Tourist Information on Seattle is available by writing to the **Seattle–King County Convention & Visitors Bureau,** 520 Pike Street, Suite 1300, Seattle, WA 98101 (206/461-5840). You can stop by their office located at the Washington State Convention & Trade Center, 800 Convention Place, Galleria Level, at the corner of Eighth Avenue and Pike Street. For information on the rest of Washington State, call the **Washington State Visitor Information Office,** at 206/586-2102, or 206/586-2088, or toll free 800/544-1800.

For information about Portland and the state of Oregon contact the **Portland/Oregon Visitors Association,** Three World Trade Center, 26 SW Salmon St., Portland, OR 97204-3299 (tel. 503/222-2223). For further information on Oregon State, contact the **Oregon Tourism Division,** 775 Summer St., Salem, OR (tel. 503/373-1200; or toll free in Oregon only 800/233-2306; or toll free out of state 800/547-7842).

ENTRY REQUIREMENTS
DOCUMENTS

Canadian nationals need only proof of Canadian residence to visit the United States. Citizens of Great Britain and Japan need only a current passport. Citizens of other countries, including Australia and New Zealand, usually need two documents: (1) a valid **passport** with an expiration date at least six months later than the scheduled end of their visit to the United States, and (2) a **tourist visa,** which is available at no charge from a U.S. embassy or consulate.

To get a tourist or business visa to enter the United States, contact the nearest American embassy or consulate in your country. If there is none, you will have to apply in person in a country where there is a U.S. embassy or consulate. Present your passport, a passport-size photo of yourself, and a completed application, which is available through the embassy or consulate.

You may be asked to provide information about how you plan to finance your trip or show a letter of invitation from a friend with whom you plan to stay. Those applying for a business visa may be asked to show evidence that they will not receive a salary in the United States.

Be sure to check the length of stay on your visa; usually it is six months. If you want to stay longer, you may file for an extension with the Immigration and Naturalization Service once you are in the country. If permission to stay is granted, a new visa is not required unless you leave the United States and want to reenter.

The visitor arriving by air, no matter what the port of entry—San Francisco, Los Angeles, New York, Anchorage, Honolulu, or any other—should cultivate patience and resignation before setting foot on U.S. soil. Getting through immigration control may take as long as 2 hours on some days, especially summer weekends; and then it takes additional time to clear Customs. When planning connections between international and domestic flights, you should allow an average of 2 to 3 hours at least for any delays.

In contrast, for the traveler arriving by car or by rail from Canada, the border-crossing formalities have been streamlined to the vanishing point. And for the traveler by air from Canada, you can sometimes go through Customs and Immigration at the point of departure, which is much quicker. If arriving in Seattle by ferry from Victoria, you will go through Customs at the ferry terminal in Seattle.

MEDICAL REQUIREMENTS

No inoculations are needed to enter the United States unless you are coming from, or have stopped over in, areas known to be suffering from epidemics, especially of cholera or yellow fever. Applicants for immigrants' visas (and only they) must undergo a screening for AIDS under a law passed in 1987.

If you have a disease requiring treatment with medications containing narcotics or drugs, or requiring injections with syringes, carry a valid signed prescription from your physician to allay any suspicions that you are smuggling drugs.

CUSTOMS REQUIREMENTS

Every adult visitor may bring in, free of duty: 1 liter of wine or hard liquor; 200 cigarettes or 100 cigars (but no cigars from Cuba) or 3 pounds of smoking tobacco; $400 worth of gifts. These exemptions are offered to travelers who will spend at least 72 hours in the United States and who have not claimed these exemptions within the preceding six months. It is altogether forbidden to bring into the country foodstuffs (particularly cheese, fruit, cooked meats, and canned goods) and plants (vegetables, seeds, tropical plants, etc.). Foreign tourists may bring in or take out up to $10,000 in U.S. or foreign currency with no formalities; larger sums must be declared to Customs on entering or leaving.

INSURANCE

Unlike most other countries, the United States has no national health-care system. Because the cost of medical care is extremely high, we strongly advise every traveler to secure health coverage before setting out. In addition, you may want to take out a travel policy that covers (for a relatively low premium) loss or theft of your baggage; trip-cancellation costs; guarantee of bail in case you are arrested; sickness or injury cost (medical, surgical, and hospital); cost of accident, repatriation, or death. Such packages (for example, "Europe Assistance" in Europe) are sold by automobile clubs at attractive rates, as well as by insurance companies and travel agencies.

MONEY

CURRENCY & EXCHANGE

The U.S. monetary system has a decimal base: 1 American dollar ($1) = 100 cents (100¢).

Dollar bills commonly come in $1 ("a buck"), $5, $10, $20, $50, and $100 denominations (the last two are not welcome when paying for small purchases and are not accepted in taxis). There are also $2 bills (seldom encountered).

There are six denominations of coins: 1¢ (one cent, or "penny"); 5¢ (five cents, or "nickel"); 10¢ (ten cents, or "dime"); 25¢ (twenty-five cents, or "quarter"); 50¢ (fifty cents, or "half dollar"); and the $1 piece (this includes the older, larger silver dollars and the newer, small Susan B. Anthony coin). *Note:* Outside of Las Vegas, Nevada, and Atlantic City, New Jersey, you will rarely encounter a $1 piece.

For currency exchange in Seattle, go to the **American Express Travel Agency,** 600 Stewart St., Plaza 600 (tel. 441-8622), or **Deak International,** 906 Third Ave. (tel. 623-6203). They are open Monday through Friday from 9am to 5pm.

In Portland, go to the **American Express Travel Service Office,** 1100 SW Sixth Ave. (tel. 226-2961). They are open Monday through Friday from 9am to 5pm.

TRAVELERS CHECKS

Travelers checks in U.S. dollar denominations are readily accepted at most hotels, motels, restaurants, and large stores. Travelers checks in other than U.S. dollars will almost always have to be changed at a bank or currency-exchange office, with the possible exception of those in Canadian dollars. Because of the proximity of the Canadian border, many hotels, restaurants, and shops will accept Canadian currency.

CREDIT CARDS

The method of payment most widely used for paying hotel and restaurant bills and for making major purchases is the credit card.

The following are the major credit cards listed in descending order of acceptance: **VISA** (BarclayCard in Britain), **MasterCard** (EuroCard in Europe, Access in Britain, Diamond in Japan), **American Express, Diners Club,** and **Carte Blanche.** You can save yourself trouble by using "plastic money," rather than cash or travelers checks, in 95% of all hotels, motels, restaurants, and retail stores (except for those selling food or liquor). A credit card can serve as a deposit for renting a car, as proof of identity (often carrying more weight than a passport), or as a "cash card," enabling you to draw money from banks that accept them.

Note: The "foreign-exchange bureaus" so common in Europe are rare even at airports in the United States; these exchange bureaus do not exist outside of major cities. Try to avoid having to change foreign money or travelers checks denominated in other than U.S. dollars; in fact, leave any currency other than U.S. dollars at home—it may prove more nuisance to you than it's worth.

2. GETTING TO & AROUND THE U.S.A.

Travelers from overseas can take advantage of the **APEX (Advance Purchase Excursion)** fares offered by all the major U.S. and European carriers. Aside from these, attractive values are offered by **Icelandair** on flights from Luxembourg to New York and by **Virgin Atlantic** from London to New York/Newark.

Some large airlines—for example, **TWA, American Airlines, Northwest, United,** and **Delta**—offer travelers on their transatlantic and transpacific flights special discount tickets under the name **Visit USA,** allowing travel between any U.S. destinations at minimum rates. These tickets are not on sale in the United States, and must therefore be purchased before you leave your foreign point of departure. This system is the best, easiest, and fastest way of seeing the country at low cost. You should obtain information well in advance from your travel agent or the office of the airline concerned, since the conditions attached to these discount tickets can be changed without advance notice.

For further information about travel to and around Seattle and Portland, see "Getting There" in Chapters 2 and 13, and "Getting Around" in Chapters 4 and 14.

FAST FACTS **FOR THE FOREIGN TRAVELER**

Accommodations It is always a good idea to make hotel reservations as soon as you know your trip dates. Reservations require a deposit of one night's payment. Seattle and Portland are particularly busy during the summer months, and hotels book up in advance—especially on weekends when there is some sort of festival going on. If you do not have reservations, it is best to look for a room in the mid-afternoon. If you wait until the evening, you run the risk that hotels will already be filled.

In the United States, major downtown hotels, which cater primarily to business travelers, commonly offer weekend discounts of as much as 50% to entice vacationers to fill up the empty rooms. Note that rates in Seattle and Portland tend to go up in the summer months, when there is a greater demand. If you wish to save money and don't mind cloudy or rainy weather, you should consider visiting sometime other than summer, though these cities really are at their best when the sun is shining.

Auto Organizations If you are planning to drive a car while in the United States and you are a member of an automobile organization in your home country, check before leaving to see if they have a reciprocal agreement with one of the large U.S. automobile associations such as **AAA**. However, if you plan to drive a rented car, the rental company should provide free breakdown service.

Business Hours **Banks** are open weekdays from 9am to 3pm, and usually have later hours on Friday; many banks are now open on Saturday also. There is also 24-hour access to banks through automatic teller machines. Most offices are open weekdays from 9am to 5pm. Most post offices are open weekdays from 8am to 5pm. In general, stores open between 9 and 10am and close between 5 and 6pm, Monday through Saturday; some department stores stay open till 9pm on Thursday and Friday evening; and many stores are open on Sunday from 11am to 5 or 6pm.

Climate See "Climate" in Section 2 of Chapter 2.

Currency & Exchange See "Money" in Section 1 of this chapter for an explanation of U.S. currency. To exchange money in Seattle, go to **American Express,** 600 Stewart St. (tel. 441-8622), or **Deak International,** 906 Third Ave. (tel. 623-6203). To exchange money in Portland, go to the **American Express,** 1100 SW Sixth Ave. (tel. 226-2961).

Customs & Immigration See "Entry Requirements" in Section 1 of this chapter.

Drinking Laws The legal drinking age in both Washington and Oregon is 21. The penalties for driving under the influence of alcohol are stiff.

Electricity U.S. wall outlets give power at 110–120 volts, 60 cycles, compared to 220–240 volts, 50 cycles, in most of Europe. Besides a 110-volt converter, small appliances of non-American manufacture, such as hairdryers or shavers, will require a plug adapter with two flat, parallel pins.

Embassies & Consulates All embassies are located in the national capital, Washington, D.C. Some consulates are located in major cities, and most nations have a mission to the United Nations in New York City. Listed here are the embassies and consulates of the major English-speaking countries—Australia, Canada, Ireland, New Zealand, and the United Kingdom. If you are from another country, you can get the telephone number of your embassy by calling **Information** in Washington, D.C. (tel. 202/555-1212).

- **Australia** The **embassy** is at 1601 Massachusetts Ave. NW, Washington, DC 20036 (tel. 202/797-3000). There is no consulate in Seattle or Portland; the nearest is in San Francisco—360 Post St., CA 94108 (tel. 415/362-6160).
- **Canada** The **embassy** is at 501 Pennsylvania Ave. NW, Washington, DC 20001 (tel. 202/682-1740). The local **consulate** is at 600 Stewart St., Seattle, WA 98101 (tel. 206/443-1777).
- **Ireland** The **embassy** is at 2234 Massachusetts Ave. NW, Washington, DC 20008 (tel. 202/462-3939). There is no consulate in Seattle or Portland; the nearest is in San Francisco—655 Montgomery St., Suite 930, CA 94111 (tel. 415/392-4214).
- **New Zealand** The **embassy** is at 37 Observatory Circle NW, Washington, DC 20008 (tel. 202/328-4800). The only **consulate** is in Los Angeles—Tishman Bldg., 10960 Wilshire Blvd., Suite 1530, Westwood, CA 90024 (tel. 213/477-8241).
- **United Kingdom** The **embassy** is at 3100 Massachusetts Ave. NW, Washington, DC 20008 (tel. 202/462-1340). There is a **consulate** in Seattle—999 Third Ave., Seattle, WA 98101 (tel. 206/622-9255).

Emergencies Call 911 for fire, police, ambulance. If you encounter such problems as sickness, accident, or lost or stolen baggage, it will pay you to call **Travelers Aid,** an organization that specializes in helping distressed travelers, whether American or foreign. In Seattle, phone 461-3888.

Gasoline [Petrol] Most cars in the United States now use unleaded gasoline (gas) only, and leaded gasoline is not available in many parts of the country. However, it is available in both Washington and Oregon. In Oregon you are not allowed to pump your own gasoline, but in Washington "self-service" gas stations are common and are less expensive than full-service stations.

Holidays On the following legal national holidays, banks, government offices, post offices, and many stores, restaurants, and museums are closed:

> January 1 (New Year's Day)
> Third Monday in January (Martin Luther King Day)
> Third Monday in February (President's Day, Washington's Birthday)
> Last Monday in May (Memorial Day)
> July 4 (Independence Day)
> First Monday in September (Labor Day)
> Second Monday in October (Columbus Day)
> November 11 (Veterans Day/Armistice Day)
> Last Thursday in November (Thanksgiving Day)
> December 25 (Christmas Day)

The Tuesday following the first Monday in November is Election Day, and is a legal holiday in presidential-election years.

Information Information on Seattle is available by writing to the **Seattle–King County Convention & Visitors Bureau,** 520 Pike Street, Suite 1300, Seattle, WA 98101 (206/461-5840). You can stop by their office located at the Washington State Convention & Trade Center, 800 Convention Place, Galleria Level, at the corner of Eighth Avenue and Pike Street. For information on the rest of Washington State, call the **Washington State Visitor Information Office,** at 206/586-2102, or 206/586-2088, or toll free 800/544-1800.

For information about Portland and the state of Oregon contact the **Portland/Oregon Visitors Association,** Three World Trade Center, 26 SW Salmon St., Portland, OR 97204-3299 (tel. 503/222-2223). For further information on Oregon State, contact the **Oregon Tourism Division,** 775 Summer St., Salem, OR (tel. 503-373-1200; or toll free in Oregon only 800/233-2306; or toll free out of state 800/547-7842).

Legal Aid The foreign tourist, unless positively identified as a member of the Mafia or a drug ring, will probably never become involved with the American legal system. If you are pulled up for a minor infraction (for example, of the highway code, such as speeding), never attempt to pay the fine directly to the police officer; you may wind up arrested on the much more serious charge of attempted bribery. Pay fines by mail, or directly into the hands of the clerk of the court. If accused of a more serious offense, it is wise to say and do nothing before consulting a lawyer. Under U.S. law, an arrested person is allowed one telephone call to a party of his or her choice. Call your embassy or consulate.

Liquor Laws See "Drinking Laws," above.

Mail Mailboxes are blue with a red-and-white logo, and carry the inscription "U.S. Mail." The international postage rates at the time of publication are 40¢ for a ½-ounce letter and 30¢ for a postcard mailed to Canada. All other countries cost 50¢ for a ½-ounce letter and 40¢ for a postcard.

Medical Emergencies Dial **911** for an ambulance.

Post Office In Seattle the main post office is at the intersection of Third Avenue and Union Street (tel. 206/442-6340). In Portland the main post office is at 715 NW Hoyt St. (tel. 503/294-2424).

Radio & Television Audiovisual media—with three coast-to-coast networks (ABC, CBS, and NBC), along with the Public Broadcasting System (PBS) and a growing network of cable channels—play a major part in American life. In Seattle there are six channels, most of which broadcast 24 hours a day, and in Portland there are seven. In addition, there are pay-TV channels showing sports events or recent movies. Both Seattle and Portland have more than 30 local radio stations, each broadcasting a particular type of music—classical, country, jazz, Top 40, oldies—along with news broadcasts and frequent commercials.

Safety Whenever you're traveling in an unfamiliar city or country, stay alert. Be aware of your immediate surroundings. Wear a moneybelt and don't flash expensive jewelry and cameras in public. This will minimize the possibility of your becoming a crime victim. Be alert even in heavily touristed areas. Seattle and Portland are both particularly prone to car break-ins, so never leave any valuables in your car. The entertainment districts of Seattle and Portland are both adjacent to areas frequented by homeless people. Do not travel alone in these areas late at night.

Taxes In the United States there is no VAT (Value-Added Tax), or other indirect tax at a national level. But every state, and each city in it, can levy their own local taxes on all purchases, including hotel and restaurant checks, airline tickets, etc. In Seattle and the rest of Washington State, the **sales tax rate** is 8.1%. In Portland and the rest of Oregon, there is no sales tax.

Telephone, Telex & Fax Pay phones can be found on street corners, in bars, restaurants, hotels, public buildings, stores, and service stations, etc. **Local calls** cost 25¢.

For **long-distance or international calls,** stock up with a supply of 25¢ coins (quarters); the pay phones will instruct you when, and in what quantity, you should put them into the slot. For direct overseas calls, first dial 011, followed by the country code (Australia, 61; Republic of Ireland, 353; New Zealand, 64; United Kingdom, 44; and so on), and then by the city code (for example, 71 or 81 for London, 21 for Birmingham) and the number of the person you wish to call. For long-distance calls in Canada and the United States, dial 1, followed by the area code and number you want.

Before calling from a hotel room, always ask the hotel phone operator if there are any telephone surcharges. These are best avoided by using a public phone, calling collect, or using a telephone charge card.

For **reverse-charge or collect calls,** and for **person-to-person calls,** dial 0 (zero, not the letter "0"), followed by the area code and number you want; an operator will then come on the line and you should specify that you are calling collect or person-to-person or both. If your operator-assisted call is international, ask for the overseas operator.

For local **directory assistance ("information"),** dial 555-1212; for long-distance information, dial 1, then the appropriate area code and 555-1212.

Like the telephone system, **telegraph** and **telex** services are provided by private corporations like ITT, MCI, and, above all, Western Union. You can bring your telegram in to the nearest Western Union office (there are hundreds across the country), or dictate it over the phone (a toll-free call, 800/325-6000). You can also telegraph money, or have it telegraphed to you very quickly over the Western Union system.

Time The United States is divided into six time zones. From east to west these are: **Eastern Standard Time (EST), Central Standard Time (CST), Mountain Standard Time (MST), Pacific Standard Time (PST), Alaska Standard Time (AST),** and **Hawaii Standard Time (HST).** Always keep in mind the different time zones when traveling (or even telephoning) long distances. For example, noon in Seattle (PST) is 1pm in Denver (MST), 2pm in Chicago (CST), 3pm in New York City (EST), 11am in Anchorage (AST), and 10am in Honolulu (HST). **Daylight Saving Time** is in effect from 1am on the first Sunday in April until 2am on the last Sunday in October except in Arizona, Hawaii, part of Indiana, and Puerto Rico.

Tipping In restaurants if the service has been good, tip 15 to 20% of the bill. Taxi drivers expect about 10% of the fare. Airport porters and bellhops should be tipped about 50¢ per bag. For chambermaids, $1 per night is an appropriate tip.

Toilets Often euphemistically referred to as restrooms, public toilets can be found in bars, restaurants, hotel lobbies, museums, department stores, and service stations—and will probably be clean (although those at gas stations sometimes leave much to be desired). Note, however, that some restaurants and bars display a notice that "Toilets Are for the Use of Patrons Only." You can ignore this sign, or better yet, avoid arguments by ordering a cup of coffee or a soft drink, which will qualify you as a patron. The cleanliness of toilets at railroad stations and bus depots may be questionable; some public places are equipped with pay toilets, which require you to insert one or two 10¢ coins (dimes) into a slot on the door before it will open.

White Pages & Yellow Pages The local phone company provides two kinds of telephone directories. The general directory, called the White Pages, lists subscribers (business and personal residences) in alphabetical order. The inside front cover lists emergency numbers for police, fire, and ambulance, as well as other vital numbers (like the Coast Guard, poison control center, crime-victims hotline, etc.). The first few pages are devoted to community-service numbers, including a guide to long-distance and international calling, complete with country codes and area codes.

The second directory, the Yellow Pages, lists local services, businesses, and industries by type, with an index at the back. The listings cover not only such obvious items as automobile repair services by make of car, or drugstores (pharmacies)—often by geographical location—but also restaurants by type of cuisine and geographical location, bookstores by special subject, places of worship by religious denomination, and other information that the tourist might otherwise not readily find. The Yellow Pages also include city plans or detailed area maps, often showing postal Zip Codes and public transportation.

THE AMERICAN SYSTEM OF MEASUREMENTS

LENGTH

1 inch (in.)	=	2.54cm
1 foot (ft.)	=	12 in. = 30.48 cm = .305m
1 yard (yd.)	=	3 ft. = .915 m
1 mile	=	5,280 ft. = 1.609 km

To convert miles to kilometers, multiply the number of miles by 1.61. Also use to convert miles per hour (m.p.h.) to kilometers per hour (kmph). **To convert kilometers to miles,** multiply the number of kilometers by .62. Also use to convert kmph to m.p.h.

CAPACITY

1 fluid ounce (fl.oz.)	=	.03 liters
1 pint	=	16 fl. oz. = .47 liters
1 quart	=	2 pints = .94 liters
1 gallon (gal.)	=	4 quarts = 3.79 liters = .83 Imperial gal.

To convert U.S. gallons to liters, multiply the number of gallons by 3.79. **To convert liters to U.S. gallons,** multiply the number of liters by .26. **To convert U.S. gallons to Imperial gallons,** multiply the number of U.S. gallons by .83. **To convert Imperial gallons to U.S. gallons,** multiply the number of Imperial gallons by 1.2.

WEIGHT

1 ounce (oz.)	=	28.35g
1 pound (lb.)	=	16 oz. = 453.6g = .45kg
1 ton	=	2,000 lb. = 907kg = .91 metric tons

To convert pounds to kilograms, multiply the number of pounds by .45. **To convert kilograms to pounds,** multiply the number of kilograms by 2.2.

TEMPERATURE

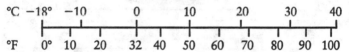

To convert degrees Fahrenheit to degrees Celsius, subtract 32 from °F, multiply by 5, then divide by 9 (example: 85°F − 32 × 5/9 = 29.4°C). **To convert degrees Celsius to degrees Fahrenheit,** multiply °C by 9, divide by 5, and add 32 (example: 20°C × 9/5 + 32 = 68°F).

CLOTHING SIZE CONVERSION

The following charts should help foreign visitors choose the correct clothing sizes in the U.S. However, sizes can vary, so the best guide is simply to try things on.

WOMEN'S DRESSES, COATS, AND SKIRTS

American	3	5	7	9	11	12	13	14	15	16	18
Continental	36	38	38	40	40	42	42	44	44	46	48
British	8	10	11	12	13	14	15	16	17	18	20

WOMEN'S BLOUSES AND SWEATERS

American	10	12	14	16	18	20
Continental	38	40	42	44	46	48
British	32	34	36	38	40	42

WOMEN'S STOCKINGS

American	8	8½	9	9½	10	10½
Continental	1	2	3	4	5	6
British	8	8½	9	9½	10	10½

WOMEN'S SHOES

American	5	6	7	8	9	10
Continental	36	37	38	39	40	41
British	3½	4½	5½	6½	7½	8½

MEN'S SUITS

American	34	36	38	40	42	44	46	48
Continental	44	46	48	50	52	54	56	58
British	34	36	38	40	42	44	46	48

MEN'S SHIRTS

American	14½	15	15½	16	16½	17	17½	18
Continental	37	38	39	41	42	43	44	45
British	14½	15	15½	16	16½	17	17½	18

MEN'S SHOES

American	7	8	9	10	11	12	13
Continental	39½	41	42	43	44½	46	47
British	6	7	8	9	10	11	12

MEN'S HATS

American	6⅞	7⅛	7¼	7⅜	7½	7⅝
Continental	55	56	58	59	60	61
British	6¼	6⅞	7⅛	7¼	7⅜	7½

CHILDREN'S CLOTHING

American	3	4	5	6	6X
Continental	98	104	110	116	122
British	18	20	22	24	26

CHILDREN'S SHOES

American	8	9	10	11	12	13	1	2	3
Continental	24	25	27	28	29	30	32	33	34
British	7	8	9	10	11	12	13	1	2

GETTING TO KNOW SEATTLE

Water, water, everywhere—that's Seattle. This rapidly growing city has water on three sides. Sailboats, seaplanes, kayaks, and sailboards are permanent fixtures of the cityscape and one of the main reasons why many people live here. Any visit to Seattle should include some manner of waterborne activity, and even if you never leave dry land, you'll find your visit affected by water. There are drawbridges all over the Seattle area, and if you're in a hurry, you can bet that the one you have to cross will be delaying traffic. If you happen to be driving across Lake Washington, you might notice that the bridge you are on is rather close to the water; in fact, it's floating on the water. Seattle has some of the only floating bridges in the world.

In between Elliott Bay, Lake Union, and Lake Washington, there are hills—not gentle hills, but the same kind that San Francisco is famous for. There used to be seven hills, just as in Rome, but one of them was relocated to the bay to make more land for building. This combination of hills and water makes for some spectacular views, so be sure to take extra care when driving: Don't let the natural beauty of the city's surroundings distract you. Unfortunately, Seattle has been busy erecting huge skyscrapers in recent years, and many excellent views have been lost to development. The city is now trying to put some controls on its rapid growth in order to preserve its unique character.

All these hills and water have turned Seattle into a city of neighborhoods. People here identify with their neighborhood even more than they identify with the city itself. Although the best way to explore the different neighborhoods is by car, there is an excellent public bus system that will get you in from the airport and all over the city.

1. ORIENTATION

ARRIVING

BY PLANE

Seattle-Tacoma (Sea-Tac) International Airport (tel. 206/431-4444) is located 14 miles south of Seattle and is connected to the city by Interstate 5 (I-5). Generally, allow 30 minutes for the trip between the airport and downtown, and more during rush hour. See "Getting There" in Chapter 2 for information on airlines serving Seattle.

Gray Line Airport Express (tel. 206/626-6088) provides service between the airport and downtown Seattle daily from 5am to midnight. This shuttle van stops at the Stouffer Madison, Holiday Inn–Crowne Plaza, Best Western Executive Inn, Days Inn Town Center, Four Seasons Olympic, Seattle Hilton, hotels along Eighth and Bell streets, Sheraton Seattle, Westin, Warwick, and WestCoast Roosevelt. Rates are $8 one way and $14 round trip.

Shuttle Express (tel. 206/622-1424, or toll free 800/942-0711) provides 24-hour service between Sea-Tac and the Seattle area. Their rates vary from $10 to $16. You need to make a reservation to get to the airport, but to leave the airport, just give them a call when you arrive. Push **48** on one of the courtesy phones outside the baggage-claim areas.

Metro Transit (tel. 206/553-3000) operates three buses between the airport and downtown. It's a good idea to call for the current schedule when you arrive in town. At this writing, **no. 174** operates every 20 to 30 minutes from about 5am to midnight; it makes local stops and takes about an hour. On Saturday and Sunday the first buses leave between 6 and 6:30am. For nightowls, there's local bus no. 184 that leaves the airport every night at 2:48 and 4:03am. **No. 194,** an express taking only 30 minutes, also departs every 30 minutes but operates only between 5am and 7:30pm Monday through Saturday. The fare is $1 during off-peak hours and $1.50 during peak hours. Nos. 174 and 184 operate to Ninth Avenue and Stewart Street. No. 194 operates to either Third Avenue and Union Street or the Convention Place Station of the Bus Tunnel, depending on the time of day.

A **taxi** into downtown Seattle will cost you about $20. There are usually plenty of taxis around, but if not, call **Yellow Cab** (tel. 206/622-6500) or **Farwest Taxi** (tel. 206/622-1717). The flag-drop rate is $1.20; after that, it's $1.40 per mile.

BY TRAIN

If you arrive in Seattle on an Amtrak train, you will find yourself at the **King Street Station** (tel. 206/382-4128), right across the parking lot from the Kingdome. The heart of downtown Seattle is only a few blocks north.

BY BUS

The **Greyhound bus station,** Eighth Ave. and Stewart St. (tel. 206/624-3456), is slightly northeast of downtown Seattle.

BY CAR

I-5, the Seattle Freeway, is the main north–south artery through Seattle, continuing south to Portland and north to the Canadian border. **I-90** comes into Seattle from Spokane and ends just after

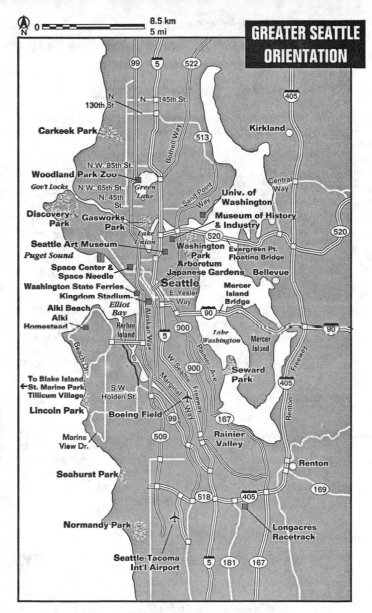

GREATER SEATTLE
ORIENTATION

23rd Avenue. **Washington Hwy. 99,** the Alaskan Way Viaduct, is another major north–south highway through downtown Seattle; it passes through the waterfront section.

BY SHIP

Washington State Ferries (tel. 206/464-6400, or toll free in Washington State 800/542-7052) dock at Pier 52. The *Victoria*

Clipper (tel. 206/448-5000, or toll free 800/888-2535) docks at Pier 69.

TOURIST INFORMATION

Tourist Information on Seattle and the surrounding area is available by writing to the **Seattle–King County Convention & Visitors Bureau,** 520 Pike Street, Suite 1300, Seattle, WA 98101 (206/461-5840). The bureau is open Monday through Friday from 8:30am to 5pm. You can stop by their office located at the Washington State Convention & Trade Center, 800 Convention Place, Galleria Level, at the corner of Eighth Avenue and Pike Street. To find this information center, walk up Pike Street until it goes into a tunnel under the Convention Center. You'll see the information center on your left as you enter the tunnel. This same office operates two **Visitor Information Centers** in the baggage-claim area at Sea-Tac Airport. One is by carousel no. 9 (open daily from 9:30am to 7:30pm; tel. 206-433-5218) and the other is by carousel no. 1 (open daily from 9am to 1:30pm; tel. 206/433-4679).

For information on the rest of Washington State, call the **Washington State Visitor Information Office,** at 206/586-2102, or 206/586-2088, or toll free 800/544-1800.

For British Columbia tourism information, contact **Tourism British Columbia,** 720 Olive Way, Suite 930, Seattle, WA 98101 (tel. 206/623-5937), open Monday through Friday from 8:30am to 4:30pm.

CITY LAYOUT

Although downtown Seattle is quite compact and can easily be navigated on foot, finding your way through this area by car can be frustrating. Seattle has been experiencing phenomenal growth in the past few years, and the city has begun to sprawl. This has created traffic-congestion problems that must be anticipated. Here are some guidelines to help you find your way around.

MAIN ARTERIES & STREETS

There are only three interstate highways serving Seattle. **I-90** comes in from the east and ends downtown. **I-405** bypasses the city completely, traveling up the east shore of Lake Washington through Bellevue. The main artery is **I-5,** which runs smack through the middle of Seattle. This can be both a convenience and a hassle,

---

IMPRESSIONS

Its streets are so steep, like those of San Francisco, that you practically need spikes in your shoes, and its politics are almost as spectacular as the scenery.
—JOHN GUNTHER, *INSIDE U.S.A.*, 1947

depending on which side of the exit you're on. Take the James Street exit west if you're heading for the Pioneer Square area; take the Seneca Street exit for Pike Place Market; or the Olive Way exit for Capitol Hill.

Downtown is roughly defined as extending from **Yesler Way** on the south to **Denny Way** on the north and from Elliott Bay on the west to **Broadway** on the east. Within this area most of the avenues are numbered, whereas the streets have names. The exceptions to this rule are the first two streets parallel to the waterfront. They are Alaskan Way and Western Avenue. Spring Street is one way eastbound, and Seneca Street one way westbound. Likewise, Pike Street is one way eastbound, and Pine Street one way westbound. First Avenue and Third Avenue are two-way streets, but Second and Fifth are one way southbound. Fourth Avenue and Sixth Avenue are one way northbound.

FINDING AN ADDRESS

After you become familiar with the streets and neighborhoods of Seattle, there is really only one important thing to remember to find an address: Pay attention to the compass point of the address. Downtown streets have no directional designation attached to them, but when you cross I-5 going east, most streets and avenues are designated "East." South of Yesler Way, which runs through Pioneer Square, streets are designated "South." West of Queen Anne Avenue, streets are designated "West." The University District is designated "NE" (Northeast); the Ballard, "NW" (Northwest). Therefore, if you are looking for an address on First Avenue South, you'd better be heading south of Yesler Way or you're not going to have any luck.

Another helpful hint is that odd-numbered addresses are likely to be on the west and south sides of streets, whereas even-numbered addresses will be on the east and north sides of the street. Also, in the downtown area, address numbers increase by 100 as you move away from Yesler Way going north or south, and as you go east from the waterfront.

STREET MAPS

Even if the streets of Seattle seem totally unfathomable to you, rest assured that even longtime residents sometimes have a hard time finding their way around. Don't be afraid to ask directions. You can get a free map of the city from the Seattle–King County Convention & Visitors Bureau, Convention Center, Galleria Level, Eighth Ave. and Pike St. (tel. 206/461-5840), or at one of the Visitor Information Centers in the baggage-claim area at Sea-Tac Airport.

If you happen to be a member of AAA, you can get free maps of Seattle and Washington State from them, either at an office near you or at the Seattle office, 330 Sixth Ave. North, (tel. 206/448-5353). They're open Monday through Friday from 8:30am to 5pm (Wednesday until 6pm).

NEIGHBORHOODS IN BRIEF

Seattle is a city disjointed by bodies of water, and it is also a city of neighborhoods.

International District   The most immediately recognizable of Seattle's neighborhoods, the International District is home to the city's Asian population.

Pioneer Square   Bordering the International District, the Pioneer Square Historic District is known for its restored old buildings. It's full of shops, galleries, restaurants, and bars.

Capitol Hill   Centered along Broadway near Volunteer Park, this is Seattle's cutting-edge shopping district and gay community.

Ballard   In northwest Seattle, you'll find Ballard, a former Scandinavian community that is now known for its busy nightlife, but remnants of its past are still visible.

First Hill   Known as Pill Hill by most Seattleites, this hilly neighborhood, just east of downtown across I-5, is home to several hospitals.

Queen Anne Hill   This neighborhood is where you'll find some of Seattle's oldest homes, several of which are now bed-and-breakfast inns. Queen Anne is located just northwest of Seattle Center and offers great views of the city. This is one of the most prestigious Seattle neighborhoods.

University District   As the name implies, this neighborhood surrounds the University of Washington in the northeast section of the city. The U District, as it's known to locals, provides all the amenities of a college neighborhood.

2. GETTING AROUND

BY PUBLIC TRANSPORTATION

BY BUS

Seattle's **Metro bus system** has been voted the best in the country, so be sure to avail yourself of it while you're in town. The best part of riding the bus in Seattle is that as long as you stay within the downtown area, you can ride for free between 4am and 9pm. The **Ride Free Area** is between Alaskan Way in the west, Sixth Avenue in the east, Battery Street in the north, and South Jackson Street in the south. Within this area are Pioneer Square, the waterfront attractions, Pike Place Market, and all the major hotels. Two blocks from South Jackson Street is the Kingdome, and six blocks from Battery Street is Seattle Center. Keeping this in mind, you can visit nearly every tourist attraction in Seattle without having to spend a dime on transportation. For more information, phone 206/553-3000.

The Metro's latest innovation is the **Bus Tunnel,** which allows buses to drive underneath downtown Seattle, thus avoiding traffic congestion. The tunnel extends from the International District in the south to the Convention Center in the north, with three stops in between. Commissioned artworks decorate each of the stations, making a trip through the tunnel more than just a way of getting from point A to point B. In fact, the tunnel is becoming a regular tourist attraction. The tunnel is served by buses no. 71, 72, 73, 106, 107, 175, 176, 177, 178, 190, 194, 195, and 196, and it's open Monday through Friday from 5am to 7pm, on Saturday from 10am to 6pm. When the Bus Tunnel is closed, the above-mentioned bus lines operate on surface streets. Because the tunnel is within the Ride Free Area, there is no charge for riding through it, unless you are traveling to or from outside of the Ride Free Area.

If you travel outside the Ride Free Area, fares range from 75¢ to $1.50, depending on the distance and time of day, and you pay when you get off the bus. When traveling into the Ride Free Area, you pay when you get on the bus. Exact change is required.

Discount Passes If you plan to make several trips beyond the Ride Free Area in one day, be sure to request a **Transit Pass.** This costs $3 and allows you unlimited rides on buses and the Waterfront Streetcar, one round trip on the monorail, and discounts on restaurants, shopping, services, entertainment, and attractions. You can pick up these passes at the Seattle–King County Convention & Visitors Bureau, Level 1 Galleria, Convention Center, Eighth Ave. and Pike St. (tel. 206/461-5840); at the Metro Customer Service Offices, Marion St. and Second Ave., or the Westlake Tunnel station; or at monorail stations. To order passes by mail, phone 206/624-PASS. On Saturday, Sunday, and holidays, you can purchase an **All Day Pass** for $1.50; it's available on any Metro bus or the Waterfront Streetcar.

BY FERRY

Washington State Ferries is the most extensive ferry system in the United States and serves numerous cities and towns around the Puget Sound area such as Bremerton, Edmonds, and Winslow; Vashon Island; Victoria, B.C.; and the San Juan Islands. At time of press, the fare from Seattle to Bremerton via car ferry service (a 60-minute crossing) was as follows: car and driver one way, $6.65 (summer), $5.55 (off season), passengers, $3.30; children and senior citizens, $1.65; children under age 5, free; eastbound from Bremerton to the main land, there was no charge for passengers. For ferry boat schedule and rate information, you can call via touch-tone phone the Seattle Times Info Line at 206/464-2000 ext. 5500. For information, you can also call the state ferry system at 206/464-6400, or toll free 800/84-FERRY within Washington State.

IMPRESSIONS

. . . on a famous ferry going into famous Seattle, dusk on a November night, the sky, the water, the mountains are all the same color: lead in a closet. Suicide weather. The only thing wrong with this picture is that you feel so happy.
—ESQUIRE MAGAZINE

BY MONORAIL

If you are planning a visit to Seattle Center, there is no better way to get there from downtown than on the monorail. It leaves from Westlake Center shopping mall (Fifth Ave. and Pine St.). The once-futuristic elevated trains cover the 1.2 miles in 90 seconds and provide a few nice views along the way. The monorail leaves every 15 minutes daily from 9am to midnight during the summer; the rest of the year, Sunday through Thursday from 9am to 9pm, on Friday and Saturday until midnight. The one-way fare is only 60¢ for adults and 25¢ for senior citizens and the handicapped.

BY WATERFRONT STREETCAR

Old-fashioned streetcars run along the waterfront from Pier 70 to Fifth Avenue South and South Jackson Street on the edge of the International District, providing another unusual means of getting around in downtown Seattle. The trolley operates Monday through Friday from 7am to 6:15pm, departing every 30 minutes; on Saturday, Sunday, and holidays from 10:30am to 5:30pm, departing every 30 minutes. One-way fare is 75¢ in off-peak hours and $1 in peak hours. If you plan to transfer to a Metro bus, you can get a transfer good for 90 minutes of bus travel.

BY TAXI

If you decide not to use the free public-transit system, call **Yellow Cab** (tel. 622-6500) or **Farwest Taxi** (tel. 622-1717). Taxis can be difficult to hail on the street in Seattle, so it's best to call or wait at the taxi stands at the major hotels. The flag-drop rate is $1.20; after that, it's $1.40 per mile.

BY CAR

Before you venture into downtown Seattle by car, remember that traffic congestion is severe, parking is limited, and streets are almost all one way. Be forewarned that you're better off leaving your car outside the downtown area.

RENTALS

For the very best deal on a rental car, make your reservation at least one week in advance. It also pays to shop around and call the same companies a few times over the course of a couple of weeks; the last time I visited Seattle, I was quoted different rates each time I called the major car-rental agencies. If you decide on the spur of the moment that you want to rent a car, check to see whether there are any weekend or special rates available. If you are a member of a frequent-flier program, be sure to mention it: You might get mileage credit for renting a car. Currently, daily rates are around $50, with weekly rates at around $140.

All the major car-rental agencies have offices in Seattle, and there are also plenty of independent companies. I recommend that you try to rent a car from **Budget Rent A Car** (tel. toll free 800/527-0700). They have several offices throughout the Seattle area, including one right in the airport. When you rent from Budget, you not only get low rates, but you also get to park free in any of the hundreds of Diamond parking lots all over the city. This can save you more than $10 a day! Budget offices are at Sea-Tac Airport (tel. 206/682-2277), downtown at Fourth Ave. and Columbia St. (tel. 206/682-8989), and at Westlake Ave. and Virginia St. (tel. 206/682-2277).

Other car-rental companies include **Avis** (tel. toll free 800/331-1212), at Sea-Tac Airport (tel. 206/433-5231) and 1919 Fifth Ave. (tel. 206/448-1700); **Dollar,** at 17600 Pacific Hwy. South (tel. 206/433-6777) and Seventh Ave. and Stewart St. (tel. 206/682-1316); **Hertz** (tel. toll free 800/654-3131), at Sea-Tac Marriott Hotel (tel. 206/433-5275), Sea-Tac Red Lion Hotel (tel. 206/246-0159), and 722 Pike St. (tel. 206/682-5050); and **Thrifty,** at 18836 Pacific Hwy. South (tel. 206/246-7565) and 801 Virginia St. (tel. 206/625-1133).

PARKING

There are **Diamond parking lots** all over Seattle, and if you rent a car from Budget Rent A Car, you can park free in any of them.

On-street parking is another matter altogether. It is extremely limited and rarely available near your destination. Pay attention to the color of the parking meter when you park your car. Meters are color-coded according to time limits: **Aluminum-colored** meters allow you 2 to 4 hours; **green** meters, 30 minutes; and **yellow** meters, 15 minutes.

DRIVING RULES

A right turn at a red light is permitted after coming to a full stop. A left turn at a red light is permissible from a one-way street onto another one-way street. If you park your car on a sloping street, be sure to turn your wheels to the curb—you may be ticketed if you don't. When parking on the street, be sure to check the time limit on parking meters; it ranges from 15 minutes to 4 hours. Also be sure to check whether or not you can park in a parking space during rush hour. Don't leave your keys in the ignition and walk away from your car—you might get a ticket.

When on foot, cross streets only at corners and only with the lights. Jaywalking is a ticketable offense.

BY BICYCLE

Downtown Seattle is congested with traffic and is very hilly. Unless you have experience with these sorts of conditions, I wouldn't recommend riding a bicycle downtown. However, there are many bike paths that are excellent for recreational bicycling, and some of these can be accessed from downtown by routes that avoid the steep hills and heavily trafficked street. See "Recreation" in Section 5 of Chapter 7 for details.

ON FOOT

Seattle is a surprisingly compact city. You can easily walk from Pioneer Square to Pike Place Market. Remember, though, that the city is also very hilly. When you head in from the waterfront, you will be climbing a very steep hill. If you get tired of walking around downtown Seattle, remember that between 4am and 9pm you can always catch a bus for free as long as you plan to stay within the Ride Free Area.

FAST FACTS *SEATTLE*

Airport Seattle-Tacoma International Airport (Sea-Tac) is located 14 miles south of Seattle; for information call 206/431-4444.

American Express In Seattle, their office is in the Plaza 600 building at 600 Stewart St. (tel. 441-8622). The office is open Monday through Friday from 9am to 5pm.

Area Code The area code in Seattle is **206.**

Babysitters Check at your hotel first if you need a babysitter. If they don't have one available, contact **Rent-A-Mom** (tel. 547-4080).

Business Hours **Banks** are generally open weekdays from 9am to 3pm, with later hours on Friday, and some have Saturday morning hours. **Offices** are generally open Monday through Friday from 9am to 5pm. In general, **stores** open Monday through Saturday between 9 and 10am and close between 5 and 6pm. Some department stores have later hours on Thursday and Friday evenings until 9pm; many stores are open on Sunday from 11am to 5 or 6pm. **Bars** stay open until 1am; **dance clubs** and **discos** often stay open much later.

Car Rentals See "By Car" in Section 2 of this chapter.

Climate See "Climate" in Section 2 of Chapter 2.

Dentist If you need a dentist while you are in Seattle, contact the **Dentist Referral Service,** the Medical Dental Building, Fifth Ave. and Olive Way (tel. 623-4096).

Doctor To find a doctor in Seattle, check at your hotel for a reference, or call the Medical-Dental Referral line (tel. 623-4096).

Driving Rules See "By Car" in Section 2 of this chapter.

Drugstores Conveniently located downtown, **Peterson's Pharmacy,** 1629 Sixth Ave. (tel. 622-5860), has been serving Seattle for more than 50 years. It's open Monday through Friday from 8:30am to 6pm, on Saturday from 9am to 1pm. **Pacific Drugs,** 822 First Ave. (tel. 624-1454), another convenient choice, is open Monday through Friday from 7am to 6:30pm, on Saturday from 10am to 5pm.

Emergencies For police, fire, or medical emergencies, phone **911.**

Eyeglasses   If you have problems with your glasses while in Seattle, try **Davis Optical Center,** 314 Stewart St. (tel. 623-1758). They are a full-service store and can replace your glasses in an hour.

Hairdressers/Barbers   **Gene Juarez Salons** has two downtown locations: Four Seasons Olympic Hotel, 411 University St. (tel. 628-0011), and 1501 Fifth Ave. (tel. 628-1405). These full-service beauty salons charge between $22.50 and $45 for a man's or woman's haircut. For an inexpensive haircut, try **Supercuts,** 1550 East Olive Way (tel. 325-4855), on Capitol Hill.

Holidays   See "Calendar of Events" in Chapter 2, and "Holidays" in "Fast Facts: For the Foreign Traveler" in Chapter 3.

Hospitals   One of the hospitals most convenient to downtown Seattle is the **Virginia Mason Hospital & Clinic,** 925 Seneca St. (tel. 583-6433 or 624-1144). There is also the **Virginia Mason Fourth Avenue Clinic,** 1221 Fourth Ave. (tel. 223-6490), open daily from 7am to 5:30pm, which provides medical treatment for minor ailments without an appointment.

Hotlines   If you have a touch-tone phone, you'll want to call the **Seattle Times Info Line** at 206/464-2000; this service provides a wealth of information on topics that range from personal health to business news, from entertainment listings to the weather report and marine forecast; you can even obtain complete information on ferry schedules and rates. The local **rape hotline** is 632-7273.

Information   For information on Seattle and the surrounding area, call or write to **Seattle–King County Convention & Visitors Bureau,** Convention Center, 520 Pike Street, Galleria Level, Seattle, WA 98101 (tel. 206/461-5840); their office is located at Eighth Ave. and Pike Street. For information on the state of Washington, contact the **Washington State Tourism Office** at 206/586-2102, 206/586-2088, or toll free 800/544-1800. For information on British Columbia, contact **Tourism British Columbia,** 720 Olive Way, Suite 930, Seattle, WA 98101 (tel. 206/623-5937).

Laundry/Dry Cleaning   The **Waterfront Place Cleaners,** 1017 First Ave. (tel. 206/583-0005), is a dry cleaner, open Monday through Friday from 8am to 6pm, on Saturday from 10am to 5pm. **Dick's,** 115 12th Ave. (tel. 624-0318), offers same-day dry cleaning and hotel/motel valet service; it's open Monday through Friday from 7:30am to 6pm, on Saturday from 7:30am to 3pm. **Downtown St. Regis,** 116 Stewart St. (tel. 448-6366), is a 24-hour coin-operated laundry.

Library   The main branch of the **Seattle Public Library** is at 1000 Fourth Ave. (tel. 386-4636).

Liquor Laws   The legal drinking age in Washington is 21.

Lost Property   If you left something on a Metro bus, call **684-1585;** if you left something at the airport, call **433-5312.**

Luggage Storage/Lockers   There is a luggage-storage facility at Amtrak's King Street Station. It costs $1 per day. The Greyhound Bus station, 811 Stewart St., has luggage lockers.

Mail   You can receive mail c/o General Delivery at the main post office (see "Post Office," below).

Maps   You can get a free map of Seattle at the **Visitors**

Information Centers in the baggage-claim area at Sea-Tac Airport or at the **Seattle–King County Convention & Visitors Bureau.** See "City Layout" in this chapter.

Newspapers/Magazines The *Seattle Post-Intelligencer* is Seattle's morning daily, and *The Seattle Times* is the evening daily. The arts and entertainment weekly for Seattle is the *Seattle Weekly.*

Photographic Needs Cameras West, 1908 Fourth Ave. (tel. 622-0066), is the largest-volume camera and video dealer in the Northwest. Best of all, it's right downtown and also offers 1-hour film processing. It's open Monday through Friday from 10am to 7pm, on Saturday from 10am to 6pm, and on Sunday from noon to 5pm.

Police For police emergencies, phone **911.**

Post Office Besides the main post office, Third Ave. and Union St. (tel. 442-6340), there are also convenient postal stations in Pioneer Square at 91 Jackson St. South (tel. 623-1908), and at Federal Station, 909 First Ave. (tel. 624-4977). Hours are 8am to 5:30pm Monday through Friday.

Radio Seattle has dozens of AM and FM radio stations broadcasting every conceivable type of music, in addition to news, traffic updates, sports, and weather.

Religious Services The **Church Council of Greater Seattle** (tel. 525-1213) can give you the location of the nearest church of your choice.

Restrooms There are public restrooms in Pike Place Market and the Convention Center.

Safety Although Seattle is rated as one of the safest cities in the United States, it has its share of crime. Take extra precautions with your wallet or purse when you're in the crush of people at Pike Place Market—this is a favorite spot of pickpockets. Whenever possible try to park your car in a garage, not on the street, at night.

Shoe Repairs If you lose a heel or need a new sole, **Busy Shoes/Instant Shoe Repair,** 306 Union St. (around the corner from Third Ave.) (tel. 624-6391), and also at 1116 Fourth Ave. (tel. 467-7386), will get you back on your feet in a hurry.

Taxes The state of Washington makes up for its lack of an income tax with its heavy **sales tax** of 8.1%. **Hotel-room tax** varies from 12% to 14%.

Taxis To get a cab, call **Yellow Cab** at 622-6500, or **Farwest Taxi** at 622-1717. See also "By Taxi" in section 2 of this chapter.

Television The six local television channels are 4 (ABC), 5 (NBC), 7 (CBS), 9 (PBS), 11 (Independent), and 13 (Fox).

Time Seattle is on **Pacific Standard Time (PST),** and **Daylight Saving Time,** depending on the time of year, making it 3 hours behind the East Coast.

Tipping In restaurants if the service has been good, tip 15 to 20% of the bill. Taxi drivers expect about 10% of the fare. Airport porters and bellhops should be tipped about 50¢ per bag. For chambermaids, $1 per night is an appropriate tip.

Transit Information For 24-hour information on Seattle's **Metro bus sytem,** call 206/553-3000. For information on the **Washington State Ferries,** call 206/464-6400 or toll free **800/84-FERRY.** For **Amtrak information,** call 206/382-4128. To contact the **King Street Station** (trains), call 206/382-4128. To contact the **Greyhound bus station,** call 206/624-3456.

Useful Telephone Numbers For police, fire, or medical emergencies, phone **911.** If you have a touch-tone phone, you'll want to call the **Seattle Times Info Line** at 206/464-2000; this service provides a wealth of information on topics that range from personal health to business news, from entertainment listings to the weather report and marine forecast; you can even obtain complete information on ferry schedules and rates.

Weather If you can't tell what the weather is by looking out the window, or you want to be absolutely sure that it's going to rain the next day, call **526-6087.**

3. NETWORKS & RESOURCES

FOR STUDENTS

The **University of Washington,** located in northeast Seattle, is the largest state university in Washington and also happens to have the second-largest student bookstore in the country. The university's **Information Center** is located at 4014 University Way NE (tel. 543-9198), and the bookstore is at 4326 University Way NE (tel. 634-3400). **Seattle Pacific University,** 3307 Third Ave. West (tel. 281-2000), is a private university, as is **Seattle University,** Broadway and Madison St. (tel. 296-6000).

If you don't already have one, get an **official student ID** from your school. Such an ID will entitle you to discounts at museums and on performances at different theaters and concert halls around town.

Seattle's **AYH youth hostel** is at 84 Union St. (tel. 206/682-0462). Besides being a place to stay, this hostel has a bulletin board with information on rides, other hostels, camping equipment for sale, and the like.

FOR GAY MEN & LESBIANS

Seattle's large gay community is centered around Capitol Hill. In this chic shopping and residential district, you can find gay restaurants, bars, bookstores, and more. For a guide to Seattle's gay community, get a copy of the *Greater Seattle Business Association (GSBA) Guide Directory.* Their mailing address is P.O. Box 20263, Seattle, WA 98102 (tel. 206/329-9949). The *Seattle Gay News* is the community's newspaper. Their offices are at 704 E. Pike St., Seattle, WA 98122 (tel. 206/324-4297).

Two of Seattle's long-time favorite gay bars are the **Ritz Café,** 429 15th Ave. East (tel. 328-0440), and **Thumpers,** 1500 E. Madison St. (tel. 328-3800). These are both in the vicinity of Capitol Hill. **The Connection** and **Brass Connection,** 722 E. Pike St.

(tel. 322-6572 and 324-3436), are a popular restaurant and disco in the heart of Capitol Hill. Although not strictly a lesbian establishment, **Wildrose,** 1021 E. Pike St. (tel. 324-9210), is a tavern primarily for women, with frequent live music.

Beyond the Closet, 1501 Belmont Ave. (tel. 322-4609), is a gay and lesbian bookstore.

Shafer Mansion and the **Gaslight Inn** are bed-and-breakfasts in the Capitol Hill area. See "Moderate" in Section 3 of Chapter 5 for details.

FOR WOMEN

Seattle is a large city, and all the normal precautions that apply in other cities hold true here. The Pioneer Square area is particularly unsafe for either sex late at night.

Wildrose, 1021 E. Pike St. (tel. 324-9210), is a women's tavern with a friendly atmosphere and frequent live music performances.

The local **rape hotline** is 632-7273.

FOR SENIORS

Be sure to carry some form of photo ID with you when touring Seattle. Most attractions, some theaters and concert halls, and the Washington State Ferries all offer senior-citizen discounts. Also, if you aren't already a member, you should consider joining the **American Association of Retired Persons (AARP),** 1909 K St. NW, Washington, DC 20049 (tel. 202/872-4700). One of the many benefits of belonging to this organization is the 10% discount offered at many motels and hotels.

IMPRESSIONS

What the Mediterranean Sea was to the Greeks, breaking the bond of custom, offering new experiences, calling out new institutions and activities, that the ever retreating Great West has been to the eastern United States directly, and to the nations of Europe more remotely.
—F. J. TURNER, *THE SIGNIFICANCE OF THE FRONTIER*, 1893

CHAPTER 5

SEATTLE ACCOMMODATIONS

1. DOWNTOWN
- FROMMER'S SMART TRAVELER: ACCOMMODATIONS
- FROMMER'S COOL FOR KIDS: ACCOMMODATIONS
2. NEAR SEA-TAC AIRPORT
3. FIRST HILL & CAPITOL HILL
4. NORTH SEATTLE

You generally get a lot for your money in Seattle. Even the most expensive hotel in the city is less expensive than a comparable one in San Francisco or New York. In the following listings, very expensive hotels are those costing more than $120 per night for a double room; expensive hotels, $90 to $120 per night for a double; moderate hotels, $60 to $90 per night for a double; and budget hotels, less than $60 per night for a double. These rates do not include the state hotel tax, which varies from about 12% to 14%. A few of the hotels include breakfast in their rates; others offer complimentary breakfast only on certain deluxe floors. In most cases you will need to tip the bellhops and chambermaids. If tips are included in a hotel's rates, this has been noted.

Finally, make your reservations as far in advance as possible, especially if you plan a visit during Seafair or one of the other Seattle festivals (see "Seattle Calendar of Events" in Chapter 2 for dates of festivals). Also, the San Juan Islands are very busy in summer, so make reservations early.

There are a number of fine bed-and-breakfast establishments in Seattle, and I have listed a few of my favorites in this chapter. In addition, the **Pacific Bed & Breakfast Agency,** 701 NW 60th St., Seattle, WA 98107 (tel. 206/784-0539), offers many accommodations, mostly in private homes, in the Seattle area; rates range from $45 to $85 for a single, and from $50 to $150 for a double. They charge $5 for a directory of their members.

1. DOWNTOWN

VERY EXPENSIVE

ALEXIS HOTEL, 1007 First Ave. (at Madison St.), Seattle, WA 98104. Tel. 206/624-4844, or toll free 800/426-7033 (outside Washington). Fax 206/621-9009. 54 rms, 15 suites. A/C TV TEL

$ Rates (including continental breakfast and service): $145–$180 single; $165–$180 double; $205–$310 suite. AE, CB, DC, MC, V. **Parking:** $9 per night.

★ Unbelievable as it sounds, this elegant little hotel was once a parking garage. Now listed on the National Register of Historic Places, this 90-year-old building is a sparkling gem. The hotel also has an enviable location halfway between Pike Place Market and Pioneer Square, only two blocks from the waterfront.

In the understated lobby, the peach walls fairly glow in the light of frosted-glass torchères, bouquets of flowers soften the angular lines, and large contemporary paintings add a touch of modern sophistication. Throughout, the hotel is a pleasant mix of old and new, contemporary and antique, giving the Alexis a very special atmosphere. The cheerful service—from doormen to chambermaids, none of whom you need to tip—will make you feel as if you are visiting old friends.

Each of the 54 rooms is furnished with antique tables, overstuffed chairs, and brass reading lamps. There are four pillows on every bed, with chocolates on them in the evening. In the black-tiled bath, you'll find a marble counter, luxurious terry-cloth robes, a shaving mirror, a telephone, and a basket of special toiletries. Each of the rooms is a little different (there are 18 floor plans), but the nicest by far are the fireplace suites, which have raised king-size beds, whirlpool baths, and wet bars.

Dining/Entertainment: The Café Alexis, serving some of the best Northwest cuisine in Seattle, is a small but elegant restaurant with a balcony for warm weather and a fireplace for cold (see "Hotel Dining" in Section 5 of Chapter 6 for details). Complimentary breakfasts, as well as lunches of straightforward American food, are served at 92 Madison St., the hotel's casual café; there is also a juice bar here. You'll think you are staying at a French château when you sit down to eat in this spacious room. Just off the lobby, the Bookstore Bar serves light lunches as well as drinks, and is filled with books, magazines, and newspapers for browsing. The Cajun Corner, another casual restaurant run by the hotel, is just down Madison Street.

Services: Room service, concierge, valet/laundry service, morning paper, evening turn-down service, complimentary sherry, shoeshine service, no tipping (except in restaurant and lounge).

Facilities: Steamroom, privileges at two sports clubs, wheelchair accommodations, parfumerie.

THE EDGEWATER, Pier 67, 2411 Alaskan Way, Seattle, WA 98121-1398. Tel. 206/728-7000, or toll free 800/624-0670. Fax 206/441-4119. 238 rms, 2 suites. A/C TV TEL
$ Rates: $95–$125 single; $95–$165 double; $250 suite. AE, CB, DC, DISC, MC, V. **Parking:** $6.

Built in 1962, Seattle's only waterfront hotel underwent an extensive renovation in 1989 and is now once again one of the finest hotels in the city. Set back from Alaskan Way on Pier 67, the Edgewater has the feel of a fishing lodge, albeit with all the amenities you'd expect from a deluxe hotel. A vaulted open-beamed ceiling and river-stone fireplace greet you as you enter the lobby, whose wall of windowpaned glass looks out on ships and sailboats on Elliott Bay. Above the lobby's living-room arrangement is a chandelier made from deer antlers. Throughout the building, tartan carpets remind you that this is not your standard stuffy hotel. With such a relaxed atmosphere, it's difficult to believe that the crowded streets of downtown Seattle are only steps away.

The fishing-lodge theme continues in the rooms, which feature rustic lodge-pole pine furniture and plaid comforters on the beds. Half the rooms have balconies over the water, and all have clock-radios, minibars, and remote-control TVs. In each bright red-and-green bathroom, you'll find a basket of soaps and a shoeshine kit.

Dining/Entertainment: With its dark-green color scheme and duck motif, Ernie's Bar & Grill could have been designed by Eddie Bauer or Ralph Lauren. You'll find Northwest cuisine featured on the menu and a stunning view of the harbor from all the tables. In the pine-walled Lobby Lounge, there is live piano music in the evenings and a fireplace to warm your toes in winter.

Services: Room service, concierge, same-day laundry/valet service, courtesy shuttle to downtown locations, in-room movies.

Facilities: Wheelchair accommodations, gift shop, no-smoking rooms.

FOUR SEASONS OLYMPIC HOTEL, 411 University St., Seattle, WA 98101. Tel. 206/621-1700, or toll free 800/332-3442 or 800/821-8106 (in Washington) or 800/268-6282 (in Canada). Fax 206/682-9633. Telex 152477. 450 rms, 26 suites. A/C MINIBAR TV TEL

$ Rates: $170–$200 single; $200–$230 double; $220–$1,300 suite. Weekend rates available. AE, CB, DC, MC, V. **Parking:** $10 per day, $12 per day valet.

Old-fashioned grandeur fit for kings is what you'll find when you step through the doors of this Italian Renaissance palace. Gilt-and-crystal chandeliers hang from the high-arched ceiling; ornate cornices and moldings grace the glowing natural wood walls and pillars. A huge floral arrangement sits in the middle of the expansive lobby, surrounded by new and antique furnishings and subdued pink-and-gray carpets. At either end, curving stairways lead to the mezzanine level. The owners spent $65 million on renovating the hotel nine years ago, and just last year redecorated all the guest rooms and the lobby.

In the halls of this 11-floor building are original art and fresh flower arrangements. There were originally 800 rooms here, but during renovation these were enlarged by taking out walls. Now the 450 rooms are all quite spacious and tastefully appointed with modern furnishings. Remote-control TVs and minibars are standard here, as are hairdryers, plush bathrobes, and large baskets of scented toiletries.

Dining/Entertainment: The Georgian Room is the most elegant restaurant in Seattle. Marble terraces lead from the lobby to its doors, and inside, luxurious drapes, a marble floor, antique chairs, and the same ornate moldings that cover the lobby all contribute to the strong feeling of courtly elegance. The menu combines creative

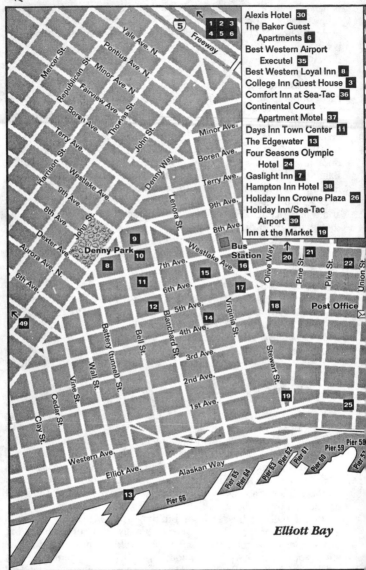

Alexis Hotel **30**
The Baker Guest
   Apartments **6**
Best Western Airport
   Executel **35**
Best Western Loyal Inn **8**
College Inn Guest House **3**
Comfort Inn at Sea-Tac **36**
Continental Court
   Apartment Motel **37**
Days Inn Town Center **11**
The Edgewater **13**
Four Seasons Olympic
   Hotel **24**
Gaslight Inn **7**
Hampton Inn Hotel **38**
Holiday Inn Crowne Plaza **26**
Holiday Inn/Sea-Tac
   Airport **39**
Inn at the Market **19**

Elliott Bay

Northwest and continental cuisines. (See "Hotel Dining" in Section 5 of Chapter 6 for details.) Downstairs from the lobby is the distinctly different Shuckers, an English pub featuring fresh seafood. In the spacious skylighted lobby court, more Northwest cuisine is served— but at half the price of The Georgian Room.

Services: 24-hour room service, concierge, same-day valet/ laundry service, one-hour pressing, complimentary shoeshine, valet parking, massages available.

SEATTLE ACCOMMODATIONS

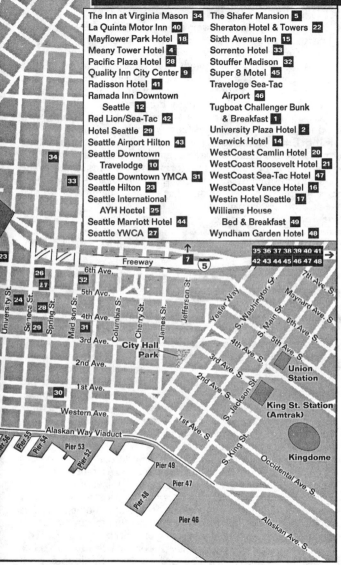

The Inn at Virginia Mason **34**
La Quinta Motor Inn **40**
Mayflower Park Hotel **18**
Meany Tower Hotel **4**
Pacific Plaza Hotel **28**
Quality Inn City Center **9**
Radisson Hotel **41**
Ramada Inn Downtown Seattle **12**
Red Lion/Sea-Tac **42**
Hotel Seattle **29**
Seattle Airport Hilton **43**
Seattle Downtown Travelodge **10**
Seattle Downtown YMCA **31**
Seattle Hilton **23**
Seattle International AYH Hostel **25**
Seattle Marriott Hotel **44**
Seattle YWCA **27**

The Shafer Mansion **5**
Sheraton Hotel & Towers **22**
Sixth Avenue Inn **15**
Sorrento Hotel **33**
Stouffer Madison **32**
Super 8 Motel **45**
Travelodge Sea-Tac Airport **46**
Tugboat Challenger Bunk & Breakfast **1**
University Plaza Hotel **2**
Warwick Hotel **14**
WestCoast Camlin Hotel **20**
WestCoast Roosevelt Hotel **21**
WestCoast Sea-Tac Hotel **47**
WestCoast Vance Hotel **16**
Westin Hotel Seattle **17**
Williams House Bed & Breakfast **49**
Wyndham Garden Hotel **48**

Facilities: Indoor swimming pool, whirlpool, sauna, sundeck, health club, wheelchair accommodations, exclusive shopping arcade, no-smoking rooms.

HOLIDAY INN–CROWNE PLAZA, 113 Sixth Ave., Seattle, WA 98101-3048. Tel. 206/464-1980, or toll free 800/521-2762 or 800/858-0511 (in Washington). Fax 206/340-1617. 415 rms, 28 suites. A/C TV TEL

$ Rates: $135–$160 single or double; $225–$500 suite. AE, CB, DC, DISC, MC, V. **Parking:** $9 per day valet.

This 34-story shiny glass tower is popular with businesspeople attending conventions at the nearby Washington State Trade and Convention Center. Almost all the rooms offer views of Puget Sound or the Cascade Mountains through large picture windows; ask for one of the higher floors to take advantage of them. The guest rooms are done in pastels and soothing shades of gray. On the concierge floors, guests receive a complimentary breakfast and afternoon hors d'oeuvres, an afternoon bar, and specially furnished rooms with dark-wood furnishings and royal-blue drapes.

Dining/Entertainment: The Parkside Café offers international meals and informal dining in a mezzanine-level atrium that looks out on Freeway Park. In the evening, Northwest cuisine is served in the adjacent formal dining room, where granite walls and glass blocks combine to create a very contemporary setting. There is also a quiet lounge area on the mezzanine.

Services: Room service, concierge, valet/laundry service, airport shuttle ($7), in-room movies.

Facilities: Whirlpool, sauna, exercise facilities, gift shop, no-smoking rooms.

INN AT THE MARKET, 86 Pine St., Seattle, WA 98101. Tel. 206/443-3600, or toll free 800/446-4484. 65 rms, 9 suites. A/C MINIBAR TV TEL

$ Rates: $85–$155 single; $95–$155 double; $180–$200 suite. AE, CB, DC, DISC, MC, V. **Parking:** $12 per day.

French country decor is the theme of this inconspicuous little hotel in the middle of Pike Place Market. There is no grand entrance, no large sign—only a plaque on the wall to indicate that this simple brick building in fact houses a very elegant hotel. In the courtyard a fountain bubbles. A small lobby with a fireplace, antique tables, and carved-wood display cabinets will make you think you've stepped into the living room of a French country home. A rooftop deck overlooking the harbor provides a tranquil spot to soak up the sun on summer afternoons.

In the guest rooms, wide bay windows overlook Puget Sound and can be opened to let in refreshing sea breezes. Antiqued furniture (including pine armoires to hide TVs), stocked minibars and refrigerators, coffee makers with complimentary coffee, and well-lit writing desks are amenities that will make you feel right at home here. The huge bathrooms are equipped with telephones and feature baskets of special toiletries from the market. If you check into one of the spacious suites, you'll also have an elegant daybed on which to relax.

Dining/Entertainment: The Gravity Bar is an ultrahip, postmodern juice bar that also provides the hotel's in-room breakfast. Café Dilletante offers light meals, espresso, and handmade chocolates. The hotel's formal dining room is Campagne, an excellent southern French restaurant located across the courtyard from the lobby (see "Hotel Dining" in Section 5 of Chapter 6 for details). In summer, Campagne offers terrace dining.

Services: Limited room service, concierge, valet/laundry service, complimentary limousine service in downtown Seattle.

Facilities: Health spa, wheelchair accommodations, gift shop, hair salon, no-smoking rooms.

SEATTLE HILTON HOTEL, Sixth Ave. and University St., Seattle, WA 98101. Tel. 206/624-0500, or toll free 800/426-0535 or 800/542-7700 (in Washington). 237 rms, 6 suites. A/C TV TEL
$ Rates: $123–$173 single; $138–$188 double; $250–$375 suite. Weekend rates available. AE, CB, DC, DISC, MC, V. **Parking:** $8.50 per day.

When you walk in the street-level lobby of the Seattle Hilton, you won't find the check-in desk, no matter how hard you look. The main lobby is actually up on the 13th floor, though the elevator labels it the lobby floor or second floor. When you finally do reach the lobby, you'll find an attractive pink-marble floor, black-wood pillars, and lots of pink tones and black accents. The overall effect is art deco, with a grand piano and frosted-glass windows further adding to the elegance.

Unfortunately, you won't find a swimming pool or any other athletic facilities here, but you will find very comfortable rooms that are everything you'd expect from a Hilton. Blond woods and pastel walls and carpets give the place a stylish and contemporary feeling. In the bathroom you'll find plenty of fragrant toiletries on hand.

Dining/Entertainment: Macaulay's Restaurant and Lounge is a casual spot serving good old-fashioned American food. Up at the Top of the Hilton, there is international cuisine with a Northwest accent. The views are superb, and there is live music in the evenings. (See "Dining with a View" in Section 5 of Chapter 6 for details.)

Services: 24-hour room service, concierge, valet/laundry service.

Facilities: Gift shop.

SHERATON SEATTLE HOTEL & TOWERS, 1400 Sixth Ave., Seattle, WA 98101. Tel. 206/621-9000, or toll free 800/325-3535 or 800/268-9393 (in eastern Canada) or 800/268-9330 (in western Canada). Fax 206/621-8441. 880 rms, 46 suites. A/C TV TEL
$ Rates: $155–$210 single; $155–$235 double; $215–$500 suite. Weekend rates available. AE, CB, DC, MC, V. **Parking:** $12 per day self-park, $14 valet.

This 35-story tower is the largest hotel in Seattle, and you'll always find the building buzzing with activity. In the spacious lobby, pink and green pastels are highlighted by glowing tripod lamps. Above a sunken lounge area with a grand piano hangs a very unusual lighted ceiling sculpture of string baffles that gently sway in the breezes of the air-conditioning system. Potted plants, flower arrangements, and comfortable couches around the lobby offer plenty of places for a quiet moment alone or an opportunity for lively conversation. The top floor of the hotel contains the exercise room and swimming-pool area.

The standard-size rooms are unfortunately not as luxurious as the lobby would suggest. However, if you book a room in the Towers, the hotel's club floors, you'll get the kind of attention and service you would expect only from a small luxury hotel. Whichever type of room you stay in, make sure it's as high up as possible to take advantage of the great views.

Dining/Entertainment: The subdued elegance and outstanding meals at Fuller's continue to win this restaurant awards and recommendations. The very finest and most innovative Northwest cuisine is what has the critics raving (see "Hotel Dining" in Section 5 of Chapter 6 for details). Banners is a less formal restaurant. Gooey's, a reference to a gigantic local clam, is the hotel's popular lounge and disco. Complimentary happy-hour buffets and live dance music on the weekends keep the crowds content.

Services: 24-hour room service, concierge, valet/laundry service.

Facilities: Indoor swimming pool, whirlpool, sauna, exercise room, wheelchair accommodations, gift shop, no-smoking floors.

STOUFFER MADISON HOTEL, 515 Madison St., Seattle, WA 98104. Tel. 206/583-0300, or toll free 800/468-3571. Fax 206/622-8635. Telex 882730. 554 rms, 90 suites. A/C TV TEL

$ Rates: $144–$159 single; $169–$184 double; $174–$194 single suite; $199–$219 double suite. Weekend packages available. AE, CB, DC, DISC, MC, V. **Parking:** $9 per day.

Despite its size, the Stouffer Madison provides the friendly service and attention to detail that you'd expect only from a smaller hotel. A spacious lobby graced by attractive Japanese prints is only the beginning of the comforts and amenities here.

All the rooms are larger than average and most have views of either Puget Sound or the Cascade Mountains. Custom-made furniture (including walnut armoires with brass trim), separate seating areas, remote-control TVs, contemporary art, and soft color schemes make every room a winner. Many also have minirefrigerators and marble counters. In the bath you'll find a nice selection of toiletries.

Dining/Entertainment: Prego, way up on the 28th floor, serves northern Italian cuisine amid eye-catching views of Seattle. (See "Dining with a View" in Section 5 of Chapter 6 for details.) Down on the second floor, Maxwell's serves American food in a casual café atmosphere; Sunday brunch here is very popular. The lobby court is a convivial lounge, and when the weather permits, tables spill out onto an outdoor terrace complete with waterfall. There's live piano music here in the evenings.

Services: 24-hour room service, concierge, complimentary morning coffee and newspaper, valet/laundry service, complimentary shoeshine, in-room movies, airport shuttle service ($7), turn-down service on club floors, massages available.

Facilities: Indoor swimming pool, whirlpool, fitness room, wheelchair accommodations, no-smoking rooms, gift shops.

WARWICK HOTEL, 401 Lenora St., Seattle, WA 98121. Tel. 206/443-4300, or toll free 800/426-9280. 230 rms, 4 suites. A/C TV TEL

$ Rates: $190–$210 single or double; $450 suite. Weekend rates available. AE, CB, DC, DISC, MC, V. **Parking:** $7.50 per day.

The name sounds European, and European ambience is just what you get at this high-rise hotel in the heart of downtown Seattle, only six blocks from Pike Place Market and two blocks from the monorail terminal. A sunken lobby with a copper fireplace provides a quiet setting for relaxing conversation. Black mirrored walls, spotlighted bouquets of flowers, and Asian art offer just the right touch of sophistication. A Belgian tapestry depicting woodcutters evokes both the European styling and the Northwest setting of this hotel.

Rooms come with either two double beds or a king-size bed, and many have stocked minibars or minirefrigerators. Modern furnishings in greens and warm beiges, a desk for working, and a couch or an easy chair for relaxing complete the amenities that will help you settle in for your visit to Seattle. On the upper floors, a marble bath with a basket of toiletries and a terry-cloth robe assure you of a fresh start each day, and a telephone in the bath lets you keep in touch.

Dining/Entertainment: Liaison, The Restaurant is the hotel's distinctive eatery, serving innovative Northwest cuisine that uses only the freshest local ingredients, as well as a few traditional favorites. The menu here changes biweekly, and there is live piano music in the adjacent lounge every evening. L'été is a casual sidewalk café specializing in delicious pastries.

Services: 24-hour room service, concierge, valet/laundry service, complimentary limousine service in downtown Seattle.

Facilities: Indoor swimming pool, whirlpool, sauna, fitness room, wheelchair accommodations.

WESTIN HOTEL SEATTLE, 1900 Fifth Ave., Seattle, WA 98101. Tel. 206/728-1000, or toll free 800/228-3000. Fax 206/728-2259. Telex 152900. 875 rms, 47 suites. A/C TV TEL
$ Rates: $160–$195 single; $185–$220 double; from $300 suite. Children 18 and under stay free in parents' room. AE, CB, DC, DISC, MC, V. **Parking:** $11 per day, $13 per day valet.

The hallmark cylindrical towers of the Westin chain rise above the downtown Seattle skyline like a pair of honeycombs. Within, you'll find a veritable beehive of activity as tour groups assemble and conventioneers register. Although the hotel has the amenities you'd expect, service can be impersonal and the crowds overwhelming. All rooms have modern furnishings and are done in subdued colors. The rooms on the upper floors are certainly the best, with fine views of Seattle and Puget Sound.

Dining/Entertainment: The Palm Court is the Westin's premier, award-winning purveyor of Northwest cuisine. This restaurant sparkles with wide windows, large mirrors, and bright lights, and is considered the most romantic restaurant in Seattle. (See "Hotel Dining" in Section 5 of Chapter 6 for details.) The Market Café is a casual place done up to look as if it belongs in Pike Place Market. Every month there's a different themed food festival here. In the lobby court you can sip a drink while listening to a pianist tickle the ivories. For music, videos, and dancing, head to Fitzgerald's on Fifth.

Services: 24-hour room service, one-day valet/laundry service, in-room movies, airport shuttle ($7).

Facilities: Indoor swimming pool, exercise room, whirlpool, sauna, wheelchair accommodations, no-smoking floors, gift shop, barber, beauty salon.

EXPENSIVE

MAYFLOWER PARK HOTEL, 405 Olive Way, Seattle, WA 98101. Tel. 206/623-8700, or toll free 800/426-5100 or 800/562-4504 (in Washington). Fax 206/382-6997. 182 rms, 14 suites. A/C TV TEL

$ Rates: $90–$110 single; $100–$120 double; from $140 suite. Children under 18 stay free in parents' room. AE, CB, DC, MC, V. **Parking:** $6 per day.

If shopping is your favorite sport, you'll really like this hotel. The Mayflower Park is connected by a covered walkway to the shops of Westlake Center, and several department stores are within a block. (If you want to spend time at Seattle Center, the monorail starts at Westlake Center and takes you to the center faster than you could cross a street.) Built in 1927, the Mayflower Park provides subdued elegance. In the high-ceilinged lobby an antique Chinese screen, Chinese cabinet, grandfather clock, and skylights complement the deep-green carpets and aquamarine overstuffed chairs. Fresh flowers add a colorful touch. Overhead hangs a tubular glass chandelier that once hung in the lobby of the Olympic Hotel.

All of the rooms have been remodeled in the past few years and now sport attractive bureaus. The modern bathrooms have large old tubs that are great for soaking. If you crave space, ask for one of the large corner rooms. In the larger queen-size rooms and suites, cherry furniture, floral-print bedspreads, and unusual tables all add up to special elegance. Some rooms even have brass Chinese garden seats—an unusual touch.

Dining/Entertainment: Clippers restaurant, open for dinner only, features fresh seafood and French and Italian cuisine. The intimate bilevel restaurant is bright and airy, with marble tables, brass rails, and blond-wood decor. Oliver's lounge provides another cheerful spot for light lunches or drinks and conversation. The room once housed a pharmacy, in which the floor-to-ceiling windows were completely painted over.

Services: Room service, valet/laundry service.

Facilities: Privileges at private athletic club.

WESTCOAST CAMLIN HOTEL, 1619 Ninth Ave., Seattle, WA 98101. Tel. 206/682-0100, or toll free 800/426-0670. 137 rms, 16 suites. A/C TV TEL

$ Rates: $70–$99 single; $88–$109 double; $175 suite. AE, CB, DC, MC, V. **Parking:** $6.

S The WestCoast hotel chain has latched onto a brilliant idea and has certainly made the very most of it in the Seattle area, where they will have eight hotels by the end of 1992. Their hotels offer convenient locations as well as European style and service without charging an arm and a leg. The Camlin has been around for years, but it took new ownership and extensive remodeling to create this stylish transformation.

The marble floor of the quiet lobby is covered with Oriental carpets, and comfortable chairs and couches are set in living-room arrangements. Large potted plants give the room a homey feeling, while marble walls echo with polish and sophistication. Whenever the weather cooperates, you can visit the outdoor pool with its small sundeck. The accommodations here offer plenty of elbow room, are done in subtle pastel shades, and have attractive floral-print bedspreads and drapes. A few choice toiletries await you in the modern bath.

Dining/Entertainment: The Cloud Room Restaurant & Lounge, on the top floor, serves a varied menu, with an emphasis on fresh seafood. Great views!

Services: Room service, laundry service, in-room movies.

Facilities: Heated outdoor swimming pool, wheelchair accommodations.

WESTCOAST ROOSEVELT HOTEL, 1531 Seventh Ave., Seattle, WA 98101. Tel. 206/621-1200, or toll free 800/ 426-0670. 150 rms, 44 suites. A/C TV TEL

$ Rates: $82–$93 single; $92–$103 double; $110–$150 suite. AE, DC, DISC, MC, V. **Parking:** $7 per day.

When you walk through the doors of this small hotel, conveniently located only a block from the Washington State Convention and Trade Center, you walk into a modern art deco room. A long wall of glass blocks illuminates the lobby. Near one entrance stands a shimmering black grand piano beside an Oriental screen. It is all so simple—perfect understated elegance.

The $10 million it cost to renovate this building was well spent. In the guest rooms, which are decorated in eye-pleasing pastels, there are king-size beds, couches, wet bars, recessed lighting, and modern sparklingly white bathrooms. If you choose to stay in one of the limited-edition suites, you can also enjoy your own private whirlpool bath, honor bar, hairdryer, shoeshine machine, and soft terry-cloth robes.

Dining/Entertainment: Just off the lobby is Von's Grand City Café and Manhattan Memorial bar. The restaurant, which can trace its history back 80 years, dedicates itself to preparing juicy steaks, lamb, veal, chicken, and salmon cooked over applewood. Be sure to have one of the special desserts that are prepared at your table. In the bar you'll be fascinated by the wild array of "objets d'junk" that hangs from the ceiling. Old water skis, a taxi door, and a totem pole are just three of the suspended surprises.

Services: Room service, concierge, valet/laundry service, in-room movies.

Facilities: Exercise room, no-smoking rooms.

MODERATE

BEST WESTERN LOYAL INN, 2301 Eighth Ave., Seattle, WA 98121. Tel. 206/682-0200, or toll free 800/528-1234. Fax 206/467-8894. 91 rms, 3 suites. A/C TV TEL

$ Rates: $52–$62 single; $62–$74 double. AE, DC, DISC, MC, V. **Parking:** Free.

A new remodeling has turned this place into a very attractive and inexpensive city-center accommodation. The deluxe rooms have wet bars, coffee makers, remote-control TVs, king-size beds, and two

**FROMMER'S SMART TRAVELER:
ACCOMMODATIONS**

VALUE-CONSCIOUS TRAVELERS SHOULD TAKE
ADVANTAGE OF THE FOLLOWING:

1. Weekend discounts of 30% to 50%.
2. Lower room rates in the late spring and early fall, when the weather is still good and summer rates are no longer in effect. Rates usually go up in early June.
3. Apartment hotels, which are very good value, help save on dining bills, and often offer free local calls.
4. The Ys and the AYH youth hostels offer very inexpensive lodgings in downtown Seattle.
5. Lower rates outside of downtown. Downtown hotels are used primarily by business travelers, and their prices reflect this. You can get the same amenities (often more) at lower prices by staying at a hotel away from downtown. The inconvenience is that you must travel into the city each day.
6. Senior citizens and families often get discounts, as do members of AAA. Be sure to ask if there are any such discounts.

QUESTIONS TO ASK IF YOU'RE ON A BUDGET:

1. Is there a parking charge? In downtown Seattle, parking charges can add as much as $14 per day to your hotel bill.
2. Does the quoted rate for a given stay include the room tax?
3. Is there a charge for local calls? A surcharge on long-distance calls?
4. Is breakfast included in the rate? Not only bed-and-breakfast inns include breakfast in their service; some moderately priced hotels and even some motels do, too (often only coffee and doughnuts).
5. Does the hotel have a complimentary airport shuttle? This can save you taxi or other airport shuttle fares.

sinks in the bathrooms. Even the standard rooms come with remote-control TVs. There's no restaurant on the premises, but because the Loyal Inn is only 5 minutes' walk from Seattle Center, it makes a good choice for families.

Services: Complimentary coffee.

Facilities: 24-hour sauna, whirlpool, no-smoking rooms.

DAYS INN TOWN CENTER, 2205 Seventh Ave., Seattle, WA 98121. Tel. 206/448-3434, or toll free 800/648-6440 or 800/325-2525. 90 rms. A/C TV TEL

$ Rates: $74 single; $79 double (discount card good for 10% off regular rates is available). AE, CB, DC, DISC, MC, V. **Parking:** Free.

Conveniently located close to Seattle Center and within walking distance or a free bus ride to the rest of downtown Seattle, this three-story hotel offers large clean accommodations. Modern furniture and pastel color schemes make every room comfortable and attractive.

Dining/Entertainment: The Greenhouse Café & Bar—as its name implies—is a sunny, cheerful place serving breakfast, lunch, and dinner. In the lounge you can sit by the fire or watch the big-screen TV.

Services: Valet/laundry service.

HOTEL SEATTLE, 315 Seneca St., Seattle, WA 98101. Tel. 206/623-5110, or toll free 800/426-2439. Telex 321234. 81 rms, 4 suites. A/C TV TEL

$ Rates: $56–$60 single; $62–$66 double; $70–$90 suite. AE, CB, DC, DISC, MC, V. **Parking:** $11 per day.

The 11-story Seattle has seen better days but is still worth considering, since it's one of the least expensive hotels in the heart of downtown that's still acceptable. Rooms are small but clean. I suspect that this hotel will soon be bought up and renovated because of its valuable location. If you want convenience and economical rates, this is the place for you.

Dining/Entertainment: Bernard's on Seneca serves inexpensive German and American food in large portions.

Services: Room service.

Facilities: Gift shop, hair salon.

PACIFIC PLAZA HOTEL, 400 Spring St., Seattle, WA 98104. Tel. 206/623-3900, or toll free 800/426-1165. Fax 206/623-3900. 160 rms, 2 suites. A/C TV TEL

$ Rates (including continental breakfast): $64–$80 single; $72–$88 double; $130–$170 suite. AE, DC, DISC, MC, V. **Parking:** $11 per day.

Built in 1929, this old hotel was renovated a few years back and offers attractive rooms and excellent value. The building, in the heart of the financial district, is now dwarfed by some of the surrounding skyscrapers. However, you're halfway between Pike Place Market and Pioneer Square, and just about the same distance from the waterfront. Rooms are small but they come with such amenities as ceiling fans and alarm clocks. Wingback chairs and cherrywood finishes on the furnishings give each guest room an elegant touch. Bathrooms are small and dated, but luckily they still have their old-fashioned porcelain shower knobs.

Dining/Entertainment: A Red Robin Restaurant serving gourmet hamburgers is in the basement of the hotel. You can see it through a window in the first-floor lobby.

Services: Valet/laundry service.

Facilities: No-smoking rooms.

SEATTLE DOWNTOWN TRAVELODGE, 2213 Eighth Ave., Seattle, WA 98121. Tel. 206/624-6300, or toll free 800/255-3050. Fax 206/233-0185. 72 rms. A/C TV TEL

$ Rates: $50–$60 single; $60–$75 double. AE, CB, DC, DISC, MC, V. **Parking:** Free.

This conveniently located and moderately priced downtown motel is located about midway between the Convention Center and Seattle Center, so it's convenient whether you are here on business or pleasure. The rooms are attractive and some even have balconies. There are clock-radios in all rooms, and the baths are large, with baskets of toiletries on the counters.

Dining/Entertainment: There is an adjacent restaurant (The Dog House) serving straightforward meals at economical prices.

Services: Complimentary coffee, in-room movies.

Facilities: No-smoking rooms.

SIXTH AVENUE INN, 2000 Sixth Ave., Seattle, WA 98121. Tel. 206/441-8300, or toll free 800/648-6440. 166 rms, 1 suite. A/C TV TEL

$ Rates: $71–$81 single; $79–$89 double; $105–$115 suite (lower rates are for off-season). AE, CB, MC, V. **Parking:** Free.

You won't have to wonder what time it is here: The huge railway clock behind the front desk seems to take up an entire wall. Royal-blue carpeting and oversize wicker chairs provide an interesting contrast of casualness and sophistication in the lobby. The deep-blue color scheme is continued throughout the hotel, from the awning over the entrance to the bedspreads and draperies in every guest room. And if you haven't already realized that this is more than your standard moderately priced hotel, one look at your room will convince you: On a small wall shelf is a selection of old hardcover books, and old photos of Seattle provide a glimpse into the city's past. Wicker furniture and a large potted plant give the room the feeling of a tropical greenhouse.

Dining/Entertainment: The Sixth Avenue Bar & Grill, located on the second floor, looks out to a Japanese garden that makes dining a very tranquil experience. Prime rib, steaks, and seafood are featured on the menu. In the lounge, warm dark-wood paneling and a fireplace are part of the cozy environment.

Services: Room service, valet/laundry service.

Facilities: No-smoking rooms.

WESTCOAST VANCE HOTEL, 620 Stewart St., Seattle, WA 98101. Tel. 206/441-4200, or toll free 800/426-0670. 165 rms. A/C TV TEL

$ Rates: $65–$85 single; $75–$95 double. AE, DC, DISC, MC, V. **Parking:** $7.

Built in the 1920s by lumber baron Joseph Vance, the Vance Hotel recently underwent a $7-million restoration and re-opened as a WestCoast hotel. Typically, the high-ceilinged lobby is very elegant—wood paneling, marble floors, Oriental carpets, tapestry-cloth upholstered chairs and couches, and ornate plasterwork wainscoting and pediments. Accommodations vary in size and some are quite small; the corner rooms compensate with lots of windows. Furniture, in keeping with the style of the lobby, includes an armoire for the TV. Bathrooms have pedestal sinks and windows.

Dining/Entertainment: Salute in Citta Ristorante is a bright Italian restaurant that has been garnering praise since it opened.

Services: Room service, valet/laundry service.
Facilities: No-smoking rooms, wheelchair accommodations.

BED-AND-BREAKFAST

TUGBOAT CHALLENGER BUNK & BREAKFAST, 809 Fairview Place North, Seattle, WA 98109. Tel. 206/ 340-1201. 7 rms (4 with private bath). A/C TEL
$ Rates (including full breakfast): $50–$110 single; $65–$110 double. Children by reservation only. AE, MC, V. **Parking:** Free.
Directions: Henry Pier, on Chandler's Cove at the south end of Lake Union.

⭐ This has to be the most unusual bed-and-breakfast I've ever seen. If you need lots of space, this place is definitely not for you. However, if you love ships and the sea and don't mind cramped quarters, don't pass up this opportunity to spend the night on board a restored and fully operational 45-year-old tugboat. (The only other waterfront hotel in Seattle is the much-pricier Edgewater.) You're welcome to visit the bridge for a great view of Lake Union and the Seattle skyline, or delve into the mechanics of the tug's enormous diesel engine. A conversation pit with granite fireplace fills the cozy main cabin, and in each of the guest cabins you'll find lots of polished wood.

Dining/Entertainment: There is a small bar in the main cabin and several excellent restaurants are nearby.
Facilities: Laundry facilities available, nearby boat-rental center.

BUDGET

Ys

SEATTLE DOWNTOWN YMCA, 909 Fourth Ave., Seattle, WA 98104. Tel. 206/382-5000. 185 rms. TEL
$ Rates: $33–$35 single; $37–$39 double ($1 discount to YMCA members). Weekly rates available. MC, V.
This is one of the nicest YMCAs I've ever seen. They welcome men, women, and families, and have rooms with or without private baths. If you want, you can get a room with a TV or just walk down the hall to the TV lounge. All the rooms are fully carpeted and equipped with modern furnishings and comfortable beds. Best of all, you have full use of all the athletic facilities when you stay here. You'd have to stay at the most expensive hotel in the city for facilities like these.

Services: Free local phone calls, baggage storage.
Facilities: Indoor pool, running track, weight room, racquetball and squash courts, TV lounges, coin-operated laundry, tailor, barbershop.

SEATTLE YWCA, 1118 Fifth Ave., Seattle, WA 98101. Tel. 206/461-4888. 30 rms (3 singles with private bathroom, 2 with shared bathroom; 6 doubles with private bathroom).
$ Rates: $26–$31 single; $37–$43 double. Weekly rates available. MC, V.
This downtown choice for budget-minded women is quite attractive

FROMMER'S COOL FOR KIDS
Accommodations

Sheraton Seattle Hotel & Towers *(see p. 47)* The V.I.K. (very important kids) program provides four hours of supervised activities on Saturdays for kids aged 5 to 12: There is a cooking class in Fullor's restaurant, a behind-the-scenes tour of the hotel, a special lunch, and a movie.

Seattle Marriott Hotel *(see p. 57)* With a huge jungly atrium containing a swimming pool and whirlpool spas, kids can play Tarzan and never leave the hotel. There is also a game room that will keep the young ones occupied for hours if need be.

Seattle Downtown YMCA *(see p. 55)* One of the nicest YMCA's I've ever seen. They welcome families and have rooms with or without private baths. You get to use all of the athletic facilities here; for facilities like these, you'd have to stay at the most expensive hotel in Seattle.

inside. The rooms are small and offer the barest essentials for comfort, but they are economical and clean. Security is also tight, so women traveling alone can sleep peacefully at night. The YWCA offers the same very convenient downtown location as the YMCA, which is only two blocks away. There is a small deli on the premises.

Facilities: Indoor pool ($5).

HOSTEL

SEATTLE INTERNATIONAL AYH HOSTEL, 84 Union St., Seattle, WA 98101. Tel. 206/682-0462. 126 beds.

$ Rates: $10 for members. MC, V.

This conveniently located hostel is housed in the former Longshoreman's Hall, which was built in 1915. To find it, walk down Post Alley, which runs through and under Pike Place Market, to the corner of Union Street. You must be an AYH member to stay at this hostel, but they'll sell you a one-night introductory membership for $3 per night. A full one-year membership will cost you $25. If you don't provide your own sheets, you can rent them for $2 for the duration of your stay.

Facilities: Kitchen, self-service laundry.

2. NEAR SEA-TAC AIRPORT

VERY EXPENSIVE

RED LION INN/SEA-TAC, 18740 Pacific Hwy. South,

Seattle, WA 98188. Tel. 206/246-8600, or toll free 800/547-8010. Fax 206/242-9727. 850 rms, 33 suites. A/C TV TEL
$ Rates: $119–$143 single; $129–$154 double; $175–$395 suite. Weekend packages available. AE, CB, DC, DISC, MC, V. **Parking:** Free.

You'll find Red Lions throughout the Northwest, and they're almost all like this one—big, sprawling, glitzy, with lots of amenities. Built on the banks of a small lake, this Red Lion has seven wings and a 14-story tower. With so many rooms, it isn't surprising that the hotel frequently plays host to large conventions. On a sunny day the lobby is filled with light streaming through the greenhouse-type walls. A shake-shingle roof and a Northwest Coast Native American design on the portico are reminders that you're in the Pacific Northwest now.

Take a room in the tower and a glass elevator will whisk you up to your floor, providing a great view of the airport all the way. Red Lion rooms are consistently large—in fact, some of the largest in the hotel business. Whether you book one with two double beds, a queen-size bed, or a king-size bed, you'll have plenty of space to move around. All the rooms have been recently remodeled in relaxing subdued colors.

Dining/Entertainment: Maxi's, up on the 14th floor, is a very elegant large restaurant. The adjacent lounge is on three levels so that you can enjoy the view no matter where you're sitting. In the evenings there's live big-band or rock dance music. Down on the first floor you'll find Seaports, a seafood restaurant open for breakfast, lunch, and dinner. There's a delicious seafood buffet Monday through Friday from 5 to 7pm. The Coffee Garden is a very casual coffee shop in the lobby.

Services: Room service, concierge, free airport shuttle, valet/laundry service.

Facilities: Heated outdoor swimming pool, exercise room, gift shop, wheelchair accommodations, beauty salon, barbershop.

SEATTLE MARRIOTT HOTEL, Sea-Tac Airport, 3201 S. 176th St., Seattle, WA 98188. Tel. 206/241-2000, or toll free 800/228-9290. 459 rms, 2 suites. A/C TV TEL
$ Rates: $83–$132 single; $83–$144 double; $195 and up suite. AE, CB, DC, DISC, MC, V. **Parking:** Free.

With its soaring atrium and tropical greenhouse garden full of flowering plants, a swimming pool, and two whirlpools, this airport-side resort hotel may keep you so enthralled you won't want to leave. There are even waterfalls and totem poles for that Northwest outdoorsy feeling. Best of all, it's always sunny and warm in here, unlike in the real outdoorsy Northwest. In the lobby, there is a huge stone fireplace that will make you think you're at some remote mountain lodge. The waiting area for the Yukon Landing Restaurant has a stuffed moosehead and shingle walls that continue the rugged-outdoors theme. You can't pick a better place to stay in the airport area.

Although all the rooms are relatively large and attractively decorated in seafoam green and lavender, the concierge-level rooms are particularly appealing. Here you'll find a copy of *Business Week* waiting for you. Attractive Oriental prints decorate the walls. In the bathroom, there are scales, a hairdryer, and a basket of elegantly bottled toiletries. And, of course, there's the concierge on hand to help you and a special lounge with complimentary coffee.

Dining/Entertainment: Yukon Landing Restaurant will have you thinking you're in the middle of the gold rush. Stone pillars; rough-hewn beams and wooden walls; moose, deer, and elk heads on the walls; and deer-antler chandeliers—all make this rustic restaurant very popular. For that gold-rush high life, enjoy the Sunday champagne brunch. The lobby lounge is a greenhouse that looks into the larger greenhouse of the atrium.

Services: Room service, free airport shuttle, valet/laundry service, in-room movies.

Facilities: Atrium swimming pool, whirlpool, health club, tanning center, sauna, game room, wheelchair accommodations, no-smoking rooms.

EXPENSIVE

HOLIDAY INN, SEA-TAC AIRPORT, 17338 Pacific Hwy. South, Seattle, WA 98188. Tel. 206/248-1000, or toll free 800/465-4329. 260 rms. A/C TV TEL
$ Rates: $88–$103 single or double. AE, CB, DC, DISC, MC, V. **Parking:** Free.

An extensive remodeling was recently completed here, and the lobby now looks as if it were in some small European hotel. There are slate and marble floors, as well as a fireplace with slate hearth. The swimming pool has been enclosed within a very contemporary building with a glass-block wall that keeps the room very bright.

Guest rooms feature gray carpets and dark-wood furniture with black trim, including armoires for the TVs. The overall effect is subtly Asian. Very comfortable easy chairs with hassocks are great for relaxing after a long business day. The King Leisure rooms come with sofas, desks, king-size beds, and a bit more room than the standard accommodations.

Dining/Entertainment: In its rotating dining room on the 12th floor, the Top of the Inn features a sweeping vista of the airport and the surrounding area, plus continental and American fare prepared with fresh local ingredients. To entertain you while you dine, there are singing waiters and waitresses, a pianist, and a violinist. The lobby lounge is a dark and lively place serving drinks and complimentary afternoon hors d'oeuvres.

Services: Room service, courtesy airport shuttle, valet/laundry service, in-room movies.

Facilities: Heated indoor pool, exercise room, whirlpool, wheelchair accommodations.

RADISSON HOTEL, 17001 Pacific Hwy. South, Seattle, WA 98188-3593. Tel. 206/244-6000, or toll free 800/333-3333. Fax 206/246-6835. 301 rms, 6 suites. A/C TV TEL
$ Rates: $89–$110 single; $89–$120 double; $150–$350 suite. Weekend and special packages available. AE, CB, DC, DISC, MC, V. **Parking:** Free.

An abundance of marble and a grand angular entrance give this low-rise hotel more glitz than you might expect. The predominantly green-and-brown decor suggests the Northwest forests, while a garden courtyard planted with spruces and ferns actually brings these famous woods right into the hotel. On sunny days you can dine on a courtyard terrace, although the sound of jets overhead might be a bit too much for you.

Rooms, done in the same brown-and-green color scheme as the rest of the hotel, are furnished with modern appointments. On the Plaza Club level you'll receive a continental breakfast, turn-down service, beverages, hors d'oeuvres, and newspaper.

Dining/Entertainment: Chaps, with exposed ceiling beams and rattan furniture, has popular lunch specials, as well as a menu featuring Northwest specialties and fresh local seafood at dinner. In the evenings there's live piano music, and later still, live bands perform as guests take to the dance floor. Colorful pastels of fresh produce decorate the walls of the Marketplace Café, where standard American fare is offered.

Services: Room service, laundry/valet service, courtesy airport shuttle, massages available.

Facilities: Heated outdoor swimming pool (in garden court-yard), sauna, florist, gift shop, wheelchair accommodations, no-smoking rooms.

SEATTLE AIRPORT HILTON, 17620 Pacific Hwy. South, Seattle, WA 98188. Tel. 206/244-4800, or toll free 800/445-8667. 173 rms, 3 suites. A/C TV TEL

$ Rates: $89–$113 single; $104–$128 double. AE, CB, DC, DISC, MC, V. **Parking:** Free.

The theme here could best be described as upscale mountain lodge. Contemporary Northwest art takes the place of moose heads, but the unusual chandeliers have a definite rustic appeal. You're right next door to the airport and within 20 minutes of downtown Seattle, so the hotel is convenient for both business and pleasure. If the hustle and bustle have you stressed out, you can escape to the beautifully landscaped courtyard gardens.

The large deluxe guest rooms have their own tiled lanais complete with rattan furniture for that tropical feeling. In the combination bath, you'll find a basket of assorted toiletries.

Dining/Entertainment: Buckwell's Restaurant is a sophisti-cated place with curtained booths for those seeking a little privacy while they dine. Seafood is the star of the menu here, but steaks and other meals are also available. The Sports Edition is the hotel's popular sports bar, with a big-screen TV and an old-fashioned popcorn machine.

Services: Room service, free airport shuttle, valet/laundry service.

Facilities: Heated outdoor swimming pool, whirlpool, exercise room, gift shop, wheelchair accommodations.

WYNDHAM GARDEN HOTEL, 18118 Pacific Hwy. South, Seattle, WA 98188. Tel. 206/244-6666, or toll free 800/

822-4200. Fax 206/244-6666, ext. 515. 204 rms, 24 suites. A/C TV TEL

$ Rates: $119 single; $129 double; $129 single suite, $139 double suite. AE, CB, DC, DISC, MC, V. **Parking:** Free.

Opened in late 1988 as a Ramada Inn, this hotel was soon taken over by the Wyndham hotel chain. Immediately inside the hotel's front door is a plush seating area that is made to look like a private library. A wood-paneled wall features a fireplace, and old books rest on the shelves. Directly behind this "library" wall, the motif is repeated but here there are far more chairs and couches, as well as a bar where you can order a drink before sitting down by the fire.

Request one of the extra-large rooms with a king-size bed and you'll find a number of amenities aimed at business travelers. L-shaped dark-wood desks with well-lit work spaces, two phones, and remote-control TVs are standard in these rooms. Suites include the same amenities, as well as separate living rooms with wet bars and two TVs. Bathrooms have long counters for spreading out all your toiletries and come equipped with hairdryers and coffee makers.

Dining/Entertainment: The Garden Café serves tried-and-true American meals for breakfast, lunch, and dinner. The lounge centers around a warm fireplace and is a pleasant spot for a drink and a bit of conversation.

Services: Room service, free airport shuttle, valet/laundry service, in-room movies.

Facilities: Indoor swimming pool, exercise room, whirlpool, coin-operated laundry, gift shop, wheelchair accommodations.

MODERATE

BEST WESTERN AIRPORT EXECUTEL, 20717 Pacific Hwy. South, Seattle, WA 98188. Tel. 206/878-3300, or toll free 800/528-1234. Fax 206/824-9000. 137 rms. A/C TV TEL

$ Rates: $65–$89 single; $75–$99 double. AE, DC, DISC, MC, V. **Parking:** Free.

Located 1 mile south of the airport, this hotel provides the service and amenities of a large hostelry. In the surprisingly elegant lobby, there are granite-topped tables, modern Louis XIV chairs, and floor lamps that resemble old pillars. Be sure to notice the unusual work of art behind the check-in counter; it's made from old hotel towels. An attractive atrium houses the swimming pool, whirlpool, and a terrace for poolside relaxation. The rooms are large and done in mauve and soft grays. In the bathroom you'll find a tray of toiletries.

Dining/Entertainment: Jimmy's is a casual restaurant with reasonable prices.

Services: Room service, free airport shuttle, valet/laundry service, complimentary morning newspaper.

Facilities: Indoor swimming pool, sauna, whirlpool, exercise room, wheelchair accommodations, no-smoking rooms.

COMFORT INN AT SEA-TAC, 19333 Pacific Hwy. South, Seattle, WA 98188. Tel. 206/878-1100, or toll free 800/228-5150 or 800/268-8900 (in Canada). 120 rms, 7 suites. A/C TV TEL

$ Rates (including continental breakfast): $65–$71 single; $75–

$81 double; $100–$150 suite. Children under 18 stay free in parents' room. AE, CB, DC, DISC, MC, V. **Parking:** Free.

You can't miss this building just south of the airport. It's painted an eye-catching orange-sherbet color. Inside, the elegant lobby is done in shades of peach. You may think that you'll be staying in a fruit salad, but the service is fine and everything is in top shape. You, too, can keep in shape in the exercise room or relax your sore muscles in the whirlpool.

Dining/Entertainment: There is no restaurant on the premises, but you'll find several nearby.

Services: Room service, free airport shuttle, valet/laundry service, in-room movies.

Facilities: Whirlpool, exercise room, wheelchair accommodations, no-smoking rooms.

HAMPTON INN HOTEL, Seattle, 19445 Pacific Hwy. South, Seattle, WA 98188. Tel. 206/878-1700, or toll free 800/426-7866. Fax 206/824-0720. 131 rms, 1 suite. A/C TV TEL

$ Rates (including continental breakfast): $65–$67 single; $75–$77 double; $100 suite (rates lower in winter). AE, CB, DC, DISC, MC, V. **Parking:** Free.

You'll get much more at the Hampton Inn than you'd expect from a small hotel in this price range. All the rooms are attractively furnished with modern appointments and decorated in pleasing pastels. A friendly service-incentive plan assures that each and every member of the staff here will do all that he or she can to make your stay enjoyable. There's even a "satisfaction guaranteed" policy that allows you to stay for free if you aren't entirely satisfied with your stay.

Dining/Entertainment: No restaurant on the premises, but several nearby.

Services: Room service, free restaurant and airport shuttle, valet/laundry service, free local calls, in-room movies.

Facilities: Heated outdoor swimming pool, exercise room, wheelchair accommodations, no-smoking rooms.

WESTCOAST SEA-TAC HOTEL, 18220 Pacific Hwy. South, Seattle, WA 98188. Tel. 206/246-5535, or toll free 800/426-0670. Fax 206/246-5535. 146 rms, 32 suites. A/C TV TEL

$ Rates: $73–$78 single; $83–$88 double; $82 single suite, $92 double suite. AE, CB, DC, MC, V. **Parking:** Free valet.

S Step into this WestCoast hotel and you enter a world of European styling, comfort, and service. The simple, elegant lines of the lobby—done in subtle pastels and shades of gray—are accentuated by a grand piano, this hotel chain's trademark. Feel free to play whenever the urge strikes.

The spacious, elegantly furnished guest rooms have queen- or king-size beds, writing table-, and art deco–style chairs. On the fifth floor, you get special service, including evening turn-down, coffee and a newspaper in the morning, plush terry-cloth robes, hairdryers, free local phone calls, and an honor bar. In all the rooms, you'll find bath scales and shoeshine machines.

Dining/Entertainment: Gregory's Bar & Grill is across the parking lot from the main hotel facility. Six nights a week, there is karäoke music in the lounge, which features an aeronautical theme; there is even part of an old plane hanging from the ceiling. In the restaurant a tropical feeling prevails. Fresh seafood is the specialty here, and there is a daily fresh sheet of specials. Sunday brunch is a good deal at $10.95.

Services: Room service, free airport shuttle, valet/laundry service, in-room movies.

Facilities: Heated outdoor swimming pool, whirlpool, sauna, wheelchair accommodations, no-smoking rooms.

BUDGET

CONTINENTAL COURT APARTMENT MOTEL, 17223 32nd Ave. South, Seattle, WA 98188. Tel. 206/241-1500. 140 rms. A/C TV TEL
$ Rates: $40 single; $45–$50 double. AE, DC, MC, V. **Parking:** Free.

If you think you've stumbled into an apartment complex while searching for this motel, you're there. You'd never know this complex wasn't strictly apartments unless I told you. Persevere and watch for the signs directing you to the office. Most of the rooms here are set up as spacious suites with full kitchens, and many of them also have cozy fireplaces.

Dining/Entertainment: Restaurants nearby.
Services: Free airport shuttle.
Facilities: Heated outdoor pool.

SUPER 8 MOTEL, 3100 S. 192nd St., Seattle, WA 98168. Tel. 206/433-8188, or toll free 800/843-1991. 119 rms. A/C TV TEL
$ Rates: $50 single; $55–$60 double. AE, CB, DC, MC, V. **Parking:** Free.

There's nothing fancy about Seattle's link of this popular budget-hotel chain—just low prices and clean rooms. The long low-rise simulated-Tudor building is within 5 minutes of the airport, which makes it very convenient.

Dining/Entertainment: There is no restaurant on the premises, but there are several in the area. Complimentary morning coffee in the lobby.
Services: Free airport shuttle.
Facilities: Coin-operated laundry, wheelchair accommodations, no-smoking rooms.

TRAVELODGE SEATTLE AIRPORT, 2900 S. 192nd St., Seattle, WA 98188. Tel. 206/241-9292, or toll free 800/255-3050. Fax 206/241-9292, ext. 123. 104 rms. A/C TV TEL
$ Rates: $45–$55 single; $50–$65 double. AE, CB, DC, DISC, MC, V. **Parking:** Free.

One more conveniently located and economically priced motel, the Travelodge offers standard motel rooms, although rose carpets and contemporary furnishings give the rooms a bit more appeal than usual.

Dining/Entertainment: Restaurants nearby.

Services: Complimentary coffee, room service, park and fly program, in-room movies.

Facilities: Sauna, coin-operated laundry, wheelchair accommodations.

3. FIRST HILL & CAPITOL HILL

VERY EXPENSIVE

SORRENTO HOTEL, 900 Madison St., Seattle, WA 98104. Tel. 206/622-6400, or toll free 800/426-1265. Fax 206/625-1059. 76 rms, 35 suites. A/C MINIBAR TV TEL

$ **Rates:** $140–$160 single or double; $170–$700 suite. AE, DC, DISC, MC, V. **Parking:** $10 per day.

Sit by the tiled fireplace in the lobby of the Sorrento and try to imagine all these dark mahogany-paneled walls painted white. Even the beautiful fireplace is hidden, covered over with plywood. That's the state this building was in before it was renovated. Today an old-fashioned European atmosphere reigns at this small hotel. From the wrought-iron gates and palm trees of the courtyard entrance to the plush seating of the octagonal lobby, the Sorrento whispers style and grace, and the service here is as fine as you can expect anywhere in town. One of the hotel's few drawbacks is the single elevator, which is slow at the best of times and which has been known to break down. If you can't climb stairs, ask for a room on a lower floor to be on the safe side.

When the Sorrento opened in 1909, there were 150 rooms. Today there are only 76. What this means is that your room will be spacious and unique. No two rooms are alike, but all have remote-control TVs and stereos hidden inside large armoires, minibars and mini-refrigerators, plush terry-cloth robes, and dual-line telephones. A couch or easy chair and hassock let you put your feet up and relax after a hard day of touring or working. In the bathroom you'll find a basket of toiletries, including a small sachet to keep your wardrobe smelling fresh. You even have a choice of down or fiber-filled pillows on the bed.

Dining/Entertainment: The Hunt Club, a dark restaurant with exposed brick walls and louvered doors that can be closed to create private dining areas, serves superb Northwest cuisine (see "Hotel Dining" in Section 5 of Chapter 6 for details). In the adjacent Fireside Room bar, dark-wood paneling continues the clublike, old-world atmosphere. Several nights a week a pianist provides musical atmosphere in this lounge.

Services: Room service, concierge, valet/laundry service, complimentary limousine service in downtown Seattle, morning paper, in-room movies.

Facilities: Health-club privileges, wheelchair accommodations.

MODERATE

THE INN AT VIRGINIA MASON, 1006 Spring St., Seattle,

WA 98104. Tel. 206/583-6453, or toll free 800/283-6453. Fax 206/223-7545. 79 rms, 3 suites. A/C TV TEL

$ Rates: $69–$99 single or double; $119–$159 suite. Senior-citizen discounts available. Children under 18 stay free in parents' room. AE, CB, DC, DISC, MC, V. **Parking:** Free.

S You may think I've sent you to a hospital rather than a hotel when you first arrive at this small European-style hotel on Pill Hill. It takes its name from the Virginia Mason Hospital, which is right next door; in fact, the two buildings are connected. The lobby is small but elegant, with a little brick courtyard just outside. Room sizes vary a lot, since this is an old building, but most have large closets, modern bathrooms (some with windows), and wingback chairs. The larger deluxe rooms and suites are quite large, and some have whirlpool baths, fireplaces, dressing rooms, hairdryers, and minirefrigerators.

Dining/Entertainment: The Rhododendron Restaurant serves Northwest and traditional cuisine. There is live piano music several nights per week.

Services: Valet/laundry service, concierge, room service, massages, in-room movies.

Facilities: Privileges at nearby fitness center, no-smoking rooms, wheelchair accommodations.

APARTMENT HOTEL

THE BAKER GUEST APARTMENTS, 528 15th Ave. East, Seattle, WA 98112. Tel. 206/323-5909. 20 rms. A/C TV TEL

$ Rates: $70–$80 studio; $85–$95 one-bedroom; $110–$120 two-bedroom. DC, DISC, MC, V. **Parking:** Free.

These apartments are located in the Capitol Hill district only a block off Broadway, where there are lots of inexpensive restaurants and unusual shops. You'll find the quiet residential setting to be relaxing and yet still quite accessible to downtown. Located in several buildings, the apartments are furnished with a combination of contemporary and period furniture. If you're planning a long stay or are traveling with your family, these apartments are a good choice. There are studios, one- and two-bedroom apartments, even two-bedroom town houses with fireplaces. Several of the rooms have excellent views of Seattle, Puget Sound, and the Olympic Mountains.

Services: Twice-weekly maid service, free local phone calls.

Facilities: Exercise room, spa, fully equipped kitchens, coin-operated laundry.

BED-AND-BREAKFASTS

GASLIGHT INN, 1727 15th Ave., Seattle, WA 98122. Tel. 206/325-3654. 9 rms (5 with private bath). TV

$ Rates (including continental breakfast): $58–$84 single or double. AE, MC, V. **Parking:** On street.

This 1906-vintage home was an early spec house—that is, it was considered to be a model home by real-estate investors—and the first house in this neighborhood. Capitol Hill was on the outskirts of the city, but eventually became one of Seattle's poshest neighborhoods.

That turn-of-the-century poshness prevails here, with some modern amenities as well. I'm sure you'll enjoy the backyard swimming pool and sundecks in the summer, the fireplace in the living room in the winter. Each of the rooms is individually decorated and even has a small refrigerator. Continental breakfast is served either in the dining room or in your room.

Services: Valet/laundry service.

Facilities: Outdoor swimming pool.

THE SHAFER MANSION, 907 14th Ave. East, Seattle, WA 98102. Tel. 206/329-4628. 6 rms, 2 suites.

$ Rates (including continental breakfast): $59–$65 single; $75–$95 double; $125–$145 suite. AE. **Parking:** On street.

⭐ Only a block away from Volunteer Park and the Seattle Art Museum in a neighborhood filled with elegant mansions, the Shafer is quiet and convenient. A huge entrance hall leads to oak-paneled rooms. Beamed ceilings, Oriental carpets, and a grand staircase leading to the second-floor rooms complete the picture of elegance. The guest rooms, especially the suites, are spacious and open, and some have views of the Olympic Mountains and the Space Needle. The continental breakfast includes freshly baked muffins, a fruit compote, juice, and coffee or tea, and is served either in the sunny paneled dining room or in your room.

4. NORTH SEATTLE

MODERATE

MEANY TOWER HOTEL, 4507 Brooklyn Ave. NE, Seattle, WA 98105. Tel. 206/634-2000, or toll free 800/648-6440. 155 rms. A/C TV TEL

$ Rates: $86–$90 single; $98–$102 double. AE, DC, MC, V. **Parking:** Free.

If you need to be near the university and want a view of downtown Seattle and the surrounding hills and water, book a room in this moderately priced high-rise hotel. There is no swimming pool or fitness room here, but the views are superb. Every room is a corner room, and all are pleasingly appointed in peach and deep-green tones. You'll also find an extremely large TV in each room, as well as a clock-radio. Though the tiled combination baths are small, they do have baskets of toiletries.

Dining/Entertainment: The Meany Grill features prime rib, steak, and fresh seafood in an elegant atmosphere of deep greens and soft pinks. Brass rails and exposed ceiling beams give it the feeling of an old-fashioned club. The adjacent lounge includes an oyster bar.

Services: Room service, valet/laundry service, complimentary newspaper.

Facilities: Exercise room.

UNIVERSITY PLAZA HOTEL, 400 NE 45th St., Seattle, WA 98105. Tel. 206/634-0100, or toll free 800/343-7040. Fax 206/633-2743. 135 rms, 2 suites. A/C TV TEL

$ Rates: $70–$78 single; $75–$86 double; $125–$165 suite. AE, CB, DC, DISC, MC, V. **Parking:** Free.

You'll think you've been transported to Merrie Olde England when you step through the front door of this hotel (formerly the Robin Hood Motel). The walls in the lobby and along an adjacent hall are done in scaled-down half-timbered cottage facades. Alas, the guest rooms do not continue the English-village theme. They were, however, recently remodeled in soothing pastels with blond-wood accents. There are comfortable chairs and a remote control for the TV so you won't have to get up. In the bath is a large vanity and a basket of soaps and shampoos. Located near the university.

Dining/Entertainment: Excalibur's Restaurant and Lounge is a baronial dining room that completes the English-village theme. Fridays and Saturdays, there is a singer in the lounge, and on Sundays guests can do their own karäoke singing.

Services: Room service, valet/laundry service, in-room movies.

Facilities: Wheelchair accommodations, heated outdoor swimming pool, fitness room, hair salon.

BUDGET

BED-AND-BREAKFAST

COLLEGE INN GUEST HOUSE, 4000 University Way NE, Seattle, WA 98105. Tel. 206/633-4441. 25 rms (none with private bath).

$ Rates (including continental breakfast): $38–$48 single; $48–$54 double. AE, CB, DC, DISC, MC, V. **Parking:** On street.

⑤ The nearby University Plaza gives you imitation Tudor; this small lodging gives you the real thing, albeit in a distinctly urban environment. This 100-year-old Tudor building is on the National Register of Historic Places. No rooms have private baths, but all are furnished with period antiques and do have sinks. There are pretty floral-print duvets on every bed, and some rooms have window seats. For the musically inclined, Room 305 even has a piano. The separate men's and women's baths on each floor are tiled, and boast antique vanities. A continental breakfast is served each morning in the fourth-floor dining room. If you're a light sleeper, ask for a room away from the street.

Dining/Entertainment: Down at street level there is a small café and a properly dark and smoky pub.

SEATTLE DINING

Consider yourself very lucky. Seattle is on the cutting edge of culinary creativity these days. For a lot of people, the opportunity to dine at Seattle's many excellent restaurants is reason enough to visit the city. Not only is the cuisine highly innovative, but prices are relatively reasonable. For these listings, a restaurant is considered expensive if it serves meals with wine or beer averaging $25 or more. Moderate restaurants offer complete dinners in the $15 to $25 range, and budget eateries are those where you can get a complete meal for less than $15.

Northwest cuisine has been generating a lot of publicity recently. Today Seattle is "like California a decade ago," says *The New York Times Magazine*. What is Northwest cuisine? First and foremost, it is fresh and almost always made with local ingredients. The Northwest has been blessed with a mild climate that's ideal for growing fruits and vegetables; wild mushrooms and greens fill the forests. The grassy hills produce excellent beef and lamb. The rivers and coastal waters abound in seafood. Put these local ingredients together in unexpected combinations, such as fresh salmon with raspberry butter, and you have quintessential Northwest cuisine.

The Northwest is also attracting a great deal of attention among wine lovers. Its climate almost reproduces that of Europe's prime wine-growing regions. Be sure to accompany your dinner with one of these fine local wines.

Seattle is not a late-night city. Many of the finest restaurants open for dinner at 5 or 5:30pm and close by 9:30 or 10pm. There are a few exceptions to this rule and I have noted these. Because the restaurants of Seattle are so popular with both locals and visitors, reservations are advised. If you plan a short stay, especially one over a weekend in summer, I highly recommend making a reservation before you arrive in Seattle if you want to dine at any of the restaurants serving Northwest cuisine.

1. DOWNTOWN

EXPENSIVE

IL BISTRO, 93-A Pike St. and First Ave. (inside Pike Place Market). Tel. 206/682-3049.

Cuisine: ITALIAN. **Reservations:** Recommended.
$ Prices: Appetizers $9–$12; pastas $11.50–$12.50; main dishes
$14–$30. CB, DC, MC, V.
Open: Lunch, Mon–Fri 11:30am–2pm; Dinner Sun–Thurs 5:30–
10pm, Fri–Sat 5:30–11pm; bar nightly until 2am.

Il Bistro takes Italian cooking very seriously and puts the Northwest's
bountiful ingredients to good use. The region is damp most of the
year and brings forth excellent crops of wild and cultivated mush-

SEATTLE DINING

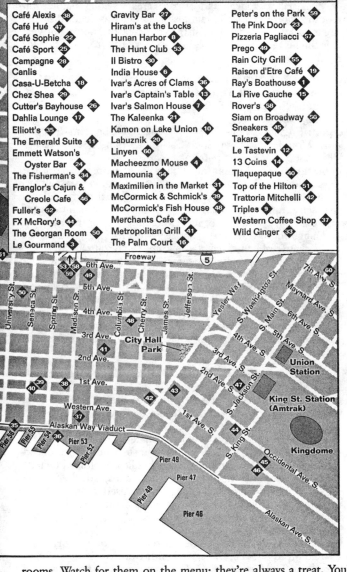

Café Alexis 38
Café Hué 47
Café Sophie 22
Café Sport 25
Campagne 28
Canlis
Casa-U-Betcha 18
Chez Shea 29
Cutter's Bayhouse 26
Dahlia Lounge 17
Elliott's 35
The Emerald Suite 11
Emmett Watson's Oyster Bar 24
The Fisherman's 34
Franglor's Cajun & Creole Cafe 46
Fuller's 52
FX McRory's 44
The Georgan Room 50
Le Gourmand 3

Gravity Bar 27
Hiram's at the Locks
Hunan Harbor 8
The Hunt Club 53
Il Bistro 30
India House 6
Ivar's Acres of Clams 36
Ivar's Captain's Table 13
Ivar's Salmon House 7
The Kaleenka 21
Kamon on Lake Union 10
Labuznik 20
Linyen 60
Macheezmo Mouse 4
Mamounia 54
Maximilien in the Market 31
McCormick & Schmick's 39
McCormick's Fish House 48
Merchants Cafe 43
Metropolitan Grill 41
The Palm Court 16

Peter's on the Park 59
The Pink Door 23
Pizzeria Pagliacci 57
Prego 49
Rain City Grill 55
Raison d'Etre Café 19
Ray's Boathouse 1
La Rive Gauche 15
Rover's 58
Siam on Broadway 56
Sneakers 45
Takara 32
Le Tastevin 12
13 Coins 14
Tlaquepaque 40
Top of the Hilton 51
Trattoria Mitchelli 42
Triples 9
Western Coffee Shop 37
Wild Ginger 33

rooms. Watch for them on the menu; they're always a treat. You'll find Il Bistro directly below the famous Pike Place Market sign. The entrance is from the ramp that leads into the bowels of the market, and once inside you'll have the feeling that you're dining in a wine cellar.

You won't find the usual antipasti of pickled vegetables here. Instead, the menu lists such mouthwatering starters as mussels sautéed with garlic, basil, tomato, and white wine. Pasta can be a genuine revelation when served with the likes of shiitake mushrooms, hot pepper flakes, vodka, and tomato cream. Long before you arrived, the choice of which main dish to order was decided by the hundreds of loyal fans who insist that the rack of lamb with wine sauce is the best in Seattle. Don't take their word for it—decide for yourself.

CAFE SPORT, 2020 Western Ave. Tel. 206/443-6000.

Cuisine: NORTHWEST. **Reservations:** Highly recommended.
$ Prices: Appetizers $4–$10; salads $4–$9; main dishes $8–$21. AE, CB, DC, MC, V.
Open: Breakfast Mon–Fri 7–10:30am, Sat–Sun 8am–2:30pm; lunch Mon–Fri 11:30am–3pm, Sat–Sun 11am–2:30pm; dinner Mon–Sat 5–10pm, Sun 5–9pm.

Seattleites and visitors alike just can't get enough of the excellent food and service here at this *très moderne* restaurant, only steps away from Pike Place Market. The design and decor are geometric, and the lighting tends to accent the many angles. These are softened, however, by niches holding vases of fresh flowers. Small dining rooms with glass walls are perfect for large parties. The animated chatter of contented guests keeps the restaurant lively.

If the black-bean soup is on the menu, as it almost always is, start with that—you'll be glad you did. The charred rare tuna with wasabi aioli, tobiko caviar, and an ocean salad is a cross between sushi and Cajun that shows off the imagination of the chef. Creamy desserts are all the rage these days in the Northwest, so be sure to try Café Sport's entry—a smooth-as-velvet crème caramel. In addition to the regular menu items, there are daily specials, including light meals and desserts.

CHEZ SHEA, 94 Pike St., Suite 34, Pike Place Market. Tel. 206/467-9990.

Cuisine: NORTHWEST. **Reservations:** Essential.
$ Prices: Fixed-price four-course dinner $34. AE, MC, V.
Open: Dinner only, Tues–Thurs 6–9:30pm; Fri–Sun 5:30–10pm.

It's hard to believe that there could be a quiet corner of Pike Place Market, but here it is. Quiet, dark, and intimate, Chez Shea is one of the finest restaurants in Seattle. A dozen candlelit tables, with views across Puget Sound to the Olympic Mountains, are the perfect setting for a romantic dinner. The ingredients used in preparing the meals here come from the market below, and they are always the freshest and the finest. Dinner is strictly fixed-price—four courses with a choice of five main dishes.

On my last visit, Canadian poussin roasted with a savory wild-mushroom bread pudding and served with Gorgonzola-fennel sauce was excellent. The first and second courses were a pasta terrine with Parmesan, olives, thyme, and an eggplant-tomato coulis, followed by an asparagus bisque made with sablefish. I know it will be difficult, but you'll have to make your own decision about which dessert to choose from the dessert cart. Apple-brandy steamed pudding and pear-almond custard tart were two of the temptations awaiting me.

DAHLIA LOUNGE, 1904 Fourth Ave. Tel. 206/682-4142.

Cuisine: NORTHWEST. **Reservations:** Highly recommended.
$ Prices: Appetizers $4.50–$7.50; main dishes $11–$20. AE, CB, DC, MC, V.
Open: Lunch Mon–Fri 11:30am–2:30pm; dinner Sun–Thurs 5:30–10pm, Fri–Sat 5:30–11pm, Sun 5–9pm.

The attractive decor of this stylish restaurant virtually disappears when your first serving arrives and all attention focuses on the creations of chef Tom Douglas, who put Café Sport on the Seattle and national map. The specialty of the house is Dungeness crab cakes with horseradish sauce—a bow to Douglas's Maryland roots. An appetizing concoction like shrimp and shiitake dumplings with sake sauce makes a tasty starter. If you are feeling extremely hungry, have one of the pasta dishes—black-walnut ravioli with roma tomato salsa, for example. If for some reason you can't eat crab, there are plenty of other succulent main dishes from which to choose, including daily salmon specials. The lunch menu features many of the same offerings at slightly lower prices. You can even get half an order of the crab cakes. There is live jazz on Thursday nights.

ELLIOTT'S, Pier 56 (near Seneca St.). Tel. 206/623-4340.

Cuisine: SEAFOOD. **Reservations:** Recommended.
$ Prices: Appetizers $6–$10.50; salads $4–$16; main dishes $11–$37. AE, DISC, MC, V.
Open: Sun–Thurs 11am–10pm, Fri–Sat 11am–11pm (later in summer).

Elliott's oyster bar is widely hailed as having the best selection in Seattle. A new menu is printed daily and lists the available oysters, fresh seafood, and smoked seafood (smoked on the premises). You'll find the long, narrow restaurant enclosed by glass and packed full of junior and senior achievers in business suits. Overhead, the massive timbers of this former pier warehouse have been exposed, while down at floor level etched and frosted glass and pale-aquamarine lighting offer a striking contrast.

Seafood is everything here, and the preparations are almost exclusively Northwestern. Instead of fried fish, you'll encounter such regional creations as king salmon with raspberry-soy glaze and smoked salmon fettuccine. Meat eaters will find only five menu items to satisfy them; so if you don't eat seafood, it's best not to eat at Elliott's. The extensive wine list offers many excellent vintages, and most are available by the glass.

FX MCRORY'S STEAK, CHOP & OYSTER HOUSE, 419 Occidental Ave. South. Tel. 206/623-4800.

Cuisine: SEAFOOD/STEAKS. **Reservations:** Recommended.
$ Prices: Appetizers $3.50–$13; main dishes $10–$26. AE, CB, DC, MC, V.
Open: Lunch Mon–Fri 11:30am–2pm; dinner Sun–Thurs 5–10pm, Fri–Sat 5–11pm; bar Sun–Thurs 11:30am–midnight, Fri–Sat 11:30am–2am.

The close proximity to the Kingdome necessitates a sports theme at this very popular steak-and-seafood restaurant. Walk through the doors and up a flight of stairs and you'll be facing a counter covered with microbrewery souvenirs and imported cigars and cigarettes. Leroy Neiman sports scenes hang from the walls, and huge pillars hold up the high ceiling. Grand arches, brass rails, and lots of glass and marble create a classic atmosphere. In the oyster bar, stand-up tables invite you to toss back a few cold ones—oysters, that is. The menu is limited to a few choice treatments of fresh seafood and hand-cut locker-aged steaks, although lamb, chicken, prime rib, and pork chops also show up on the bill of fare. The wine list features the best of Washington and California wines, and there are 30 microbrews on tap.

LABUZNIK, 1924 First Ave. Tel. 206/682-1624.

Cuisine: EASTERN EUROPEAN. **Reservations:** Recommended.

$ Prices: Appetizers $3.50–$4.50; main dishes $12–$23. AE, CB, DC, MC, V.

Open: Dinner only, Tues–Sat 4:30–11pm.

These days when we think of ethnic food we tend to think of Thai, Moroccan, Caribbean, and other exotic cuisines. But before all of these began to appear on the American scene, there was a very different sort of ethnic cuisine—Eastern European. Well, at Labuznik, the meat-and-potatoes meals of Eastern Europe have never been forgotten. Instead, they have been perfected. In Czechoslovakian, *labuznik* means "lover of good food." Dine here and you'll be a happy labuznik when you leave.

You'll have as much trouble pronouncing the names of the dishes here as you do at a Thai restaurant—but maybe that's what makes this such a good ethnic restaurant. *Vepro knedlo zelo* translates into a filling plate of roast pork with cabbage and dumplings. The veal Orloff is deliciously rich with mushrooms, capers, pickle, and cream. A meal here would not be complete without the Sachertorte. A lighter and less expensive menu is served in the bar.

MAXIMILIEN IN THE MARKET, 85 Pike St. Tel. 206/682-7270.

Cuisine: FRENCH. **Reservations:** Recommended.

$ Prices: Mon–Thurs fixed-price dinners $13.50; Fri–Sat appetizers $6.50–$8.50; main dishes $9–$22. AE, DC, MC, V.

Open: Mon–Sat 7:30am–10pm; brunch Sun 9:30am–4pm.

Maximilien is not your usual highbrow French restaurant. Dark-green walls and old, well-used tables speak volumes about the ambience here. It is country French, the sort of place you might find in a small village. And the fare is as no-nonsense as the decor, especially on weeknights, when the meals are fixed-price and served family-style. On Friday and Saturday evenings, however, dinner is a bit more formal, with such standards as beef tenderloin with béarnaise sauce; escargots bourguignons; and broiled rack of lamb with mint-butter sauce. If you're at the market early, you might stop by for breakfast or lunch, which are less expensive than dinner.

McCORMICK & SCHMICK'S, 1103 First Ave. Tel. 206/623-5500.

Cuisine: SEAFOOD. **Reservations:** Recommended.

$ Prices: Appetizers $4–$10; main dishes $10–$20; box lunches $6–$9.50. AE, CB, DC, DISC, MC, V.

Open: Mon–Fri 11am–11pm, Sat–Sun 5–11pm.

Force your way past the crowds of business suits at the bar and you'll find yourself in a classic fish house. From the café curtains on the windows to the highly polished brass to the sparkling cut glass to the dark-wood paneling, everything about this restaurant shines. Waiters wearing black bow ties will help you find your way through the exhaustingly long sheet of daily specials and equally long wine list.

The well-prepared seafood, lamb, veal, steak, and wild game have made McCormick & Schmick's extremely popular with executives from Seattle's surrounding financial community. You, too, can hobnob with the wheelers and dealers for the price of blackened yellowfin tuna with a tomato-ginger jam. From 3 to 6pm daily, you can get appetizers in the bar for only $1.95, and if you're in the mood for a downtown picnic, they also prepare box lunches.

MCCORMICK'S FISH HOUSE & BAR, 722 Fourth Ave. (at Columbia St.). Tel. 206/682-3900.

Cuisine: SEAFOOD. **Reservations:** Recommended for lunch and dinner.

$ Prices: Appetizers $5–$11; main dishes $9–$30. AE, CD, DC, DISC, MC, V.

Open: Lunch Mon–Fri 11am–3pm; dinner Sun–Thurs 5–11pm, Fri 3pm–midnight, Sat 5pm–midnight.

A recent menu here listed 31 different seafoods from such far-flung locations as Florida, Chile, Hawaii, Idaho, and, of course, Washington—to give you some idea of how committed McCormick's is to bringing you the very best. However, 23 of the listed seafoods were from the Northwest, and this was noted on the menu for those who insist that the freshest is always local. It is immediately apparent that McCormick's is determined to please. The ambience is old-fashioned, with dark-wood booths and a tile floor around the long bar, and the service is fast. The crowds are large; the clientele tends to be very upscale, especially in the bar after the financial offices let out. Both traditional and imaginative Northwest-style cuisine is served, with the menu broken into categories based on how the seafood is cooked.

METROPOLITAN GRILL, 818 Second Ave. Tel. 206/624-3287.

Cuisine: STEAKS. **Reservations:** Recommended.

$ Prices: Appetizers $4–$8; main dishes $12–$28. AE, DC, MC, V.

Open: Lunch Mon–Fri 11am–3pm; dinner Mon–Sat 5–11pm, Sun 5–10pm.

Another reliable restaurant for aspiring financial whiz kids and their mentors, this one is dedicated to meat eaters rather than to seafood lovers. Green-velvet booths, bar stools, and floral-design carpets are the keynote of the sophisticated atmosphere at the Metropolitan. Mirrored walls and a high ceiling trimmed with elegant plasterwork make the dining room feel larger than it actually is, while murals depicting scenes from Seattle history make the local movers and shakers feel secure that one day they, too, will be part of Seattle history.

Perfectly cooked steaks are the primary attraction here, and you'd be foolish not to order one of them. They're considered the best steaks in Seattle by those in the know. A baked potato and a pile of crispy onion rings complete the perfect steak dinner.

RAISON D'ETRE CAFE, 113 Virginia St. Tel. 206/728-1113.
   Cuisine: NORTHWEST. **Reservations:** Recommended.
$ **Prices:** Appetizers $9; pastas $9; salads $9; main dishes $11. AE, MC, V.
   Open: Sun–Thurs 7:30am–10pm, Fri–Sat 7:30am–midnight.
The young and the artistic, the chic and the wealthy, these are the Seattleites who can't get enough of the eclectic combinations that show up daily here. Amid outlandish decor and contemporary art, a noisy café atmosphere prevails. The menu is very simple and straightforward: Appetizers, salads, and pastas are all priced at $9, with main dishes coming in at only $11. Such pricing equality eliminates budget gourmets' frequent predicament of wishing they could afford the most expensive item on the menu. The offerings range the world. Cheese fondue showed up recently at the beginning of its American revival, and chicken satay and chicken curry are respectable versions of a couple of Asian favorites. Artistic mixed drinks have become a specialty of this restaurant.

LA RIVE GAUCHE, 2214 Second Ave. Tel. 206/441-8121.
   Cuisine: FRENCH. **Reservations:** Recommended.
$ **Prices:** Appetizers $3–$7.50; main dishes $13–$17; light meals $6.50–$10; fixed-price dinner $25; Mon–Thurs simple fixed-price meal $8.95. AE, DISC, MC, V.
   Open: Dinner only, Mon–Thurs 5–11pm, Fri–Sat 5pm–1am; bar open later.
⑤ The crowds here are a bit younger than you would expect, especially on the weekends when there is live jazz in the evening. The color scheme is red, white, and blue, but you won't find any American flags—these are French colors. Though the food is nothing fancy, it is typically Gallic. Couscous, borrowed from France's years in North Africa, is a staple. You'll also find steak and pommes frites, as well as a French-style hot dog. More refined tastebuds may prefer rabbit with mustard sauce or steak au poivre. For a more imaginative meal, you might opt for the fixed-price dinner special. Don't be intimidated by the long dessert list; simply order the homemade Armagnac ice cream laced with golden raisins.

MODERATE

CAFE HUE, 312 Second Ave. South. Tel. 206/625-9833.
   Cuisine: VIETNAMESE. **Reservations:** Recommended.
$ **Prices:** Appetizers $1–$4; main dishes $4.50–$19.50. MC, V.
   Open: Mon–Thurs 11am–10pm, Sat–Sun noon–10pm.

FROMMER'S SMART TRAVELER: RESTAURANTS

1. Eat your main meal at lunch, when prices are lower. You can eat at some of the city's best restaurants and try Northwest cuisine for substantially less than what it would cost at dinner.
2. Always ask the price of daily specials; they are almost always several dollars more expensive than the highest-priced main dish on the regular menu.
3. Eat early, between 5 and 7pm. Some restaurants offer sunset dinner specials at greatly reduced prices (and you aren't likely to have to wait as long).
4. Make reservations whenever possible. Even at lunchtime, downtown restaurants fill up. If there is someplace where you particularly want to eat, don't risk being disappointed.
5. Pay attention to how much alcohol you drink; even local wines and beers can be expensive.
6. Eat ethnic—there are lots of good inexpensive Asian restaurants all over the city.
7. Eat at Pike Place Market. There are more than 50 eating establishments here serving all types of food in all price categories.

The decor is simple urban chic with exposed brick walls, artful flower arrangements, and a Buddhist altar. Even the flatware and chopsticks are artfully arranged on each table. As you may have already guessed, this is Vietnamese as you have never known it—contemporary and with a French flair. You absolutely must start with the escargots stuffed with pork and ginger. Each little snail comes with its own lemon-grass pull tab. Other unexpected and equally succulent dishes are the stuffed crab and the roast quail. The location is convenient to both Pioneer Square and the International District.

CAFE SOPHIE, 1921 First Ave. Tel. 206/441-6139.
   Cuisine: INTERNATIONAL. **Reservations:** Highly recommended.
$ Prices: Appetizers $3–$9.50; main dishes $10–$14; desserts $3–$6. MC, V.
   Open: Mon 11:30am–2pm, Tues–Thurs 11:30am–midnight, Fri 11:30am–1am, Sat 9am–1am, Sun 10am–10pm.

A self-consciously stylish restaurant for self-consciously stylish patrons, Café Sophie hearkens back to the grand old days of supper clubs on the Continent. The booths are terribly romantic and there are a couple of tables up front in the lounge area, plus a few more out on the sidewalk, where you can sit and watch the Pike Place Market foot traffic. The menu pulls its gastronomic references from all over the world and changes frequently to keep the loyal patrons returning. On a recent evening, straightforward wienerschnitzel shared the menu with pork chili verde. Be sure to save plenty of room for one of the luscious desserts; they're the main reason most people come here.

IVAR'S ACRES OF CLAMS, Pier 54. Tel. 206/624-6852.

Cuisine: SEAFOOD. **Reservations:** Suggested.
$ Prices: Appetizers $4.50–$10; main dishes $12–$19. AE, MC, V.
Open: Summer daily 11am–11pm; winter daily 11am–10pm.

Opened in 1938, this is the original Seattle Ivar's. The entrance is directly across Alaskan Way from the Clam Central Station trolley stop, and a few steps from the door is a statue of old Captain Ivar himself, feeding seagulls. The lofty warehouse that houses Ivar's is filled with historic photos of old Seattle and its waterfront. Gleaming brass is everywhere, and there is a spacious lounge area with its own menu of lighter fare. Clams are the main attraction here, as you might have guessed, but every other type of seafood also shows up on the menu. Cajun, Northwest, Italian, French—however you can prepare fish, Ivar's does it and does it well. During happy hour, from 4 to 6:30pm on weekdays, there are half-price appetizers.

LINYEN, 424 Seventh Ave. South. Tel. 206/622-8181.

Cuisine: CHINESE. **Reservations:** Recommended.
$ Prices: Appetizers $5–$8; main dishes $6–$12; fixed-price dinners $12–$15.50. AE, DC, MC, V.
Open: Mon–Fri 11:30am–1:30am, Sat–Sun 3pm–1:30am.

⑤ It started out as a neighborhood coffee shop, a hangout for single men, but today Linyen is one of the most respected Chinese restaurants in Seattle. This is the heart of Chinatown, and there are dozens of other good Chinese restaurants all around. However, what makes Linyen stand out is its dedication to freshness and its excellent seafood dishes. Every day, there are fish, shellfish, and vegetarian specials listed on a blackboard just inside the front door. Spicy clams and crab in black-bean sauce are two of the restaurant's most popular specials, and they show up frequently. The decor is postmodern industrial, with exposed air ducts snaking around the ceiling of the main dining area. Just across the street is the Wing Luke Asian Museum, which is worth a visit while you are here in the International District.

MERCHANTS CAFE, 109 Yesler Way. Tel. 206/624-1515.

Cuisine: AMERICAN/CONTINENTAL. **Reservations:** Recommended.
$ Prices: Appetizers $2–$7; main dishes $7–$14. CB, DC, MC, V.
Open: Sun–Thurs 11am–8pm, Fri–Sat 11am–11pm.

If you have already been on the highly recommended Seattle Underground Tour, you've already had this place pointed out to you. It's Seattle's oldest restaurant and looks every bit of its 100 years. A well-scuffed tile floor surrounds the bar, which came around the Horn in the 1800s. An old safe and gold scales are left over from the days when Seattle was the first, or last, taste of civilization for those bound for, or returning from, the Yukon gold fields. This bar/restaurant has had a long and colorful history. At one time the basement was a card room and the upper floors were a brothel. In fact, this may be the original Skid Row saloon, since Yesler Way was the original Skid Road down which logs were skidded to a sawmill. Straightforward sandwiches and steaks are the mainstays of the menu, though a few more imaginative main dishes also appear.

THE PINK DOOR, 1919 Post Alley. Tel. 206/443-3241.
   Cuisine: ITALIAN. **Reservations:** Suggested.
$ Prices: Lunch appetizers $4.50–$7; pastas $6–$7; main dishes $7–$9; four-course fixed-price dinner $16.50. MC, V.
   Open: Tues–Sat 11:30am–midnight.

If I didn't tell you about this one, you'd never find it. There is no sign out front, only the pink door for which the restaurant is named (watch for a pale-gray wall with flowerboxes in the windows between Stewart Street and Virginia Street). Open the door and you step into a cool, dark room with a high ceiling and a fountain in the middle of the floor. Don't worry if you don't see anyone—the action is in the back dining room and on the deck, both of which are decorated with hanging Chianti bottles. Tuesday through Thursday, there's a palm reader working the tables so you can find out before your meal whether you're going to enjoy your evening or not. There are also cabaret singers in the evening, and on the weekend there's an accordion player. Be sure to start your meal with the fragrant roasted garlic and ricotta-Gorgonzola spread. I can never get enough seafood when I'm in Seattle, so I highly recommended the cioppino, a flavorful seafood stew. On the other hand, you can opt for the $16.50 four-course fixed-price meal and you won't go wrong.

TAKARA, 1501 Western Ave. Tel. 206/682-8609.
   Cuisine: JAPANESE. **Reservations:** Recommended.
$ Prices: Appetizers $1–$7; sushi $2.50–$8; main dishes $7.50–$16. AE, MC, V.
   Open: Mon–Thurs 11:30am–9pm, Fri–Sat 11:30am–9:30pm, Sun (June–Aug) noon–7pm.

If the sight of all the fresh fish in Pike Place Market has you craving some sushi, head down the Pike Market stairs. One flight below Western Avenue, you'll come to Takara, one of the city's best sushi bars. The decor is simple—tile floors, low walls separating booths, and a framed kimono on the wall. You can sit at a table inside or out on the patio (when the weather is good), or pull up a stool at the sushi bar. There is a long menu of Japanese soups, appetizers, and main dishes, but the sushi is the real attraction here. Be sure to order the Seattle roll—made with smoked salmon, of course.

TLAQUEPAQUE BAR, 1122 Post Ave. Tel. 206/467-8226.
   Cuisine: MEXICAN. **Reservations:** Recommended.
$ Prices: Appetizers $4–$6; main dishes $8–$16; lunches $5.50–$8.50. AE, DC, DISC, MC, V.
   Open: Mon–Thurs 11am–10:30pm, Fri–Sat 11:30am–11pm, Sun 2–10pm.

If you enjoy good Mexican food amid noisy revelry, then you are sure to find contentment here. Every evening a strolling mariachi band whoops it up in this cavernous open room, which was once a warehouse. A chandelier made from beer bottles leaves no doubt as to whether or not this restaurant/bar means good times. The menu features regional Mexican fare with the occasional Northwest twist. Cabrito—mesquite-broiled baby goat in ancho chile sauce, a favorite in Monterrey, Mexico—makes a rare North American appearance here. If you have a few friends along, you can order the Tlaquepaque Botana Platter, a dinner that includes 10 of the restaurant's specialties. To help you learn a little about the food you are consuming, the menu includes a glossary of chiles. During happy hour, from 4 to 6:30pm on weekdays, there are half-price appetizers.

TRATTORIA MITCHELLI, 84 Yesler Way. Tel. 206/623-3883.

Cuisine: ITALIAN. **Reservations:** Recommended.

$ **Prices:** Appetizers $3.50–$6.75; pastas $7.50–$10; main dishes $8–$13; lunches $4.50–$7.50. AE, DC, MC, V.

Open: Tues–Fri 7am–4am, Sat 8am–4am, Sun 8am–11pm, Mon 7am–11pm.

Located only a few steps from Pioneer Square toward the water, Trattoria Mitchelli is a cozy place with a friendly old-world atmosphere. The white-tiled waiting area has large windows that let in the warm summer air and salty breezes. An old circular bar in the lounge is a popular after-work and late-night gathering spot; candles flicker in Chianti bottles, and conversation is lively. There is a wide selection of veal dishes, all of which are worth trying. If you're in the mood for a salad, order the *insalata di salmone affumicato* just so you can say "smoked salmon salad" in Italian. It has quite a ring to it. If you're a night owl, keep Mitchelli's in mind—they serve full meals right through to 4am.

WILD GINGER ASIAN RESTAURANT & SATAY BAR, 1400 Western Ave. Tel. 206/623-4450.

Cuisine: INDONESIAN/MALAYSIAN. **Reservations:** Recommended.

$ **Prices:** Appetizers $1.50–$3.75; main dishes $8–$19. AE, DC, MC, V.

Open: Lunch Mon–Sat 11:15am–3pm; dinner Sun–Thurs 5–11pm, Fri–Sat 5pm–midnight.

With sushi bars old hat these days, the satay bar may be a worthy replacement. Pull up a comfortable stool around the large grill and watch the cooks grill little skewers of anything from fresh produce to fish to pork to prawns to lamb. Each skewer is served with a small cube of sticky rice and a dipping sauce. Order three or four satay sticks and you have a meal. If you prefer to sit at a table and have a more traditional dinner, Wild Ginger can accommodate you. Try the pungent Prawns Assam—tiger prawns in a curry of tamarind, tumeric, candlenuts, chilis, and lemon grass. Accompany your meal with a pot of chrysanthemum tea or a beer from China, Japan, or Singapore for a real Southeast Asian experience. As in Asia, the lunch menu is primarily noodle dishes.

BUDGET

EMMETT WATSON'S OYSTER BAR, 1916 Pike Place. Tel. 206/448-7721.

⒡ FROMMER'S COOL FOR KIDS
Restaurants

Ivar's Salmon House *(see p. 86)* This restaurant is built to resemble a Northwest Coast Native American longhouse and is filled with artifacts that kids will find fascinating. If they get restless, they can go out to the floating patio and watch the boats passing by.

Gravity Bar *(p. 80)* If you're traveling with teenagers, they'll love this place where Seattle's young and hip and health-conscious crowd comes to dine. The decor is post-modern neo-industrial and the food is wholesome, with juices called Saturn Return and 7 Year Spinach.

Merchants Café *(p. 76)* Seattle's oldest restaurant may be the original Skid Row saloon. This bar/restaurant looks every bit of its 100 years. The kids will go for the straightforward sandwiches and steaks.

Cuisine: SEAFOOD. **Reservations:** Not taken.
$ Prices: Soups $1.50–$6; main dishes $3.50–$6. No credit cards.
Open: Sun–Thurs 11:30am–8pm, Fri–Sat 11:30am–9pm.

Tucked away in a rare quiet corner of Pike Place Market (well, actually, it's across the street in the market overflow area), Emmett Watson's looks like a fast-food place, but the service here in fact is infamously slow. The battered booths are tiny, so it's best to come here on a sunny afternoon when you can sit in the courtyard. The restaurant is named for a famous Seattle newspaper columnist, and there are clippings about him all over the walls. Oysters on the half shell are the raison d'être for this little place, but the fish dishes are often memorable as well. Check the blackboard for daily specials.

FRANGLOR'S CAJUN & CREOLE CAFE, 547 First Ave. South. Tel. 206/682-1578.
Cuisine: CAJUN. **Reservations:** Not accepted.
$ Prices: Main dishes $7.25–$12. AE, MC, V.
Open: Tues–Sat noon–9pm.

Ⓢ Despite what Paul Prudhomme has led us to believe, Cajun food does not have to be expensive. In fact, the staples of the bayou are just down-home cookin' and ought to be cheap. Here at Franglor's the cookin' is both cheap and authentic. You won't find ham hocks and greens on too many menus, but here you will. Slightly more cultured palates might prefer crabs stuffed with spicy sausage, ham, and crabmeat. The charice Creole sausages, with red beans and rice, are spicy enough for any fire eater. This is a very casual café, with Mardi Gras masks and New Orleans posters on the walls.

GRAVITY BAR, 86 Pine St. Tel. 206/443-9694. Also at 415
E. Broadway, on Capitol Hill (tel. 206/325-7186).
  Cuisine: NATURAL. **Reservations:** Not taken.
$ **Prices:** Breakfast and lunch $2.50–$5.75; juices $1.50–$4.75.
No credit cards.
  Open: Downtown—Mon–Sat 7am–6pm, Sun 8am–5pm;
Broadway—Mon–Thurs 8am–10pm, Fri–Sat 8am–11pm, Sun
9am–10pm (later in summer).

★ If you're young and hip and concerned about the food that you
put into your body, this is the place you frequent in Seattle.
The postmodern neo-industrial decor (lots of sheet metal on
the walls) is the antithesis of the wholesome juices and meals they
serve here. The juice list includes all manner of unusual combinations, all with catchy names like Saturn Return or 7 Year Spinach. Be
there or be square.

**WESTERN COFFEE SHOP, 911½ Western Ave. Tel. 206/
682-5001.**
  Cuisine: AMERICAN. **Reservations:** Not accepted.
$ **Prices:** Complete meal $4–$6. No credit cards.
  Open: Mon–Fri 7am–3pm, Sat 8am–3pm, Sun 9am–3pm.

Ⓢ This place is so narrow that you'll probably walk right past it
the first time, and once you do find it, you won't be able to get
past that big guy on the first counter stool. Persevere and you'll
be treated to a real Seattle experience. The Western is a very casual
coffee shop sporting a Western theme—toy horses on the counter,
cowboy hats here and there, cowboy music on the stereo. The
cooking is good old-fashioned home cooking, no fruit-and-meat
combos here. Don't miss the espresso milk shake.

2. SEATTLE CENTER/
LAKE UNION AREA

EXPENSIVE

CANLIS, 2576 Aurora Ave. North. Tel. 206/283-3313.
  Cuisine: CONTINENTAL. **Reservations:** Highly recommended; jacket and tie required for men.
$ **Prices:** Appetizers $7–$9.50; main dishes $17.50–$33. AE, CB,
DC, MC, V.
  Open: Dinner only, Mon–Sat 5:30–10:30pm.
Peter Canlis opened his first restaurant on Waikiki Beach in 1947. It
proved very popular with Seattleites fleeing the Northwest damp, and
they wished they had a Peter Canlis restaurant of their own. And in
1950 they got their wish. The restaurant has enjoyed unflagging
popularity for more than 40 years now. The reason? It could be the
perfectly prepared steaks and seafood, or it could be the excellent
service by kimono-clad waitresses, or it could be the view across Lake
Union from high on a hillside. Why not find out for yourself?

A huge stone fireplace and stone columns lend a cool, dark air to
the main dining room, while outside the tops of fir trees jut into your

view of the lake far below. Unusual Asian antiques, including an old door, are displayed throughout the restaurant. A pianist fills the room with his melodies. This is the perfect place to close a big deal or celebrate a very special occasion. The perfect meal? Steak tartare with the restaurant's legendary baked potato, plus a salad tossed at your table, finished off with a Grand Marnier soufflé.

KAMON ON LAKE UNION, 1177 Fairview Ave. North. Tel. 206/622-4665.
  Cuisine: JAPANESE/INTERNATIONAL. **Reservations:** Recommended.
$ **Prices:** Appetizers $5–$10; main dishes $14–$23. AE, DC, MC, V.
  Open: Lunch Mon–Fri 11:30am–2:30pm; dinner Sun–Thurs 5–10pm, Fri–Sat 5–11pm.

If you crave Japanese tonight and your dinner partner can't stand it, try Kamon on Lake Union. You'll both be happy. You can also enjoy the sunset over the lake from either the formal dining room or the open-air deck. This is a grand restaurant, with wide steps leading up to the entrance, a spacious lounge with a piano bar, and the longest sushi bar in Seattle.

If you're still not convinced this is the place for you, consider your choices. For an appetizer, you might have smoked Northwest seafood, sushi, oysters on the half shell, or Italian-style calamari. The teppanyaki dinners, cooked tableside by talented chefs, are both entertaining and delicious. Or let the sushi master make a selection of his favorite sushi rolls for you. Filet mignon with wild mushrooms is sure to appeal to anyone who loves steak. There's no question about it—Kamon on Lake Union is the place to go if you have different cravings.

LE TASTEVIN, 19 W. Harrison St. Tel. 206/283-0991.
  Cuisine: FRENCH. **Reservations:** Recommended.
$ **Prices:** Appetizers $7–$32; main dishes $17–$24. AE, CB, DC, DISC, MC, V.
  Open: Lunch Tues–Fri 11:30am–2:30pm; dinner Mon–Sat 5–11:30pm.

Conjure up your image of a classic French restaurant and I bet this is about what it looks like. The use of skylights, picture windows, and trellises (on both walls and ceiling) creates an open, gardenlike atmosphere. Not only is Le Tastevin the largest French restaurant in Seattle, but it also has the best wine cellar, which features a surprising number of vintage French wines. In fact, wine is nearly an obsession at Le Tastevin. The back of the restaurant's business card has the following old German saying, "Drink and go to heaven, drink wine and you will sleep, sleep and you will avoid sin, avoid sin and you will be saved, ergo, drink wine and be saved." You'll find Le Tastevin between Seattle Center and the waterfront.

If wine isn't your cup of tea, you might start your meal with an exotic frozen, flavored Russian vodka. Don't miss the appetizer of pheasant pâté with Pommery mustard sauce. The salmon baked in a puff-pastry shell and served with pomegranate Chardonnay sauce is delicious. For a special meal, try the roast pheasant or chateaubriand

Wellington, both of which are prepared at your table. The dessert menu includes old favorites and unusual creations. Lunch prices are half those at dinner.

MODERATE

IVAR'S CAPTAIN'S TABLE, 333 Elliott Ave. Tel. 206/284-7040.

Cuisine: SEAFOOD. **Reservations:** Suggested.

$ Prices: Appetizers $2–$8; main dishes $12–$24. AE, MC, V.

Open: Mon–Fri 11am–11pm, Sat 4–11pm, Sun 4–10pm; Sun brunch 10am–2pm.

Not nearly so large as Ivar's Acres of Clams—but with better views, including several of the distant Olympic Mountains—the Captain's Table is said to have the best food of the three Ivar's restaurants. Because it is outside the normal tourist routes, this one tends to have slightly better service. There is free parking, too, which is enough to recommend it over Acres of Clams. For the more daring and delicious offerings, head straight for the restaurant's daily fresh sheet of specials.

3. FIRST HILL, CAPITOL HILL & EAST SEATTLE

EXPENSIVE

PETER'S ON THE PARK, 4000 E. Madison St. Tel. 206/323-7686.

Cuisine: NORTHWEST. **Reservations:** Recommended.

$ Prices: Appetizers $4–$13; pastas $11–$12; main dishes $11–$19. MC, V.

Open: Lunch Tues–Fri 11:30am–2pm; dinner Tues–Sat 5:30–10pm, Sun 5–9pm.

Amid the greenery of the Madison Park neighborhood, not far from the banks of Lake Washington and the botanical gardens, stands this cheery little neighborhood restaurant. The entrance is framed by lattices, and lots of potted plants and trees bring the greenery in from outdoors.

There are four nightly specials, including a low-calorie spa special for the fit-and-trim, on-the-go crowd that frequents Peter's. Each day also sees a Northwest catch-of-the-day special. Shish kebabs and Thai-influenced dishes both find their way on the menu, but I suggest sticking to one of the more interesting main dishes, such as orange prawns sautéed in garlic, oregano, scallions, and orange juice. Northwest wines are a specialty of the house.

RAIN CITY GRILL, 2359 Tenth Ave. East. Tel. 206/325-5003.

Cuisine: NORTHWEST. **Reservations:** Recommended.

$ Prices: Appetizers $2–$8; main dishes $14–$20; lunches $7–$10. MC, V.

Open: Lunch Mon–Fri 11:30am–2pm; dinner Sun–Thurs 5:30–9:30pm, Fri–Sat 5:30–10pm.

So you came to Seattle expecting to experience one of those legendary crystal-clear days when the mountain is out, but all it's done is rain, rain, rain. Cheer up. Seattleites have learned to laugh about the miserable weather, and the very best weather joke in town is the Rain City Grill. The restaurant's ceiling is decorated with dozens of umbrellas hanging upside down. The walls, of course, are painted overcast gray.

All the open umbrellas obviously have not brought bad luck—the meals served here are some of the best in town and display the imaginative flair of Northwest cuisine. On my last visit—a tempestuously rainy day, of course—the sautéed Dungeness crab cakes with saffron-lime mayonnaise were what most appealed to me, but the seared Washington venison with a date, black-pepper demi-glace was equally mouthwatering. Be sure to save room for one of the delectable desserts.

ROVER'S, 2808 E. Madison St. Tel. 206/325-7442.
  Cuisine: NORTHWEST. **Reservations:** Essential.
$ Prices: Appetizers $5–$8.50; main dishes $22–$28; five-course menu dégustation $41.50. AE, MC, V.
  Open: Dinner only, Tues–Sat 5:30–11pm.

Tucked away in a quaint clapboard house behind a chic little shopping center is one of Seattle's most talked about restaurants. Chef Thierry Rautureau received classic French training before falling in love with the Northwest and all the wonderful ingredients it had to offer an imaginative chef.

Voilà! Northwest cuisine with a French accent. Or is it French cuisine with a Northwest accent? Find out for yourself. If the salad of wild greens and edible flowers is on the daily-changing menu, don't pass it by; the flavors are delicately Northwest. Warm squab salad with wild mushrooms and balsamic vinegar dressing offers more emphatic flavors. The distinctive but subtle tastes of salmon and saffron come together in a grilled-salmon main course served with a leek-and-saffron sauce. In summer, don't miss the raspberry desserts—or, for that matter, the desserts at any time of year.

MODERATE

SIAM ON BROADWAY, 616 Broadway East. Tel. 206/324-0892.
  Cuisine: THAI. **Reservations:** Suggested.
$ Prices: Appetizers $4.50–$5.75; main dishes $5.75–$9.50; lunches $5–$7. AE, MC, V.
  Open: Mon–Thurs 11:30am–10pm, Fri 11:30am–11pm, Sat 5–11pm, Sun 5–10pm.

All the way at the north end of the Broadway shopping district in trendy Capitol Hill is one of Seattle's best inexpensive Thai restaurants. In fact, the food's generally as good as you'll get in Thailand, and that's saying a lot when you can't always come up with all the necessary ingredients. Siam on Broadway is small and very casual. The tom yum soups, made with either shrimp or chicken, are the richest and creamiest I've ever had—also some of the spiciest. If you prefer your food less fiery, let your server know; the cooks will prepare any meal with one to four stars, depending on how much fire you can handle. But remember that they mean it when they say super-hot. The phad thai (spicy fried noodles) is excellent, and the muu phad bai graplau (spicy meat and vegetables, one of my all-time favorites) is properly fragrant with chilis and basil leaves.

BUDGET

PIZZERIA PAGLIACCI, 426 Broadway Ave. East. Tel. 206/324-0730. And also at 550 Queen Anne Ave. North (tel. 206/285-1232), and 4529 University Way NE (tel. 206/632-1058).

Cuisine: PIZZA. **Reservations:** Not taken.

$ Prices: Pizza $8–$17. AE, MC, V.

Open: Mon–Thurs 11am–11pm, Fri–Sat 11am–1am, Sun noon–11pm.

Pagliacci's pizza was voted the best in Seattle, and they now have three popular locations. Although you can order a traditional cheese pizza, there are much more interesting pies on the menu, like pesto pizza or the sun-dried-tomato primo. It's strictly counter service here, but there are plenty of seats at each of the bright restaurants. For those in a hurry or who just want a snack, there is pizza by the slice.

4. NORTH SEATTLE

EXPENSIVE

LE GOURMAND, 425 NW Market St. Tel. 206/784-3463.

Cuisine: FRENCH. **Reservations:** Essential.

$ Prices: Three-course fixed-price dinners $18–$28. AE, CB, DC, MC, V.

Open: Dinner only, Wed–Sat 5:30–9:30pm.

On an otherwise forgettable corner in the Ballard neighborhood of North Seattle stands a tiny building that looks as if it might once have been a laundry or dry cleaner. Chefs Bruce Naftaly and Robin Sanders, former music students who came to Seattle to study voice, have converted this aging storefront into a memorable French restaurant. With only a handful of tables, service is very personal and the atmosphere is homey, with a hint of the country.

On the back of the menu you'll find a list of all the ingredients used at the restaurant, from Sumatran coffee to organically grown herbs and vegetables, and where they come from (neighborhood gardens, in the case of some of the herbs). A nice touch. On my last visit the menu included nettle soup, longline lingcod baked in paper with homemade nasturtium caper butter, and a house salad made with a variety of lettuces, wild greens, and edible flowers. A choice from the tempting pastry tray is not included in the fixed-price dinner.

HIRAM'S AT THE LOCKS, 5300 34th Ave. NW. Tel. 206/784-1733.

Cuisine: SEAFOOD/STEAKS. **Reservations:** Recommended.
$ **Prices:** Appetizers $6–$10; main dishes $13–$22. AE, CB, DC, MC, V.
Open: Lunch Mon–Sat 11am–3pm, Sat 11:30am–3pm; dinner Mon–Sat 4–11pm, Sun 4:30–9:30pm; Sun brunch 9am–2:30pm.

Seattle is surrounded by water, both fresh and salt. Here at Hiram's the two come together at the Hiram M. Chittenden Locks, where commercial and private boats of all sizes are raised or lowered during their journey between Puget Sound and Lake Union. The action here makes wonderful entertainment during a meal, and at night the locks are lit up. The restaurant's exterior, constructed of corrugated sheet metal, looks as if it belonged in a warehouse district; however, the interior is as elegant as the prices are high.

The menu is about equally divided between the regular dishes and the daily specials—and either way, you can't lose. Preparations are frequently in the Northwest style, but more traditional fare can also be found. The steaks are also quite good, and the Sunday buffet is a veritable seafood feast.

RAY'S BOATHOUSE, 6049 Seaview Ave. NW. Tel. 206/789-3770.

Cuisine: SEAFOOD. **Reservations:** Recommended.
$ **Prices:** Appetizers $6–$10; main dishes $11–$19; prices slightly higher downstairs. AE, CB, DC, MC, V.
Open: Lunch Mon–Fri 11:30am–2pm; dinner Mon–Thurs 5:30–9pm, Fri–Sat 5–10pm.

Upstairs at Ray's, where you'll find the lounge, the crowd of suntanned boating types can get pretty rowdy. The restaurant compensates by reducing the price of the food here, but waits of up to an hour for a table are not unusual. Downstairs, everything is quiet, cozy, and sophisticated.

Luckily, everyone gets the same fine meals. As at other Seattle restaurants, fresh herbs are making bold appearances on the menu, in dishes such as poached ling cod with mustards, tarragon, and cream. There are many delicious reasons why this is considered one of the best restaurants in Seattle. Grilled black cod in sake kasu with ginger is a bow to the Japanese influence that has crept into Northwest kitchens.

TRIPLES, 1200 Westlake Ave. North. Tel. 206/284-2535.

Cuisine: SEAFOOD. **Reservations:** Recommended.
$ **Prices:** Appetizers $4.50–$9; main dishes $10–$19. AE, MC, V.
Open: Lunch Mon–Fri 11:15am–3pm; dinner Sun–Thurs 5–10pm, Fri–Sat 5–11pm. Light meals served 3pm–1am.

The marina in front of Triples brings a very upscale yachting crowd to this large seafood restaurant on Lake Union, but the prices are extremely reasonable. Overhead fans turn languidly, and through the floor-to-ceiling windows you can watch sailboats drift slowly by and the skyscrapers of Seattle loom. It's all very casually sophisticated.

Proud of their fresh seafood, Triples also serves sushi and sashimi. This truly is "breakthrough" seafood, as the restaurant claims. The extensive menu also lists steaks, pastas, and chicken, as well as daily specials. Cajun preparations are a staple here, and so are Northwest, Italian, and French dishes. To accompany your meal, there is an excellent selection of wines by the glass or by the bottle. The beer list was chosen by a Mr. Michael Jackson, one of the world's leading beer authorities.

MODERATE

IVAR'S SALMON HOUSE, 401 Northlake Way. Tel. 206/ 632-0767.

Cuisine: SEAFOOD. **Reservations:** Suggested.

$ Prices: Appotizers $2–$7; main dishes $10–$19; fish bar $4–$7. AE, MC, V.

Open: Main restaurant—lunch Mon–Fri 11am–2pm; dinner Mon–Thurs 5–11pm, Fri 5–11pm, Sat 4–11pm, Sun 4–10pm; Sun brunch 10am–2pm. Fish bar—Sun–Thurs 11am–11pm, Fri–Sat 11am–midnight.

Ivar's Salmon House commands an excellent view of the Seattle skyline at the far end of Lake Union. Floating docks out back act as magnets for weekend boaters, who abandon their own galley fare in favor of the restaurant's clam chowder and famous alder-smoked salmon. The theme here is Northwest Coast Native American, and the building has even won an award from the Seattle Historical Society for its replica of a tribal longhouse. Inside are many artifacts, including long dugout canoes, and historic photographic portraits of Native American chiefs. The dinners even come with Native American cornbread and wild blueberry ice cream. Kids, and adults, love this place.

---

5. SPECIALTY DINING

LOCAL FAVORITES

I don't know for certain, but I suspect that Seattle is the espresso capital of America. Seattleites are positively rabid about coffee. Coffee isn't just a hot drink or a caffeine fix anymore, it's a way of life. Coffeehouses are rapidly overtaking bars as the most popular places to hang out and visit with friends. Espresso and its creamy cousin the latte (made with one part espresso to three parts milk) are the stuff that this city runs on, and you never have to be more than a block away from your next cup. There are espresso carts parked on the sidewalks, walk-up espresso windows, espresso bars, espresso milk shakes, espresso chocolates, even eggnog lattes at Christmas. The ruling coffee king is **Starbuck's,** a chain of dozens of coffee shops where you can buy your java by the cup or by the pound. They sell 36 blends of coffee, and you can find their shops all over the city. (Of course, there is one in Pike Place Market). **SBC,** formerly Stewart Brothers Coffee and also known as Seattle's Best Coffee, doesn't have as many shops as Starbuck's but it does have a very devoted clientele.

HOTEL DINING

CAFE ALEXIS, Alexis Hotel, 1007 First Ave. Tel. 206/624-3646.

Cuisine: NORTHWEST. **Reservations:** Essential.
$ **Prices:** Appetizers $4–$8.50; main dishes $18–$21. AE, CB, DC, DISC, MC, V.
Open: Lunch Mon–Fri 11:30am–2pm, Sat noon–4pm; dinner daily 5:30–10pm.

In keeping with the intimate European atmosphere of the Hotel Alexis, its premier restaurant is also small and elegant. The subdued lighting is perfect for romantic, special-occasion dinners. In warm weather French doors open onto a small balcony; in winter a marble fireplace fills the room with its cheery warmth. Flawless service and excellent food make this one of the best restaurants in Seattle.

The menu changes with the seasons and always features the freshest ingredients. The offerings at lunch are slightly different from those at dinner, and prices are slightly reduced. At dinner you might encounter Vashon Island rabbit accompanied by sun-dried-tomato polenta, or Penn Cove mussels on sorrel pasta in Asiago cream sauce. For an appetizer, the baked phyllo purse with Cambozola cheese and marjoram pesto is both fragrant and irresistible. Though the menu is short, the wine list is lengthy. The desserts are always delicious.

CAMPAGNE, Inn at the Market, 86 Pine St. Tel. 206/728-2800.

Cuisine: FRENCH. **Reservations:** Essential.
$ **Prices:** Appetizers $4.50–$13; main dishes $15–025. AE, MC, V.
Open: Lunch Mon–Sat 11:30am–2:30pm; dinner daily 5:30–10pm.

On the far side of the fountain that bubbles in the courtyard of the Inn at the Market, French country decor continues inside the aptly named Campagne. Large windows let in precious sunshine and provide a view of Elliott Bay over the top of Pike Place Market. Cheerful and unpretentious, Campagne is one of the most enjoyable French restaurants in Seattle.

The cuisine of Provence is the specialty of the house, and meals are consistently excellent. The rough-textured pâté de Campagne garnished with niçoise olives and cornichons is delicious, and the sautéed oysters breaded with Provençal herbs and served with aioli will give you a real taste of the south of France. There are daily fresh fish specials that feature whatever happens to be in season—and of high quality—at the nearby market. However, the menu's focus is definitely on locally raised meats, including Vashon Island rabbit on a bed of lemon-thyme fettuccine tossed with a green-peppercorn-and–wild-mushroom sherry sauce; rack of Ellensburg lamb fragrant with a sauce of rosemary, juniper berries, anchovies, and garlic; and beef tenderloin served with a red-wine, shallot, and fresh oregano sauce. Desserts are the equal of any other dish on the menu.

FULLER'S, Seattle Sheraton Hotel & Towers, 1400 Sixth Ave. Tel. 206/447-5544.

Cuisine: NORTHWEST. **Reservations:** Highly recommended.
$ **Prices:** Appetizers $6–$10; main dishes $16–$24. AE, CB, DC, DISC, MC, V.
Open: Lunch Mon–Fri 11:30am–2pm; dinner Mon–Sat 5:30–10pm.

★ Fuller's, named for the founder of the Seattle Art Museum, is dedicated to both the culinary and the visual arts of the Northwest. Each dish is as artfully designed as it is superbly prepared. Surrounding you in this elegant dining room are works of art by the Northwest's best artists. A tiny circle of light illuminates each table as if it were a stage, and it is—a stage for the creative productions of chef Caprial Pence's kitchen. The service is gracious and attentive.

You never know what influences might show up on Fuller's menu. On my last visit an excellent appetizer of grilled scallops was served with a South American chipotle sauce, while coconut prawns came with marinated rice noodles. If you are in town only for a short visit and wish to sample as much food here as possible, order from Fuller's Premier Menu, which gives you smaller portions of two main dishes. Lamb rack with marionberry sauce and venison loin with huckleberry sauce are just two examples of what you can expect from the Northwest kitchen at Fuller's. If you haven't yet grown to appreciate fruit with your meat, try the kasu cod with spicy cabbage salad. Local fruits are also put to excellent use in the restaurant's desserts, which should be accompanied by the special coffee tray. Shaved chocolate, cinnamon sticks, whipped cream, and other accompaniments make the coffee alone a dessert unto itself. Lunch, with its lower prices, is especially popular. The wine list reflects the seasonal changes on the menu.

THE GEORGIAN ROOM, Four Seasons Olympic Hotel, 411 University St. Tel. 206/621-1700.
   Cuisine: CONTINENTAL/NORTHWEST. **Reservations:** Recommended.
$ Prices: Appetizers $7–$17.50; main dishes $22–$30. AE, CB, DC, MC, V.
   Open: Breakfast Mon–Fri 6:30–11am, Sat 6:30am–noon, Sun 7–11am; lunch Mon–Fri 11:30am–2pm; dinner Mon–Thurs 6–10pm, Fri–Sat 6–10:30pm; Sun brunch 10am–2pm.

★ Nowhere in Seattle is there a more elegant restaurant—to dine at The Georgian Room is to dine in a palace. The soaring ceiling is decorated with intricate moldings, and the huge windows are framed by luxurious draperies. On a small marble floor in the center of the room stands a baby grand piano on which a pianist plays soothing music at dinner. An antique table nearby holds the evening's dessert selection as well as an immense flower arrangement. The green-and-rose decor beneath the sparkling crystal chandelier is perfectly sophisticated. The excellent service will convince you that your table is the only one being served.

The menu offerings are primarily continental, which is appropriate to the European setting. For less daring diners, the few touches of Northwest flair are a suitable introduction to that cuisine. Wild game makes regular appearances, as does caviar, so if you have ever craved caviar and pheasant for dinner, you might just have your wish fulfilled here. Of course, you'll also find those staples of the Northwest— salmon and Dungeness crab—in several guises. For dessert, there's that table in the middle of the room. As you would expect, the wine list is well suited to both the cuisine and the dining room. Sunday brunch is the best in the city.

THE HUNT CLUB, Sorrento Hotel, 900 Madison St. Tel. 206/622-6400.

Cuisine: NORTHWEST. **Reservations:** Recommended.

$ Prices: Appetizers $6.50–$8; main dishes $19–$25. AE, DC, MC, V.

Open: Daily 7am–10pm.

The Hunt Club is just the sort of place its name would indicate— dark, intimate, well suited to business lunches and closing big deals. Mahogany paneling lines the walls, and stained glass adds splashes of color. If you need a little privacy, folding louvered doors can create private dining areas.

Although chef Barbara Figueroa prepares Northwest-style meals in her kitchen, they're not as flowery or as fruity as in other Seattle restaurants. Some of the most adventurous creations are to be found in the appetizers section, where such delicacies as oyster-mushroom timbales with smoked duck and hazelnuts tempted me to make a meal of only starters. Always a fan of Indian food, I couldn't resist the rack of lamb accompanied by sautéed spinach with cumin and black-mustard seed and minted yogurt sauce with rhubarb. The always popular filet mignon with smoked tomato demi-glace and elephant garlic wafers will appeal to less adventurous diners. For dessert, there are pastries, cakes, and homemade ice cream. Lunch, with equally delicious main dishes, is about half the price of dinner.

THE PALM COURT, Westin Hotel, Seattle, 1900 Fifth Ave. Tel. 206/728-1000.

Cuisine: NORTHWEST. **Reservations:** Recommended.

$ Prices: Appetizers $5–$6; main dishes $16–$20. AE, DC, MC, V.

Open: Lunch Mon–Sat 11:30am–2pm; dinner Mon–Sat 6:30–10:30pm.

The Palm Court's gardenlike dining rooms are the antithesis of those of other highly acclaimed local hotel restaurants such as Fuller's and the Hunt Club—bright and well lit. Walls of glass and sparkling lights turn it into a giant jewelbox. Despite the glimmer and glitz, service is friendly and the atmosphere is always relaxed and casual.

The fare here is solidly Northwest, with a distinctive emphasis on sauces made with fruit. From the moment you open the menu, you realize that you're going to be tasting some flavor combinations you have never before encountered. The prawn cocktail comes with a creamy and brightly tasty ginger-orange mayonnaise. The salads here are another arena for chef Peter Mueller's imagination. Scallop–and–Jerusalem artichoke salad is served with a hazelnut vinaigrette, while a salad of Bibb lettuce and port-marinated pear is served with an avocado vinaigrette. The main dishes are almost equally divided between seafood and meat, and all are tempting. Grilled red snapper with tomatillo rice and mango sauce is a classic example of Northwest cuisine, as is grilled marinated duck breast with eggplant pudding and port-wine sage sauce. For dessert, there is no question— order one of the soufflés, such as that made with Whidbey Island loganberry liqueur. Lunches are much less expensive than dinners, but the menu is not as imaginative.

DINING WITH A VIEW

THE EMERALD SUITE AND SPACE NEEDLE RESTAURANT, Seattle Center. Tel. 206/443-2150.

Cuisine: NORTHWEST. **Reservations:** Essential.

$ Prices: Emerald Suite—appetizers $6.50–$10; main dishes $22–$36. Space Needle Restaurant—appetizers $4.50–$9, main dishes $18–$34. AE, CB, DC, MC, V.

Open: Summer—breakfast Mon–Sat 7:30–9:30am; lunch Mon–Sat 11am–3pm; dinner Mon–Sat 5pm–midnight, Sun 5pm–midnight; Sun brunch 8am–3pm. Winter (Labor Day to Memorial Day)—lunch 11am–3pm; dinner Sun–Thurs 5–11pm, Fri–Sat 5pm–midnight; Sun brunch 10am–3pm.

There may not be a more difficult restaurant in Seattle to get into than the Emerald Suite at the Space Needle. With seating for only 50, the attractively decorated restaurant is cozy, elegant, and almost always booked solid. Both the prices and the views are some of the highest in the city. The dining room rotates, assuring you a new vista with each course.

The long appetizers list can be difficult to get past. You'll want to try everything—for example, calamari with basil mayonnaise or a Northwest sampler of prawns, smoked salmon, and smoked chicken. A salad of seasonal greens and flowers topped with champagne-raspberry vinaigrette is filled with the delicate flavors of summer in the Northwest. Main dishes are savory and mouthwatering, with an emphasis on fragrant sauces. Try the veal medallions sautéed in olive oil with mushrooms, garlic, tomato concasse, and Madeira.

PREGO, Stouffer Madison Hotel, 515 Madison St. Tel. 206/583-0300, ext. 3900.

Cuisine: ITALIAN. **Reservations:** Recommended.

$ Prices: Appetizers $4–$6; pastas $13–$23; main dishes $18–$25. AE, CB, DC, MC, V.

Open: Lunch Mon–Fri 11:30am–2:30pm; dinner Sun–Thurs 5:30–10pm, Fri–Sat 5:30–11pm.

You'll be surrounded by the bold colors and shapes of Matisse originals when you dine at this very stylish northern Italian restaurant. The dining room is split into two levels, so all diners get a view. Service is attentive and accommodating.

There is a distinct emphasis on seafood at this outstanding place, where a meal might start with deep-fried calamari with warm basil aioli, followed by a pasta course of Dungeness crabmeat ravioli with caviar, and then by a main dish of sautéed prawns and sea scallops with wild mushrooms and sherry sauce. Luckily, the pasta courses are available in appetizer proportions for those who were not born with an Italian appetite. In addition to the delicious seafood dishes, there are also plenty of meat dishes, such as rack of lamb with rosemary and garlic. Lunches are quite a bit less expensive than dinners, but there are far fewer seafood dishes offered.

TOP OF THE HILTON, Seattle Hilton Hotel, Sixth Ave. and University St. Tel. 206/624-0500.
Cuisine: CONTINENTAL. **Reservations:** Recommended.
$ Prices: Appetizers $7–$9; main dishes $17–$36; Sun brunch $13–$16. AE, CB, DC, DISC, MC, V.
Open: Lunch Tues–Fri 11:30am–2pm; dinner Sun, Tues–Thurs 5:30–10pm, Fri–Sat 5:30–11pm; Sun brunch 9:30am–2pm.

There's just no getting around the fact that if you want to dine with a million-dollar view, it's going to cost you a pretty penny. One difference here is the live music in the evenings, which neither the Emerald Suite nor Prego offers. The decor is sparkling sophistication; you'll dine amid shining chrome furniture arranged on two levels. Service is excellent and I'm sure you'll be happy with the food.

The appetizers here are not calculated to astound or surprise—just simple but flavorful stalwarts such as prawn cocktail, pâté, peppered brie, and oysters on the half shell. The marinated teng dah beef, with its hints of Asian spices, is always popular. The tempting display of fresh desserts is placed close to the entrance so that you will be sure to notice it as you arrive; save room. Stop by for lunch and you can get an inexpensive sandwich, or come for the Sunday brunch. Any time of day or night, the view is great.

LIGHT, CASUAL, & FAST FOOD

MACHEEZMO MOUSE, 211 Broadway Ave. East. Tel. 206/325-0072.
Cuisine: MEXICAN. **Reservations:** Not taken or necessary.
$ Prices: Complete dinner $3–$6.
Open: Mon–Thurs 11am–9pm, Fri–Sat 11am–10pm, Sun noon–9pm. Also at 4129 University Way NE (tel. 206/633-4658).

Portland has such a problem with mice these days that it has started exporting them to Seattle. The Macheezmo Mouse concept of healthy fast food is catching on with the young and active crowd. They come here for delicious low-fat, low-salt, low-cholesterol, low-calorie Mexican food. Everything on the menu tastes even better with plenty of tangy, spicy Boss sauce.

BREAKFAST/BRUNCH

If a restaurant serves brunch, I have noted it in the listings above. The best bets for brunches are the major downtown hotels, and although the prices are high, the spreads are lavish. By far the most lavish is to be found at the Four Seasons Olympic Hotel amid the greenery and glass of the greenhouselike Garden Court restaurant (tel. 206/621-1700). If you're in town on a Sunday, put on your finery and enjoy the feast for $25; it is served from 10am to 2pm. If you prefer an even tonier brunch, head for the Olympic's Georgian Room instead. It's à la carte only and will cost you even more than at the Garden Court. Another notable brunch, for $15.95, is the one served at the Top of the Hilton (tel. 206/624-0500), where the spectacular views are as impressive as the display of food (see "Dining with a View," above). The hours here are also 9:30am to 1:30pm.

LATE-NIGHT/24-HOUR RESTAURANTS

CUTTER'S BAYHOUSE, 2001 Western Ave. Tel. 206/448-4884.

Cuisine: INTERNATIONAL. **Reservations:** Suggested.

$ Prices: Appetizers $5–$7.50; salads $3.50–$12; main dishes $9–$20. AE, DC, MC, V.

Open: Lunch Mon–Fri 11am–3pm, Sat–Sun 11am–4:30pm; dinner Mon–Fri 5–11pm, Sat–Sun 4:30–11pm; bar until 2am.

Cutter's is a difficult place to classify: It serves delicious seafood, steaks, and pastas, with influences as far-flung as Japanese, Indian, and Italian. With its varied menu, casual and friendly atmosphere, convenient location, and long hours, Cutter's considers itself the quintessential American bistro. It's as American as Cajun fettuccine or yaki soba (Japanese noodles) or Thai shrimp salad or veal pepperonata or coconut curry or . . . you get the picture. This is where Seattle comes to graze, and it's best to visit after Pike Place Market has closed, late at night, or on a weekday. When the weekend crowds throng to the market across the street, Cutter's can be just as crowded, despite its immense dining room.

13 COINS RESTAURANT, 125 Boren Ave. North. Tel. 206/682-2513. And also at 18000 Pacific Hwy. South (tel. 206/243-9500).

Cuisine: CONTINENTAL. **Reservations:** Suggested during usual dinner hours.

$ Prices: Appetizers $4.50–$8.75; pastas $9–$12.50; main dishes $12–$29. AE, CB, DC, MC, V.

Open: Daily 24 hours.

The name comes from a Peruvian legend about a poor boy who had only 13 coins in his pocket to offer for the hand in marriage of the girl he loved. Embedded in each of the tables at these two restaurants you will find 13 coins. For 25 years the restaurants have been preparing meals with "care and concern." The star attraction is the exhibition cooking, but what keeps fans loyal are the gargantuan proportions. Every meal is enough for two people! The menu offers all the standard continental favorites from calf's liver and onions to veal parmigiana. There's a nice selection of pastas, plus plenty of fresh seafood. At the airport restaurant, there is live jazz several nights each week.

CHAPTER 7

WHAT TO SEE & DO IN SEATTLE

Seattle is a very new city, and until recently it was considered a cultural backwater rich in natural beauty. Things are changing on the cultural front, but the city's natural surroundings are still one of its primary attractions. You can easily cover all of Seattle's museums and major sights in two or three days. With the help of the itineraries below, you should have a good idea of what not to miss. After that, rent a car and head for the great outdoors. You have your choice of islands, ocean beaches, or mountains, all of which can be enjoyed in any season.

The itineraries outlined here will give you an understanding of the history, natural resources, and cultural diversity that have made Seattle the city it is today.

SUGGESTED ITINERARIES

IF YOU HAVE 1 DAY

Day 1 Start your day in the historic Pioneer Square District and take the earliest Seattle Underground Tour you can. You'll have fun and get a good idea of Seattle's early history. From Pioneer Square, walk down to the waterfront and head north. You'll pass numerous seafood restaurants, all of which are quite good; Ivar's Acres of Clams is the most famous. Stop in at the Seattle Aquarium and learn about the sealife of the region. At Pier 55 you can get a 1-hour harbor tour cruise. Continue along the waterfront until you reach the signs for Pike Place Market, which is on the far side of the elevated highway and up a hill. In the market, you can buy fresh salmon and Dungeness crabs packed to go, and much more. From Pike Place Market, walk to the monorail station in Westlake Center, which is at the corner of Pine Street and Fourth Avenue. The monorail will take you to Seattle Center, where you can take

❓ DID YOU KNOW . . . ?

- KJR radio became the second radio station in America when it opened in 1920.
- There used to be seven hills in Seattle, but now there are only six. Denny Hill was leveled by high-powered water hoses because it was just too steep.
- Seattleites buy more sunglasses per capita than the people of any other U.S. city—they lose the last pair during the year's long stretch of gray skies.
- It rains fewer inches per year in Seattle than it does in New York, Boston, or Washington, D.C.
- The term Skid Row is derived from Skid Road, a road down which logs were skidded to a lumber mill. The very first Skid Road was in Seattle. Today it is called Yesler Way.
- The first Boeing airplane took off from Lake Union in 1916. Boeing is now the largest employer in the Seattle area.
- The geoduck (pronounced "gooeyduck") clam, harvested from around the Puget Sound, can weigh more than 5 pounds.

an elevator to the top of the Space Needle, Seattle's best-known landmark. Finish the day with dinner at one of the city's many restaurants serving seafood or Northwest cuisine.

IF YOU HAVE 2 DAYS

Day 1 Start your first day in Pioneer Square, as outlined above. After the Seattle Underground Tour, head over to the nearby International District (Chinatown) and have lunch in a Chinese restaurant. Linyen is my favorite. After lunch, head over to the waterfront for a harbor cruise, a stop at the aquarium and Ye Olde Curiosity Shop, and have dinner at one of the seafood restaurants.

Day 2 Start your second day at Pike Place Market, and be sure to get there early to get the freshest fish (they'll pack it to take on the plane). From here it is only two blocks to the new Seattle Art Museum. After touring the museum, take the lunch tour to Tillicum Village. You'll get to see Northwest Native American dances while dining on alder-smoked salmon. When you get back to Seattle, head for Seattle Center and the Space Needle.

IF YOU HAVE 3 DAYS

Days 1-2 Follow the two-day strategy, as outlined above.

Day 3 Take a trip out of the city to the Olympic Peninsula, the San Juan Islands, or the Mount Rainier area. All these trips can be turned into overnighters or longer, but if you plan on just doing a day trip, leave early.

IF YOU HAVE 5 DAYS OR MORE

Days 1-2 Follow the two-day strategy, as outlined above.

Days 3-4 Stay a night or two somewhere such as Port Townsend on the Olympic Peninsula or at a bed-and-breakfast in the beautiful

San Juan Islands. Or better yet, take the ferry from the San Juans to the Olympic Peninsula and then back to Seattle. This makes a great loop.

Day 5 Visit Mount St. Helens, and stop at the Museum of Flight on your way south.

---

1. THE TOP ATTRACTIONS

MUSEUM OF FLIGHT, 9404 E. Marginal Way South. Tel. 764-5720.

⭐ Located right next door to busy Boeing Field, 10 miles south of Seattle, is one of the world's best museums dedicated to the history of flight. Aviation buffs will be walking on air when they visit this cavernous repository of some of history's most famous planes. A six-story glass-and-steel building holds most of the collection, and a viewing area lets you watch planes take off and land at the adjacent airport. There is a replica of the Wright brothers' first glider to start things off, and then the exhibits bring you right up to the present state of flight. Suspended in the Great Hall are 20 planes, including a DC-3 and the first air force F 5 supersonic fighter. Commuters will look longingly on the prototype flying car that would have solved highway congestion problems. Other planes have been grounded and can be examined up close. See Section 4, below, for information on a tour of the Boeing plant.

Admission: $5 adults and senior citizens, $3 ages 6–16, under age 6 free.

Open: Daily 10am–5pm (until 9pm Thurs). **Bus:** 174. **Directions:** Take exit 158 on I-5.

MUSEUM OF HISTORY & INDUSTRY, 2700 24th Ave. East. Tel. 324-1125.

You can learn more about the history of Seattle and the Northwest in this museum at the north end of Washington Park Arboretum. There is a Boeing mail plane from the 1920s, plus an exhibit on the 1889 fire that leveled the city. If the Seattle Underground Tour's vivid description of prefire life has you curious about what the city's more respectable citizens were doing back in the 1880s, you can find out here, where re-created storefronts provide glimpses into their lives. This museum also hosts touring exhibitions that address history outside the Northwest.

Admission: $3 adults, $1.50 senior citizens and ages 6–12, under 6 free. Free to all on Tuesday.

Open: Daily 10am–5pm. **Closed:** Thanksgiving, Christmas, and New Year's Day. **Bus:** 43.

OMNIDOME FILM EXPERIENCE, Pier 59, Waterfront Park. Tel. 622-1868.

This huge wraparound theater is located adjacent to the Seattle Aquarium, and on my last visit was showing one film about the

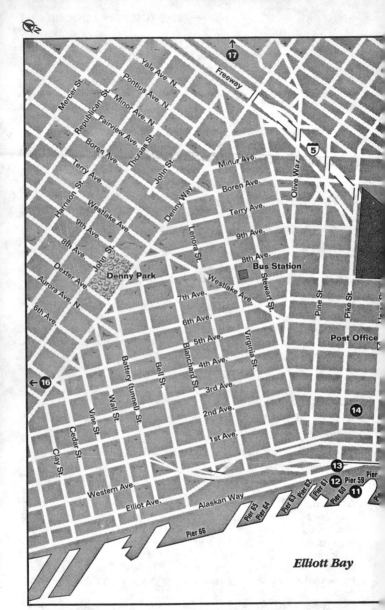

eruption of Mount St. Helens and another about the ocean and Puget Sound. The Omnidome, for those who have never experienced it, is a movie theater with a 180° screen that fills your peripheral vision and puts you right in the middle of the action. People with hangovers or who get motion sickness should stay away!

Admission: $5.95 adults, $4.95 senior citizens and ages 13–18, $3.95 ages 6–12, under 6 free.

SEATTLE ATTRACTIONS

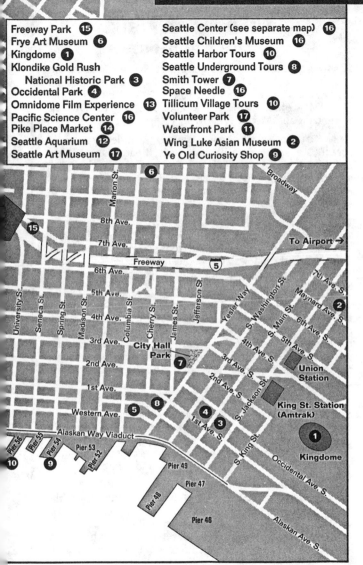

Open: Sun–Thurs 10am–9pm, Fri–Sat 10am–11pm. **Bus:** 15, 18, or 91; then walk down Pike Place stairs.

PACIFIC SCIENCE CENTER, 200 Second Ave. North, Seattle Center. Tel. 443-2001 or 443-2880 (information).

Although its exhibits are aimed primarily at children, the Pacific Science Center is fun for all ages. The primary goal of this sprawling

FROMMER'S FAVORITE

SEATTLE EXPERIENCES

Riding the Ferry   There are harbor tours, but for my money you can't beat the ferries of the Washington State ferry system. For $3.30 you can ride across the sound and back with a great view of the Seattle skyline, and sometimes the Olympic Mountains and Mount Rainier.

Sea Kayaking on Lake Union   Seattle is a city of speedboats, sailboats, sailboards, even floatplanes, but my favorite is the sea kayak. This is the nation's sea-kayak capital, and the waters all around the city are ideal for an afternoon of leisurely paddling. You can even pull up at waterfront restaurants for a meal.

The Seattle Underground Tour   The humor is slightly off-color and the history is not what you learn in grade school, and that's what makes this tour so interesting and fun. Go beneath the sidewalks and old buildings of the Pioneer Square area to see what Seattle was like before the Great Seattle Fire of 1889.

A Day at Pike Place Market   There is no better place in Seattle to shop for fresh local and gourmet produce, fish, or meats. The displays are beautiful, even if you don't buy; but the fishmongers will gladly pack a few crabs or a salmon for you to take home on the plane. The market maze also is home to hundreds of craftspeople, vendors, and shops filled with all manner of amazing goods.

A Latte from an Espresso Cart   Seattle is a city of espresso addicts, so you never have to be more than a block or so from your next cup. Colorfully painted espresso carts park on the sidewalks in busy neighborhoods, providing commuters with a quick cup on the way to work. Lattes are the best—they are a three-to-one mixture of milk and espresso coffee. Delicious!

Watching the Salmon Return to Spawn   At the Seattle Aquarium, a fish ladder allows salmon that were hatched here to return from the sea as adults and spawn right on the aquarium grounds. These graceful and powerful fish are an integral part of Northwest culture and it is always reassuring to see them return.

complex at Seattle Center is to teach kids about science and hopefully to instill a desire to study it. To that end, there are dozens of fun hands-on exhibits addressing the biological sciences, physics, and chemistry. Kids learn how their bodies work, blow giant bubbles, put on shows, build a dam, and play in a rocketship. There is a planetarium for learning about the skies, plus laser shows. Even more interesting are the many special exhibits. There are also special events, such as kayaking classes, reptile shows, a bubble festival, and a science circus. An IMAX theater has daily screenings of short films on its huge screen.

Admission: $5 adults, $4 ages 6–13 and senior citizens, $3 ages 2–5, under 2 free. IMAX $4 adult, $3 ages 6–13 and senior citizens, $2 ages 2–5, under 2 free ($1 as add-on to general-admission ticket). Laser show $5.50 for evening performances, $1 for matinee performances as add-on to general-admission ticket only.

Open: July–Sept, daily 10am–6pm; Oct–June, Mon–Fri 10am–5pm, Sat–Sun 10am–6pm. **Bus:** 3, 4, 6, 16, 19, 24, or 33. **Monorail:** To Seattle Center station.

PIKE PLACE MARKET, between Pike St. and Pine St. (at First Ave.). Tel. 682-7453.

Pike Place Market, a farmers' market, was founded in 1907 when housewives complained that middlemen were raising the price of produce too high. The market allowed shoppers to buy directly from the producers, and thus save on their grocery bills. However, by the 1960s the market was no longer the popular spot it had once been. World War II had deprived it of nearly half its farmers when Japanese-Americans were moved to internment camps. The postwar flight to the suburbs almost struck the last blow for the market, and the site was being eyed for a major redevelopment project. However, a grass-roots movement to save the 7-acre market culminated in its being declared a National Historic District.

Today it is once again bustling, but the 100 or so farmers and fishmongers who set up shop here are only a small part of the attraction. More than 200 local craftspeople and artists can be found selling their creations at different times of the year. There are excellent restaurants, and dozens of shops fill the market area. Street performers—including mimes, sitar players, and hammered-dulcimer players—serenade the milling crowds. There is an information booth almost directly below the large Pike Place Market sign, where you can pick up a free map of the market as well as a shopper's guide for $1. Watch for the flying fish.

Admission: Free.

Open: Mon–Sat 9am–6pm, Sun 11am–5pm. **Bus:** 15, 18, 22, or 23.

SEATTLE AQUARIUM, Pier 59, Waterfront Park. Tel. 386-4320.

The highly acclaimed Seattle Aquarium, in the heart of the waterfront, is a fascinating place to spend a few hours learning about marine and freshwater life in the Northwest. From the underwater viewing dome, you'll get a fish's-eye view of life beneath the waves. A salmon ladder is particularly exciting when the salmon return to the aquarium to spawn (autumn). There is a beautiful large coral-reef tank, as well as many smaller tanks that exhibit fish from local and distant waters. A telling exhibit on the pollution of Puget Sound shows the effect of human population expansion not only on the sound but also on the area's salmon-spawning streams.

Admission: Memorial Day–Labor Day—$5.75 adults, $3.50 ages 13–18 and senior citizens, $2.50 ages 6–12, ages 5 and under free. Labor Day–Memorial Day—$4.75 adults, $2.75 ages 13–18 and senior citizens, $2 ages 6–12, ages 5 and under free.

Open: Labor Day–Memorial Day, daily 10am–5pm; Memorial Day–Labor Day, daily 10am–7pm. **Bus:** 15, 18, or 91; then walk down Pike Place stairs.

SEATTLE ART MUSEUM, First Ave. and University St. Tel. 625-8901.

By the time you arrive in Seattle, you should be able to visit the new Seattle Art Museum. Located only two blocks from Pike Place Market and six blocks from Pioneer Square, it is sure to be popular with tourists and Seattleites alike. The museum is already known for its extensive collection of Asian art and its commitment to displaying the works of Northwest artists. Its African art collection contains more than 2,000 objects, including masks, furniture, textiles, and jewelry. Pre-Columbian, Oceanic, and Native American art is also represented, and there is even a collection of European masters and contemporary art. Classic films are screened regularly at the museum.

The old museum in Volunteer Park will be closed for renovation until 1993, when it will reopen as a museum of Asian art.

Admission: $2 adults, $1 senior citizens and students, ages 6 and under free. Free to all on Thursday.

Open: Tues–Sat 10am–5pm (Thurs until 9pm), Sun noon–5pm. **Bus:** 15, 18, 22, or 23.

SPACE NEEDLE, 203 Sixth Ave. North, Seattle Center. Tel. 443-2100.

From a distance it resembles a flying saucer on top of a tripod, and when it was built it was meant to suggest future architectural trends. Erected for the 1962 World's Fair, the 600-foot-tall tower is the most popular tourist sight in Seattle. At 518 feet above ground level, the views from the observation deck are stunning, and there are displays identifying more than 60 sites and activities in the Seattle area. High-powered telescopes let you zoom in on things. You'll also find a history of the Space Needle, a lounge, and two very expensive restaurants. If you don't mind standing in line and paying quite a bit for an elevator ride, make this your first stop in Seattle so you can orient yourself.

Admission: $4.75 adults, $2.75 ages 5–12, ages 4 and under free.

Open: Mid-June–Labor Day, daily 8am–1am; Sept, Sun–Thurs 9am–midnight, Fri–Sat 9am–1am; Oct–mid-June, Sun–Thurs 10am–midnight, Fri–Sat 10am–1am. **Bus:** 3, 4, 6, 16, 19, 24, or 33. **Monorail:** To Seattle Center station.

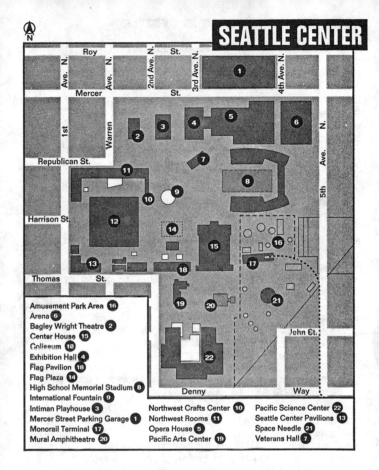

SEATTLE CENTER

Amusement Park Area **16**
Arena **6**
Bagley Wright Theatre **2**
Center House **15**
Coliseum **18**
Exhibition Hall **4**
Flag Pavilion **18**
Flag Plaza **14**
High School Memorial Stadium **8**
International Fountain **9**
Intiman Playhouse **3**
Mercer Street Parking Garage **1**
Monorail Terminal **17**
Mural Amphitheatre **20**

Northwest Crafts Center **10**
Northwest Rooms **11**
Opera House **5**
Pacific Arts Center **19**

Pacific Science Center **22**
Seattle Center Pavilions **13**
Space Needle **21**
Veterans Hall **7**

2. MORE ATTRACTIONS

MUSEUMS

BURKE MUSEUM, 17th Ave. NE and NE 45th St. Tel. 543-5590.

Located in the northwest corner of the University of Washington campus, the Burke Museum is noteworthy primarily for its archeological and anthropological displays of Native American culture. The museum's collection includes artifacts from 900 sites around Washington State, as well as from cultures around the Pacific Rim. There are also full-size Native American dwellings from different parts of the state. Down in the basement, there is a large collection of minerals and fossils. In front of the museum stand replicas of totem poles carved in the 1870s and 1880s. There is also an ethnobotanical garden displaying plants used by Northwestern tribes. Campus parking is very expensive on weekdays and Saturday mornings, so try to visit on a Saturday afternoon or a Sunday.

Admission: Donation, $2.50 adults, $1.50 students and seniors.
Open: Daily 10am–5pm (Thurs until 8pm).
Bus: 70, 71, 72, 73, or 74.

FRYE ART MUSEUM, 704 Terry St. (at Cherry St.). Tel. 622-9250.

Most of the paintings in this small museum date from the second half of the 19th century and are primarily by European artists, but there are also paintings by 19th-century Americans and the prolific Wyeth family. A few Russian and Alaskan paintings complete the collection.

Admission: Free.
Open: Mon–Sat 10am–5pm, Sun noon–5pm.
Bus: 3, 4, or 12.

KLONDIKE GOLD RUSH NATIONAL HISTORICAL PARK, 117 S. Main St. Tel. 442-7220.

It isn't in the Klondike (which isn't even in the United States) and it isn't a park (it's a single room in an old store), but it is a fascinating little museum. "At 3 o'clock this morning the steamship *Portland,* from St. Michaels for Seattle, passed up [Puget] Sound with more than a ton of gold on board and 68 passengers." When the *Seattle Post-Intelligencer* published that sentence on July 17, 1897, they started a stampede. Would-be miners heading for the Klondike gold fields in the 1890s made Seattle their outfitting center and helped turn it into a prosperous city. When they struck it rich up north, they headed back to Seattle, the first outpost of civilization, and unloaded their gold, making Seattle doubly rich. It seems only fitting that this museum should be here. Film buffs can catch a free screening of Charlie Chaplin's *The Gold Rush* here any day of the week.

Admission: Free.
Open: Daily 9am–5pm. **Closed:** Thanksgiving, Christmas, and New Year's Day. **Bus:** 15, 18, 21, 22, 23, 56, 91, or 99.

WING LUKE ASIAN MUSEUM, 407 Seventh Ave. South. Tel. 623-5124.

In the heart of the International District, Asian-American culture, art, and history are explored. The emphasis is on the life of Asian immigrants in the Northwest, and special exhibits are meant to help explain customs to non-Asians. Asians, primarily the Chinese and Japanese, played an integral role in settling the Northwest, and today the connection of this region with the far side of the Pacific is opening up many new economic and cultural doors.

Admission: $2.50 adults, $1 students and senior citizens, 50¢ ages 5–12, under 5 free. Free to all on Thursday.

Open: Tues–Fri 11am–4:30pm, Sat–Sun noon–4pm. **Bus:** 7, 14, 36, or 91.

YE OLDE CURIOSITY SHOP, Pier 54, Alaskan Way. Tel. 682-5844.

★ It's a museum. It's a store. It's weird! It's tacky! If you have a fascination with the bizarre—and I think we all do—shoulder your way into this crowded shop and erstwhile museum. See Siamese-twin calves, a natural mummy, the Lord's Prayer on a grain of rice, a narwhal tusk, shrunken heads, walrus and whale oosiks (the bone of the male reproductive organ)—in fact, all the stuff that fascinated you as a kid. The collection of oddities was started in 1899 by Joe Standley, who had developed a more-than-passing interest in strange curios.

Admission: Free.

Open: Daily 9am–9pm. **Bus:** 15, 18, or 91; then walk down Pike Place stairs.

NEIGHBORHOODS

INTERNATIONAL DISTRICT, Fifth Ave. South to Eighth Ave. South (between South Main St. and South Lane St.).

Seattle's large and prosperous Asian neighborhood is called the International District rather than Chinatown because so many Asian nationalities call this area home. This has been the traditional Asian neighborhood for 100 years or more and you can learn about its history at the Wing Luke Museum (see above for details). There are of course lots of import and food stores, including the huge Uwajimaya (see "Markets" in Section 2 of Chapter 9 for details). Both the Nippon Kan Theatre, 628 South Washington Street (tel. 624-8800), and the Northwest Asian–American Theater, 409 Seventh Avenue South (tel. 340-1049), feature performances with an Asian flavor.

TOTEM POLES

OCCIDENTAL PARK, Occidental Ave. South and South Washington St.

Totem poles are the quintessential symbol of the Northwest, and although this Native American art form actually comes from farther north, there are quite a few totem poles around Seattle. The four in this shady cobblestoned park were carved by local artist Duane Pasco. The tallest is 35-foot-high *The Sun and Raven,* which tells the story of how Raven brought light into the world. Next to this pole is the *Man Riding a Whale*. This type of totem pole was traditionally carved to help villagers during their whale hunts. The other two figures that face each other are symbols of the Bear Clan and the Welcoming Figure.

PIONEER PLACE, First Avenue and Yesler Way.

The totem pole in this little triangular park at the heart of Pioneer Square has a rather unusual history. The one you see now is actually a copy of the original that stood here, which arrived in Seattle in 1890 after a band of drunken men stole it from a Tlingit village up the coast. In 1938 the pole was set afire by an arsonist. The Seattle city fathers sent a $5,000 check to the Tlingit village requesting a replacement. Supposedly, the response from the village was, "Thanks for paying for the first totem pole. If you want another, it will cost another $5,000." The city of Seattle paid up, and so today Pioneer Square has a totem pole and the city has clear conscience.

PANORAMAS

SMITH TOWER, 508 Second Ave. Tel. 682-9393.

Despite all the shiny glass skyscrapers crowding the Seattle skyline these days, you can't miss the Smith Tower. It sits off all by itself, a tall white needle on the edge of the Pioneer Square District. At only 42 stories, it was still the tallest building west of the Mississippi for many years. It isn't nearly as popular as the Space Needle, but there is an observation platform way up near the top. It's worth the trip for not only the view of the city from this end of town, but also for the ride up in the shiny brass-and-copper elevator, which still uses an operator and has glass doors. You should call ahead if you are going out of your way, since the observation floor is sometimes closed due to special functions.

Admission: $2 adults, $1 children.

Open: Daily 10am–10pm. **Bus:** 15, 17, 18, 21, 22, 23, 56, or 91.

PARKS & GARDENS

FREEWAY PARK, Sixth Ave. and Seneca St.

What do you do when a noisy interstate runs right through the middle of your fair city and you haven't got enough parks for all the suntanners and Frisbee throwers? You could tear up the whole darn thing and turn it into a park, as Portland did with its river-front freeway, or you could put a roof on the highway and build a park over all the rushing cars and trucks, as Seattle did. Terraced gardens, waterfalls, grassy lawns—they're all here, and they're all smog-resistant. They have to be to survive in this environment. You'd never know there's a roaring freeway beneath your feet.

Admission: Free.

Open: Daily dawn to dusk.
Bus: Any bus that goes to the downtown bus tunnel; Convention Center stop.

THE HIRAM M. CHITTENDEN LOCKS, 3015 NW 54th St. Tel. 783-7059.

These locks connect Lake Washington and Lake Union to Puget Sound and allow boats to travel from the lakes onto open water. The difference between the water levels of the lakes and the sound varies from 6 to 26 feet, depending on the tides and rainfall levels. Mostly used by small boats, the locks are a popular spot for salmon-watching. People watch salmon jumping up the cascades of a fish ladder as they return to spawn in the stream where they were born, and windows below the waterline give you an idea of what it's like to be a salmon. The best months to see salmon are July and August.
Admission: Free.
Open: Daily 7am–9pm; visitors center 10am–7pm. **Bus:** 17, 43, or 46.

JAPANESE GARDENS, Washington Park Arboretum, Lake Washington Blvd. East (north of E. Madison St.). Tel. 684-4725.

Situated on 3½ acres of land, the Japanese Gardens are a perfect little world unto themselves. Babbling brooks, a lake rimmed with Japanese irises and filled with colorful koi (Japanese carp), and a cherry orchard for spring color are peaceful any time of year. Unfortunately, noise from a nearby road can be distracting at times. A special Tea Garden encloses a Tea House, where, on the third Sunday of each month at 2 and 3pm, you can attend a traditional tea ceremony.
Admission: $2 adults; $1 senior citizens, the disabled, and ages 6–18.
Open: June–Sept, daily 10am–8pm, Sept–Oct, daily 10am–6pm. Oct–Nov, daily 10am–4pm. **Bus:** 11, 43, or 48.

VOLUNTEER PARK, E. Prospect St. and 14th Ave. East. Tel. 684-4743.

Home of the old Seattle Art Museum—which will be reopening as an Asian art museum in 1993—Volunteer Park is surrounded by the elegant mansions of Capitol Hill and is a popular spot for suntanning and playing Frisbee. A stately conservatory houses a large collection of tropical plants, including palm trees, orchids, and cacti.
Admission: Free (park and conservatory).
Open: Daily dawn to dusk; conservatory daily 10am–7pm. **Bus:** 10.

WASHINGTON PARK ARBORETUM, 2300 Arboretum Dr. East. Tel. 543-8800.

Acres of manicured lawns and trees stretch from the far side of Capitol Hill all the way to the Montlake Cut, a canal connecting Lake Washington to Lake Union. Within the arboretum, there are quiet trails that are most beautiful in spring, when azaleas, cherry trees, rhododendrons, and dogwoods are all in flower. There are more than 5,000 varieties of plants in the 200-acre park. The north end, a marshland that is home to ducks and swans, is popular with kayakers and canoeists (see below for where you can rent a canoe or kayak).
Admission: Free.
Open: Daily dawn to dusk; visitors center Mon–Fri 10am–4pm, Sat–Sun noon–4pm. **Bus:** 11, 43, or 48.

WOODLAND PARK ZOO, 5500 Phinney Ave. North. Tel. 684-4800.

Although the zoo in Portland is known for its elephants, the new elephant habitat here at the Woodland Park Zoo is more impressive. It includes a tropical forest, pool, Thai logging camp, and an elephant house designed to resemble a Thai Buddhist temple. The gorilla exhibit and the African savannah display are equally impressive. Together, these well-designed habitats have helped to make this zoo one of the top 10 zoos in America. A new rain forest exhibit will be opening in 1992. The zoo also includes the Family Farm, where kids can marvel at animal babies.
Admission: $4.50 adults; $2.25 children ages 6–17, senior citizens, and disabled; ages 5 and under free. **Parking:** $1.
Open: Daily 9:30–6pm (shorter hours in winter). **Bus:** 5, 6, 43.

3. COOL FOR KIDS

Look under "The Top Attractions" and "More Attractions," above for the following Seattle attractions that have major appeal for kids: the **Pacific Science Center,** the **Seattle Aquarium,** and **Ye Olde Curiosity Shop.**

The places listed in this section are also great for kids. They'll be interested in the arcades and rides at **Seattle Center,** as well as their very own museum, the **Seattle Children's Museum.**

Or you can take them to a sports event. Seattle has professional football, basketball, and baseball teams (see Section 5 in this Chapter). And what could be more fun than exploring the **Seattle Underground** (see Section 4 of this chapter)!

ENCHANTED VILLAGE & WILD WAVES, 36201 Enchanted Parkway S., Federal Way. Tel. 838-8828.

The littlest kids can watch the clowns and ride on miniature trains, merry-go-rounds, and the like at Enchanted Village. The older kids, teenagers, and adults will want to spend the hot days of summer riding the wild waves, tubing down artificial streams, and swooshing down water slides.
Admission (to both parks): $17.50 age 10–adult, $15.50 ages 3–9, under age 2 free.

Open: Apr–Memorial Day Fri–Sat 10am–6pm; Memorial Day–late June daily 10am–6pm; late June–Labor Day daily 11am–8pm; Sept Sat–Sun 10am–6pm. Wild Waves closes Labor Day for season.

Directions: By car from Seattle, Take I-5 south to Exit 142-B, Puyallup.

SEATTLE CENTER, 305 Harrison St. Tel. 684-7200.

This 74-acre amusement park and cultural center was built for the Seattle World's Fair in 1962 and stands on the north edge of downtown at the end of the monorail line. The most visible building at the center is the Space Needle, which provides an outstanding panorama of the city from its observation deck. However, of much more interest to children are the rides (a roller coaster, log flume, merry-go-round, and ferris wheel) and arcade games. This is Seattle's main festival site, and in the summer months hardly a weekend goes by without some festival or another filling its grounds. (See map page 101.)

Admission: Free; pay per ride or game.

Open: Summer, daily 9am–midnight; rest of year, Sun–Thurs 9am–9pm, Fri–Sat 9am–midnight.

Bus: 1, 2, 3, 4, 6, 13, 15, 16, or 18.

SEATTLE CHILDREN'S MUSEUM, Center House, Seattle Center. Tel. 441-1767.

Kids have their very own museum in the basement of Center House at Seattle Center. The museum includes plenty of hands-on cultural exhibits, workshops, a child-size neighborhood, an infant and toddler play center, and a soap-bubble center that will keep kids entertained for hours. Summer weekends feature fun workshops.

Admission: $3 adults or children.

Open: Tues–Sun 10am–5pm.

Bus: 1, 2, 3, 4, 6, 13, 15, 16, or 18.

4. ORGANIZED TOURS

BOEING TOUR CENTER, State Rte. 526, Everett. Tel. 342-4801.

Anyone interested in how planes are built will enjoy this free 90-minute tour of the Boeing assembly plant, 30 miles north of Seattle (not at Boeing Field, which is south of the city). This is the single largest building, by volume, in the world. Gigantic 747s easily fit inside, and the Seattle Seahawks football team would have no problem playing here. A window opening onto the plant allows you to observe the assembly-line production. There is also a slide and movie presentation in the visitor's center auditorium.

Tours: Mon–Fri on first-come, first-served basis, free of charge. Call for current schedule. Children under age 10 not permitted.

CASUAL CABS, (tel. 623-2991) and CARRIAGE HORSE TOURS OF SEATTLE (tel. 292-8372).

One of the most enjoyable ways to tour the Seattle waterfront and Pioneer Square area is by horse-drawn carriage. You will usually find a few carriages parked along the waterfront near the Seattle Aquarium, and you can hire one on the spur of the moment.

Price: $25 per half hour for up to five adults.

SAIL SEATTLE, 809 Fairview Place North, Seattle, WA 98109. Tel. 624-3931.

The islands and bays of Puget Sound are a favorite with the yachting crowd, and if you want to find out why this is such a popular sailing destination, why not step aboard the *Kaholo Makani* for a full-day, half-day, or sunset cruise? On the full-day cruise, you might even stop at Tillicum Village. A minimum number of people are required for each of these trips, so call in advance to make reservations.

Prices: $70 per person for a full-day cruise, $45 per person for a half-day, $35 per person for a sunset sail.

SEATTLE HARBOR TOURS, Pier 55. Tel. 623-1445.

For your basic see-Seattle-from-the-water cruise, you can't beat this one. You'll learn about the history, geography, and important sights of Seattle on the one-hour cruise that takes in the Seattle waterfront as well as the harbor facilities.

Prices: $8.50 adults, $7.50 senior citizens, $6 ages 13–18, $4 ages 5–12, under 5 free.

Tours: Daily March-Dec.

SEATTLE UNDERGROUND TOURS, 610 First Ave. Tel. 682-1511 for information, 682-4646 for reservations.

Dirt, corruption, sewers, scandal! With a come-on like that, how can you resist this unusual tour? Never have I enjoyed a guided tour as much as I enjoyed this one, and I'm sure you'll be equally entertained and enlightened (though an appreciation for off-color humor is a prerequisite). Early Seattle had its problems, and when a fire raged through the city in 1889, leveling most of downtown, the city authorities had to start all over again. Part of their solution was to build on top of the old city, and today you can still see parts of the old Seattle beneath the busy streets of the modern-day metropolis. Best of all, you'll learn a side of local history that official versions avoid. Don't miss this one!

Prices: $4.75 adults, $3.50 senior citizens and students aged 13–17 or with valid ID, $2.25 ages 6–12.

Tours: Daily (hours vary with the month).

TILLICUM VILLAGE TOURS, Pier 56. Tel. 443-1244.

Northwest Native American culture comes alive at Tillicum Village, across Puget Sound from Seattle at Blake Island Marine State Park. Totem poles stand vigil outside a huge cedar longhouse fashioned after the traditional dwellings of the Northwest tribes. You'll enjoy a meal of alder-smoked salmon while watching traditional masked dances. All around stand the carved and painted images of fanciful animals, and you can see the park's resident wood-carver create more of these beautiful works of art. After the dinner and dances, you can explore the deep forest that surrounds the clearing in which the lodge stands. There are even beaches on which to relax.

Prices: $35 adults, $32 senior citizens, $24 ages 13–19, $14 ages 6–12, $7 ages 4–5.

Tours: Daily May–Oct.

5. SPORTS & RECREATION

SPECTATOR SPORTS

BASEBALL

The **Seattle Mariners** (AL) are Seattle's professional baseball team, and they play in the Kingdome from April to October. Monday nights are family nights, with the more expensive seats being sold on a two-for-one basis. Prices range from $2.50 to $11.50; call for schedule and ticket information (tel. 800/950-FANS). Tickets are available at the box office or by calling TicketMaster (tel. 206/628-0888). Parking is next to impossible, so plan to leave your car behind.

BASKETBALL

The **Seattle SuperSonics** (NBA) play in the Seattle Center Coliseum from November to May. Games start at 7pm, and tickets are $7 to $35. Call for schedule and ticket information (tel. 281-5800).

FOOTBALL

The **Seattle Seahawks** (NFL) play in the Kingdome from September to December. Games are on Sunday at 1pm, and tickets, at $12 to $32, are very difficult to get. Call for schedule and ticket information (tel. 827-9777). Parking in the Kingdome area is nearly impossible during games, so take the bus.

HORSE RACING

Watch the thoroughbreds run and wager a bit on your favorites at **Longacres Race Course,** 1621 SW 16th St., Renton (tel. 226-3131 or 251-8717), south of downtown Seattle. The season runs from April to September. On Saturday, Sunday, and holidays, the first race is at 1pm; Wednesday through Friday, the first race is at

5pm. Admission is $3.25 and children under age 10 are admitted free.

MARATHONS

Seattle has two major marathons each year: The **Emerald City Marathon** takes place in April, and the **Seattle Marathon** takes place in November. There's a runners' hotline in Seattle that you can call to find out more about races in the area (tel. 524-RUNS).

RECREATION

BEACHES

Alki (rhymes with sky) **Beach,** on Puget Sound, is the nearest beach to downtown Seattle. It stretches for 2½ miles down the west side of the Alki Peninsula, which is the promontory you see across Elliott Bay from Seattle's waterfront. This is a busy beach, but the views across the sound to the Olympic Mountains can be stunning on a clear day. There are also several miles of beaches at **Blake Island State Park,** site of Tillicum Village (see above). You'll need your own boat to get here, though, if you don't plan to come on the Tillicum Village tour.

BICYCLING

The most convenient bicycle rental shop is **U-Pedal Bike Rental,** 1416 Post Alley (tel. 223-3645), just around the corner from the AYH hostel on the corner of Union Street. Rates for 21-speed mountain bikes with locks and helmets are $6 per hour, $10 per half day, and $15 per full day. This shop is only two blocks from the ferry terminal, which opens up some beautiful biking possibilities on Vashon and Bainbridge islands.

Gregg's Green Lake Cycle, 7007 Woodlawn St. NE (tel. 523-1822); the **Bicycle Center,** 4529 Sand Point Way NE (tel. 523-8300); and **Sammamish Valley Cycle,** 8451 164th Ave. NE, Redmond (tel. 881-8442)—all also rent bikes by the hour and by the day, as well as by the week. Rates range from $4 to $6 per hour and $15 to $25 per day. These latter three are all convenient to the **Burke-Gilman Trail** and the **Sammamish River Trail.** The former is a 12.5-mile trail created from an old railway bed. It starts at **Gasworks Park** and continues to **Kenmore Logboom Park** at the north end of Lake Washington by way of the University of Washington. Serious riders can then connect to the Sammamish River Trail, which leads to Lake Sammamish. There are lots of great picnicking spots along both trails.

FISHING

As you might have guessed from the plethora of seafood restaurants in Seattle, the waters around here are brimming with fish. You can fish the rivers for salmon and steelhead trout, or try the salt water of Puget Sound for salmon or bottom fish. **Major Northwest Tours,** 1415 Western Ave., Suite 503, Seattle, WA 98101 (tel. 292-0595), will outfit you completely (including licenses) and take you where the fish are biting. Boats depart daily. The rates are $55 per person, $40 for children 12 and under. Reservations are required, and boats leave from Pier 54.

Trophy Guide Service, P.O. Box 1232, Forks, WA 98331 (tel. 374-6237), offers fishing on rivers and streams of the Olympic Peninsula. The charge is $225 per day for two people.

GOLF

There are more than a dozen public golf courses in the Seattle area. **Jackson Park Municipal Golf Course,** 1000 NE 135th St. (tel. 363-4747); **Jefferson Park Municipal Golf Course,** 4101 Beacon Ave. South (tel. 762-4513); and **West Seattle Municipal Golf Course,** 4470 35th Ave. SW (tel. 935-5187)—these are three of the most convenient courses. Greens fees are $16.50 if you're not a King County resident, $11 if you are.

HIKING

The areas surrounding Seattle are a hiker's paradise, and hiking, backpacking, and camping are some of the most popular activities in the region. Within an easy drive of the city are three national parks, Mount St. Helens National Volcanic Monument, and numerous national forests, all of which offer hikes of varying lengths and degrees of difficulty.

Mount Rainier National Park, Tahoma Woods/Star Route, Ashford, WA 98304 (tel. 569-2211), is the easiest to reach from Seattle. **Olympic National Park,** 600 E. Park Ave. Port Angeles, WA 98362 (tel. 452-4501), is the most varied of the national parks in this region. There are long stretches of isolated beaches, snow-capped mountains, lush rain forests, and hot springs. The **North Cascades National Park,** 2105 Washington Hwy. 20, Sedro Woolley, WA 98284 (tel. 856-5700), is adjacent to the Canadian border northeast of Seattle.

Mount St. Helens National Volcanic Monument, 3029 Spirit Lake Hwy., Castle Rock, WA 98611-9719 (tel. 274-4038), has been left as a monument to the power of a volcanic eruption and is an amazing site that should not be missed. A limited number of hikers are allowed to climb the peak each day, but you have to make reservations far in advance.

The **Interagency Committee for Outdoor Recreation,** 4800 Capitol Blvd., KP-11, Tumwater, WA 98504-5611 (tel. 753-7140), will send you a trails directory that lists most of Washington's parks with hiking trails.

HORSEBACK RIDING

Down at the south end of Lake Washington near the airport are three outfits that rent horses. **Aqua Barn Ranch,** 15227 SE Renton-Maple Valley Hwy., Renton (tel. 255-4618), offers guided rides at the rate of $17.50 per hour; reservations are required.

Kelly's Riding and Boarding Ranch, 7212 Issaquah-Renton Rd. SE, Issaquah (tel. 392-6979), charges $15 an hour for similar rides. **Tiger Mountain Outfitters,** 24508 SE 133rd St., Issaquah (tel. 392-5090), offers a 3-hour ride up Tiger Mountain for $35; reservations required.

KAYAKING/CANOEING

Although there is no white water around Seattle, kayaking is still a very popular recreational activity. The boats used are not the tiny white-water boats, but long sea kayaks, often with a rudder for better steering in choppy or windy seas.

Northwest Outdoor Center, 2100 Westlake Ave. North (tel. 281-9694), is located on Lake Union, and they will rent you a sea kayak for only $7 to $9 per hour. Your third and fourth hours are free on weekdays, and on the weekend your fourth hour is free. From April to September, the center is open Monday through Friday from 10am to 8pm, on Saturday, Sunday, and holidays from 9am to 6pm; in March and October, daily from 10am to 6pm; and from November to February, Wednesday through Sunday from 10am to 5pm.

The **University of Washington Waterfront Activities Center,** on the university campus behind Husky Stadium (tel. 543-9433), is open to the public and rents canoes for only $3.50 per hour. Rentals are available from February to October, daily from 10am to 7:30pm.

SAILBOARDING

Sailboarding is one of Seattle's favorite sports. The local waters are ideal for learning—the winds are light and the water is flat. **Bavarian Surf/Seattle,** 711 NE Northlake Way (tel. 545-WIND), will rent you a board and give you lessons if you need them. Rates are $35 per day for a board. Private lessons are $30 per hour, and a 6-hour group class is $80. The shop is open Monday through Friday from 10am to 6pm, on Saturday from 10am to 5pm.

SAILING

The **Center for Wooden Boats,** 1010 Valley St. (tel. 382-BOAT), has its museum and boat-rental shop at Waterway 4 at the south end of Lake Union. Dedicated to the preservation of wooden boats, the center is unique in that all exhibits can be rented and taken out on Lake Union. There are rowboats and large and small sailboats. Rates range from $8 to $25 per hour. Individual sailing instruction is also available. There is a wooden-boat show held here every year on the Fourth of July. From June 15 to Labor Day, the center is open daily from 7am to 7pm; the rest of the year, Wednesday through Tuesday from noon to 6pm.

SKIING

One of the reasons Seattleites put up with their long, wet winters is because they can go skiing within an hour of the city. With many slopes set up for night skiing, it's possible to leave work and be on the slopes before dinner, ski for several hours, and be home in time to get a good night's rest. The ski season in the Seattle area generally runs from mid-November to the end of April.

Equipment can be rented at the ski areas listed below, and at **REI,** 1525 11th Ave. (tel. 323-8333).

The largest ski area at Snoqualmie Pass, which is less than 50 miles east of Seattle on I-90, is actually made up of three separate ski areas. **Alpental, Ski Acres,** and **Snoqualmie Summit,** 3010 77th Ave. SE, Mercer Island, WA 98040 (tel. 232-8182, or 236-1600 for snow conditions), are all part of a single gigantic complex with 50 runs, 21 chair lifts, and 12 rope tows. There are also plenty of cross-country ski trails here. You can rent both cross-country and downhill equipment, and can take lessons at the ski school. Daily lift rates are $10–$14 Monday through Friday, $23 on weekends and holidays. Lift rates for night skiing (5pm to closing) are $14.

Alpental and Snoqualmie Summit are open Tuesday through Friday from 9:30am to 10:30pm, on Saturday from 9am to 10:30pm, and on Sunday from 9am to 6pm (at Alpental) or 9pm (at Snoqualmie Summit). Ski Acres is open Wednesday through Friday from 9:30am to 10:30pm, on Saturday from 9am to 10:30pm, and on Sunday from 9am to 9pm (from December 29 through March 17, on Friday and Saturday until 11pm).

Crystal Mountain Resort, P.O. Box 1, Crystal Mountain, WA 98022 (tel. 663-2265, or 634-3771 for snow conditions), is a little bit farther away (76 miles southeast of Seattle on Washington Hwy. 410), but the facilities are better than those at Snoqualmie Pass: 10 chair lifts, 34 trails, and night skiing on the weekends. There are rentals, a ski school, a repair shop, and child-care services. The Crystal Mountain Express bus leaves daily at 7am from the Ravenna Park & Ride at I-5 and NE 65th Ave. Round-trip fares are $17 for adults and $12 for children Monday through Friday, $19 for adults and $12 for children on Saturday and Sunday.

Monday and Thursday lift rates are $15 for adults and children, $13 for senior citizens; Friday through Sunday, lift rates are $28 for adults, $19 for children, and $15 for senior citizens. Night skiing costs $14 for adults and seniors, $10 for children. Lift hours are 9am to 4:30pm Monday through Friday, and 8:30am to 10pm on Saturday and Sunday.

Cross-Country Skiing   The Seattle area abounds in cross-country skiing opportunities. In the Snoqualmie Pass area, less than 50 miles east of Seattle on I-90, **Ski Acres Cross-Country Center,** P.O. Box 134, Snoqualmie Pass, WA 98068 (tel. 434-6646), offers rentals, instruction, and many miles of groomed trails. Ski Acres even has lighted trails for night skiing. The trail fee runs $5 to $8.

If you happen to be in town on a rare clear winter day, head for **Hurricane Ridge,** Olympic National Park, 600 E. Park Ave., Port Angeles, WA 98362 (tel. 452-0330). The views of the Olympic Mountains from here are spectacular. Rental equipment is available, but the area is open only on weekends and holidays.

When renting skis, be sure to get a **Sno-Park permit.** These are required in most cleared parking areas near ski trails. They are available at ski shops.

TENNIS

Seattle Parks and Recreation operates dozens of outdoor tennis courts all over the city. The most convenient are at **Volunteer Park,** 15th Ave. East and E. Prospect St., and at **Lower Woodland Park,** West Green Lake Way North. If it happens to be raining and you had your heart set on playing tennis, there are indoor public courts at the **Seattle Tennis Center,** 2000 Martin Luther King Jr. Way South (tel. 684-4764). Rates here are $10 for singles and $12 for doubles for 1¼ hours.

WHITE-WATER RAFTING

Seattle is surrounded by water, but it's flat water. For more thrilling boating experiences you have to head to the Olympic or Cascade Mountains. **Olympic Raft and Guide Service,** 464 U.S. 101 West, Port Angeles, WA 98362 (tel. 457-7011), offers trips down the Olympic Peninsula's Elwha River. Rates range from $25 to $75 per person. Another outfit that runs trips down rivers all over the state is **Northern Wilderness River Riders,** 23312 77th Ave. SE, Woodinville, WA 98072 (tel. 485-RAFT). They charge $55 for a 4-hour trip.

CHAPTER 8

STROLLING AROUND SEATTLE

WALKING TOUR — PIONEER SQUARE AREA
Although downtown Seattle is easy to explore on foot, there are only a few specific areas that offer the visitor much of interest. Foremost, of course, are the Pike Place Market and the waterfront, which together form the busiest neighborhood in Seattle. You really don't need a guided tour of this area: Just follow the hoards of people. The historic Pioneer Place neighborhood is a different story. This latter area has some interesting buildings and history that you will probably not want to miss.

WALKING TOUR — Pioneer Square Area

Start: Pioneer Place at the corner of Yesler Way and First Avenue.
Finish: Washington Street Public Boat Landing.
Time: Approximately 2 hours, not including shopping, dining, museum, and other stops.
Best Times: Weekdays, when Pioneer Square and the Seattle Underground Tour are not so crowded.
Worst Times: Weekends, when the area is very crowded.

Seattle is a very young city, and although it was founded in 1851, the buildings surrounding Pioneer Square were erected after the fire of 1889. Today this small section is all that remains of old Seattle. You will probably notice a uniformity of architectural style. This is because many of the buildings were designed by one architect, Elmer Fisher.

Start your tour of this historic neighborhood at the corner of Yesler Way and First Avenue on:

1. **Pioneer Place,** the triangular park in the middle of Pioneer Square. The totem pole here is a replacement of one that burned in 1938. The original pole had been stolen from a Tlingit village up the coast in 1890. Legend has it that the city fathers sent a check for $5,000 requesting a new totem pole. The tribe's response was, "Thanks for paying for the first one. Send another $5,000 for a replacement." The cast-iron pergola in the park was erected in 1905 as a shelter for a large underground lavatory. Facing the square is the:

2. **Pioneer Building,** one of the architectural standouts of this neighborhood. It houses an antiques mall and several bars, including:

3. **Doc Maynard's** (610 First Ave.), a nightclub featuring live rock bands, which is also the starting point of the Seattle Underground Tour, which takes a look at the Pioneer Square area from beneath the sidewalks. (See p. 108.) Forming the south side of Pioneer Square is the:

4. **Yesler Way,** which is the original Skid Row. In Seattle's early years, logs were skidded down this road to a lumber mill on the waterfront, and the road came to be known as Skid Road. These days it's trying hard to live down its reputation, but there are still quite a few homeless people who call this neighborhood home.

REFUELING STOP Across Yesler Way from the pergola is **5. Merchants Café** (109 Yesler Way), the oldest restaurant in Seattle. If it happens to be time for lunch or dinner, this makes a good place to stop. Meals are moderately priced and well prepared. (See p. 76.)

Glance up Yesler Way past the triangular parking deck and you'll see the:

6. **Smith Tower,** which was the tallest building west of the Mississippi for a long time. (See p. 104.) There's a great view of the city from an observatory near the top. This 1914 building is worth a visit just to view the ornate lobby and elevator doors.

Walk down Second Avenue (take the right fork, not Second Avenue Extension) to Main Street and you'll find the shady little:

7. **Waterfall Park,** with a roaring waterfall that looks as if it had been transported here straight from the Cascade Mountains. The park was built by United Parcel Service and makes a wonderful place for a rest or a picnic lunch. Two more blocks down Main Street toward the water is cobblestoned:

8. **Occidental Park,** with four totem poles that were carved by a Northwestern artist. Unfortunately, this shady park serves as a gathering spot for homeless people. On the west side of the park is the:

9. **Grand Central Arcade,** a shopping and dining center created from a restored brick building. Inside, you can watch craftspeople at work in their studios. Across Main Street from Occidental Park is the:

10. **Klondike Gold Rush National Historic Park** (117 S. Main St.), a small museum dedicated to the history of the Klondike gold rush, which helped Seattle grow from an obscure little town into a booming metropolis. (See p. 102.) A couple of doors toward the water from this museum is:

11. **The Elliott Bay Book Company,** on the corner of Main Street and First Avenue. This is one of Seattle's most popular bookstores and has an extensive selection of books on Seattle and the Northwest. Continue down Main Street to the water and turn right. In one block you will come to the:

12. **Washington Street Public Boat Landing.** This iron open-

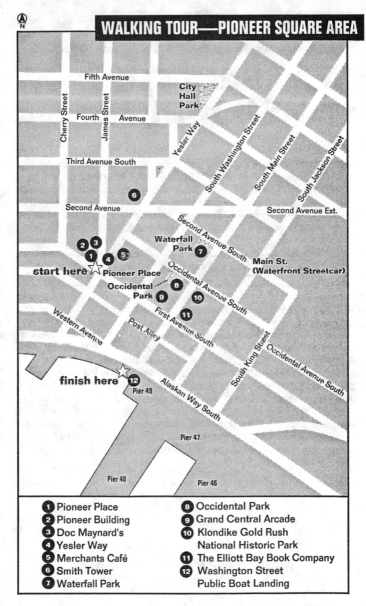

N

Fifth Avenue

City Hall Park

Cherry Street

James Street

Fourth Avenue

Yesler Way

Third Avenue South

South Washington Street

South Main Street

South Jackson Street

6

Second Avenue

Second Avenue Ext.

Second Avenue South

Waterfall Park
7

2 **3**

1 **4** **5**

Main St. (Waterfront Streetcar)

start here ☆ Pioneer Place

Occidental Avenue South

Occidental Park

8

9 **10**

Western Avenue

11

Post Alley

First Avenue South

South King Street

Occidental Avenue South

finish here ☆ **12**

Pier 49

Alaskan Way South

Pier 47

Pier 48

Pier 46

1 Pioneer Place	**8** Occidental Park	
2 Pioneer Building	**9** Grand Central Arcade	
3 Doc Maynard's	**10** Klondike Gold Rush	
4 Yesler Way	National Historic Park	
5 Merchants Café	**11** The Elliott Bay Book Company	
6 Smith Tower	**12** Washington Street	
7 Waterfall Park	Public Boat Landing	

air building was erected in 1920 and today serves as a public dock where people can tie up their boats while they are in Seattle. As recently as 100 years ago, this was a mud flat, but dredging deepened the bay.

SEATTLE SHOPPING

Seattle's most famous shopping area is **Pike Place Market,** a produce market but also much more. It's located at the foot of Pine Street overlooking the waterfront. (See p. 99 for details.) The nearby waterfront, with its many restored piers, has numerous souvenir and gift shops.

1. THE SHOPPING SCENE

The heart of Seattle's shopping district is at the corner of Pine Street and Westlake Avenue. Within one block of this intersection are four major department stores and a new shopping mall. These stores include **Nordstrom,** which is rapidly gaining a name as the best department store in the country; The **Bon Marche,** which is known simply as **"The Bon"** here in Seattle; **Frederick & Nelson,** which has been in business since 1890; and **I. Magnin,** which is smaller than the other three but still offers a wide selection.

If you're young at heart and possess a very personal idea of style, you head over to Broadway on Capitol Hill to do your shopping. Pioneer Square, Seattle's historic district, is filled with art galleries, antiques shops, and other unusual shops.

Hours Shops in Seattle are generally open Monday through Saturday from 9 or 10am to 5 or 6pm, with shorter hours on Sunday. The major department stores usually stay open later on Friday evenings, and many shopping malls stay open until 9pm Monday through Saturday.

2. SHOPPING A TO Z

ANTIQUES

The three shops listed here are located in Seattle, but for an even larger selection of antiques, head north of Seattle to the town of **Snohomish**—where you'll find one of the largest concentrations of antiques dealers in the Northwest and more than 150 shops to keep antiques hunters happy.

HONEYCHURCH ANTIQUES, 1008 James St. Tel. 622-1225.

For high-quality Asian antiques, including Japanese woodblock prints, textiles, furniture, and ivory and wood carvings, few Seattle antiques stores can approach Honeychurch Antiques. Regular special exhibits give this shop the feel of a tiny museum.

THE CRANE GALLERY, 1203-B Second Ave. Tel. 622-7185.

Chinese, Japanese, and Korean antiquities are the focus of this shop, which prides itself on selling only the best pieces. Imperial Chinese porcelains, bronze statues of Buddhist deities, rosewood furniture, Japanese ceramics, netsukes, snuff bottles, and Chinese archeological artifacts are just some of the quality antiques you will find here. Some Southeast Asian and Indian objects are also available.

PIONEER SQUARE MALL, 602 First Ave. Tel. 624-1164.

This underground antiques mall is in the heart of Pioneer Square and contains 80 shops selling all manner of antiques and collectibles. There are also art galleries and restaurants.

ART GALLERIES

Pioneer Square also has Seattle's greatest concentration of art galleries. Wander around south of Yesler Way and you are likely to stumble upon a gallery showing the very latest contemporary art from the Northwest. There are also many antiques stores and galleries selling Native American art in the Pioneer Square area.

THE LEGACY, 1003 First Ave. Tel. 624-6350.

Located in the same building as the prestigious Alexis Hotel, The Legacy claims to be Seattle's oldest gallery. It's certainly the city's premier gallery of contemporary and traditional Native American Indian and Inuit art. You'll find a large selection of masks by Northwest Coast Indian, as well as boxes, bowls, baskets, ivory and stone carvings, jewelry, prints, and books. Craftsmanship and prices are the highest in Seattle. For the serious collector.

NORTHWEST TRIBAL ART, 1417 First Ave. Tel. 467-9330.

Located next to Pike Place Market, this is another of Seattle's galleries selling Northwest Coast Native American and Eskimo art. Traditional and contemporary wood carvings, masks, fossilized ivory carvings, soapstone carvings, scrimshaw, jewelry, drums, and even totem poles are available.

There is another shop at 400 Pine St., Suite 308 (tel. 623-9236).

FOSTER/WHITE GALLERY, 311½ Occidental Ave. South. Tel. 622-2833.

Seattle's largest fine-arts dealer represents the foremost contemporary artists of the Northwest, including glass artists from the Pilchuk School of Glass, which is renowned for its creative glass sculptures.

There is another Foster/White Gallery in the Frederick & Nelson department store, 502 Pine St. (tel. 206/382-8538).

THE GLASS EYE, 1902 Post Alley, Pike Place Market. Tel. 441-3221.

The Glass Eye is one of Seattle's oldest art-glass galleries, specializing in glass made with Mount St. Helens ash. These hand-blown pieces all contain ash from the volcano's 1980 eruption.

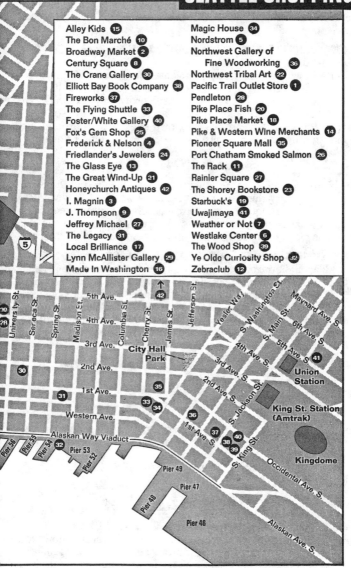

Alley Kids **15**	Magic House **34**
The Bon Marché **10**	Nordstrom **5**
Broadway Market **2**	Northwest Gallery of
Century Square **8**	Fine Woodworking **36**
The Crane Gallery **30**	Northwest Tribal Art **22**
Elliott Bay Book Company **38**	Pacific Trail Outlet Store **1**
Fireworks **37**	Pendleton **28**
The Flying Shuttle **33**	Pike Place Fish **20**
Foster/White Gallery **40**	Pike Place Market **18**
Fox's Gem Shop **25**	Pike & Western Wine Merchants **14**
Frederick & Nelson **4**	Pioneer Square Mall **35**
Friedlander's Jewelers **24**	Port Chatham Smoked Salmon **26**
The Glass Eye **13**	The Rack **11**
The Great Wind-Up **21**	Rainier Square **27**
Honeychurch Antiques **42**	The Shorey Bookstore **23**
I. Magnin **3**	Starbuck's **19**
J. Thompson **9**	Uwajimaya **41**
Jeffrey Michael **27**	Weather or Not **7**
The Legacy **31**	Westlake Center **6**
Local Brilliance **17**	The Wood Shop **39**
Lynn McAllister Gallery **29**	Ye Olde Curiosity Shop **32**
Made In Washington **16**	Zebraclub **12**

BOOKS

THE SHOREY BOOK STORE, 110 Union St. Tel. 624-0221.
In business since 1890, Shorey's will be happy to find you books from the year they opened (or any other year for that matter). Rare, antiquarian, and out-of-print books are their specialty. With more than a million items in stock, Shorey's is sure to have that obscure

tome you've been seeking for years. If they don't have it, they'll search the world to find it for you. The store's motto is "The oldest, the biggest, the best!"

ELLIOTT BAY BOOK COMPANY, 101 S. Main St. Tel. 624-6600.

With heavy wooden fixtures, balconies, and a staircase descending to the deli/café in the basement, this could very well be the most aesthetically pleasing bookstore in the Northwest. They have an excellent selection of books on Seattle and the Northwest, so if you want to learn more or are planning further excursions around the region, stop by. It's located just two blocks from Pioneer Square.

CRAFTS

The Northwest seems to be a mecca for craftspeople, and the place to see what crafty things they are creating is at Pike Place Market. Although there are quite a few permanent shops within the market that sell local crafts, you can meet the artisans themselves on the weekends when they set up tables on the main floor of the market.

FIREWORKS, 210 First Ave. South. Tel. 682-8707.

Playful, outrageous, bizarre, beautiful—these are just some of the terms that can be used to describe the eclectic collection of Northwest crafts on sale at this Pioneer Square–area gallery. A table with place setting and food painted onto its top, cosmic clocks, wildly creative jewelry, and children's furniture painted with fun designs are some of the fine and unusual items you'll find here.

NORTHWEST GALLERY OF FINE WOODWORKING, 202 First Ave. Tel. 625-0542.

This store is a showcase for some of the most amazing woodworking you'll ever see. Be sure to stroll through here while in the Pioneer Square area. The warm hues of the exotic woods are soothing and the designs are beautiful. Furniture, boxes, sculptures, vases, bowls, and much more are created by more than 35 Northwest artisans.

A second shop can be found at 317 NW Gilman Blvd., Issaquah (tel. 206/391-4221).

DEPARTMENT STORES

NORDSTROM, 1501 Fifth Ave. Tel. 628-2111.

This is my pick for best department store in Seattle. Known for its personal service, the Nordstrom stores are rapidly gaining a reputation as the premier department stores in the United States. The company originated here in Seattle, and its customers are devotedly loyal. Whether it's your first visit or your 50th, the knowledgeable staff will help you in any way they can. Prices are not low, but you're paying for the best service available. Fans of the store will convince you that it's worth the extra money. There are very popular sales in June, July, and November (for women), and in January and June (for men).

THE BON MARCHE, Third Ave. and Pine St. Tel. 344-2121.

Slightly less expensive than Nordstrom, The Bon (as it's known here in Seattle) offers nine floors of merchandise. You'll find nearly anything you could possibly want at this store.

FREDERICK & NELSON, Fifth Ave. and Pine St. Tel. 682-5500.

Founded in 1890, Frederick & Nelson is Seattle's oldest department store. You'll realize that this is not your ordinary department store as soon as you see the doorman out front. Inside, there are 10 floors of merchandise, including an antiques store and a Steuben Glass shop. At Christmas the store windows are filled with animated decorations.

I. MAGNIN, 601 Pine St. Tel. 682-6111.

Though smaller than the other downtown department stores, I. Magnin provides the same excellent service and a surprising selection of merchandise.

DISCOUNT STORES

J. THOMPSON, 1501 Fourth Ave. Tel. 623-5780.

This store sells designer men's and women's clothing at 30% to 70% off retail. Styles are rather conservative.

THE RACK, 1601 Second Ave. Tel. 448-8522.

Discounts similar to those at J. Thompson are available at The Rack, which sells clearance items from Nordstrom.

FASHIONS

PENDLETON, 1313 Fourth Ave. Tel. 682-4430.

For Northwesterners, and many other people across the nation, Pendleton is and always will be *the* name in conservative wool fashions. This store features the Northwest company's full line of men's and women's wool clothes. The styles are classic and the wool is only the finest.

A second store can be found in Bellevue Square, Bellevue (tel. 453-9040).

WEATHER OR NOT, 400 Pine St. Tel. 682-3797.

Seattle's inclement weather is legendary, and so it comes as no surprise that there is a store here devoted exclusively to weathering this climate. Weather or Not sells everything from umbrellas and raincoats to underwater paper, waterproof matches, and floating briefcases.

CHILDREN'S

ALLEY KIDS, 1904 Post Alley. Tel. 728-0609.

Tucked away on Post Alley, between Pike Place and First Avenue, Alley Kids sells both locally designed and imported children's clothing. If you don't mind spending a bundle on clothes that will be outgrown in a few months, you'll love the selection here.

MEN'S

JEFFREY MICHAEL, 1318 Fourth Ave. (in Rainier Sq.). Tel. 625-9891.

With five floors of top men's fashions, Jeffrey Michael is Seattle's leading menswear store. Excellent service and reasonable prices.

ZEBRACLUB, 1901 First Ave. Tel. 448-7452.

If you're young and hip and believe that clothes shopping should be an audiovisual experience, make the scene at ZebraClub, where rock videos playing on overhead monitors set the shopping tempo. If you need to get wired beforehand, grab a double espresso from the espresso cart out front. Clothing is casual.

WOMEN'S

THE FLYING SHUTTLE, 607 First Ave. Tel. 343-9762.

★ Fashion becomes art and art becomes fashion at this chic boutique-cum-gallery on Pioneer Square. Hand-woven fabrics and hand-painted silks are the specialties here, but of course such unique fashions require equally unique body decorations in the form of exquisite jewelry creations. Designers and artists from the Northwest and the rest of the nation find an outlet for their creativity at The Flying Shuttle.

LOCAL BRILLIANCE, 1535 First Ave. Tel. 343-5864.

If you want to return from your trip to Seattle wearing a dress you know no one else at the office will have ever seen before, visit Local Brilliance. The shop carries a wide selection of fashions by the Northwest's best fashion designers.

FOOD

COFFEE

STARBUCK'S, Pike Place Market. Tel. 448-8762.

★ Seattle has developed a reputation as a city of coffee-holics, and Starbuck's is probably the reason why. This company has coffeehouses all over town, but this is probably the most convenient if you are just visiting Seattle. With 36 blends available by the cup or by the pound, you can do a bit of taste-testing before making a decision.

FISH

After tasting the bounty of seafood available in Seattle, it's almost impossible to do without. Any of the seafood vendors in Pike Place Market will pack your fresh salmon or Dungeness crab in an airline-approved container that will keep it fresh for up to 48 hours.

PIKE PLACE FISH, 86 Pike Place, Pike Place Market. Tel. 682-7181.

★ Located just behind Rachel, the life-sized bronze pig, this fishmonger is famous for flying fish. Pick out a big silvery salmon, ask them to fillet it, and watch the show. The floor salesman, who usually keeps up a loud sales patter, calls out to the folks behind the counter that a fish is on the way, and the next thing you know, your salmon is flying over the counter and in moments is filleted and wrapped. They'll also deliver your packaged order to your hotel, ready for you to carry it onto the plane.

PORT CHATHAM SMOKED SALMON, 1306 Fourth Ave., Rainier Sq. Tel. 623-4645.

Northwest Coast Native Americans relied heavily on salmon for sustenance; to preserve the fish for times of the year when the fish weren't running, they used alderwood smoke. This tradition is still carried on today to produce one of the Northwest's most delicious food products. This store sells smoked sockeye, king salmon, rainbow trout, black cod, and oysters—all of which will keep without refrigeration until the package is opened.

GIFTS/SOUVENIRS

Pike Place Market is the Grand Central Station of Seattle souvenirs, with stiff competition from Seattle Center and Pioneer Square.

MADE IN WASHINGTON, Pike Place Market (Post Alley at Pine St.). Tel. 467-0788.

Washington takes pride in what it produces, whether it's salmon, wine, or Northwest Native American masks. You'll find a selection of Washington State products in this shop, which is an excellent place to pick up gifts for all the unfortunates who didn't get to come with you on your visit to Seattle.

Other Made in Washington locations include Westlake Center, third floor (tel. 623-9753); and Bellevue Square, second level, Bellevue (tel. 454-6907).

JEWELRY

FOX'S GEM SHOP, 1341 Fifth Ave. Tel. 623-2528.

This is Seattle's premier jeweler (with prices to prove it). Among other elegant lines, they feature the Tiffany Collection.

FRIEDLANDER'S JEWELERS, 1400 Fifth Ave. Tel. 223-7474.

This company has been doing business in Seattle since before the great fire of 1889 and stocks a wide selection of jewelry, watches, and fine crystal.

MALLS/SHOPPING CENTERS

WESTLAKE CENTER, 400 Pine St. Tel. 467-1600.

This is a new covered shopping mall in the heart of the downtown shopping district. The monorail terminal is on the second floor of the mall.

RAINIER SQUARE, 1326 Fifth Ave. Tel. 628-5058.

Only two blocks away from Westlake Center, Rainier Square is filled with 50 upscale shops and restaurants. Built on the bottom floors of several skyscrapers, the Rainier Square mall is a veritable maze.

CENTURY SQUARE, 191 Fourth Ave. and Pike St.

More fine stores are to be found in this upscale mall a block from Westlake Center.

BROADWAY MARKET, 401 Broadway East. Tel. 322-1610.

A trendy mall located in the stylish Capitol Hill neighborhood, the Broadway Market houses numerous small shops and restaurants with reasonable prices.

MARKETS

PIKE PLACE MARKET, Pike St. and First Ave. Tel. 682-7453.

★ Pike Place Market is one of Seattle's most famous landmarks and tourist attractions. Not only are there produce vendors, fishmongers, and butchers, but also artists, craftspeople, and performers. A trip here can easily be an all-day affair. Hundreds of shops are tucked away in hidden nooks and crannies on the seemingly endless levels. Many of Seattle's best restaurants are located in or near this megamarket.

UWAJIMAYA, 519 Sixth Ave. South. Tel. 624-6248.

Typically, your local neighborhood supermarket has a section of Chinese cooking ingredients; it's probably about 10 feet long, with half that space taken up by various brands of soy sauce. Now imagine your local supermarket with nothing *but* Asian foods, housewares, produce, and toys. That's Uwajimaya, Seattle's Asian supermarket in the heart of the International District.

TOYS

MAGIC MOUSE, 603 First Ave. Tel. 682-8097.

★ Adults and children alike have a hard time pulling themselves away from this, the most fun toy store in Seattle. It is conveniently located on Pioneer Square.

THE WOOD SHOP, 320 First Ave. Tel. 624-1763.

Just two blocks away is another Seattle favorite that sells wooden toys and puppets. This place is worth a look even if you're not in the market for toys.

THE GREAT WIND-UP, Pike Place Market. Tel. 621-9370.

You guessed it—they sell wind-up toys (and battery-operated toys, too).

WINES

The Northwest is rapidly becoming known as a producer of fine wines. The relatively dry summers with warm days and cool nights provide the perfect climate for growing grapes. After you have sampled a few Washington or Oregon vintages, you might want to take a few bottles home.

PIKE & WESTERN WINE MERCHANTS, Pike Place Market. Tel. 441-1307.

For an excellent selection of Northwest and French wines. The extremely knowledgeable management here will be happy to send you home with the very best wines available in Seattle.

CHAPTER 10

SEATTLE NIGHTS

1. THE PERFORMING ARTS

• **MAJOR CONCERT & PERFORMANCE HALLS**

2. THE CLUB & MUSIC SCENE

3. THE BAR SCENE

4. MORE ENTERTAINMENT

Though Seattleites spend much of their free time enjoying their natural surroundings, they have not overlooked the more cultured evening pursuits. Theater, opera, and ballet flourish here, and music lovers will find a plethora of classical, jazz, and rock venues. If you are a fan of chamber music, you're in good company in Seattle. Much of the evening entertainment is clustered in the Seattle Center or Pioneer Square area, which makes a night out on the town surprisingly easy. To make things even easier, you can buy half-price tickets at **Ticket/Ticket,** which has two sales booths. The Pike Place Market location, First Ave. and Pike St. (tel. 324-2744), is the more convenient location if you are staying downtown. This booth is open Tuesday through Sunday from noon to 6pm. The other booth is on the second floor of the Broadway Market, 401 Broadway East (same telephone number). It's open Tuesday through Sunday from 10am to 7pm. The booths offer day-of-show tickets only and charge an additional 50¢ to $3 depending on the ticket price, but you still save lots of money. If you want to pay full price with your credit card, call **Ticketmaster Northwest** (tel. 206/628-0888), open Monday through Saturday from 8am to 10pm, on Sunday from 10am to 6pm.

To find out what's going on when you are in town, pick up a copy of *Seattle Weekly* (75¢), which is Seattle's weekly arts-and-entertainment newspaper. You'll find it in bookstores, convenience stores, grocery stores, and newsstands. The Friday *Seattle Times* also has a guide, "Tempo," to the week's arts and entertainment offerings. Another free weekly guide is the *Seattle Guide,* which you can pick up at the Seattle–King County Convention & Visitors Bureau information center, Convention Center, Level 1 Galleria, Eighth Ave. and Pike St. (tel. 206/461-5840).

1. THE PERFORMING ARTS

The main venues for the performing arts in Seattle are clustered in the Seattle Center. Here, in the shadow of the Space Needle, you'll find the Seattle Center Opera House, Bagley Wright Theater, Intiman Playhouse, Center House Theatre, Pacific Arts Center, Coliseum, and Arena.

MAJOR CONCERT & PERFORMANCE HALLS

A Contemporary Theater. Tel. 285-5110.
Bagley Wright Theater. Tel. 443-2222.
Broadway Performance Hall. Tel. 323-2623.
Empty Space Theatre. Tel. 467-6000 or 587-3737.
The 5th Avenue Theatre. Tel. 625-1900.
Intiman Playhouse. Tel. 626-0782.
Meany Theater. Tel. 543-4880.
New City Theatre and Art Center. Tel. 323-6800.
Seattle Center Opera House. Tel. 443-4711.
Paramount Theatre. Tel. 682-1414.

MAJOR PERFORMING ARTS COMPANIES

OPERA & CLASSICAL MUSIC

NORTHWEST CHAMBER ORCHESTRA, Seattle Center, 201 Mercer St. Tel. 343-0445.

Chamber music is very popular in Seattle, and the Northwest Chamber Orchestra presents some of the very finest. Active for 20 seasons now, it is a showcase for Northwest performers. The annual "Bach by Popular Demand" baroque music festival is the highlight of the season, which runs from September to April.

Prices: $19; student and senior-citizen discounts.

SANTA FE CHAMBER MUSIC FESTIVAL IN SEATTLE, Meany Theater, University of Washington. Tel. 233-0993.

The stars of the Santa Fe cultural scene have been bringing their music to Seattle every August for 14 years now. Chamber music fans who may have missed them in the Southwest can catch them here in the Northwest. The festival series extends over two weeks.

Prices: $10–$20; student and senior-citizen discounts for some performances.

SEATTLE OPERA ASSOCIATION, Seattle Center Opera House, Fourth Ave. and Mercer St. Tel. 389-7676.

The Seattle Opera is a first-rate company best known for its productions of Wagner's four-opera *The Ring of the Nibelungen,* which returned to the Opera House stage in the fall of 1991. The company gives five productions during its season, which runs from September to May.

Prices: $30–$125.

SEATTLE SYMPHONY ORCHESTRA, Seattle Center Opera House, Fourth Ave. and Mercer St. Tel. 443-4747.

The Seattle Symphony Orchestra is conducted by Gerard

Schwarz, who also conducts the New York Chamber Symphony and is music director of New Jersey's Waterloo Music Festival and New York City's Mostly Mozart Festival. The season here runs from September to May, and performances are on Monday and Tuesday evenings. On Sunday afternoons, there are pops concerts and children's programs.

Prices: $9–$45.

THEATER COMPANIES

A CONTEMPORARY THEATER [ACT], 100 W. Roy St. Tel. 285-5110.

This theater offers slightly more adventurous productions than the other major theater companies in Seattle, although it is still not as avant-garde as some of the smaller companies. The season runs from May to December, when they close the year with a well-loved version of *A Christmas Carol*.

Prices: $10.50–$21.50.

EMPTY SPACE THEATRE, 107 Occidental Ave. South. Tel. 467-6000, or 587-3737.

In the Pioneer Square area, this theater's six-play season runs from October to June. If you enjoy the new and the unusual, the Empty Space will more than likely have something for you.

Prices: $13–$18.

INTIMAN THEATRE COMPANY, Intiman Playhouse, Seattle Center, 201 Mercer St. Tel. 626-0782.

This company has a very dedicated following in the Seattle area. The theater season runs from June to October, with a different play being presented each month. The theater is small, seating only 424 people, so you are always assured a good seat. Past seasons have included *The Kentucky Cycle, Misalliance* and *A Streetcar Named Desire*.

Prices: $11.50–$19.50 for most tickets.

SEATTLE REPERTORY THEATER, Bagley Wright Theater, Seattle Center. Tel. 443-2222.

The Rep season picks up where the Intiman leaves off, giving Seattle excellent year-round theater. The season is October to May, with six plays performed in the main 856-seat theater and three more in the intimate PONCHO theater, which seats only 142. The Rep has been around for more than a quarter century and is consistently outstanding. Productions range from classics to contemporary to Broadway musicals.

Prices: $8–$26.

DANCE COMPANIES

ON THE BOARDS, Washington Hall Performance Gallery, 153 14th Ave. Tel. 325-7901.

This is Seattle's premier modern-dance company, satisfying the

city's year-round craving for innovative dance. The Northwest New Works Festival, which is held every summer, is one of the season's highlights. In addition to performances by the company, there are special appearances by internationally known artists.
Prices: $4–$18.

PACIFIC NORTHWEST BALLET, Opera House, Seattle Center, Fourth Ave. and Mercer St. Tel. 628-0888.

If you happen to be in Seattle in December, try to get a ticket to this company's performance of *The Nutcracker*. In addition to the outstanding dancing, you'll enjoy sets and costumes by children's book author Maurice Sendak. During the rest of the season, which runs from October to May, the company presents a wide range of classics and world premieres, with an emphasis on the choreography of George Balanchine.
Prices: $11–$47.

THEATERS

THE 5TH AVENUE THEATRE, 1308 Fifth Ave. Tel. 625-1900.

First opened in 1926 as a vaudeville house, The 5th Avenue Theatre is a loose re-creation of the imperial throne room in Beijing's Forbidden City. When vaudeville lost popularity, this opulent setting was used as a movie theater. In 1980 a $2.6-million renovation was undertaken and the theater once again opened as a venue for live stage performances. Since then, major touring companies—with such stars as Katharine Hepburn, Richard Harris, and Lauren Bacall—have played The 5th Avenue. In addition to national touring shows, the theater now has its own resident musical-theater company. Don't pass up an opportunity to attend a show at Seattle's most beautiful theater.
Prices: $18–$35.

NEW CITY THEATRE AND ART CENTER, 1634 11th Ave. Tel. 323-6800.

Located on Capitol Hill, Seattle's hippest neighborhood, this is the city's most daring theater venue. As you would expect, the productions here are calculated to keep the local art crowd talking. You'll find everything from performance artists to plays by local playwrights, even a bit of cabaret now and then.
Prices: $2–$12.

2. THE CLUB & MUSIC SCENE

NIGHTCLUBS/CABARETS

If you have the urge to do a bit of nightclubbing and bar hopping while in Seattle, there's no better place to start than in Pioneer Square. The last time I visited, the fleet was in and the sailors were having a grand old time. It isn't always so noisy, but good times are guaranteed whether you want to laugh it up at a comedy club, hang out in a good old-fashioned bar, or do a little dancing.

COMEDY CLUBS

SEATTLE IMPROV, 1426 First Ave. Tel. 628-5000 or 628-0888.

What's the difference between December and June in Seattle? Answer: June has only 30 days. If you're a fan of the Showtime Comedy Club Network, you'll probably be able to catch someone you've seen on TV while you are in Seattle. Not all the jokes are about the local weather, but you can bet there will be a few on any given night. The Seattle Improv also has a very good restaurant serving Northwest cuisine. Reservations are required for dinner. Open: Showtimes Tues–Sun 8:30pm.

Admission: Sun, Tues–Thurs $6; Fri–Sat $10. Two-drink minimum if you aren't having dinner.

COMEDY UNDERGROUND, 622 South Main St. Tel. 628-0303.

What is it about the Seattle Underground that induces people to tell jokes? Remember all those horrendous ones you heard during the Seattle Underground Tour? Maybe it's all those sewer gases that affect people down here. Whatever the reason, this underground (literally) nightspot in the Pioneer Square area is dedicated to laughter. Local and nationally known comedians whiff their fair share of the laughing gases when they perform here.

Admission: $3–$7.50.

FOLK, COUNTRY & ROCK

BACKSTAGE, 2208 Northwest Market St. Tel. 781-2805.

This is Seattle's top venue for contemporary music of all kinds and packs in the crowds most nights. The audience ranges from drinking age up to graying rock 'n' rollers. The music runs the gamut from Afro pop to zydeco. If you want to find out who's hot in the Northwest, check this place out.

Admission: $7–$14.

BALLARD FIREHOUSE, 5429 Russell Ave. Tel. 784-3516.

A similarly eclectic assortment of musical styles finds its way onto the bandstand of this converted firehouse in the old Scandinavian section of northwest Seattle. Now it's just the music that's hot, and that's the way they want to keep it. You might catch one of your jazz favorites here, or maybe someone who used to be famous but decided to make good music instead of selling out for big bucks. People having dinner here get the best tables.

Admission: $5–$12.

CENTRAL TAVERN AND CAFE, 207 First Ave. Tel. 622-0209.

Seattle's only "second class tavern"—that's what the sign out front claims, and more than a few people wind up inside just to find out what a second-class tavern is really all about. The crowd is young and the music is rock and rhythm-and-blues. You can catch both local and out-of-town bands here. On weekends this is one of the clubs participating in the "joint cover" program: For $7 you can get into seven different clubs in the Pioneer Square area.

Admission: $4–$7.

DOC MAYNARD'S, 610 First Ave. Tel. 682-4649.

By day it's the starting point of the family-oriented Seattle Underground Tour, but by night it's one of Seattle's most popular clubs for live rock 'n' roll. This place attracts all types of rock-music lovers, and you'll be welcome as long as you like your music loud.

Admission: $6–$12.

KELLS, 1916 Post Alley, Pike Place Market. Tel. 728-1916.

⭐ This friendly Irish pub has the look and feel of a casual Dublin pub. They pull a good Guinness stout and feature live traditional Irish music Wednesday through Saturday. This is also a restaurant serving traditional Irish meals, and there's even a patio dining area (something you aren't likely to find in a pub in Ireland, where it rains even more than in Seattle).

Admission: $2.

JAZZ & BLUES

DIMITRIOU'S JAZZ ALLEY, 2033 Sixth Ave. Tel. 441-9729.

⭐ This is *the* place for great jazz music in Seattle. Cool and sophisticated, Dimitriou's books only the very best performers and is reminiscent of New York jazz clubs. There is also a $5 per set drink minimum.

Admission: $5–$10.

NEW ORLEANS CREOLE RESTAURANT, 114 First Ave. South. Tel. 622-2563.

If you like your food and your jazz hot, check out the New Orleans. There's live music seven nights a week. Tuesday is Cajun night, but the rest of the week you can hear Dixieland, R&B, jazz, and blues. This is one of the "joint cover" clubs (seven clubs for $7).

Admission: Weeknights free, weekends $7.

DANCE CLUBS/DISCOS

GOOEY'S, Seattle Sheraton, Sixth Ave. and Pike St. Tel. 621-9000.

Artsy high-tech styling and a multilevel dance floor make Gooey's a hit with the young and restless crowd. During happy hour there's a free appetizer buffet that features some surprisingly tasty and unusual dishes. The dance music goes on late into the night. The peculiar name is a reference to the amazing giant clam of the Northwest, which is spelled geoduck but pronounced "goo-ee-duck."

Admission: $3.

PIER 70 RESTAURANT AND CHOWDER HOUSE, 2815 Alaskan Way. Tel. 728-7071.

Over on the waterfront is a cavernous place popular with Seattle's singles set. There's live Top 40 dance music six nights a week, and the restaurant has great views of Elliott Bay. However, the folks here are usually too busy checking each other out to notice the romantic parade of lights as the ferry leaves the harbor. Oh well. Let's dance.

Admission: $3–$6.

GAY CLUBS

NEIGHBOURS, 1509 Broadway. Tel. 324-5358.

This has been the favorite disco of Capitol Hill's gay community for years, and recently the word has gotten out to straights that it's a fun place in which to dance. Still, the clientele is primarily gay. Weekend buffets are extremely popular.

Admission: $1–$3

3. THE BAR SCENE

BREW PUBS

BIG TIME BREWERY AND ALEHOUSE, 4133 University Way NE. Tel. 545-4509.

Located in the University District, the Big Time serves up four of its own brews, which you can see being made on the premises.

THE TROLLEYMAN, 3400 Phinney Ave. North. Tel. 548-8000.

This is the taproom of the Red Hook Brewery, one of the Northwest's most celebrated microbreweries. It's located in a restored trolley barn on the Lake Washington Ship Canal. You can sample the ales brewed here, have a bite to eat, and even tour the brewery if you are interested.

SPECIALTY BARS

SPORTS BARS

SNEAKERS, 567 Occidental Ave. South. Tel. 625-1340.

Located almost directly across the street from the Kingdome, Sneakers is a favorite of Seattle sports fans, especially before and after Seahawks games. The walls are covered with celebrity signatures and old sports photos; the day's sports pages are plastered on the restroom walls so you can keep current; and a TV broadcasting sports events is never out of view.

FX MCRORY'S STEAK, CHOP, AND OYSTER HOUSE, 419 Occidental Ave. South. Tel. 623-4800.

Also very popular, FX McRory's is a glittery drinking-and-dining establishment with an old-fashioned saloon feel to it. However, the clientele is upscale, and you're likely to see members of the Seahawks or the Supersonics at the bar. The original Leroy Neiman paintings on the walls lend an abundance of class to this sports bar.

BANKERS' BARS

MCCORMICK & SCHMICK'S, 1103 First Ave. Tel. 623-5500.

If the mahogany paneling, sparkling cut glass, and waiters in bow ties don't convince you that you're drinking with money, a glance at the clientele will. Happy hour is very busy as brokers wind down with a few stiff drinks. If you long to rub shoulders with the movers and shakers of Seattle, this is the place for you.

MCCORMICK'S FISH HOUSE & BAR, 722 Fourth Ave. Tel. 682-3900.

This dining-and-drinking establishment provides the same atmosphere as McCormick's & Schmick's. Elbow your way up to the bar during after-work hours and you just might overhear a hot tip on the market. Be sure to look your best when you stop in here for a drink or two.

ATMOSPHERIC BARS

TLAQUEPAQUE, 1122 Post Alley. Tel. 467-8226.

There are rowdier bars in Seattle, but few have the atmosphere of this cavernous Mexican cantina. Strolling mariachi musicians, strumming for their lives and wailing at the tops of their lungs, keep the crowds of diners and drinkers happy. Overhead is a massive chandelier made from Mexican beer bottles. The bar used to be a warehouse, and still they need more space!

Bars for the Chic

CAFE SPORT, 2020 Western Ave. Tel. 443-6000.

Certainly better known as one of Seattle's most innovative restaurants, Café Sport also happens to have a very lively bar. The subdued tones and angular modern deco decor let you know at a glance what sort of place this is. The folks in the bar are young, attractive, and working on their first million. There isn't much space here, so grab a seat early.

CUTTERS BAYHOUSE, 2001 Western Ave. Tel. 448-4884.

Located right across the street from Café Sport, this much larger place attracts a slightly less affluent but equally stylish crowd. Cutters Bayhouse claims to have invented grazing, and their extensive appetizer menu is perfect for a long night of drinking.

A BILLIARD PARLOR

JILLIAN'S BILLIARD CLUB AND CAFE, 731 Westlake Ave. North. Tel. 223-0300.

There was a time when people who wore a suit and tie to work wouldn't dream of going into a pool hall after a hard day at the office, but not anymore. Jillian's has changed all that. The bar here is from the famous Algonquin Bar and fits in nicely with the view of the lake.

A GAY BAR

THUMPERS, 1500 E. Madison St. Tel. 328-3800.
Perched high on Capitol Hill with an excellent view of downtown Seattle, Thumpers is a classy little bar. The seats by the fireplace are perfect on a cold and rainy night. Great snacks to go with the drinks.

4. MORE ENTERTAINMENT

MOVIES

The **Seattle International Film Festival** has become quite an affair in recent years. It's held every May, with 150 films being screened during the festival. They are shown at **The Egyptian,** 801 E. Pine St. (tel. 206/323-4978), and the **Market Theater,** 1428 Post Alley (tel. 206/382-1171).

The **Market Theater,** mentioned above, shows foreign and independent films year round. **Harvard Exit,** 807 E. Roy St. (tel. 206/323-8986), often shows films that can't find a screen elsewhere in the city. However, the most eclectic programming is to be found in the University District at **Grand Illusion,** 1403 NE 50th Ave. (tel. 206/523-3935); **Seven Gables,** 911 NE 50th Ave. (tel. 206/682-8820), which books top foreign films; and **Neptune,** NE 45th Ave. and Brooklyn St. NE (tel. 206/633-5545), which is Seattle's repertory theater.

CHAPTER 11

EASY EXCURSIONS FROM SEATTLE

I strongly recommend that you make one or more of these trips so that you get a sense of what life is like in the Northwest. Seattleites are nearly inseparable from their natural surroundings—the forests, the mountains, and the waters—and spend as much time in them as they can. At least some part of each of the areas described below can be visited on long day trips. However, to circle the Olympic Peninsula, visit all of the major San Juan Islands, or to fully explore the Cascade Mountains requires an overnight trip or longer. Regardless of how much time you have, be sure to get at least a taste for the Northwest's natural beauty by visiting one of these areas.

1. MOUNT RAINIER

Weather forecasting for Seattle laymen is a simple matter: Either "The Mountain" is out and the weather is good, or it isn't (out or good). "The Mountain" is of course Mount Rainier, the 14,410-foot-tall dormant volcano that looms over Seattle on clear days. Mount Rainier may look as if it were on the edge of town, but it's actually 90 miles southeast of the city.

WHAT TO SEE & DO

If you're planning a day trip, be sure to leave early so you can have plenty of time to do a bit of walking in the **Mount Rainier National Park,** Tahoma Woods–Star Route, Ashford, WA

IMPRESSIONS

There is a great deal in the remark of the discontented traveller: 'When you have seen a pine forest, a bluff, a river, and a lake, you have seen all the scenery of western America. Sometimes the pine is three hundred feet high, and sometimes the rock is, and sometimes the lake is a hundred miles long. But it's all the same don't you know. I'm getting sick of it.'
—RUDYARD KIPLING

98304 (tel. 206/569-2211). Backpackers interested in overnight and longer trips can hike the **Wonderland Trail,** which circles Mount Rainier.

On the way to the park on Washington Hwy. 706, you might want to stop in the town of **Elbe** to take a ride on the **Mount Rainier Scenic Railroad** (tel. 206/569-2588). The old steam trains pull vintage cars through lush forests and over old bridges, then wind up at Mineral Lake. The trip covers 14 miles and takes an hour and a half. Fares are $6.75 for adults, $5.75 for senior citizens, $4.75 for ages 12 to 17, and $3.75 for children under age 12. The train operates daily from June 15 to Labor Day, with departures at 11am, 1:15pm, and 3:30pm. From Memorial Day to June 15 and from Labor Day to the end of September, the train operates on weekends only.

There is a **national park visitors center** in the town of **Paradise** on the south side of the mountain. Paradise, elevation 5,400 feet, is best reached by taking I-5 south from Seattle to Washington Hwy. 161 to Washington Hwy. 706. From here you have a magnificent view of the mountain, which is covered with snow and glaciers throughout the year. Paradise happens to hold the world's record for snowfall in a single year—91 feet fell in the winter of 1972. In the summer, however, the air is warm, the wildflowers are in bloom, and the snow stays on Mount Rainier's glaciers. The circular glass-walled visitors center affords 360° views of the area.

Sunrise, on the northeast side of the mountain, is the highest point in the park open to automobile traffic, and provides more spectacular views of the mountain.

WHERE TO STAY

The **Paradise Inn,** P.O. Box 108, Ashford, WA 98304 (tel. 206/569-2275), is a rustic lodge built in 1917. Exposed beams, cathedral ceilings, and huge stone fireplaces provide a warm atmosphere for those who want to stay overnight or a few days up here. There are rooms available with or without bath. People drive down from Seattle just for the Sunday brunch. There are trails and meadows all around the lodge for guests and visitors to explore. In winter, although the lodge is closed, there is excellent cross-country skiing and snowshoeing in the area. Rates are extremely reasonable: $50 single or double without bath; $70 single or double with bath; $91 single, double, or triple for a two-room unit with bath; and $95 single, double, or triple for a suite. The lodge is open only from May to October.

If you're in the area in the winter, you might want to stay at the equally rustic **National Park Inn,** P.O. Box 108, Ashford, WA 98304 (tel. 206/569-2275), which was built in 1920 and is open all year. This spot is particularly popular in winter for cross-country skiing. Rates are $45 single or double without bath; $65 single or double with bath; $86 single, double, or triple for a two-room unit with bath.

Just north of Mount Rainier National Park on Washington Hwy. 410 is **Crystal Mountain Resort,** P.O. Box 1, Crystal

Mountain, WA 98022 (tel. 206/663-2265), which offers year-round activities. The resort receives most of its visitors in winter, when skiers come for the miles of slopes. However, there is also plenty to do in summer. Chair lifts are still working and there is swimming, tennis, hiking, and horseback riding. Rates at the resort's five hotels and condominium complexes here vary from $58 to $130 double per night.

CAMPGROUNDS

There are also several campgrounds within the park for which you can make reservations through any Ticketron outlet.

2. MOUNT ST. HELENS

For many visitors to the Northwest, a trip to see Mount St. Helens is far more important than a trip to Mount Rainier. Mount St. Helens, another volcanic peak, erupted on May 18, 1980, and attracted worldwide attention for many months. The devastation wrought by this eruption is as awesome a sight as the Grand Canyon and should not be missed.

WHAT TO SEE & DO

Today the area surrounding the volcano is designated the **Mount St. Helens National Volcanic Monument.** There are numerous information centers and viewing sites, and it is even possible to climb to the top now, although only a few permits are handed out each day and reservations for weekends must be made far in advance. The main **visitors information center** is located at Silver Lake, 5 miles east of I-5 at Exit 49. Included in the extensive exhibits here are photos of the eruption and the effects on the region. There are also excellent views from here.

For a closer look, take U.S. 12 from Exit 68. Head east to the town of Randle and head south on local Route 25. You can stop at the **Iron Creek information center** for further information. This is my favorite approach to the volcano. The two-way road is only one lane wide (with turnouts), and you travel through mile after mile of tree trunks that were blown down by the force of the explosion. It's an amazing sight that will forever remind you of the power of nature.

For more information, contact **Mount St. Helens National Volcanic Monument,** 42218 NE Yale Bridge Rd., Amboy, WA 98601 (tel. 206/247-5473). For climbing permits, phone 206/247-5800.

For the most spectacular view of the volcano, take a plane or helicopter ride. **Turbotech,** 2215 Parrot Way, Kelso Airport, Kelso, WA 98626 (tel. 206/423-7699), will carry one to three people aloft for around $90. Because the fare varies depending on fuel prices, however, call for current fare.

3. THE OLYMPIC PENINSULA

On a clear day, the view west from the Seattle waterfront is almost as spectacular as the view of Mount Rainier in the east. The snow-capped Olympic Mountains shimmer in the sun on the far side of Puget Sound. All around them are lush green hills and mountains. This is the Olympic Peninsula, home of **Olympic National Park,** 600 E. Park Ave., Port Angeles, WA 98362 (tel. 206/452-4501). Of all the possible excursions from Seattle, in my opinion this is the most worthwhile. There are other mountains and islands, but nowhere else in the continental United States will you find a rain forest. The 150 inches of rain that fall annually on the **Hoh Valley** make Seattle's climate look dry. Between Winslow on the east side of the peninsula and the Hoh Valley on the west, there are spectacular mountain views, lakes, ocean beaches, museums, even a restored Victorian town full of restaurants and bed-and-breakfast inns.

If you have time only for a taste of the Olympic Peninsula, I suggest a visit to **Hurricane Ridge** to view the Olympic Mountains and a stop in **Port Townsend.** It will take you at least two days to make the trip to the Hoh Valley rain forest and back, but it's well worth it. I would happily give up a day in Seattle to make this trip.

Start by taking the **Washington State Ferry** to **Winslow** on **Bainbridge Island.** For ferry information, phone 206/464-6400, or toll free 800/84-FERRY.

SUQUAMISH MUSEUM

Your first stop, heading north on Washington Hwy. 305, should be at the Suquamish Museum, located on Sandy Hook Road (tel. 206/598-3311), which is just after you cross Agate Pass Bridge between Bainbridge Island and the mainland on Washington Hwy. 305. The museum is dedicated to the Suquamish tribe and Chief Sealth, from whom Seattle got its name. In addition to exhibits covering the tribe's early history, there are canoe-carving and Native American art demonstrations. Nearby is the grave of Chief Sealth, the site of a

---

IMPRESSIONS

What can we do with the western coast, a coast of 3,000 miles, rockbound cheerless, uninviting, and not a harbour on it? What use have we for such a country? I will never vote one cent from the public treasury to place the Pacific Ocean one inch nearer Boston than it is now.
—DANIEL WEBSTER, QUOTED IN NANCY WILSON ROSS,
FARTHEST REACH, 1944

Suquamish village and longhouse, and the Suquamish Fish Hatchery. The museum is open from Memorial Day to September, daily from 10am to 5pm; and October to May, Wednesday through Sunday from 11am to 4pm. Admission is $2.50 for adults, $2 for senior citizens, and $1 for children.

PORT TOWNSEND

North of here, watch for the turnoff to Port Townsend. This busy little town has become very popular in recent years after being neglected for a long time. The downtown area is lined with turn-of-the-century brick buildings that are filled with interesting shops and restaurants. On a bluff above town are the Victorian homes for which the town is now so famous. There are dozens of the ornately decorated and brightly painted houses looking out across the sound. Many of them are now bed-and-breakfast inns, and the best part of a visit to Port Townsend is the chance to stay in one of these old homes.

WHAT TO SEE & DO

Built in 1867, the **Rothschild House,** at the corner of Taylor and Jefferson streets, is open to the public. Although the house is filled with Victorian antiques, the exterior is quite plain-looking compared with some of its neighbors. It's open April to September, daily from 11am to 4pm; September to April, only on Saturday and Sunday from 11am to 4pm. Admission is $1. You can also tour the **Commanding Officer's Quarters** at nearby **Fort Worden State Park.** The house is open in summer only, April to October, daily from 10am to 5pm.

For further information on Port Townsend, contact the **Port Townsend Chamber of Commerce,** 2437 E. Sims Way, Port Townsend, WA 98368 (tel. 206/385-2722).

WHERE TO STAY

Among my favorite bed-and-breakfasts here is the **F. W. Hastings House/Old Consulate Inn,** 313 Walker St., Port Townsend, WA 98368 (tel. 206/385-6753). Built in 1889, this Queen Anne Victorian is one of the most photographed homes in Washington. There are eight rooms, with rates ranging from $59 to $145 for a double room. If you can't stay but would like to see the interior of this antiques-filled house, you can make an appointment for a tour.

Ann Starrett Mansion, 744 Clay St., Port Townsend, WA 98368 (tel. 206/385-3205), is equally ornate and has rates of $68 to $125 for a double room. This house can also be toured if you call and make an appointment.

If you are searching for even greater splendor than a mere Victorian home can furnish, perhaps you should look into staying at **Manresa Castle,** at the corner of Seventh and Sheridan streets (P.O. Box 564), Port Townsend, WA 98368 (tel. 206/385-5750, or toll free 800/732-1281 in Washington). The 41-room castle was built in 1892 by the first mayor of Port Townsend for his wife, and in 1928 it was acquired by the Society of Jesus (the Jesuits) for use as a school. Today the building, restored to its original beauty, is Port Townsend's most elegant accommodation. Rates range from $70 to $175 for a double.

ON & AROUND THE PENINSULA

WEST OF PORT TOWNSEND

Continuing around the Olympic Peninsula on U.S. 101, you next come to the town of **Sequim.** This area is an Olympic Peninsula anomaly. Because Sequim is in the rain shadow of the Olympic Mountains, the town receives only about 13 inches of rain per year. For contrast, keep in mind that the Hoh Valley, on the other side of the mountains, gets upward of 200 inches per year. Because of its sunny climate, Sequim has recently become a very popular retirement community.

A little farther west is **Port Angeles,** the largest city on the Olympic Peninsula. The Olympic National Park maintains a visitors center here, the **Pioneer Memorial Museum,** 3002 Mount Angeles Rd. (tel. 206/452-0330). You can watch an orientation slide program, buy books and maps, find out about trail and road conditions throughout the park, and ask about the availability of campsites and rooms in the park's lodges. The visitors center is open daily from 8am to 6pm.

From here, you should continue up to **Hurricane Ridge** if it's a clear day. Hurricane Ridge is 17 miles from U.S. 101 and has an elevation of 5,230 feet. There are sweeping panoramas of the Olympic Mountains and the forests of the park. Drive slowly and be alert; the deer up here like to graze beside the road. There is another **visitors information center** up here that's open daily from 9:30am to 5:30pm.

Six miles west of Port Townsend, you'll see the turnoff for **Elwha Valley.** Five miles up this road are two campgrounds and trailheads for backcountry trails. There is also a short nature trail opposite the entrance station.

LAKE CRESCENT

Back on U.S. 101, you next come to Lake Crescent, which offers camping, hiking, boating, and fishing on a beautiful lake that looks as if it could be a fjord. The road runs alongside the lake for 11 miles, providing many excellent views.

Lake Crescent Lodge, HC 62, Box 11, Port Angeles, WA 98362 (tel. 206/928-3211), is a historic hotel on the edge of the lake. Accommodations are available in the lodge, cottages, and modern motel rooms. Rates range from $55 to $105 single or double.

About 1½ miles past the western end of Lake Crescent is the turnoff for **Sol Duc Hot Springs Resort,** P.O. Box 2169, Port Angeles, WA 98362 (tel. 206/327-3583). The popular mineral hot springs are open from mid-May to mid-October. An all-day pass to the hot pools costs $4.35 for adults and $3.35 for senior citizens.

There are also modern cabins available if you want to stay overnight. Rates are $70 to $75 single or double. There is also a campground here.

NEAH BAY

Turn off U.S. 101 at the crossroads of Sappho and you'll be on your way to the northwesternmost point in the continental United States, Neah Bay, in the middle of the **Makah Indian Reservation.** The **Makah Museum and Cultural Center,** Washington Hwy. 112 (tel. 206/645-2711), will fill you in on the fascinating tribal history of this area. Most of the artifacts on display here are from a Native American village that was completely covered by mud slides 500 years ago. Admission is $4 for adults, $3 for children, students, and senior citizens. In summer the museum is open daily from 10am to 5pm; the rest of the year it is only open Wednesday through Sunday. Here at Neah Bay you finally get your first glimpse of the **Pacific Ocean.** As you walk along the beaches here, watch for whales, seals, and sea lions.

THE LA PUSH BEACHES

My favorite Olympic Peninsula **beaches** are those near the tiny town of La Push. To reach La Push from Neah Bay, it is necessary to backtrack to Sappho and then continue west on U.S. 101 until you see the signs for the La Push turnoff. **Second Beach** and **Third Beach** are both more than a mile from the road on well-maintained trails. The reward for those who make the walk is a secluded beach piled high with driftwood logs and surrounded by cliffs and deep forest. Offshore, there are rocky islands that are home to birds, seals, and sea lions.

THE HOH RIVER VALLEY & KALALOCH

South of Forks, which is the turnoff for La Push, you finally reach the Hoh River Valley and its **rain forest.** It is 12 miles from the highway to the visitors information center, campgrounds, and rain forest nature trails. There are several trails of differing lengths and difficulty originating at the visitors center, but no matter which one you choose, you will be surrounded by a verdure the likes of which you have probably never seen. Mosses 3 feet long hang from the branches of the trees. Groves of new trees sprout from decaying tree stumps. Ferns cover the forest floor.

Kalaloch, 34 miles south of Forks, is known for its beaches and tide pools. The **Kalaloch Lodge,** H.C. 80 (P.O. Box 1100), Forks, WA 98331 (tel. 206/962-2271), is the place to stay in this area. Its main lodge and cottages are perched on a bluff above water. Rates are $79 to $110 for a double.

THE QUINAULT VALLEY

The Quinault Valley, located 35 miles south of Kalaloch, is the Olympic Peninsula's other major rain forest. Lake Quinault fills the valley east of the highway. Along the North Shore Drive, there are two trails into the rain forest: One is a half mile long and the other four miles long.

Also on the shores of the lake is **Lake Quinault Lodge,** South Shore Rd. (P.O. Box 7), Quinnault, WA 98575 (tel. 206/288-2571). The lodge was built in the mid-1920s and still has many of its original furnishings. Although not all the rooms in the original building have private baths, they are much more appealing than those in the newer wing of the lodge. For those who prefer warmer water than the lake offers, there is a heated indoor pool, whirlpool baths, and a sauna. Rates are $78 to $99 for a double.

You can once again return to the ocean beaches by turning west in the town of **Humptulips. Moclips** and **Pacific Beach,** on the coast, are popular beach resort towns with all the amenities you'd expect to find.

HOQUIAM & RETURN

Continuing on to Ocean City and heading east on Washington Hwy. 109, you come to the town of Hoquiam. If you didn't stay at the Manresa Castle in Port Townsend, you can still visit the Olympic Peninsula's other castle—**Hoquiam Castle,** 515 Chenault Ave. (tel. 206/533-2005). The 20-room mansion was built in 1897 for a local timber baron. The castle is open for tours mid-June to Labor Day, daily from 11am to 5pm; the rest of the year, on Saturday and Sunday (closed in December). Tickets for the tour are $3 for adults, $2 for senior citizens, and $1 for children.

In Hoquiam you leave U.S. 101 and drive east on U.S. 12 to **Olympia,** Washington's state capital. From Olympia, I-5 will return you to Seattle in about an hour.

4. THE SAN JUAN ISLANDS

Seattleites love the water, and when they want to enjoy some serious sailing, sea kayaking, or simply the unequaled water-and-island views, they head for the San Juan Islands. Dotting the blue waters of Puget Sound, the 172 San Juans were named by early Spanish explorers who came as far north as Puget Sound, claimed the land for Spain, and then never came back. Only four islands—**Orcas, San Juan, Shaw,** and **Lopez**—have much in the way of development, but that's exactly what makes a trip to the San Juans so enjoyable. People come here to get away from crowds and traffic. For those seeking real solitude, nothing will do but to sail through the islands for a few days, anchoring in tiny coves and exploring deserted islands.

GETTING THERE

Although the islands are only about 50 miles north of Seattle, it takes several hours to get to any of them. There are no bridges to the islands, so you'll have to take one of those huge **Washington State Ferries** (tel. 206/464-6400, or toll free 800/84-FERRY). If you have the time and are planning to spend a few days in the islands, I'd recommend taking **Washington Hwy. 20** north from Seattle. This narrow road winds across scenic Whidbey Island before reaching Anacortes, where the ferries dock. If you're in a hurry, you can take **I-5** to the northern end of Washington Hwy. 20 and reach Anacortes that way. Another alternative is to fly from Seattle. **Lake Union Air,** 950 Westlake Ave. North (tel. 206/284-0300, or toll free 800/826-1890), provides regular floatplane service to five towns in the San Juans. Flights leave from the west side of Lake Union, north of downtown Seattle.

If you only have a day to spare and would like to spend it seeing as much of the San Juans as possible, contact **Gray Line Tours,** 500 Wall St., Suite 413, Seattle (tel. 206/371-5222, or toll free 800/443-4552). In summer they offer an 8-hour tour that includes four hours of cruising among the islands and 4 hours at the port town of Friday Harbor. The cruise leaves from **Resort Semiahmoo** in Blaine, Washington. The price for the daylong outing is $39 for adults and $18 for children.

If you have come north on Washington Hwy. 20, be sure to stop at **Deception Pass State Park,** which is just over the bridge from Whidbey Island and before the turnoff for Anacortes. The park isn't very far from Anacortes, so you should make a point of visiting even if you took I-5. Turbulent currents rush through the pass as tidal waters are squeezed into a narrow channel by the point and an island. The sight is as awe-inspiring as a waterfall when the water surges over the rocks below you.

If it's summer, expect a wait for the ferry from Anacortes. The San Juans are very popular. There are only about 10,000 permanent residents on the islands, but more than 200,000 people visit each summer. Weekends are the busiest.

SEEING THE ISLANDS
SAN JUAN ISLAND

One of the main destinations in the San Juans is **Friday Harbor** on San Juan Island. This is the busiest spot in the islands, but it's still a beautiful little town. The **Visitor Information Center,** 125 Spring St. (tel. 206/378-5240), can give you information on lodgings on the island, as well as information on what to see and do here.

Tops on the list is a visit to the **Whale Museum,** 62 First St. (tel. 206/378-4710), which is the only museum in the United States dedicated entirely to whales. Whale-watching is popular throughout the San Juans, and the whale most often sighted is the much-maligned killer whale, correctly known as the orca. While riding the ferries through the islands, keep your eyes peeled for their characteristic knife-edged dorsal fins. If you're lucky, you might even see one breach (jump completely out of the water). **Lime Kiln State Park,** 10 miles west of Friday Harbor, is a good spot for whale-watching. It's open June to October, daily from 10am to 5pm; October to June, Wednesday through Monday from 10am to 5pm. Admission is $4 for adults, $2 for ages 12 to 18, and $1 for children under 12 years old.

San Juan Island was nearly the site of a battle between the British and the Americans in 1859. The two countries had only recently agreed upon the border between the United States and Canada, and it seems someone forgot to tell a British pig on San Juan Island. The pig unknowingly crossed the border, illegally, to have dinner in an American garden. The owner of the garden didn't take too kindly to this and shot the pig. The Brits, rather than welcoming this succulent addition to their evening's repast, threatened redress. In less time than it takes to smoke a ham, both sides were calling in reinforcements. Luckily, this pigheadedness was defused, and armed conflict was avoided. **San Juan Island National Historic Park** (tel. 206/378-2240) commemorates the "Pig War" with two parks on different sides of the island—one called **American Camp** and the other called **English Camp.** You can visit buildings that are much as they might have looked in 1859.

The old Victorian **Roche Harbor Resort,** P.O. Box 4001, Roche Harbor, WA 98250 (tel. 206/378-2155), is the largest resort on the island. It is surrounded by forests and water that provide hiking and boating opportunities. There are also tennis, golf, bicycling, and fishing. Rates are $57 to $115 single or double.

ORCAS ISLAND

Orcas Island is a favorite of nature lovers. **Moran State Park,** which covers 5,000 acres of the island, is the largest park in the San Juans. If the weather is clear, you'll find great views from the summit of **Mount Constitution,** which rises 2,409 feet above Puget Sound. There are also five lakes in the park and 30 miles of hiking trails. There are fishing, hiking, boating, biking, and camping in the park. For campground reservations or more information, contact **Moran State Park,** Star Route, Box 22, Eastsound, WA 98245 (tel. 206/376-2326).

The **Rosario Resort and Spa,** 1 Rosario Way, Eastsound, WA 98245-2222 (tel. 206/376-2222, or toll free 800/562-8820 in Washington), is the island's premier hotel. The hotel's central building is the Moran Mansion, which was built in 1905 and is a National Historic Building. The spa features three heated pools, whirlpools, a health club, a beach, boat rentals, tennis courts, and nature trails. Rates are $85 to $190 single or double.

BED-AND-BREAKFAST INNS

On San Juan, Orcas, and Lopez islands, there are a number of bed-and-breakfast inns that are very popular in the summer. You can find out about these, and inns all over the state, by writing the **Pacific Bed & Breakfast Agency,** 701 NW 60th St., Seattle, WA 98107 (tel. 206/784-0539).

CHAPTER 12

INTRODUCING PORTLAND

1. CULTURE, HISTORY & BACKGROUND
- **WHAT'S SPECIAL ABOUT PORTLAND**
- **DATELINE**

2. RECOMMENDED BOOKS & FILMS

Portland likes to think of itself as a big little city. It long ago gave up trying to compete with Seattle for the title of the Northwest's Pacific Rim trade capital. By giving up this goal, it has been able to concentrate on being a very livable city. Compared to the rapid growth in Seattle, Portland's progress is moving at a snail's pace. However, this hasn't prevented the city from opening new cultural venues, a new convention center, and some very appealing hotels and restaurants that are as good as any you'll find elsewhere.

1. CULTURE, HISTORY & BACKGROUND

GEOGRAPHY/PEOPLE

Located at the junction of the Columbia and Willamette rivers in northwestern Oregon, Portland is a compact city of about 1.5 million people. The West Hills act as backdrop for the handful of skyscrapers in the downtown area, making the cityscape as you enter from the east one of the most impressive in the country. The view from the West Hills, looking out over the city to Mount Hood, is even more inspiring.

The individualist spirit that prompted pioneers to follow the Oregon Trail is still very much alive. Oregonians are proud of their heritage and value their active lifestyle, and the people of Portland are at the forefront of environmental policy. City planning here generally focuses on the quality of life rather than on economic progress at any cost, as is so often the case in other cities. Of course, it does rain quite a bit, but residents will tell you that's what keeps the land

IMPRESSIONS

Oregon is seldom heard of. Its people believe in the Bible, and hold that all radicals should be lynched. It has no poets and no statesmen.
—H. L. MENCKEN, *AMERICANA*, 1925

WHAT'S SPECIAL ABOUT PORTLAND

Beaches
- ☐ Cannon Beach has Haystack Rock, just offshore.
- ☐ Oswald West State Park—the beach is a mile walk through dense forests.

Buildings
- ☐ The Portland Building, by Michael Graves, is considered the first postmodern building in the United States.
- ☐ The Oregon Convention Center, with its twin glass spires, has become Portland's most readily identifiable landmark.

Museums
- ☐ The American Advertising Museum is the only museum of its kind in the country.

Parks/Gardens
- ☐ The gardens of the Japanese Garden Society of Oregon, in Washington Park, are considered the equivalent of any in Japan.

Events/Festivals
- ☐ The Portland Rose Festival, which had its start more than 100 years ago, is a three-week-long extravaganza celebrating the start of the rose-blossoming season.

Natural Spectacles
- ☐ The Columbia Gorge boasts dozens of waterfalls, high cliffs, and scenic highways.
- ☐ Mount Hood, an extinct volcano, has year-round skiing and hiking.

Shopping
- ☐ At Portland's Saturday Market, which is held on Sundays also, local artisans sell their creations.

Zoos
- ☐ Metro Washington Park Zoo, known for its elephant-breeding program, recently opened an African rain forest exhibit.

Great Neighborhoods
- ☐ Old Town (also known as the Skidmore District) has outstanding examples of cast-iron-fronted buildings from 100 years ago. There are also dozens of boutiques and galleries, as well as the Portland Saturday Market.
- ☐ Nob Hill is Portland's trendiest neighborhood. Old Victorian homes have been converted into boutiques and restaurants.

Offbeat Oddities
- ☐ The Church of Elvis offers 24-hour psychic readings.

Regional Food & Drink
- ☐ Innovative chefs are cooking up a quiet storm at Portland's restaurants—and at very reasonable prices.
- ☐ Portland is the microbrewery capital of America. These small breweries produce delicious and unusual ales.
- ☐ The Oregon wine industry is maturing well and local wines are winning awards in international competitions.

green. Portlanders are happy to put up with the drizzly months in exchange for the glorious summers. The same aspects that make Portland one of the most livable cities in the world also make it one of the most visitable.

HISTORY/POLITICS

THE EARLY DAYS

Portland was once a very expensive piece of property. In 1844 it sold for $50, double the original price of Manhattan Island. Before that, it had been purchased for just 25¢, although the original purchaser had to borrow the quarter. Remember that there was nothing here at the time. This was a wilderness, and anyone who thought it would ever be anything more was either foolish or extremely farsighted.

Asa Lovejoy and William Overton, the two men who staked the original claim to Portland, were the latter: farsighted. From this spot on the Willamette River they could see snow capped Mount Hood 50 miles away; they liked the view and figured other people might also. These two characters were as disparate as a pair of founding fathers could be. Overton was a penniless drifter. No one is sure where he came from, or where he went when he left less than a year later. Lovejoy had attended Harvard University and graduated from Amherst. He was one of the earliest settlers to venture by wagon train to the Oregon country.

These two men were traveling by canoe from Fort Vancouver, the Hudson's Bay Company fur-trading center on the Columbia River, to the town of Oregon City on the Willamette River. Midway through their journey they stopped to rest at a clearing on the west bank of the Willamette. Overton suggested that they stake a claim to the spot. It was commonly believed that Oregon would soon become a U.S. territory and that the federal government would pass out free 640-acre land claims. Overton wanted to be sure that he got his due. Unfortunately, he didn't have the 25¢ required to file a claim. In exchange for half the claim, Lovejoy loaned him the money. Not a bad return on a 25¢ investment!

DATELINE

- **1804** The Lewis and Clark expedition passes down the Columbia River on its journey to the Pacific Ocean.
- **1834** Methodist missionaries settle at the confluence of the Columbia and Willamette rivers.
- **1843** Asa Lovejoy and William Overton file a claim for 640 acres on the site of present-day Portland. Filing fee: 25¢.
- **1844** Francis Pettygrove enters into partnership with Lovejoy, buying Overton's share for $50.
- **1845** The name Portland wins over Boston in a coin toss between Pettygrove and Lovejoy.
- **1851** Portland is incorporated.
- **1872** Fire levels most of city.
- **1873** A second fire devastates Portland.
- **1888** The first Portland rose show.
- **1905** Centenary celebration of the Lewis and Clark expedition.
- **1907** The annual rose show becomes *(continues)*

DATELINE

the Portland Rose Festival.

• **1927** Downtown wharves are demolished and a seawall is built.

• **1974** Expressway removed from west bank of Willamette River to create Waterfront Park.

• **1980** The design for Pioneer Courthouse Square, which has become the city's heart and focal point of downtown activities, was chosen.

• **1988** Portland is named "Most Liveable U.S. City" by the U.S. Conference of Mayors.

Wanderlust struck Overton before he could do anything with his claim, and he bartered his half to one Francis Pettygrove for $50 worth of supplies and headed off for parts unknown. Overton must have thought he had turned a pretty deal—from a borrowed quarter to $50 in under a year is a respectable return. Pettygrove, a steadfast Yankee like Lovejoy, was a merchant with that species' ideas on how to make a fortune. Alas, poor Overton, all he got in the end was a single street named after him.

Pettygrove lost no time in setting up a store on the waterfront, and now with a single building on the site, it was time to name the town. Pettygrove was from Maine and wanted to name the new town for his beloved Portland; Lovejoy was from Boston and wanted that name for their new settlement. A coin was flipped, Pettygrove called it, and a new Portland was born.

Portland was a relative latecomer to the region. Oregon City, Fort Vancouver, Milwaukie, and St. Helens were all busily doing business in the area when Portland was still just a glimmer in the eyes of Lovejoy and Overton. But in 1846 things changed quickly. Another New Englander, Capt. John Couch, sailed up the Willamette River, dropped anchor in Portland, and decided to make this the headquarters for his shipping company.

Another enterprising gentleman, this one a Southerner named Daniel Lownsdale, opened a tannery outside town and helped build a road through the West Hills to the wheat farms of the Tualatin Valley. With a road from the farm country and a small port to ship the wheat to market, Portland rapidly became the most important town in the region.

With the 1848 discovery of gold in California (by a former Oregonian), and the subsequent demand for such Oregon products as grain and timber to be shipped south, Portland became a booming little town of 800.

By the late 1880s Portland was connected to the rest of the country by several railroad lines, and by 1900 the population had grown to 90,000. In 1905 the city hosted the Lewis & Clark Exposition, that year's World's Fair, which celebrated the centennial of the explorers' journey to the Northwest. The fairgrounds, landscaped by John Olmsted, successor to Central Park (New York City) designer Frederick Law Olmsted, were a great hit. The city of Portland also proved popular with visitors; by 1910 its population had exploded to 250,000.

By this time, however, there were even more roses than there were people. Since 1888 Portland had been holding an annual rose show, but in 1907 it had blossomed into a full-fledged Rose Festival. Today the annual festival, held each June, is still Portland's favorite celebration. More than 400 varieties bloom in the International Rose Test Garden in Washington Park, lending Portland the sobriquet City of Roses.

PORTLAND TODAY

The 20th century has been a roller-coaster ride of boom and bust for Portland. The phenomenal growth of the city's first 50 years has slowed. Timber and agriculture have been the mainstays of the Oregon economy, but the lumber-industry recession of recent years has nearly crippled the Oregon economy. Luckily, Portland has developed a high-tech industrial base that has allowed it to weather the storm and continue to prosper.

However, Portlanders tend to have a different idea of prosperity than the residents of most other cities. Since its beginnings, nature and the city's relationship to it have been an integral part of life here. As far back as 100 years ago the Willamette River was a favored recreation site, with canoe clubs racing on its clean waters. But the industries of the 20th century brought the pollution that killed the river. Downtown Portland lost its preeminence as a shipping port, and eventually the wharves were torn down and replaced by a freeway. This was akin to cutting out Portland's very heart and soul. But the freeway did not last long.

With the environmental awareness of the 1960s and 1970s, Portland's basic character and love of nature began to resurface. A massive cleanup of the Willamette River was undertaken—and was eventually so successful that today salmon once again can be seen from downtown Portland. The freeway was torn up and replaced with the Tom McCall Waterfront Park, 2 miles of lawns, trees, fountains, and promenades. But this is only one in a grand network of parks.

The city is ringed with them, including Forest Park, the largest wooded city park in the United States, and Washington Park, which is home to the Rose Test Garden, Japanese Garden, Washington Park Zoo, and Hoyt Arboretum. Mount Hood, only 90 minutes from downtown, and the hundreds of thousands of acres of national forest surrounding it are well utilized by the outdoors-conscious citizens of this green city.

Being a "big little city," Portland isn't interested in growth quite

---

IMPRESSIONS

Oregon . . . a pleasant, homogeneous, self-contained state, filled with pleasant, homogeneous, self-contained people, overwhelmingly white, Protestant, and middle class. Even the working class was middle class.
—ARTHUR M. SCHLESINGER JR., *ROBERT KENNEDY AND HIS TIMES,* 1978

so much as Seattle, its main competitor in the Northwest. Economic progress is less important to the city than the quality of life. Portland is a clean city, a polite city. Littering is almost unheard of, and in case a bit of trash does make it to the streets and sidewalks, there's a special cleaning crew that works overtime to keep the downtown area looking beautiful. The city's Percent for Art program also ensures a beautiful downtown. Every new public building must spend slightly more than 1% of building costs on public art.

Portland could be considered a bit eccentric. Many Portlanders claim that the hippies of the 1960s are alive and well and selling their crafts at the Saturday Market. You won't find any Styrofoam containers at fast-food restaurants in Portland; they've been banned because of the damage they cause to the ozone layer. Likewise, damaging aerosols have also been banned. And although I haven't been able to verify this statistic, a reliable local source tells me that Portland has the county's highest per capita consumption of Grape Nuts.

2. RECOMMENDED BOOKS & FILMS

BOOKS

The Journals of Lewis and Clark (Penguin, Mentor, and American Heritage) will give you an idea of what this area was like almost two centuries ago. Although this fascinating journal does not focus directly on the Portland area, it was this report of Lewis and Clark's famous 1803–06 expedition that first introduced the rest of the world to the Pacific Northwest. *The Oregon Trail* (1849), by Francis Parkman, Jr. (New York: Penguin, 1988), chronicles the grueling travels of the first pioneers to settle in the Oregon country. It was the rich soils of the Willamette and Tualatin river valleys just outside Portland that lured families to undertake such an arduous trip. *Caesars of the Wilderness,* by Peter C. Newman (Penguin), focuses on the role of Britain's Hudson's Bay Company in opening up this part of the West.

FILMS

Come See the Paradise (1990) has a few shots of a vintage Portland in its story of a Caucasian man's love for his Japanese wife during World War II. *Drugstore Cowboy* (1989) relates the exploits of a band of drug-crazed criminals who work around Portland. The film stars Matt Dillon and received much acclaim when it was released.

CHAPTER 13

PLANNING A TRIP TO PORTLAND

1. INFORMATION
- WHAT THINGS COST IN PORTLAND
2. WHEN TO GO
- PORTLAND CALENDAR OF EVENTS
3. WHAT TO PACK
4. TIPS FOR THE DISABLED, SENIORS, SINGLES, FAMILIES & STUDENTS
5. GETTING THERE
- FROMMER'S SMART TRAVELER: AIRFARES

Making a few plans before you leave can make all the difference between enjoying your trip and wishing you had stayed home. For many people, in fact, planning a trip is half the fun of going. You can write to the addresses below for interesting packets of information that are created to get you excited about your upcoming trip. One of your first considerations should be when you want to visit. Summer is the peak season in the Northwest. That's when the sun shines and outdoor festivals and events take place. During the summer, hotel and car reservations are almost essential; the rest of the year, they are highly advisable. You usually get better rates by reserving at least one or two weeks in advance.

1. INFORMATION

For information on Portland and the rest of Oregon, contact the **Portland/Oregon Visitor Association,** Three World Trade Center, 26 SW Salmon St., Portland, OR 97204-3299 (tel. 503/222-2223). They also have an information booth by the baggage-claim area at Portland Airport. Another organization with brochures helpful in planning a Portland visit is the **Association for Portland Progress,** Suite 1015, Cascade Building, 520 SW Sixth Ave., Portland, OR 97204 (tel. 503/224-8684). This is the same group that provides the Portland Guide service, those invaluable souls who walk the streets of Portland answering any and all questions about the city. Also helpful is the **Portland Metropolitan Chamber of Commerce,** 221 NW Second Ave., Portland, OR 97209 (tel. 503/228-9411).

WHAT THINGS COST IN PORTLAND	U.S. $

Taxi from the airport to the city center	22.00
Bus or tram ride between downtown points	Free
Local telephone call	.25

	U.S. $
Double at Heathman Hotel (deluxe)	150.00
Double at the Riverside Inn (moderate)	85.00
Double at Imperial Hotel (budget)	50.00
Lunch for one at B. Moloch (moderate)	10.00
Lunch for one at Macheezmo Mouse (budget)	5.00
Dinner for one, without wine, at L'Auberge (deluxe)	45.00
Dinner for one, without wine, at Eddie Lee's (moderate)	21.00
Dinner for one, without wine, at Mayas (budget)	6.00
Pint of beer	2.75
Coca-Cola	.75
Cup of coffee	.90
Roll of ASA 100 Kodacolor film, 36 exposures	5.50
Admission to the Oregon Art Institute	3.50
Movie ticket	6.50
Theater ticket to the Arlene Schnitzer Concert Hall	20.00

2. WHEN TO GO

CLIMATE

This is the section you've all been looking for. You've all heard about the horrible weather in the Northwest. It rains all year, right? Wrong! The Portland area has some of the most beautiful summer weather in the country—warm, sunny days with clear blue skies, cool nights that are perfect for sleeping. During the months of July, August, and September, it almost never rains. And the rest of the year? Well, yes, it rains in those months and it rains regularly. However, the rain is generally a fine mist and not the torrential downpour most people associate with the word rain. In fact, it often rains less in Portland than it does in New York, Boston, Washington, D.C., and Atlanta. There, now I've let the secret out. Let the stampede begin! Winters here aren't too bad, either. They're warmer than in the Northeast, but there is still snow in the nearby mountains. In fact, there's so much snow on Mount Hood, only 90 minutes from downtown Portland, that you can ski right through the summer.

IMPRESSIONS

The green damp England of Oregon.
—ALISTAIR COOKE, *ALISTAIR COOKE'S AMERICA*, 1973

Of course you're skeptical about the amazing information I just presented, but here are the statistics.

Average Monthly Temperatures & Rainfall

	Jan	Feb	Mar	Apr	May	June	July	Aug	Sept	Oct	Nov	Dec
Temp. (°F)	40	43	46	50	57	63	68	67	63	54	46	41
Temp. (°C)	4	6	8	10	14	17	20	20	17	12	8	5
Days of Rain	18	16	17	14	12	10	4	5	8	13	18	19

A CITY OF FESTIVALS

There is nothing Portland enjoys more than a big get-together. Because of the winter weather conditions, these festivals, free concerts, and fairs tend to take place in the summer. Not a week goes by then without some sort of event. For a complete list of special events in and around Portland, send a self-addressed envelope with 50¢ postage to **Portland/Oregon Visitors Association,** Three World Trade Center, 26 SW Salmon St., Portland, OR 97204. To find out what's going on during your visit, pick up a copy of *Willamette Week* or the Sunday *Oregonian.* Some of the larger and more popular special and free events are listed there.

While you're in town, keep your ears peeled and you might find out about other free concerts, such as the Music on the Roof Friday-lunchtime concerts at Yamhill Market or the Jazz on the Water Friday-evening concerts on the patio at the Harborside Restaurant in RiverPlace.

The **Portland Bureau of Parks and Recreation** also sponsors concerts in more than half a dozen parks throughout the city every summer. Write to them at 1120 SW Fifth Ave., Portland, OR 97204, for a free schedule of concerts.

Portland is especialy proud of its Tom McCall Waterfront Park, and rightfully so. Not too many years ago this 2-mile-long park with its fountains and sweeping lawns was a busy freeway. You'll find that a lot of festivals take place here throughout the year. If you happen to be in town and see tents and crowds in the park, you can be sure it's one of Portland's favorite festivals in swing.

PORTLAND CALENDAR OF EVENTS

FEBRUARY

☐ **Portland International Film Festival** Various theaters around the city.

MARCH

☐ **Winter Games** Timberline Ski Area, Mount Hood Meadows, Mulorpor SkiBowl. Alpine and Nordic ski competitions.

APRIL

☐ **Hood River Blossom Festival.** Hood River. Celebration of the blossoming of the orchards outside the town of Hood River.

MAY

☐ **Mother's Day Rhododendron Show.** Crystal Springs Rhododendron Gardens. Mother's Day.

JUNE

☐ **Fort Vancouver Festival Days.** Fort Vancouver, across the Columbia River.

☐ **Rhythm and Zoo.** Metro Washington Park Zoo. Rhythm and blues concerts are held on Thursday nights from June to August.

☐ **Your Zoo and All That Jazz.** Metro Washington Park Zoo. Jazz concerts are held on Wednesday nights from June to August.

✪ *PORTLAND ROSE FESTIVAL   From its beginnings back in 1888, when the first rose show was held, the Rose Festival has blossomed into Portland's biggest celebration. The festivities now span 3½ weeks and include a rose show, parade, rose queen contest, music festival, airshow, car races, foot race, boat races, even a snow-skiing competition up on Mount Hood at Timberline Lodge. Most of the events take place in the first 2 weeks of June, and hotel rooms can be hard to come by. Plan ahead.*

Where: All over the city. When: First 3 weeks of June. How: Contact the Portland Rose Festival Association, 220 NW Second Ave., Portland, OR 97209 (tel. 503/227-2681), for information on tickets to specific events.

☐ **Peanut Butter and Jam Noon Concerts.** Pioneer Courthouse Square. This is the site of the Peanut Butter & Jam Sessions, free lunchtime jazz concerts (tel. 223-1613). They're held every Tuesday and Thursday, mid-June to mid-August.

JULY

☐ **Multnomah County Fair.** Portland Exposition Center.

☐ **Oregon Brewers Festival.** Waterfront Park. America's largest beer party features lots of local microbrews and music.

☐ **Fourth of July Fireworks.** Vancouver, Washington. "What about the Fourth of July?" you ask. Doesn't anything special happen in Portland then? Well, not exactly. Portland just can't compete with the fireworks spectacle that Vancouver, Washington, puts on. It's the biggest display west of the Mississippi. Vancouver is just across the river, and you can see the fireworks from plenty of spots in Portland. For a closeup view, head up to Jantzen Beach. For an elevated perspective, climb up in the West Hills.

☐ **Rose City Blues Festival.** Waterfront Park. Early July.

✪ NEIGHBORFAIR *Colorful tents and pavilions spring up in Waterfront Park, and the sounds of folk music mix with the mouthwatering aromas of ethnic foods. Art, folk dancing, and lots of folks in colorful costumes make this great fun for the whole family.*

> ***Where:*** *Waterfront Park.* ***When:*** *Mid-July.* ***How:*** *Phone 503/226-5055 for details.*

☐ **Portland Scottish Highland Games.** Mount Hood Community College, Gresham. Late July.
☐ **Cathedral Park Jazz Festival.** Under the St. John's Bridge in Cathedral Park. Free performances by nationally known jazz artists. End of July.

AUGUST

☐ **The Bite.** Portland's finest restaurants serve up sample portions of their specialties at this food and music festival. A true gustatory extravaganza.
☐ **Mount Hood Festival of Jazz.** Mount Hood Community College, Gresham (less than 30 minutes from Portland). For the serious jazz fan, this is the festival of the summer. It features the greatest names in jazz.
☐ **Waterfront Classics.** Classical music under the stars at Waterfront Park. This program continues into September.
☐ **Artquake.** Radiating out from Pioneer Courthouse Square along Broadway. Artquake is Portland's grandest festival of the arts. Visual arts, all types of music, theater, dance, festival foods, and a crafts market are all part of this celebration. Late August and early September.

OCTOBER

☐ **Hood River Harvest Festival.** Hood River. Celebration of the harvest season with crafts and food booths, pie-eating contests, and lots of entertainment.

NOVEMBER

☐ **Harvest Festival.** Oregon Convention Center. Lots of food, handmade gifts, and entertainment.

DECEMBER

☐ **Festival of Trees.** Memorial Coliseum. Extravagantly decorated Christmas trees are displayed among gingerbread houses and trains.

3. WHAT TO PACK

A raincoat, an umbrella, and a sweater or jacket are all absolutely essential any time of year. Other than that, you might want to bring skis (snow or water), hiking boots, boat shoes, running shoes, shorts, bicycling shorts, a bathing suit, and just about any other outdoor clothing or equipment you have on hand. The outdoors is a way of life in this part of the country.

4. TIPS FOR THE DISABLED, SENIORS, SINGLES, FAMILIES & STUDENTS

FOR THE DISABLED

Many of the hotels listed in this book feature special rooms for the disabled. I have noted this in all cases, but if you don't see mention in a listing, be sure to ask when making a reservation.

All MAX light-rail (trolley) system stations have wheelchair lifts, and there are two wheelchair spaces available on each train. Be sure to wait on the platform lift. Many of the Tri-Met buses also are equipped with wheelchair lifts and wheelchair spaces. Look for the wheelchair symbol on buses, schedules, and bus stops. There is also a special door-to-door service provided for people who are not able to use the regular Tri-Met service. Phone 503/238-4952 for information.

Broadway Cab (tel. 248-8294) and **Radio Cab** (tel. 227-1212) both have vehicles for transporting the disabled.

The Oregon Guide to Accessibility presents in-depth information on wheelchair access to restaurants, theaters, shopping malls, local and state parks, and travel facilities. To order a free copy, write the **Spinal Cord Association,** 825 NE Multnomah St., Suite 1075, Portland, OR 97232.

FOR SENIORS

Many hotels, museums, theaters, gardens, and tour companies offer special discounts for senior citizens. I have noted this in all listings. Also, while you are in Portland try to pick up a copy of **Senior Tribune,** a monthly newspaper for senior citizens. Call 244-2227 to find out where you can pick up a copy.

FOR SINGLE TRAVELERS

Portland has a lively singles nightlife, and the **Shanghai Lounge,** 0309 SW Montgomery St. (tel. 220-1865), is one of the liveliest spots. You'll also find popular discos at all the **Red Lion hotels.** If you're looking for someone to talk sports with, head over to **Champions,** the sports bar at the Portland Marriott, 1401 SW Front Ave. (tel. 226-7600).

FOR FAMILIES

At some of the hotels in Portland, kids stay free in their parents' room. Be sure to check the listings or ask when you contact a hotel. As many as three children under age 6 can ride free with an adult on Tri-Met buses and MAX.

FOR STUDENTS

Student discounts are available at many museums, theaters, and concert halls. Be sure to carry an ID and ask about discounts.

5. GETTING THERE

BY PLANE

Portland International Airport (PDX) (tel. 503/249-4984), Oregon's main airport, is located 9 miles northeast of downtown Portland. The airport is small and offers some amenities you wouldn't expect at a facility this size. Tops on this list is the new PDX Conference Center, which offers businesspeople a secluded and quiet working space.

THE MAJOR AIRLINES

More than 30 airlines service Portland Airport from almost 100 cities worldwide. The major airlines include: **Alaska Airlines** (tel. 503/224-2547, or toll free 800/426-0333), **America West** (tel. 503/228-0737, or toll free 800/247-5692), **American Airlines** (tel. toll free 800/433-7300), **Continental** (tel. 503/224-4560, or toll free 800/525-0280), **Delta** (tel. 503/225-0830, or toll free 800/221-1212), **Horizon** (tel. toll free 800/547-9308), **Northwest** (tel. toll free 800/225-2525), **TWA** (tel. 503/282-1111, or toll free 800/221-2000), **United Airlines** (tel. 503/226-7211, or toll free 800/241-6522), **USAir** (tel. 503/249-4416, or toll free 800/428-4322).

REGULAR AIRFARES

At the time of this writing, round-trip **Super-APEX (Advance Purchase Excursion)** fares from the East Coast were about $360, though these were special summer fares. Shortly before the summer rates went into effect, fares had been running about $500 from the East Coast.

The round-trip coach fare was $1,040, with **business class** about the same. The round-trip **first-class** fare was $1,364.

OTHER GOOD-VALUE CHOICES

Check the Sunday travel section of your nearest major-city newspaper for ads from **ticket brokers** (also called **bucket shops**). These ads are usually small boxes with a list of destinations and prices. You'll usually find that these brokers are selling airline tickets at a discount. However, when an airline runs a special deal, you won't always do better at the bucket shops.

BY TRAIN

Amtrak trains arrive at and depart from the historic Union Station, 800 NW Sixth Ave. (tel. 503/273-4865, or 503/273-4866 for arrival times only). Trains depart for Seattle at 8am, 2:10pm, and 2:40pm. The trip takes about 4 hours and costs $28 one way. A train departs for San Francisco at 3:10pm, arriving at 8:50am the next day. The one-way fare is $128. There is a train for Salt Lake City at 12:10am, arriving at 7:15am the next day. The one-way fare is $127. For Amtrak schedule and fare information reservations, call toll free 800/872-7245.

BY BUS

From the **Greyhound** bus station, 550 NW Sixth Ave. (tel. 503/243-2323), bus service connects Portland with virtually every city in the United States.

BY CAR

Portland is connected to the rest of the country by a number of major interstates and smaller highways. I-5 runs north to Seattle and south as far as San Diego. I-84 runs east as far as Salt Lake City. I-405 circles

---

 FROMMER'S SMART TRAVELER: AIRFARES

1. Shop all the airlines that fly to your destination.
2. Always ask for the lowest-priced fare, not just for a discount.
3. Keep calling the airline—availability of cheap seats changes daily. Airline yield managers would rather sell a seat than have it fly empty. As the departure date nears, additional low-cost seats become available.
4. Watch the newspapers for special offers. You may be able to save several hundred dollars per ticket by changing your vacation plans to fit in with special low-fare offers.

around the west and south of downtown Portland. I-205 bypasses the city to the east. U.S. 26 heads west to the coast.

Here are some driving distances from selected cities (in miles):

Los Angeles	1,015 miles
San Francisco	640 miles
Seattle	175 miles
Spokane	350 miles
Vancouver, B.C.	285 miles

CHAPTER 14

GETTING TO KNOW PORTLAND

1. ORIENTATION
- NEIGHBORHOODS IN BRIEF
2. GETTING AROUND
- FAST FACTS: PORTLAND
3. NETWORKS & RESOURCES

Portland's compactness makes it a wonderfully easy city to explore. Although the airport is in the northeastern part of the city, most of the important sights and hotels are in the southwestern part. The Willamette River forms a natural dividing line between the eastern and western halves of the city, while the Columbia River forms a boundary with the state of Washington on the north. The West Hills, Portland's prime residential district, are a beautiful backdrop for this attractive little city. Covered in evergreens, the hills rise to a height of 1,000 feet at the edge of downtown. Among these hills are found the Washington Park Zoo, the Rose Garden, the Japanese Garden, and several other attractions. When you're ready to leave the city and explore the beautiful Oregon countryside, it's simple to get onto one of the interstate highways and be far from the city within 30 minutes.

1. ORIENTATION

ARRIVING

BY PLANE

Portland International Airport (PDX) (tel. 503/249-4984) is located 9 miles northeast of downtown Portland. The trip into town is entirely on interstates and takes about 20 minutes. The airport is small enough not to be convenient but large enough to offer amenities you wouldn't expect. Tops on this list is the new **PDX Conference Center,** which offers businesspeople a secluded and quiet working space. There are five meeting rooms, a fax machine, computer workstations, secretarial help, and more. This is the first such airport conference center of its kind in the United States. Also at the airport is the **Oregon Market,** a shopping mall featuring Oregon-based retail stores and food and beverage vendors. You can pick up a new pair of Nike's as you run to make your flight or hook into a fresh salmon packed to go.

There's an information booth by the baggage-claim area where you can pick up maps and brochures and find out about transportation into the city.

Many of the hotels in downtown Portland provide courtesy

shuttle service to and from the airport. Be sure to check at your hotel when you make a reservation. This is by far the best way to get in from the airport.

The next best way, if you haven't rented a car at the airport, is to take the **Downtown Shuttle** (tel. 503/246-3301). They'll take you directly to your hotel for $5. They operate every 20 minutes from 5:30am to 12:05am Monday through Friday, departing at 15, 35, and 55 minutes past the hour. They leave every 30 minutes between the same hours on Saturday, Sunday, and holidays, departing at 5 and 35 minutes past the hour.

Tri-Met public buses leave the airport approximately every 15 minutes from 5:30am to 11:50pm for the trip to downtown Portland. The trip takes about 40 minutes and costs 85¢. The bus between downtown and the airport operates between 5am and 12:30am and leaves from Southwest Sixth Avenue and Main Street.

A **taxi** into town will cost you around $20.

BY TRAIN

Amtrak trains arrive at the historic **Union Station,** 800 NW Sixth Ave. (tel. 503/273-4865). For Amtrak schedule and fare information and reservations, call toll free 800/872-7245.

BY BUS

The **Greyhound bus station** is located at 550 NW Sixth Ave. (tel. 503/243-2323).

BY CAR

Portland's major interstates and smaller highways are **I-5** (north to south), **I-84** (east), **I-405** (circles around the west and south of downtown Portland), **I-205** (bypasses the city to the east), and **U.S. 26** (west).

If you have rented a car at the airport and want to get into downtown Portland, follow the signs for downtown. These signs will take you first to I-205, then I-84, which brings you to the Willamette River. Take the Morrison Bridge exit to cross the river.

TOURIST INFORMATION

The **Portland/Oregon Visitor Association Information Center** is at Three World Trade Center, 26 SW Salmon St., Portland, OR 97204-3299 (tel. 503/222-2223). They also have an information booth by the baggage-claim area at Portland Airport. If you happen to see two people walking down a Portland street wearing matching kelly-green hats and jackets, they are probably members of the Portland Guide service. They'll be happy to answer any question you have about the city.

CITY LAYOUT

Portland is located in northwestern Oregon at the confluence of the Columbia and Willamette rivers. Circling the city to the west are the West Hills, which rise to more than 1,000 feet. Some 90 miles east of

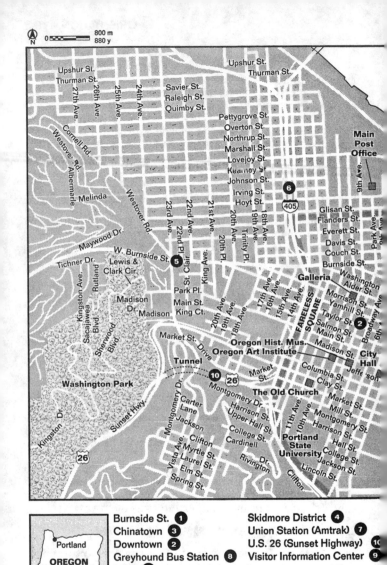

Burnside St. ①		Skidmore District ④
Chinatown ③		Union Station (Amtrak) ⑦
Downtown ②		U.S. 26 (Sunset Highway) ⑩
Greyhound Bus Station ⑧		Visitor Information Center ⑨
I-405 ⑥		
I-84 ⑪		
Nob Hill ⑤		

Portland
OREGON

the West Hills are the Pacific Ocean and the spectacular Oregon coast. To the east are rolling hills that extend to the Cascade Mountains, about 50 miles away. The most prominent peak in this section of the Cascades is Mount Hood (11,235 feet), a dormant volcanic peak that looms over the city on clear days. From some parts of Portland it's also possible to see Mount St. Helens, another volcano, which blew its top in 1980.

With only about 1.5 million people in the entire metropolitan

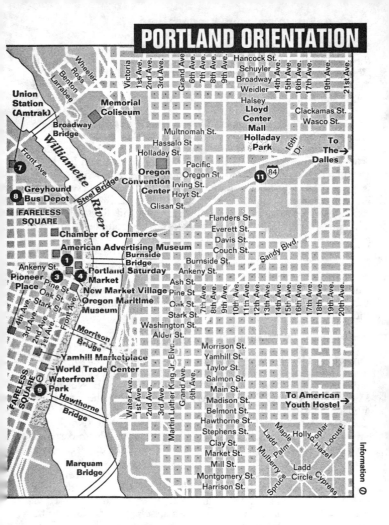

PORTLAND ORIENTATION

Union Station (Amtrak)
Broadway Bridge
Memorial Coliseum
Wheeler
Ross
Benton
Larrabee

Victoria
1st Ave.
2nd Ave.
3rd Ave.
Grand Ave.
6th Ave.
7th Ave.
8th Ave.
9th Ave.
Hancock St.
Schuyler
Broadway
Weidler
Halsey
14th Ave.
15th Ave.
16th Ave.
17th Ave.
19th Ave.
21st Ave.

Lloyd Center Mall
Holladay Park
Clackamas St.
Wasco St.
To The → Dalles

Multnomah St.
Hassalo St
Holladay St.
Pacific
Oregon St.
Irving St.
Hoyt St.
Glisan St.

Oregon Convention Center

7
8 Greyhound Bus Depot
FARELESS SQUARE
Front Ave.
Williamette River
Steel Bridge
Broadway Bridge

16th Dr.
11 84

Flanders St.
Everett St.
Davis St.
Couch St.
Burnside St.
Ankeny St.
Ash St.
Pine St.
Oak St.
Stark St.
Washington St.
Alder St.

Sandy Blvd.

Chamber of Commerce
American Advertising Museum
1 Burnside Bridge
Ankeny St.
3 **4** Portland Saturday Market
Pine St.
New Market Village
Oregon Maritime Museum
Pioneer Place
Oak St.
Stark St.
4th Ave.
3rd Ave.
2nd Ave.
1st Ave.
Front Ave.
Morrison Bridge

7th Ave.
8th Ave.
9th Ave.
10th Ave.
11th Ave.
12th Ave.
13th Ave.
14th Ave.
15th Ave.
16th Ave.
17th Ave.
18th Ave.
19th Ave.
20th Ave.

Yamhill Marketplace
World Trade Center
9 Waterfront Park
Hawthorne Bridge
FARELESS SQUARE

Water Ave.
1st Ave.
2nd Ave.
3rd Ave.
Martin Luther King Jr. Blvd.
Grand Ave.
6th Ave.

Morrison St.
Yamhill St.
Taylor St.
Salmon St.
Main St.
Madison St.
Belmont St.
Hawthorne St.
Stephens St.
Clay St.
Market St.
Mill St.
Montgomery St.
Harrison St.

To American Youth Hostel →

Maple
Holly
Poplar
Ladd
Palm
Hazel
Locust
Mulberry
Ladd Circle
Cypress
Spruce

Marquam Bridge

Information ⊘

area, Portland is a relatively small city. This is especially evident when one begins to explore the compact downtown area. Nearly everything is accessible on foot, and the city authorities are doing everything they can to encourage this.

MAIN ARTERIES & STREETS

I-84 (Banfield Freeway or Expressway) comes into Portland from the east. East of the city is **I-205,** which bypasses downtown

Portland but runs past the airport. **I-5 (East Bank Freeway)** runs through on a north–south axis, passing along the east bank of the Willamette River directly across from downtown. **I-405 (Stadium Freeway and Foothills Freeway)** circles around the west and south sides of downtown. **U.S. 26 (Sunset Freeway)** leaves downtown heading west toward Beaverton and the coast. **Washington Hwy. 217 (Beaverton–Tigard Highway)** runs south from U.S. 26 in Beaverton.

The most important street to remember in Portland is **Burnside Street.** This is the dividing line between north and south Portland. Dividing the city from east to west is the **Willamette River,** which is crossed by eight bridges in the downtown area. All these bridges are named: from north to south they are Fremont, Broadway, Steel, Burnside, Morrison, Hawthorne, Marquam, and Ross Island. In addition to these bridges, there are others farther from the downtown area.

For convenience sake I'll define downtown Portland as the area within the **Fareless Square.** This is the area in which you can ride for free on the city's public buses and the MAX light-rail system. The Fareless Square is that area bounded by I-405 on the west and south, by Hoyt Street on the north, and by the Willamette River on the east.

FINDING AN ADDRESS

Finding an address in Portland can be easy if you keep a number of things in mind. Every address in Portland, and even extending for miles out from the city, includes a map quadrant—NE (Northeast), SW (Southwest), etc. The dividing line between east and west is the Willamette River; between north and south it's Burnside Street. Any downtown address will carry a SW (Southwest) or NW (Northwest) prefix. An exception to this rule is the area known as North Portland. Streets here have a "North" designation. This is the area across the Willamette River from downtown going toward Jantzen Beach.

Avenues run north–south and streets run east–west. Street names continue on both sides of the Willamette River. Consequently, there is a Southwest Yamhill Street and a Southeast Yamhill Street. In northwestern Portland the street names are alphabetical from Burnside to Wilson. Front Avenue is the road nearest the Willamette River on the west side, and Water Avenue is the nearest on the east side. After these, the numbered avenues begin. On the west side you'll also find Broadway and Park Avenue between Sixth Avenue and Ninth Avenue. With each block, the addresses increase by 100, beginning at the Willamette River for avenues and at Burnside Street for streets. Odd numbers are generally on the west and north sides of the streets, and even numbers on the east and south sides.

Here's an example. You want to go to 1327 Southwest Ninth Avenue. Because it's in the 1300 block, you'll find it 13 blocks south of Burnside and, because it's an odd number, on the west side of the street.

Getting to the address is a different story, since streets in downtown Portland are mostly one way. Front Avenue is two way, but then First, Third, Fifth, Broadway, and Eleventh are one way southbound. Alternating streets are one way northbound.

STREET MAPS

Write, call, or stop by the **Portland/Oregon Visitors Association,** Three World Trade Center, 26 SW Salmon St., Portland, OR 97204-3299 (tel. 503/222-2223), for a free map of the city. **Powell's "City of Books,"** 1005 W. Burnside St. (tel. 503/228-4651), has an excellent free map of downtown that also includes a walking-tour route and information on many of the sights you'll pass along the way. Members of the **American Automobile Association** can get a free map of the city at the AAA office at 600 SW Market St. (tel. 503/222-6900).

NEIGHBORHOODS IN BRIEF

Downtown This term usually refers to the business and shopping district south of Burnside and north of Jackson Street between the Willamette River and 13th Avenue. You'll find the major department stores, dozens of restaurants, most of the city's performing arts venues, and almost all of the best hotels in this area.

Chinatown Portland has had a Chinatown almost since the city's earliest days. It is entered through the colorful Chinatown Gate at West Burnside Street and Fourth Avenue.

Skidmore District Also known as Old Town, this is Portland's original commercial core and overlaps with Chinatown for a few streets. The center of this district is the Skidmore Fountain at Southwest Ankeny Street and Southwest Front Avenue. Many of the restored buildings in this neighborhood have become retail stores, which, along with the presence of the Saturday Market here, has made this one of Portland's main shopping districts. There are also half a dozen or so nightclubs. Unfortunately, the city's homeless also call this neighborhood home due to the presence of several missions and welfare hotels.

Nob Hill Centered along Northwest 23rd Avenue at the foot of the West Hills, Nob Hill is an old residential neighborhood that has been taken over by interesting shops and restaurants. This is by far the most stylish neighborhood in town.

Hollywood District One of the latest neighborhoods to attract attention in Portland is the Hollywood District of northeast Portland. This area, which centers around the busy commercial activities of Sandy Boulevard near 42nd Avenue, came into being in the early years of this century. The name derives from a movie theater that is an area landmark. Throughout this neighborhood are craftsman-style houses and vernacular architecture of the period.

Sellwood This is Portland's antiques-store district and is full of restored Victorian houses.

Hawthorne District This enclave of southeast Portland is full of eclectic boutiques, moderately priced restaurants, and hip young college students from nearby Reed College.

2. GETTING AROUND

BY PUBLIC TRANSPORTATION

FREE RIDES

Portland is committed to keeping its downtown uncongested, and to this end it has invested a great deal in its public-transportation system. The single greatest innovation and best reason to ride the Tri-Met public buses and the MAX light-rail system is that they're free within an area known as the **Fareless Square.** That's right, free! There are 300 blocks of downtown included in the Fareless Square, and as long as you stay within the boundaries, you don't have to pay a cent. The Fareless Square covers the area between I-405 on the south and west, Hoyt Street on the north, and the Willamette River on the east.

BY BUS

Tri-Met buses operate daily over an extensive network. You can pick up the **Tri-Met Guide,** which lists all the bus routes with times, or individual route maps and time schedules at the **Tri-Met Customer Assistance Office,** behind and beneath the waterfall fountain at Pioneer Courthouse Square (tel. 233-3511). They're open Monday through Friday from 9am to 5pm.

Outside the Fareless Square, fares on both Tri-Met buses and MAX are 90¢ or $1.20, depending on how far you travel. You can also make free transfers between the bus and the MAX light-rail system. A **day ticket** costing $3 is good for travel to all zones and is valid on both buses and MAX. Day tickets can be purchased from any bus driver.

Portland's other great public transportation innovation is the **Portland Transit Mall.** Nearly all the Tri-Met buses pass through the Transit Mall on Southwest Fifth Avenue and Southwest Sixth Avenue. These two streets have very limited automobile access, being almost entirely devoted to pedestrians and public transit. There are brick sidewalks and streets, flower-filled planters, fountains, and sculptures to enhance the beauty of these streets, as well as umbrella-shaped glass shelters for waiting on rainy days. Each shelter indicates which bus stops there. Just walk along the street until you find the stop you need. Once you're at the right shelter, you'll see a lighted display with the next departure time.

BY MAX

The **Metropolitan Area Express (MAX)** is the new above-ground light-rail system that now connects downtown Portland with the suburb of Gresham, 15 miles to the east. Basically, Portland has reinvented the trolley. You can ride the MAX for free if you stay within the boundaries of the Fareless Square, which includes all the downtown area. However, be sure to buy your ticket before you get on the MAX if you're traveling out of the Fareless Square. Fares are the same as they are on buses. There are ticket-vending machines at all MAX stops that tell you how much to pay for your destination; these machines also give change. The MAX driver cannot sell tickets. There are ticket inspectors who randomly check tickets. If you don't have one, you can be fined $250.

The MAX light-rail system crosses the Transit Mall on Southwest Morrison Street and Southwest Yamhill Street. Transfers to the bus are free.

BY TAXI

Because most everything in Portland is fairly close together, getting around by taxi can be economical. Although there are almost always taxis waiting in line at major hotels, you won't find them cruising the streets—you'll have to phone for one. **Broadway Cab** (tel. 227-1234) and **Radio Cab** (tel. 227-1212) both offer 24-hour radio-dispatched service and accept American Express, MasterCard, and VISA credit cards. Fares are $3.50 for the first mile and $1.50 for each additional mile.

BY CAR
RENTALS

For the best deal on a rental car, I highly recommend making a reservation at least one week before you arrive in Portland. It also pays to call several times over a period of a few weeks just to ask prices; the last time I rented a car, the same company quoted me different prices every time I called to ask about rates. Remember the old Wall Street adage: Buy low! If you didn't have time to plan ahead, ask about special weekend rates or discounts that you might be eligible for. And don't forget to mention that you are a frequent flyer: You might be able to get miles for your car rental. Also, be sure to find out whether your credit card pays the collision-damage waiver, which can add a bundle to the cost of a rental. Currently, daily rates are around $45 and weekly rates are around $140.

You'll find all the major car-rental companies represented in Portland, and there are also many independent and smaller car-rental agencies listed in the Portland Yellow Pages. Inside the main arrivals terminal at Portland International Airport, right behind the baggage-claim area, you'll find the following companies:

Avis (tel. 503/249-4950, or toll free 800/331-1212).
Budget (tel. 503/249-6500, or toll free 800/527-0700), which also has offices downtown at 2033 SW Fourth Ave. (tel. 503/249-6500), on the east side at 2323 NE Columbia Blvd. (tel. 503/249-6500), and in Beaverton at 10835 SW Canyon Rd. (tel. 503/249-6500).
Dollar (tel. 503/249-4792, or toll free 800/800-4000), which also has an office downtown at NW Broadway and NW Davis St. (tel. 503/228-3540).
Hertz (tel. 503/249-8216, or toll free 800/654-3131), which also has an office downtown at 1009 SW Sixth Ave. (tel. 503/249-5727).
National (tel. 503/249-4900, or toll free 800/227-7368).

Outside the airport:

Thrifty, 10800 NE Holman St. (tel. 503/254-6563, or toll free 800/367-2277), which also has an office downtown at 632 SW Pine St. (tel. 503/227-6587).

PARKING

Portland is lucky in having far more downtown parking facilities than most cities of its size. However, as you probably know, this is never enough. Parking downtown can be a problem, especially if you show up after all the working stiffs have gotten to their offices. There are a couple of very important things to remember when parking downtown.

When parking on the street, be sure to notice the meter's time limit. These vary from as little as 15 minutes (these are always right in front of the restaurant or museum where you plan to spend 2 hours) to long-term (read long-walk). Most common are 30- and 90-minute meters. You don't have to feed the meters after 6pm or on Sunday. There is currently a move afoot to shorten meter times and raise rates to help meet the budget needs of the city.

If you're going shopping, look for a red-and-green sign that says "2 hr free park downtown" at pay parking lots. Spend $15 or more at any participating merchant and you get 2 hours of free parking.

If you rent a car from Budget Rent A Car, you can park free at the **Diamond parking lot** at the corner of Southwest 13th Avenue and Southwest Stark Street and save yourself quite a bit of money. Phone 222-6929 for the location of other Diamond parking lots. Rates in public lots range from 75¢ up to about $2 per hour.

DRIVING RULES

You may turn right on a red light after a full stop, and if you are in the far left lane of a one-way street, you may turn left into the adjacent left lane at a red light after a full stop.

BY BICYCLE

Bicycles are a very popular way of getting around Portland. The downtown stoplights are timed at 13 miles per hour, so a bicycle can easily keep up with automobile traffic. For leisurely cycling, try the seawall promenade in Waterfront Park. There's another esplanade path on the east side of the river between the Hawthorne and Burnside bridges. The Terwilliger Path runs for 10 miles from Portland State University to Tryon Creek State Park in the West Hills. You can pick up a copy of a bike map of the city of Portland at any bike shop. At **Agape Cycle & Sport,** 2610 SE Clinton St. (tel. 230-0317), you can rent a bike for $15 to $25 a day.

ON FOOT

City blocks in Portland are about half the size of most city blocks elsewhere, and the entire downtown area covers only about 13 blocks by 26 blocks. These two facts make Portland a very easy place to explore on foot. The city has been very active in encouraging people to get out of their cars and onto the sidewalks downtown. The sidewalks are wide, and there are many small parks with benches for resting, fountains for cooling off, and works of art for soothing the soul.

If you happen to spot a couple of people wearing kelly-green baseball caps and jackets and navy-blue pants, they're probably a pair of Portland Guides. These informative souls are here to answer any questions you might have about Portland—"Where am I?" for instance. Their job is simply to walk the streets and answer questions for the populace.

FAST FACTS PORTLAND

Airport **Portland International Airport (PDX)** is located 9 miles northeast of downtown Portland; for information call 503/249-4984.

American Express **The American Express Travel Service Office** (tel. 226-2961) is located at 1100 SW Sixth Ave.—corner of Sixth and Main. The office is open Monday through Friday from 9am to 5pm. You can cash American Express traveler's checks and exchange foreign currency here.

Area Code The area code for Portland and the entire state of Oregon is **503.**

Babysitters Call **Rent-A-Mom** (tel. 222-5779). However, if you are staying at a major hotel, they almost certainly will offer babysitting services. Check with the concierge first before calling an outside sitter.

Business Hours **Banks** are generally open Monday through Thursday from 9am to 3pm, with later hours (to 6pm) on Friday. **Offices** are generally open Monday through Friday from 8:30 or 9am to 5 or 5:30pm. In general, **stores** in the downtown area are open Monday through Friday from 10am to 6pm. Many stores have later hours one or two times a week—usually on Monday and Friday evenings. **Bars** stay open until 1 or 2:30am.

Car Rentals See "By Car" in Section 2 of this chapter.

Climate See "Climate" in Section 2 of Chapter 13.

Dentist If you need a dentist while you are in Portland, contact the **Multnomah Dental Society** for a referral at 223-4731. Statewide, you can call the **Oregon Dental Society** at 620-3230.

Doctor If you need a doctor while you are in Portland, contact the **Multnomah Medical Society** for a referral at 222-9977. Statewide, you can call the **Oregon Medical Society** at 226-1555.

Driving Rules See "By Car" in Section 2 of this chapter.

Drugstore Convenient to most downtown hotels, Central Discount Drug, 538 SW Fourth Ave. (tel. 226-2222), is open Monday to Friday from 9am to 6pm, on Saturday from 9am to 5pm.

Emergencies For police, fire, or medical emergencies, phone **911.**

Eyeglasses Stocking a wide range of designer eyeglass

frames, **Zell Optical,** 816 SW Morrison St. (tel. 228-0104), has been in business for more than 40 years. They perform optical examinations and will be happy to replace your lost glasses.

Hairdressers/Barbers **Dione's Hair,** 1975 SW First Ave. (tel. 227-5565), is a full-service salon for men, women, and children. They even offer computer video-graphic hair styling. Open daily.

Holidays See "Calendar of Events" in Chapter 13, and "Holidays" in "Fast Facts: For the Foreign Traveler" in Chapter 3.

Hospitals Three area hospitals available to you in case of need: **Good Samaritan,** 1015 NW 22nd Ave. (tel. 229-7711); **St. Vincent Hospital,** 9205 SW Barnes Rd. (tel. 291-2115), off U.S. 26 (Sunset Highway) before Oregon Hwy. 217; and the **Oregon Health Sciences University Hospital,** 3131 SW Sam Jackson Park Rd. (tel. 494-8311), just south of the city center.

Hotlines AIDS, 223-AIDS; **battered women,** 235-5333; **child abuse,** 238-7555; **drunk drivers,** 800/24DRUNK; **rape,** 235-5533; **suicide prevention,** 223-6161.

Information For tourist information, contact **Portland/ Oregon Visitor Information Association** at Three World Trade Center, 26 SW Salmon St. Portland, OR 97204-3299 (tel. 503/222-2223). While you're in Portland, if you spot members of the **Portland Guide service**—dressed in kelly-green hats and jackets—they'll be happy to answer any question you have about the city.

Laundry/Dry Cleaning **Downtown Cleaners** offers dry cleaning at two locations, 609 SW Third Ave. (tel. 227-7881) and 621 SW Washington St. (tel. 226-1255); open Monday through Friday from 7am to 6pm, on Saturday from 10am to 2pm. **Starting Point Laundromat,** 302 NW Sixth Ave. (tel. 222-3316) is open daily from 7am to 8pm.

Library The **Multnomah County Library,** 801 SW 10th Ave. (tel. 248-5123), is Portland's largest library. It's open Monday through Thursday from 9am to 9pm, on Friday and Saturday from 9am to 5:30pm, and on Sunday from 1 to 5pm.

Liquor Laws The legal drinking age in Oregon is 21.

Lost Property If you lose something on a bus or the MAX, call **238-4855** Monday through Friday from 10am to 5pm. If you lose something at the airport, call **234-8422.**

Luggage Storage/Lockers You'll find coin-operated luggage-storage lockers at the **Greyhound bus station,** 550 NW Sixth Ave.

Mail You can receive mail c/o General Delivery at the main post office (see "Post Office," below).

Maps For a free street map of Portland, contact the **Portland/Oregon Visitors Association,** Three World Trade Center, 26 SW Salmon St., Portland OR 97204-3299. **Powell Books** at 1005 W. Burnside St. (tel. 503/228-4651) has an excellent free map of downtown that includes a walking tour and information on the sights you'll pass. Members of **AAA** can get a free map at the AAA office, 600 SW Market St. (tel. 222-6900). See "City Layout" in this chapter.

Newspapers/Magazines Portland's morning daily

newspaper is **The Oregonian.** For arts and entertainment information and listings, pick up a free copy of **Willamette Week.** Another free weekly that has information about Portland is the **Portland Downtowner.** The **Portland Guide** is a weekly tourism guide to Portland.

Photographic Needs **Flashback Foto,** 900 SW Fourth Ave. (tel. 224-6776), offers 1-hour film processing. It's open Monday through Friday from 7am to 7pm, on Saturday from 9am to 6pm, and on Sunday from noon to 5pm. **Camera World,** 500 SW Fifth Ave. (tel. 222-0008), is the largest camera and video store in the city; open Monday through Thursday from 9am to 6pm, on Friday from 9am to 8pm, on Saturday from 10am to 6pm, and on Sunday from 11am to 5pm.

Police To reach the police, call **911.**

Post Offices The main post office, 715 NW Hoyt St. (tel. 294-2200), is open Monday through Friday from 7:30am to 6:30pm, Saturday from 8:30am to 5pm. There are also convenient postal stations at Pioneer Station, 520 SW Morrison St. (tel. 221-0282), open Monday through Friday from 8:30am to 5pm; and University Station, 1505 SW Sixth Ave. (tel. 221-0199), open Monday through Friday from 8:30am to 5pm.

Radio In the Portland area, there are more than 30 AM and FM radio stations. Together they offer every imaginable type of music, news, and sports. KOPB FM (91.5) is the local National Public Radio station.

Religious Services In the downtown area you can find the following churches and synagogues: **First Baptist,** SW 12th Ave. and SW Taylor St. (tel. 228-7465); **St. James Lutheran,** 1315 SW Park Ave. (tel. 227-2439); **First Presbyterian,** 1200 SW Alder St. (tel. 228-7331); **First Unitarian,** 1011 SW 12th Ave. (tel. 228-6389); **First Christian,** 1314 SW Park Ave. (tel. 228-9211); **St. Stephen's Episcopal,** 1432 SW 13th Ave. (tel. 223-6424); **St. Michael's Roman Catholic,** 424 SW Mill St. (tel. 228-8629); **Sixth Church (Christian Science),** 1331 SW Park Ave. (tel. 227-6024); **Congregation Beth Israel (Reform),** 1931 NW Flanders St. (tel. 222-1069); **Congregation Neveh Sholom (Conservative),** 2900 SW Peaceful Lane (tel. 246-8831); **Congregation Kesser Israel (Orthodox),** 136 SW Meade St. (tel. 222-1239); and **First United Methodist,** 1838 SW Jefferson St. (tel. 228-3195).

Restrooms There are public restrooms underneath the Starbuck coffeeshop in Pioneer Courthouse Square and in downtown shopping malls.

Safety Because of its small size and emphasis on keeping the downtown alive and growing, Portland is still a relatively safe city; in fact, strolling the downtown streets at night is a popular pastime. Take extra precautions, however, if you venture into the entertainment district along West Burnside Street or Chinatown at night. Parts of Northeast Portland are controlled by street gangs, so before visiting any place in this area, be sure to get very detailed directions so that you don't get lost. If you plan to go hiking in Forest Park, don't leave anything valuable in your car. This holds true in the Old Town district as well.

Shoe Repairs In Yamhill Market, **Busy Shoes,** SW Yamhill St. and SW First Ave. (tel. 227-5728), is the spiffiest-looking shoe-repair shop I've ever seen. They're set up to resemble a tiny diner, with bar stools and a little counter. They'll fix your shoes while you wait, any time Monday through Friday from 9am to 6pm, on Saturday from 10am to 5pm.

Taxes Portland is a shopper's paradise—there's no sales tax. However, there is a 9% tax on hotel rooms within the city of Portland. Outside the city, the room tax varies.

Taxis To get a cab, call **Broadway Cab** at 227-1234, or **Radio Cab** at 227-1212. See also "By Taxi" in Section 2 of this chapter.

Television Active channels in Portland are 2 (ABC), 6 (CBS), 8 (NBC), 10 (PBS), 12, 24 (Christian), and 49. All the major cable networks are also available.

Time Portland is on Pacific Standard **Time (PST)** or Daylight Saving Time, depending on the time of year, making it 3 hours behind the East Coast.

Tipping In restaurants if the service has been good, tip 15 to 20% of the bill. Taxi drivers expect about 10% of the fare. Airport porters and bellhops should be tipped about 50¢ per bag. For chambermaids, $1 per night is an appropriate tip.

Transit Information For bus information, call the **Tri-Met Customer Assistance Office** at 503/233-3511. They're open Monday through Friday from 9am to 5pm. You can pick up a **Tri-Met Guide** from their office located beneath the waterfall fountain at Pioneer Courthouse Square. For **Amtrak** schedule and fare information, call toll free 800/872-7245. To reach **Union Station** (for train arrival times only), call 503/273-4866. For the **Greyhound bus station,** call 503/243-2323.

Useful Telephone Numbers You may find the following telephone numbers useful during your stay in Portland: **Alcoholics Anonymous** (tel. 223-8569), **Portland Center for the Performing Arts Information Hotline** (tel. 796-9293), and the **Nike Runner's Hotline** (tel. 223-7867).

Weather If it's summer, it's sunny; otherwise, there's a chance of rain. This is almost always a sufficient weather forecast in Portland, but for specifics, call weather information (tel. 236-7575).

3. NETWORKS & RESOURCES

FOR STUDENTS

There are no large universities in Portland, but there are a number of smaller ones. **Portland State University,** 724 SW Harrison St. (tel. 464-3000), in downtown Portland, is a state-run commuter college. The **University of Portland,** 5000 N. Willamette Blvd. (tel. 283-7911), in North Portland, is operated by the Holy Cross Fathers of Notre Dame. **Reed College,** 3203 SE Woodstock St. (tel. 771-1112), a small private college in southeastern Portland, was an anachronism when it opened in 1911. It shunned the fraternities, sororities, athletics, and other aspects of college life in favor of academic excellence. Today it ranks highest in the number of Rhodes Scholars graduated for a college of its size.

FOR GAY MEN & LESBIANS

Gay men and women visiting Portland should be sure to pick up a free copy of *Just Out,* a monthly newspaper for the gay community. You can usually find copies at the **Powell's Books,** 1005 W. Burnside St., or phone 236-1252 to find out where you can get a copy. The newspaper covers local news of interest to gays. They also publish a resource guide for lesbians and gays called the *The Just Out Pocket Book.* Call the above number to find out where you can get a copy. The guide is a directory of Portland businesses that welcome gay customers.

FOR WOMEN

Old Wives' Tales, 1300 E. Burnside St. (tel. 238-0470), is a restaurant that, although not strictly for women, has a distinctively feminist slant. It's open Monday through Thursday from 8am to 10pm, on Friday from 8am to 11pm, on Saturday from 9am to 11pm, and on Sunday from 9am to 10pm. They have a small browsing library and a children's playroom.

The women's **crisis hotline** number is 235-2308.

FOR SENIORS

In addition to the discounts senior citizens can get at events, museums, hotels, and on tours, there is a local monthly newspaper specifically for older citizens: *Senior Tribune.* Call 244-2227 for information on where you can pick up a copy.

IMPRESSIONS

We want you to visit our State of Excitement often. Come again and again. But for heaven's sake, don't move here to live. Or if you do have to move in to live, don't tell any of your neighbors where you are going.
—GOV. TOM MCCALL, 1971

CHAPTER 15

PORTLAND ACCOMMODATIONS

1. **DOWNTOWN**
- **FROMMER'S SMART TRAVELER: ACCOMMODATIONS**
- **FROMMER'S COOL FOR KIDS: ACCOMMODATIONS**
2. **NORTH PORTLAND**
3. **NORTHEAST & SOUTHEAST PORTLAND**
4. **NEAR THE AIRPORT**
5. **THE BEAVERTON/ TIGARD AREA**

Although room rates are slowly creeping up to what they are in other major U.S. cities, Portland's hotels are still relatively inexpensive. Even the most expensive hotel in the city costs less than a comparable one in San Francisco or New York. In the following listings, very expensive hotels are those costing more than $120 per night for a double room; expensive hotels, $90 to $120 per night for a double; moderate hotels, $60 to $90 per night for a double; and budget hotels, less than $60 per night for a double. These rates do not include the hotel-room tax of 9%. A few of the hotels include breakfast in their rates, and this has been noted in the listing; others offer complimentary breakfast only on certain deluxe floors. In most cases you will need to tip the bellhops and chambermaids. If tips are included in a hotel's rates, I have noted this also.

If you are planning to visit during the busy summer months, make your reservations as far in advance as possible, and be sure to ask if there are any special rates available. Almost all large hotels offer weekend discounts of as much as 50%. In fact, you might even be able to get a discount simply by asking for one. Who knows—if the hotel isn't busy, you might just be able to negotiate.

1. DOWNTOWN

VERY EXPENSIVE

THE BENSON HOTEL, 309 SW Broadway, Portland, OR 97205. Tel. 503/228-2000, or toll free 800/426-0670. Fax 503/226-4603. 320 rms, 14 suites. A/C TV TEL
$ Rates: $135–$160 single; $160–$185 double; $185–$285 suite. AE, CB, DC, DISC, MC, V. **Parking:** Valet, $8 per day.
With its mansard roof and French baroque lobby, the Benson, built in 1913, exudes old-world sophistication and elegance. Circassian walnut from Russia covers the lobby walls, framing a marble fireplace. A marble staircase with wrought-iron railing leads from the grand lobby to the mezzanine. Austrian crystal chandeliers hang from

the ornate plasterwork ceiling. You'll be expecting movie stars or royalty to come rushing in surrounded by popping flashbulbs. The Benson recently underwent a $16-million facelift and is looking as fresh as the day it opened, but unfortunately, room rates took a corresponding leap upward.

The guest rooms, housed in two towers above the lobby, have all been redone in shades of pale gray, with elegant classic French Second Empire furnishings that include large desks and armoires that hide the TVs. The deluxe queens are particularly roomy and come with seven pillows per bed. Baths have also been upgraded and include pedestal sinks, but very little shelf space for spreading out your toiletries.

Dining/Entertainment: Down in the wine-cellar-like basement is the London Grill restaurant, one of Portland's best dining establishments. Open for breakfast, lunch, and dinner, it features fresh seafood specialties. (See p. 216 for details.) Trader Vic's, on the ground floor, has become an international institution over the years; and this branch of the famous Polynesian-motif restaurant and bar serves up all the expected meals and colossal cocktails. The Lobby Court serves a buffet lunch from 11:30am to 2pm Monday through Friday, and cocktails until midnight on weekdays and 1am on weekends. Both the London Grill and Trader Vic's also have their own bars.

Services: 24 hour room service, concierge, valet parking, in-room movies, airport shuttle service ($6 each way), valet/laundry service, valet parking.

Facilities: Privileges at nearby athletic club, gift shop, no-smoking floor.

THE HEATHMAN HOTEL, SW Broadway (at Salmon St.), Portland, OR 97205. Tel. 503/241-4100, or toll free 800/551-0011. Fax 503/790-7110. 152 rms, 40 suites. A/C TV TEL

$ Rates: $120–$155 single; $140–$175 double; $225–$350 suite. Weekend and other packages available. AE, CB, DC, MC, V. **Parking:** $7 per day.

Understated luxury, style, and sophistication have made the Heathman the finest hotel in Portland. Originally opened in 1927, it is listed on the National Register of Historic Places. Original art, from 18th-century oil paintings to Andy Warhol prints, give the place a museum atmosphere. A marble-and-teak lobby opens onto the Tea Court, where a fireplace, sweeping staircase, grand piano, and the original eucalyptus paneling create a warm atmosphere.

Every guest room is decorated with its own original works of art and photographs, matching bedspreads and unusual Roman shades in English chintzes, torchère lamps, rattan bedsteads, and glass-topped tables. An elegant wood armoire hides the remote-control TV. Live plants impart a homey feel to each room. In the bath you'll find European soaps and shampoos, plush terry-cloth robes, and large towels.

Dining/Entertainment: The Heathman Restaurant and Bar is

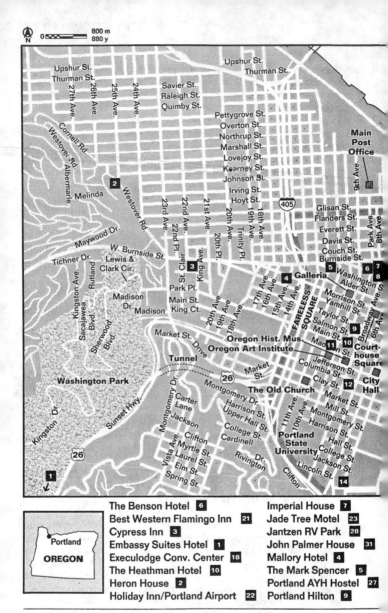

The Benson Hotel **6**	Imperial House **7**
Best Western Flamingo Inn **21**	Jade Tree Motel **23**
Cypress Inn **3**	Jantzen RV Park **28**
Embassy Suites Hotel **1**	John Palmer House **31**
Execulodge Conv. Center **18**	Mallory Hotel **4**
The Heathman Hotel **10**	The Mark Spencer **5**
Heron House **2**	Portland AYH Hostel **27**
Holiday Inn/Portland Airport **22**	Portland Hilton **9**

one of the finest restaurants in Portland, and has been receiving rave reviews since it opened. The menu, which changes seasonally, emphasizes fresh local produce, seafood, and game, all combined in imaginative and delectable creations. (See p. 216 for details.) B. Moloch, the hotel's informal, but equally popular, second restaurant is located two blocks away at 901 Southwest Salmon Street. (See p. 203 for details.) The emphasis is similar, but prices are much lower. Both restaurants have cozy bars. At the hotel's Mezzanine Bar, there

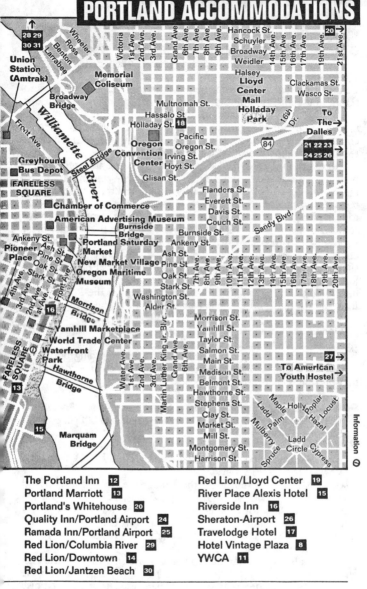

PORTLAND ACCOMMODATIONS

The Portland Inn 12		Red Lion/Lloyd Center 19
Portland Marriott 13		River Place Alexis Hotel 15
Portland's Whitehouse 20		Riverside Inn 16
Quality Inn/Portland Airport 24		Sheraton-Airport 26
Ramada Inn/Portland Airport 25		Travelodge Hotel 17
Red Lion/Columbia River 29		Hotel Vintage Plaza 8
Red Lion/Downtown 14		YWCA 11
Red Lion/Jantzen Beach 30		

is live jazz music on Wednesday evenings for most of the year. High tea is served daily in the Lobby Lounge.

   Services: 24-hour room service, concicrge, valet parking, 150-film videotape library, waterproof running maps.

   Facilities: Privileges at nearby athletic club, wheelchair accommodations, no-smoking rooms, in-room exercise equipment.

PORTLAND HILTON, 921 SW Sixth Ave., Portland, OR

97204-1296. Tel. 503/226-1611, or toll free 800/
HILTONS. Fax 503/220-2565. 455 rms, 16 suites. A/C TV TEL
$ Rates: $98–$130 single; $118–$150 double; $280–$900 suite.
Weekend and other packages available. AE, CB, DC, MC, V.
Parking: $9 per day.

Centrally located near businesses, the performing arts center, and
several museums, this modern high-rise attracts many tour groups
and conventions and is almost always bustling with activity. The
marble-walled lobby is intimate and quiet, with a small grouping of
couches arranged around a large redwood slab coffee table. Three
restaurants are located in or within steps of the lobby.

All the rooms, renovated in the past few years, are decorated in
relaxing pastels and floral prints. Comfortable wingback chairs,
tables, and desks make both businesspeople and those with time to
relax feel right at home. Be sure to request a floor as high as possible
to take advantage of the views (though these are the more expensive
rooms). The corner rooms with king-size beds are particularly nice.

Dining/Entertainment: From its 23rd-floor aerie, Alexander's
offers a striking panorama of Portland, the Willamette River, and
snow-covered Mount Hood. (See p. 217 for details.) Back down at
lobby level is the informal Twigs restaurant, with its popular
lunchtime salad buffet. Up a flight of stairs from the lobby is the
International Club and Lounge. Pettygrove's is a casual lounge just off
the lobby.

Services: Room service, concierge, in-room movies, laundry/
valet service, overnight shoeshine service.

Facilities: Fitness center, heated outdoor swimming pool, gift
shop, beauty salon/barber, business center, wheelchair accommodations, no-smoking floors.

**PORTLAND MARRIOTT, 1401 SW Front Ave., Portland,
OR 97201. Tel. 503/226-7600,** or toll free 800/228-9290.
503 rms, 28 suites. A/C TV TEL
$ Rates: $129–$142 single; $149–$169 double; $300–$350;
suite. Weekend and other packages available. AE, CB, DC, MC,
V. **Parking:** $7 per day.

Just across Front Avenue from the Willamette River, the Portland
Marriott is the flashiest of the city's hotels. A massive portico
complete with lava-rock waterfall and bamboo water clock ushers
you into a high-ceilinged lobby filled with bright lights. Red floral
carpets, small groupings of comfortable lavender chairs, and gentle
piped-in classical music tone down the glitz.

Almost all the accommodations here have small balconies. Ask
for a room overlooking the river, throw back the glass door to the
balcony, and consider that the view here used to be of a noisy
freeway. On a clear day Mount Hood looms in the distance. The
decor in the rooms is simple but attractive.

Dining/Entertainment: The King's Wharf restaurant features
fresh seafood, Northwest specialties, and a view of the river below.
Fazzio's is a family restaurant serving breakfast, lunch, and dinner.
Champions is a very popular sports bar with all the requisite sports
memorabilia on the walls; after night games there's dancing to
recorded music. The lobby bar attracts a much more sedate and

sophisticated clientele, as is obvious from the small library of books available to guests.

Services: Room service, concierge floor, in-room movies, dry cleaning/laundry service, shoeshine stand, baby-sitting service, valet parking, video checkout and message viewing, massage.

Facilities: Exercise room, indoor pool, whirlpool, saunas, games room, weight room, sundeck, beauty salon, gift shop, newsstand, no-smoking floors.

RIVERPLACE ALEXIS HOTEL, 1510 SW Harbor Way, Portland, OR 97201. Tel. 503/228-3233, or toll free outside Oregon 800/227-1333. Fax 503/295-6161. 74 rms, 35 suites. A/C TV TEL

$ Rates (including continental breakfast): $130 single; $150–$170 double; $170 junior suite, $190–$500 suite. AE, CB, DC, MC, V. **Parking:** Valet, $10 per day.

⭐ With the sloping lawns of Waterfront Park to the north and the Willamette River at its back doorstep, the RiverPlace Alexis occupies an enviable location in downtown Portland. As part of the renovation of the city's waterfront, this complex incorporates not only this fine hotel but shops, restaurants, and condominiums. The promenade along the waterfront, with a marina full of private boats floating below, is Portland's best spot for a sunset stroll. The RiverPlace Alexis is an intimate European-style hotel with the feeling of a luxurious resort.

Spacious rooms are decorated with wingback chairs, teak tables, writing desks, and lacquered armoires. Nearly half the rooms here are suites, and these come with wood-burning fireplaces, wet bars, and whirlpool baths. In all the rooms you can open the large windows to let in the cool breezes that waft down the Willamette. In the bath you'll find a delightful assortment of luxurious soaps, shampoos, lotions, and gels. In the closet are terry-cloth robes and sweatsuits (this is a fitness-oriented city)! Forget your running shoes? Don't worry. Ring down to the desk and they'll send up a pair (and a running map so you can find your way back to the hotel). Planning a long stay in town? The hotel can arrange for you to stay in one of their adjacent condominiums. Keep in mind that there is a no-tipping policy in effect except for food and beverage service.

Dining/Entertainment: The Esplanade Restaurant overlooks the river. Northwest and continental cuisines are the specialty here. (See p. 215 for details.) For al fresco dining there's the Patio, featuring sandwiches, burgers, and steaks. Just off the lobby is a very comfortable bar where light meals are served to the accompaniment of live piano music and a crackling fire in cool weather.

Services: 24-hour room service, concierge, arrival sherry, turndown service with a custom-made chocolate on each pillow, in-room movies, complimentary shoeshine, valet/laundry service, complimentary morning paper.

Facilities: Whirlpool, sauna, privileges at nearby athletic club, wheelchair accommodations.

HOTEL VINTAGE PLAZA, 422 SW Broadway, Portland, OR 97205. Tel. 503/228-1212, or toll free 800/243-0555. Fax 503/228-3598. 107 rms, 21 suites. A/C MINIBAR TV TEL

$ Rates: $115–$145 single; $125–$145 double; $145–$185 suite. AE, CB, DC, DISC, MC, V. **Parking:** Valet, $9.

Portland's newest deluxe hotel sports Italianate decor and a wine theme that plays up the budding Oregon wine industry. The intimate lobby is divided into two seating areas with low lighting and comfortable easy chairs. In the main seating area, there is a fireplace flanked by bookshelves that hold old volumes. Soaring up from the lobby is a seven-story atrium that gives this old building a very modern feel.

All the accommodations are different, and though the starlight rooms and two-level suites are real scene-stealers, the standard rooms also have much to recommend them. Roman window shades and old Italian architectural prints are elements of the Italianate decor. Long pink granite counters, gold-tone designer faucets, and green-taffeta shower curtains and walls make the bathrooms here the classiest in town. However, it is the starlight rooms that are truly extraordinary. Though small, they have greenhouse-style wall-into-ceiling windows that provide very romantic views at night and let in lots of light during the day. These rooms have wicker furniture and pale-pastel color schemes, creating a tropical feel. The two-level suites, some with Japanese soaking tubs and one with a spiral staircase, are equally stunning. On the concierge club floors, you get special treatment.

Dining/Entertainment: The Pazzo Northern Italian Restaurant is a dark and intimate trattoria just off the lobby. You can gaze into the restaurant through a wall of glass, and prominently displayed wine racks remind you of the hotel's theme once again. Hotel guests get preferential seating in the restaurant.

Services: Complimentary evening wine, morning coffee, shoe-shine service, morning newspaper, valet/laundry service, concierge floors, turn-down service.

Facilities: Executive gym, business center, no-smoking rooms, wheelchair accommodations.

EXPENSIVE

RED LION HOTEL/DOWNTOWN, 310 SW Lincoln St., Portland, OR 97201. Tel. 503/221-0450, or toll free 800/547-8010. Fax 503/226-6260. 237 rms, 2 suites. A/C TV TEL

$ Rates: $89–$97 single; $104–$112 double; $225–$325 suite. Weekend and other packages available. AE, CB, DC, MC, V. **Parking:** Free.

Situated on a shady tree-lined street on the southern edge of downtown Portland, this low-rise hotel offers convenience and comfort. The design and landscaping reflect the Northwest. A glass-enclosed walkway leads to the lobby from the parking lot, and in the courtyard surrounding the swimming pool are lush plantings of evergreens and other shrubs.

Red Lion Inns are noted for the spaciousness of their guest rooms, and this one is no exception. Large windows let in lots of precious Northwest light when the sun shines. All rooms come with king- or queen-size beds.

Dining/Entertainment: The Cityside Restaurant offers a wide variety of well-prepared meals, with the focus on fresh local seafood.

In the adjacent Cityside Lounge, there is live jazz music on weekends and recorded music other nights. Club Max is the hotel's disco, with live Top 40 bands on weekends.

Services: Room service, complimentary airport shuttle, valet/laundry service.

Facilities: Outdoor pool, gift shop, wheelchair accommodations, coin laundry.

BED-AND-BREAKFAST

HERON HAUS, 2545 NW Westover Rd., Portland, OR 97210. Tel. 503/274-1846. Fax 503/274-1846. 5 rms. TEL
$ Rates (including continental breakfast): $95–$175 single or double. AE, MC, V. **Parking:** Free.

A short walk from the bustling Nob Hill shopping and dining district of northwest Portland, the Heron Haus offers outstanding accommodations and spectacular views. There is even a small swimming pool with sundeck.

Surprisingly, the house still features some of the original plumbing. In most places this would be a liability but not here, since the plumbing was done by the same man who plumbed Portland's famous Pittock Mansion. Many of that building's unusual bath features are to be found at the Heron Haus as well. One shower has seven shower heads; another has two. In another room there's a modern whirlpool spa that affords excellent views of the city.

Facilities: Swimming pool.

MODERATE

MALLORY HOTEL, 729 SW 15th Ave. (at Yamhill St.), Portland, OR 97205-1994. Tel. 503/223-6311, or toll free 800/228-8657. Fax 503/223-0522. 143 rms, 13 suites. A/C TV TEL
$ Rates: $43–$55 single; $48–$80 double; $70–$80 suite. AE, CB, DC, MC, V. **Parking:** Free (a real plus this close to downtown).

The older and old-fashioned Mallory on the edge of Portland's business district is a sort of poor man's Benson Hotel. Although the neighborhood and the hotel's exterior are unassuming, the lobby exhibits an unexpected grandeur. It is done in deep forest greens and ornate gilt-plasterwork wainscoting. A crystal chandelier hangs from the ceiling, and soft light filters through a frosted lead-glass skylight.

Though the rooms are not as luxurious as the lobby might suggest, they are comfortable and clean. With rates as low as they are here, you might want to go for one of the king-size suites. These rooms are about as big as they come, with walk-in closets, minirefrigerators, and sofabeds. All the rooms have new carpets, drapes, and furniture.

Dining/Entertainment: The dining room at the Mallory continues the grand design of the lobby. Heavy drapes hang from the windows, and faux-marble pillars lend just the right air of imperial grandeur.

FROMMER'S SMART TRAVELER: ACCOMMODATIONS

VALUE-CONSCIOUS TRAVELERS SHOULD TAKE ADVANTAGE OF THE FOLLOWING:

1. Weekend discounts of 30% to 50%.
2. Lower room rates in the late spring and early fall, when the weather is still good and summer rates are no longer in effect. Rates usually go up in early June.
3. Apartment hotels, which are very good value, help save on dining bills, and often offer free local calls.
4. The Y and the AYH youth hostel offer very inexpensive lodgings in or near downtown Portland.
5. Lower rates outside of downtown. Downtown hotels are used primarily by business travelers, and their prices reflect this. You can get the same amenities (often more) at lower prices by staying at a hotel away from downtown. The inconvenience is that you must travel into the city each day.
6. Senior citizens and families often get discounts, as do members of AAA. Be sure to ask if there are any such discounts.

QUESTIONS TO ASK IF YOU'RE ON A BUDGET:

1. Is there a parking charge? In downtown Portland, parking charges can add as much as $14 per day to your hotel bill.
2. Does the quoted rate for a given stay include the room tax?
3. Is there a charge for local calls? A surcharge on long-distance calls?
4. Is breakfast included in the rate? Not only bed-and-breakfast inns include breakfast in their service; some moderately priced hotels and even some motels do, too (often only coffee and doughnuts).
5. Does the hotel have a complimentary airport shuttle? This can save you taxi or other airport shuttle fares.

Services: Free local calls, 2pm checkout, in-room movies, valet/laundry service.

THE PORTLAND INN, 1414 SW Sixth Ave., Portland, OR 97201. Tel. 503/221-1611, or toll free 800/648-6440. 173 rms. A/C TV TEL
$ Rates: $67 single; $72–$77 double. AE, CB, DC, MC, V.
Parking: Free.
Located in the heart of downtown, the Portland Inn is an excellent choice for budget-minded business travelers and family vacationers. From the moment you walk into the royal-blue-and-beige lobby and see the humongous railway clock behind the tiny check-in desk, you'll know you've stumbled on something unusual. You'll be even more surprised to discover a small library of old hard-bound books

in every room. In addition, there are brass beds and framed old photos of Portland. Each room has a wall of glass—to let in lots of sunlight—and may even have live plants.

Dining/Entertainment: With its art deco lamps, brass rails, and wood trim, the Portland Bar & Grill is popular for its oyster bar and free happy-hour taco bar.

Services: Valet/laundry service, complimentary newspaper.

Facilities: Outdoor swimming pool, athletic facilities.

RIVERSIDE INN, 50 SW Morrison Ave., Portland, OR 97204. Tel. 503/221-0711, or toll free 800/648-6440. 137 rms. A/C TV TEL

$ Rates: $72 single; $82–$87 double. AE, CB, DC, MC, V. **Parking:** Free.

Operated by the same company that owns the Portland Inn, the Riverside has many of the same unexpected features. As the name implies, you are only steps from the Willamette River, but you are also close to businesses, fine restaurants, and shopping. Colorful fine-art posters enliven the walls of the small lobby, giving the seating area a very homey feel. Rooms, many with excellent views of the river and Morrison Bridge, feature a small library of hard-bound books, brass beds, modern furnishings, and attractive framed posters.

Dining/Entertainment: The Riverside Café & Bar is a bright and airy restaurant with large windows looking out over the Waterfront Park and the river. Fresh seafood is the specialty here.

Services: Room service, valet/laundry service.

BUDGET

As you would expect, your options for budget accommodations in the downtown Portland area are extremely limited. However, there are a couple of options available.

IMPERIAL HOTEL, 400 SW Broadway, Portland, OR

 FROMMER'S COOL FOR KIDS
ACCOMMODATIONS

Holiday Inn, Portland Airport Hotel (see p. 193) The indoor swimming pool and video game room will keep kids entertained no matter what the weather.

Red Lion Hotel/Lloyd Center (see p. 188) Let the kids loose in the huge Lloyd Center Shopping Mall across the street and they'll stay entertained for hours. There is even an ice-skating rink in the mall.

Portland Marriott (see p. 180) The game room and indoor pool are popular with kids, and just across the street is 2-mile-long Tom McCall Waterfront Park, which runs along the Willamette River.

97205. Tel. 503/228-7221, or toll free 800/547-8282. 168 rms. A/C TV TEL

$ Rates: $40–$55 single; $45–$60 double. AE, CB, DC, MC, V. **Parking:** Free.

Although it doesn't quite live up to its regal name, this older hotel—catty-corner to The Benson Hotel—is a fine choice if you're on a budget. It recently underwent a complete renovation that, surprisingly, didn't raise the rates. Rooms here are clean and comfortable, with new furniture (psuedo-Louis XIV) and lavender color schemes. Bathrooms are older (they even have porcelain shower knobs) but in good shape. The corner king rooms, with large windows, are the best choices here. All rooms come with clock-radios.

Dining/Entertainment: The hotel's restaurant/lounge is a popular meeting place with downtown businesspeople. A stone wall and unusual pieces of driftwood evoke the Northwest, while long curving banquettes and brass rails create a clubby atmosphere.

Services: In-room movies, valet/laundry service.

Facilities: Wheelchair accommodations.

APARTMENT HOTEL

THE MARK SPENCER, 409 SW 11th Ave., Portland, OR 97205. Tel. 503/224-3293, or toll free 800/548-3934). 103 rms. A/C TV TEL

$ Rates: $49 studio, single or double; $64 one-bedroom. Lower weekly and monthly rates are also available. Children 12 and under stay free in parents' room. AE, CB, DC, MC, V.

If you're planning an extended stay in Portland and need to be within walking distance of downtown, this is the place for you. Although the hotel is not in the best neighborhood in the city, it's just around the corner from Jake's Famous Crawfish, one of Portland's oldest and most popular restaurants. The building itself has been attractively restored, with flower baskets hanging from old-fashioned streetlamps out front.

Both studios and one-bedrooms feature kitchenettes and attractive modern furnishings, including plush-velvet wingback chairs and couches in some rooms. Walk-in closets are a definite plus for those planning a long stay in town.

Services: Free housekeeping, coin-operated laundry and valet service, private mailboxes, personal phone lines.

Facilities: Privileges at nearby athletic club, no-smoking rooms.

BED-AND-BREAKFAST SERVICE

NORTHWEST BED & BREAKFAST TRAVEL UNLIMITED, 610 SW Broadway, Portland, OR 97205. Tel. 503/243-7616.

$ Rates: $25–$40 single; $30–$60 double. These are average rates; some may be higher.

This service represents more than 45 B&Bs in the Portland area, most of which are private homes. You can avail yourself of their service by paying a $20 annual membership fee, or by paying by the booking ($5 for a maximum two-night booking). Once you have paid your membership fee, you will receive the service's 160-page directory of host homes. All homes have been inspected by the service and are clean and comfortable. Many offer free airport pickup.

Y

YWCA, 1111 SW 10th Ave., Portland, OR 97205. Tel. 503/223-6281.

$ Rates: $15 in shared room with shared bath; $24 single with shared bath down the hall, $26 single with semiprivate bath; $28 double in a private room with shared bath, $36 double with semiprivate bath. MC, V.

If you are a woman and traveling on a budget, you might want to check out this very conveniently located Y. Accommodations are simple, as you would expect, but the atmosphere is friendly. There's a TV lounge for guests, as well as a microwave and refrigerator where you can store a few foodstuffs. For an additional charge you can use the athletic facilities.

2. NORTH PORTLAND

VERY EXPENSIVE

Located in north Portland on the Columbia River is the shopping and resort area of Jantzen Beach, named for the famous swimwear manufacturer that originated in Portland. Although you'll find Red Lion Inns throughout the West, including three others in Portland, the pair listed here are two of the nicest and most impressive. One warning: Both these hotels are in the flight path for the airport, and although the rooms themselves are adequately insulated against noise, the swimming pools and sundecks are not.

RED LION HOTEL/COLUMBIA RIVER, 1401 N. Hayden Island Dr., Portland, OR 97217. Tel. 503/283-2111, or toll free 800/547-8010. Fax 503/283-4718. 351 rms, 8 suites. A/C TV TEL

$ Rates: $98–$118 single; $113–$133 double; $195–$400 suite. Weekend and other packages available. Children under 18 stay free in parents' room. AE, CB, DC, MC, V. **Parking:** Free.

An attractive low-rise design that's slightly reminiscent of a North-west Native American longhouse has kept this hotel popular for many years. The lobby, completely redecorated in 1991, now features lots of cherry wood and faux green-marble accents for that Ivy League look. Unfortunately, the impressive wood carvings that previously decorated the lobby were sold off during the remodeling.

As with all Red Lions, the rooms are spacious and comfortable, and were redone in shades of seafoam green and mauve. Floral-print bedspreads with a beige background, as well as framed watercolors, give the rooms a country-cottage appeal.

Dining/Entertainment: The Coffee Garden, just off the lobby, offers coffee-shop meals from early morning to late at night. Great views of the Columbia River are to be had at Brickstone's Restaurant, which features an international menu emphasizing fresh local seafoods. For late-night entertainment, there's the Brickstone Lounge, where live rock bands perform on weekends. For a quieter atmosphere, try the aptly named Quiet Bar, a small glass-walled octagonal building just off the lobby and overlooking the pool.

Services: Room service, complimentary airport shuttle, valet/laundry service.

Facilities: Heated outdoor swimming pool, whirlpool spa, putting green, gift shop, barbershop, beauty salon.

RED LION HOTEL/JANTZEN BEACH, 909 N. Hayden Island Dr., Portland, OR 97217. Tel. 503/283-4466, or toll free 800/547-8010. Fax 503/283-4743. 320 rms, 8 suites. A/C TV TEL

$ Rates: $105–$115 single; $120–$130 double; $300–$400 suite. AE, CB, DC, MC, V. **Parking:** Free.

Everything about this resort hotel is spacious. An imposing portico that reflects Northwest tribal designs leads to the massive lobby, which is fronted by a long wall of glass. Thick carpets muffle every sound. Intricately carved dark woods impart a warmth and Northwest feel.

Arranged in wings around a central garden courtyard and swimming pool, the rooms are as large as you're likely to find in any hotel. Most have balconies and excellent views of the river and sometimes Mount St. Helens. The baths, each with a nice assortment of soaps, shampoos, and lotions, are equally spacious.

Dining/Entertainment: Elegant dining in plush surroundings can be found in Maxi's Restaurant, which specializes in traditional continental cuisine prepared with flair. For much more casual dining there's the Coffee Garden in the lobby. Thursday through Saturday nights come alive to the sound of live rock 'n' roll bands at Maxi's Lounge, an art nouveau extravaganza.

Services: Room service, complimentary airport shuttle, valet/laundry service.

Facilities: Heated outdoor pool, tennis courts, privileges at a nearby athletic club, wheelchair accommodations, gift shop, helicopter port.

3. NORTHEAST & SOUTHEAST PORTLAND

VERY EXPENSIVE

RED LION HOTEL/LLOYD CENTER, 1000 NE Multnomah St., Portland, OR 97232. Tel. 503/281-6111, or toll free 800/547-8010. Fax 503/284-8553. 476 rooms, 17 suites. A/C TV TEL

$ Rates: $96–$129 single; $111–$134 double; $199–$485 suite. AE, CB, DC, MC, V. **Parking:** Free.

In the busy lobby of this modern high-rise, glass elevators shuttle up and down through the skylighted ceiling. Massive overstuffed chairs and couches with built-in tables are surrounded by plants, which create a warm greenhouse atmosphere. Spreading out in different directions are hallways leading to the restaurants, gift shops, a swimming pool, and an elegant lounge. Large leaf patterns in bas-relief decorate the walls. Tubular-glass chandeliers sparkle overhead.

As you've come to expect, the Red Lion's rooms are spacious beyond compare, and the views from the higher floors are stunning. On a clear day you can see Mount Hood, Mount St. Helens, and Mount Rainier.

Dining/Entertainment: Maxi's Restaurant, with its stained-glass chandeliers and baffled ceiling, is just off the lobby but surrounded by a low wall of plants. Local seafood, steaks, and wild game are the well-prepared specialties here. If you're more in the mood for Mexican, cross the lobby to Eduardo's Cantina, where stucco walls, tile floors, rough-hewn wood beams, and rattan chairs will transport you down Mexico way. Family dining is possible in the Coffee Garden, which opens directly onto the lobby. For those seeking a quiet place for conversation and a drink, there's the Quiet Bar. In Maxi's Lounge you'll find two dance floors, and live music can be heard on the weekends.

Services: Room service, concierge, complimentary airport shuttle, in-room movies, valet/laundry service.

Facilities: Heated outdoor swimming pool, wheelchair accommodations, exercise room, gift shop.

EXPENSIVE

EXECULODGE CONVENTION CENTER, 1021 NE Grand Ave., Portland, OR 97232. Tel. 503/235-8433, or toll free 800/343-1822. Fax 503/238-0132. 174 rms, 2 suites. A/C MINIBAR TV TEL

$ Rates: $80 single; $90 double; $250 suite. Special packages for senior citizens. AE, CB, DC, MC, V. **Parking:** Free.

This reasonably priced hotel, located across the street from the striking new Oregon Convention Center, is a popular choice with conventioneers who don't want to spend an arm and a leg. Because Portland's MAX light-rail system stops one block from the hotel, this is also a convenient location if you want to go downtown.

You'll find all the rooms attractively furnished in pastel colors and modern decor with an Asian touch. Large tables, writing desks, and comfortable armchairs allow guests to spread out. Upper floors have good views either west to the city skyline or east to the Cascades and Mount Hood, and the twin peaks of the Convention Center loom just across the street.

Dining/Entertainment: Windows, the hotel's aptly named top-floor restaurant, provides the hotel's best views and is a popular dining spot. You can dine on fresh Northwest cuisine or just have a drink in the lounge.

Services: Room service, in-room movies, valet/laundry service, courtesy airport shuttle.

Facilities: Rooftop heated outdoor swimming pool, sauna, fitness center, business center.

MODERATE

TRAVELODGE HOTEL, 1441 NE Second Ave., Portland, OR 97232. Tel. 503/233-2401, or toll free 800/255-3050. Fax 503/238-7016. 236 rms. A/C TV TEL

$ Rates: $79 single; $85–$89 double. AE, CB, DC, MC, V. **Parking:** Free.

Convenient to both the city center and the Convention Center, the Travelodge offers excellent views from its modern 10-story building. Soothing pastels are used in the small lobby and in the guest rooms, all of which have large windows to let in as much of that rare Northwest sunshine as possible. In the baths you'll find marble countertops and tile floors. You'll also find a coffee maker in every room.

Dining/Entertainment: Traders, just off the lobby, is the hotel's restaurant, and fresh seafood is the specialty. For cocktails and conversation, there's the adjacent Encore Lounge.

Services: Room service, in-room movies, complimentary airport shuttle, valet/laundry service, free jogging maps.

Facilities: Heated outdoor swimming pool, wheelchair accommodations, no-smoking rooms, women's floor, privileges at nearby athletic facility.

BED-AND-BREAKFAST

PORTLAND'S WHITE HOUSE, 1914 NE 22nd Ave., Portland, OR 97212. Tel. 503/287-7131. 6 rms (4 with private bath).

$ Rates (including full breakfast): $60–$90 single; $68–$98 double; some rates lower in winter. MC, V.

★ This imposing Greek-revival mansion bears a more than passing resemblance to its namesake in Washington, D.C. Massive columns frame the entrance and a patio area where on sunny days you can sit at a table and enjoy a picnic lunch. A long semicircular driveway sweeps up to the entrance, and a fountain bubbles in the garden. This is a no-smoking inn, and hosts Larry and Mary Hough prefer guests who are more than 12 years old.

Behind the mahogany doors is a huge entrance hall with original hand-painted murals on the walls. To your right is the parlor, with its French windows and piano. To your left is the formal dining room, where the large breakfast is served amid sparkling crystal chandeliers. A double staircase leads past a large stained-glass window to the second-floor accommodations.

Canopy and brass beds, antique furnishings, and bathrooms with clawfoot tubs await you at the end of a weary day. Request the balcony room and you can gaze out past the Greek columns and imagine you're the master of a vast Southern plantation.

Services: Free airport pickup, afternoon tea.

BUDGET

JADE TREE MOTEL, 3939 NE Hancock St., Portland, OR 97212. Tel. 503/288-6891. 48 rms. A/C TV TEL

$ Rates: single $38; double $50. AE, CB, DC, DISC, MC, V.
Parking: Free.

Located in the Hollywood District of northeast Portland about halfway between the airport and downtown, the Jade Tree Motel is an excellent choice in the budget-accommodation range. All the rooms are exceptionally large and were renovated a few years ago. Attractive modern furniture and comfortable beds will make your stay here enjoyable. Take a stroll around the neighborhood and you'll see why they call this the Hollywood District—the same style of southern California Hollywood architecture prevails.

Dining/Entertainment: Restaurants nearby.

Services: Room service, one-day valet service, free coffee.

Facilities: Wheelchair accommodations.

BED-AND-BREAKFAST

JOHN PALMER HOUSE, 4314 N. Mississippi Ave., Portland, OR 97217. Tel. 503/284-5893. 7 rms (2 with private bath), 2 suites.

$ Rates (including continental breakfast): $30–$75 single or double; $75–$105 single or double suite. MC, V.

Even before you set foot inside the door of this restored Queen Anne Victorian home in an unassuming neighborhood in North Portland, you know that you've stumbled onto something special. Cross the Italianate veranda, step through the double stained-glass doors, and you are enveloped in the Victorian era. The interior has been done with all the flair for which that period was known. Dozens of different wallpapers turn the walls into a coordinated riot of colors and patterns.

Guest accommodations are actually in two houses: the main Palmer House and Grandma's Cottage. Each room in the main house is decorated with massive Victorian furnishings, and stained-glass windows throughout the house filter the sunlight into magical hues. In one bedroom there's a stuffed moose head that seems to take up almost the entire room. Decor in Grandma's Cottage is much simpler. In the morning you will be served a delicious gourmet breakfast. There is also a whirlpool in a gazebo, plus a croquet court.

For an additional fee, you can indulge whatever Victorian fantasy you might have. Have a horse-drawn carriage carry you to the inn. Perhaps you'd like your own private butler or maid. Lacey Victorian sleepwear might be what you need to help you sleep better at night. A massage? You name it, and the Sauters will try to accommodate you.

Dining/Entertainment: Saturday and Sunday, high tea is served from 2 to 5pm; after tea, a tour is given. The price of tea and tour is $10. The Palmer House also offers fine dining by reservation (48 hours ahead) at 6 and 8:15pm.

YOUTH HOSTEL

PORTLAND AYH HOSTEL, 3031 SE Hawthorne Blvd., Portland, OR 97214. Tel. 503/236-3380. 50 beds. **Bus:** 5 from downtown or 12 then 5 from airport.

$ Rates: $10 member, $13 nonmember. MC, V.

The Hawthorne District is a shopping and dining area popular with students, artists, and musicians, so it makes an ideal location for a youth hostel. Housed in an old house on a busy street, this hostel is small and has only dormitory beds. The common room is also small, but a large wraparound porch makes up for the lack of space inside. There is a large kitchen where guests can prepare their own meals, with a grocery store a short walk away. Located in the same building is an AYH Travel Center, where hostel members can get student IDs, and buy books, travel packs, and Eurailpasses. Membership is $10 per year for youths under 17, $25 for adults, and $15 for senior citizens over 55.

4. NEAR THE AIRPORT

EXPENSIVE

RAMADA INN/PORTLAND AIRPORT, 6221 NE 82nd Ave., Portland, OR 97220. Tel. 503/255-6511, or toll free 800/272-6232. Fax 503/255-8417. 202 rms, 108 suites. A/C TV TEL

$ Rates: $85 single; $95 double; $95–$105 suite. AE, CB, DC, MC, V. **Parking:** Free.

Located 3 miles from the airport, this Ramada Inn is convenient to the interstate for quick access to downtown Portland. Rooms are done in attractive lavenders and grays and come with queen-size or double beds. If you stay in one of the suites, you'll find a microwave, wet bar, refrigerator, and remote-control TV, in addition to the sofabed and the art deco and Asian styling. These suites are definitely worth the few dollars extra they cost.

Dining/Entertainment: O'Callahan's, the spacious two-level dining room and lounge, specializes in Cajun food, extra-large sandwiches, and seafood. Sunday brunch is only $10.95.

Services: Room service, complimentary airport shuttle, valet/laundry service.

Facilities: Heated outdoor swimming pool, whirlpool spa, sauna, fitness room, business center.

SHERATON-AIRPORT, 8235 NE Airport Way, Portland, OR 97220-1398. Tel. 503/281-2500, or toll free 800/325-3535. 210 rms, 5 suites. A/C TV TEL

$ Rates: $95–$104 single; $107–$116 double; $125–$295 suite. AE, CB, DC, MC, V. **Parking:** Free.

You can't get any closer to the airport than this unless you sleep in one of the departure lounges. Not only is this hotel convenient for business travelers, but it also offers plenty of amenities to attract vacationers. All the rooms are quite large and tastefully decorated, with your choice of a king-size or double bed. In most of the rooms you'll get two telephones, a large writing desk, and an attractive oak armoire that hides the TV when it's not in use. There are even original lithographs by Northwest artists on the walls of the guest rooms—a nice touch.

Dining/Entertainment: The Premiere, as its name implies, is the hotel's premier restaurant, serving well-prepared continental cuisine in elegant surroundings of frosted-glass and wall-sconce lighting. For less formal dining, stop in at Coffee & Things. The Lobby Bar is a quiet little niche where you can have a drink and enjoy a quiet conversation. At Harold's there's always plenty of action on the dance floor, or you can sit by the fireplace and relax. There's live rock music Tuesday through Saturday.

Services: 24-hour room service, in-room movies, complimentary airport shuttle, valet/laundry service.

Facilities: Indoor swimming pool, whirlpool, sauna, athletic facilities, wheelchair accommodations, gift shop.

MODERATE

HOLIDAY INN, PORTLAND AIRPORT HOTEL, 8439 NE Columbia Blvd., Portland, OR 97220-1382. Tel. 503/ 256-5000, or toll free 800/HOLIDAY. Fax 503/256-5000, ext 149. 286 rms, 17 suites. A/C TV TEL
$ Rates: $74–$90.50 single; $80–$97 double; $100–$245 suite. AE, CD, DC, MC, V. **Parking:** Free.
A Southwest motif reigns at this Holiday Inn in the Northwest. From the outside the building looks unremarkable, but once you're inside you enter a mezzanine-level lobby overlooking a large covered courtyard. Spanish-tile awnings, a bubbling fountain, and a swimming pool beneath a ramada all help create the Southwest flavor. The courtyard dining area has an al fresco feel. In your room you'll find pleasant subdued colors and a large bath—everything you'd expect of a Holiday Inn.

Dining/Entertainment: John Q's offers traditional gourmet dining. The Coffee Shop is open early and late. Music and dancing go on every night at the Flirts Dance Club.

Services: Room service, in-room movies, complimentary airport shuttle, valet/laundry service.

Facilities: Indoor pool, exercise room, whirlpool, sauna, video games room, wheelchair accommodations, gift shop.

QUALITY INN/PORTLAND AIRPORT, 8247 NE Sandy Blvd., Portland, OR 97220. Tel. 503/256-4111, or toll free 800/228-5151. Fax 503/254-1507. 120 rms, 8 suites. A/C TV TEL
$ Rates: $65–$70 single; $75–$80 double; $100 suite. AE, CB, DC, DISC, MC, V. **Parking:** Free.
Although the rooms here are a bit small and dark, they are very comfortable and clean, and the attractively landscaped surroundings more than make up for any inadequacies in the accommodations. If you are willing to spend a bit more, there are suites and rooms with whirlpool baths.

Dining/Entertainment: Steamers Restaurant specializes in fresh seafood. If you're a fan of the steam era, you'll love this place. There are plenty of old photos on the walls, and bits and pieces rescued from paddle-wheelers and steam locomotives.

Services: Complimentary airport shuttle, complimentary hors d'oeuvres from 5 to 7pm, same-day valet service, complimentary morning newspaper, free local phone calls.

Facilities: Heated outdoor pool, laundry facilities.

BUDGET

BEST WESTERN FLAMINGO MOTOR INN, 9727 NE Sandy Blvd., Portland OR 97220. Tel. 503/255-1400, or toll free outside Oregon 800/621-4358, or toll free in Oregon 800/556-0006. Fax 503/256-3842. 175 rms. A/C TV TEL
$ Rates: $46 single; $51 double. Children 12 and under stay free in parents' room. AE, CB, DC, DISC, MC, V.

Only 5 minutes' drive from the airport, the Flamingo offers comfortable accommodations, a few unexpected amenities, and easy access to the interstate and downtown Portland. Rooms are spacious and clean. If you're honeymooning or just feel romantic, ask for one of the Jacuzzi rooms, which also come with mirrors over the king-size bed.

Dining/Entertainment: Splash Restaurant serves seafood, steaks, and pasta. A separate coffee shop fills breakfast and snack needs.

Services: Valet/laundry service, in-room movies, courtesy airport shuttle.

Facilities: Heated outdoor swimming pool, whirlpool spa, steamroom, privileges at a nearby athletic club.

5. THE BEAVERTON/TIGARD AREA

EXPENSIVE

EMBASSY SUITES HOTEL, 9000 SW Washington Square Rd., Tigard, OR 97223. Tel. 503/644-4000, or toll free 800/EMBASSY. Fax 503/641-4654. 250 suites. A/C TV TEL
$ Rates (including full breakfast): $89–$112 single; $89–$127 double. AE, DC, DISC, MC, V. **Parking:** Free.

Beaverton and Tigard are at the heart of Oregon's rapidly growing high-tech industries, and whether you are traveling on business or for pleasure, this outstanding nine-story hotel should be your first choice in the area. It is built around a soaring atrium, with colorful kites suspended high above the gardenlike lobby and courtyard dining area. Tropical plants are everywhere, and waterfalls add their pleasant music. In the evening and during brunch there's live piano music in the lobby garden dining area. A glass elevator whisks guests to their rooms.

As the name implies, every room is a suite—each beautifully decorated in pale greens and pastels, with plush carpets. In the sitting room you'll find a huge stereo console TV, potted plants, a relaxing couch, a telephone, and a large table. There are also a microwave, minirefrigerator, and wet bar in each suite. In the bedroom you'll find another TV, a clock-radio, and a second phone. The bath is equally appealing with its generous basket of fragrant soaps, shampoos, and lotions on the large counter.

Dining/Entertainment: At the elegant Crossroads Restaurant, Northwest cuisine is the order of the day. For more casual dining and for the delicious Sunday brunch, seat yourself amid the lush foliage of the Atrium. For relaxing, socializing, and dancing, there's the Crossroads Lounge, with live entertainment and a cozy fireplace.

Services: Room service, valet/laundry service, nightly manager's reception with complimentary drinks, courtesy transportation to Washington Square Mall, complimentary newspapers.

Facilities: 24-hour indoor pool, whirlpool, sauna, fitness room and privileges at nearby health club, wheelchair accommodations.

CHAPTER 16

PORTLAND DINING

Portland may not be garnering as much praise for its Northwest cuisine as Seattle, but there are certainly a few restaurants here that are every bit the equal of Seattle's best. Young and innovative chefs are cooking up a quiet storm in Portland these days, and prices are very reasonable. For these listings, I considered a restaurant expensive if a meal with wine or beer would average $25 or more. Moderate restaurants offer complete dinners in the $15 to $25 range, and budget eateries are those where you can get a complete meal for less than $15.

To learn more about Northwest cuisine, see the introduction to Chapter 6, "Seattle Dining."

Be sure to accompany your dinner with one of Oregon's fine wines. Quite a few of them have been winning taste-test competitions with California and French wines in recent years.

Many of Portland's finest restaurants are open for dinner only between 5 or 5:30pm and 9:30 or 10pm, so you'll have to plan on dining early. There are a few exceptions to this rule and I have noted these. Reservations are always a good idea, especially if there are five or more in your group.

1. DOWNTOWN & OLD TOWN

EXPENSIVE

BRASSERIE MONTMARTRE, 626 SW Park Ave. Tel. 503/224-5552.

Cuisine: CONTINENTAL/FRENCH. **Reservations:** Recommended.

$ Prices: Appetizers $4.75–$7.25; main dishes $9–$16.75. AE, CB, DC, MC, V.

Open: Lunch Mon–Fri 11:30am–2:30pm; dinner daily 5:30–10pm; brunch Sat–Sun 10am–2:30pm; bistro menu available daily from 2pm–closing.

Though the menu lacks the creativity of other continental and French restaurants in Portland, The Bra (as it's known here in town) is hardly the stodgy and expensive place its full name implies. There is nightly jazz music from around 9pm on, and on every table you'll find a paper tablecloth and a container of crayons. Let your artistic ambitions run wild while you wait for dinner or linger over drinks. Tuesday through Saturday, a magician performs amazing feats of digital dexterity.

This playfulness is balanced out by spacious and dark formal dining rooms. Massive white pillars, black-and-white tile floors, velvet banquettes, and silk lampshades lend an air of fin de siècle Paris. With all this elegance and entertainment, prices are surprisingly reasonable. When I last visited, the most expensive item on the menu was rack of lamb with a sauce of port and tarragon for $16.75. You might start your meal with a ménage à trois of pâtés, then have a cup of onion soup with three cheeses, move on to salmon with lingonberry-and-ginger butter, and finish off with one of the divinely decadent pastries. The wine list is neither too extensive nor too expensive. And if you've grown attached to your tabletop work of art, they'll be happy to let you have it.

COUCH STREET FISH HOUSE, NW Third Ave. and Couch St. Tel. 503/223-6173.

Cuisine: SEAFOOD. **Reservations:** Highly recommended.

$ Prices: Appetizers $6.95–$8.95; main dishes $11.50–$20; four-course sunset dinners $10.95. AF, MC, V.

Open: Dinner only, Mon–Thurs 5–10pm, Fri–Sat 5–11pm.

Located in the heart of Old Town, this award-winning restaurant specializes in the Northwest's freshest seafood. The restaurant occupies two historic buildings, one of which is merely the facade of an Italianate Victorian hotel built in 1883; this, in fact, must be the only historic parking lot in the country. The other historic building has been completely remodeled into a dark and intimate restaurant. Antiques and exposed brick abound.

The succulent seafood main dishes run the gamut from pan-fried oysters coated with a crust of Oregon hazelnuts to mesquite-grilled salmon to such classics as lobster thermidor and shrimp scampi. The menu focuses on fresh seafood, but meat eaters are also served with the likes of rack of lamb and filet mignon in Madeira glacé.

CREPE FAIRE, 133 SW Second Ave. (at Pine St.). Tel. 503/227-3365.

Cuisine: FRENCH. **Reservations:** Imperative.

$ Prices: Appetizers $3.50–$7.50; main dishes $6–$16. AE, CB, DC, MC, V.

Open: Breakfast Mon–Fri 7–10:30am; brunch Sat–Sun 9am–3pm; lunch Mon–Fri 11:30am–2:30pm; dinner Mon–Sat 5:30–9:30pm.

More than any other restaurant in the Old Town district, Crepe Faire captures the mood of a past era. However, that era is not turn-of-the-century Portland, but Gay '90s Paris. Exposed brick walls and arched doors and windows showcase the historic architecture of this building. On the floor are very elegant burgundy-and-gray carpets. Rosewood paneling, leaded-glass windows, and a burgundy banquette in the waiting area further add to the elegance, and fresh flowers on each table complete a picture that is made for romance.

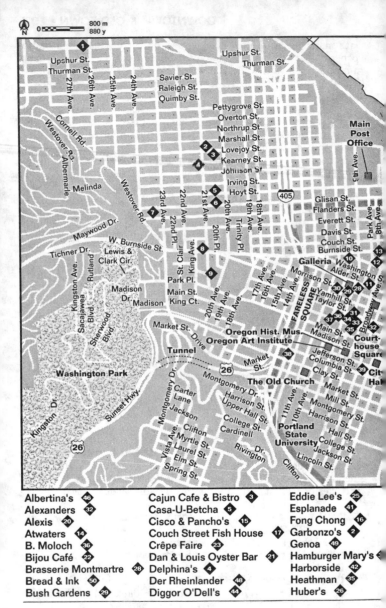

As the name implies, crepes are the specialty of the house,
although other main dishes and desserts are available. The spinach-
and-mushroom gateau—alternating layers of creamed spinach and
mushroom duxelles with mornay sauce, sandwiched between
crepes—is legendary. Be sure to save plenty of room for one of the
desserts. They're so good you may even want to have more than one!
Nougatine crepe is filled with caramel, dates, and toasted filberts.
The brandied apple gateau is another creation of layered crepes, this

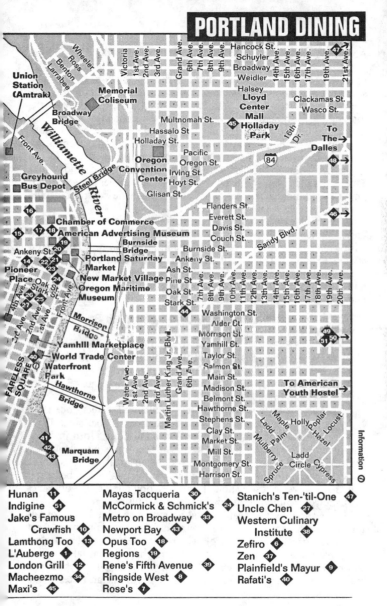

Hunan	Mayas Tacqueria	Stanich's Ten-'til-One
Indigine	McCormick & Schmick's	Uncle Chen
Jake's Famous	Metro on Broadway	Western Culinary
Crawfish	Newport Bay	Institute
Lamthong Too	Opus Too	Zefiro
L'Auberge	Regions	Zen
London Grill	Rene's Fifth Avenue	Plainfield's Mayur
Macheezmo	Ringside West	Rafati's
Maxi's	Rose's	

time filled with apples and cinnamon and dressed with an apricot-brandy sauce and whipped cream. Scrumptious!

HARBORSIDE RESTAURANT AND SHANGHAI LOUNGE,
0309 SW Montgomery St. Tel. 503/220-1865.
Cuisine: SEAFOOD. **Reservations:** Recommended.
$ Prices: Appetizers $4–$8; main dishes $5.50–$18; lunches $4.75–$10. AE, CB, DC, DISC, MC, V.

Open: Daily 11am–11pm.

Anchoring the opposite end of the RiverPlace from the Alexis Hotel is this large and very popular restaurant. The clientele is mostly upscale, especially at lunch and in the après-work hours. The sparkling cut-glass windows and doors at the restaurant's entrance are an unexpected bit of tradition in an otherwise very modern-looking establishment. Tall walls of glass are fronted by four dining levels, so everyone gets a view of the river and marina below. Because it's so popular, the place tends to be noisy and the help seems a bit harried; however, don't let this detract from the fine food. In the Shang-hai Lounge there's live jazz or rock music on Friday and Saturday nights. Nearly any time of year, if the weather is good, you'll find folks dining al fresco along the promenade in front of the restaurant.

Although seafood (such as broiled salmon with tomato hollandaise, blackened yellow fin with lime butter, and broiled swordfish with orange-jalapeño butter) is the main attraction here, the menu is quite extensive. The long list of hot and cold salads is very tempting and even includes a hot Thai salad. There are a dozen pasta dishes and even pizzas made with such unusual ingredients as blue cheese and apples.

JAKE'S FAMOUS CRAWFISH, 401 SW 12th St. Tel. 503/226-1419.

Cuisine: SEAFOOD. **Reservations:** Recommended for dinner.

$ Prices: Appetizers $2.95–$11.95; main dishes $8.50–$20. AE, CB, DC, DISC, MC, V.

Open: Lunch Mon–Fri 11am–3pm; dinner Mon–Thurs 5–11pm, Fri–Sat 5pm–midnight, Sun 5–10pm.

Jake's has been serving up these miniature lobsters since 1909 at an address that has housed a restaurant or bar since 1892. The back bar came all the way around Cape Horn in 1880, and much of the rest of the restaurant's decor looks just as old and well-worn. The noise level after work, when local businesspeople pack the bar, can be deafening, and the wait for a table can be long if you don't have a reservation. However, don't let these obstacles dissuade you from visiting this Portland institution.

A large selection of seafood and an extensive wine list make this one of the city's most popular restaurants. There's a daily menu sheet listing 15 to 20 specials, all of which are fresh from the market. However, there is really no question about what to eat at Jake's—you can order your crayfish prepared any of five different ways. If you really want something else, their other seafoods and steaks are equally delectable.

MCCORMICK & SCHMICK'S, 235 SW First Ave. Tel. 503/224-7522.

Cuisine: SEAFOOD. **Reservations:** Highly recommended.

$ Prices: Appetizers $4–$20; main dishes $10–$20; bar meals $2.25; lunches $3.25–$9.50. AE, DC, MC, V.

Open: Lunch Mon–Fri 11:30am–2pm; dinner Mon–Sat 5–11pm; bar meals Mon–Sat 1:30–6:30pm and 9:30pm–midnight.

Although it opened in 1979, McCormick & Schmick's feels as if it had been around as long as Jake's. The owners wanted to open a restaurant/bar that was based on traditional seafood establishments. What they succeeded in creating was a very popular place noted for the freshness of its ingredients. Both the up-and-coming and the already-there keep this place bustling.

Whether it's king salmon or Dungeness crab, seafood is king here. The oysters in the oyster bar go by their first names, names like Kumamoto, Willapa Bay, and Quilcene. The daily fresh menu sheet begins with a listing of what's available that day and might list 20 different types of seafood; it even lists the home port of each type of seafood. If you aren't interested in live oysters as an appetizer, there are plenty of cooked seafoods to start you out. Some outstanding main dishes on a recent visit included grilled lingcod served with raspberry vinaigrette, steamed clams with fresh oregano, and halibut sauté with morels and dill beure blanc. The extensive wine list features quite a few excellent Oregon wines, and while you're waiting for your table, you might want to try one of the more than 30 single malt scotches available.

OPUS TOO RESTAURANT & JAZZ DE OPUS BAR, 33 NW Second Ave. Tel. 503/222-6077.

Cuisine: SEAFOOD/STEAKS. **Reservations:** Recommended
$ Prices: Appetizers $4.25–$8; main dishes $10–$21. AE, CB, DC, MC, V.
Open: Lunch Mon–Sat 11am–3pm; dinner Mon–Sat 5pm–midnight, Sun 5–11pm. Bar open until 2am.

Anyone who has outgrown sushi but still enjoys the camaraderie and floor show of a sushi bar should stop by this popular restaurant in the heart of Portland's Old Town. Solo diners can sit at the grill bar and watch the cooks mesquite-broil thick seafood steaks, beefsteaks, and chops. The flames leap and dance; the steaks sizzle. What a show! You'll know you've found the right place when you see the window full of artfully arranged fresh seafood steaks. In the bar, you can listen to excellent jazz recordings and share an intimate moment with someone special. Though the menu is short compared with those of other nearby seafood restaurants, Opus Too makes up for this inadequacy by grilling your order to perfection and then offering you a choice of eight different sauces to accompany your meal.

RAFATI'S ON THE WATERFRONT, 25 SW Salmon St. Tel. 503/248-9305.

Cuisine: SEAFOOD/STEAKS. **Reservations:** Highly recommended.
$ Prices: Appetizers $5–$7; main dishes $14–$20. AE, MC, V.
Open: Lunch Mon–Fri 11:30am–2pm; dinner Mon–Thurs 5:30–9pm, Fri–Sat 5:30–10pm, Sun 4:30–8:30pm.

Popular with executives and other business types, this small restaurant overlooking Waterfront Park prides itself on its award-winning wine list, excellent service, and well-prepared steaks and seafood. The steaks are of only the finest corn-fed, dry-aged beef, and the seafood, lamb, and veal are of equal quality and freshness.

The specialty of the house is flame broiling over mesquite

charcoal. With this in mind, you might try Alaskan jumbo scallops, Stilton and blue cheese stuffed filet mignon, raspberry teriyaki chicken, or any of the other mouthwatering offerings. And Rafati's seafood paella, though not mesquite-broiled, is an outstanding mélange of fresh flavors from the sea. For dessert, there are tempting seasonal fruit tarts that are outstanding. Be sure to peruse the extensive wine list, which features dozens of local, California, and imported wines.

REGIONS, 53 NW First Ave. Tel. 503/223-5033.
　　Cuisine: INTERNATIONAL. **Reservations:** Highly recommended.
$ Prices: Appetizers $3–$6; main dishes $8–$18. AE, CB, DC, DISC, MC, V.
　　Open: Lunch Tues–Fri 11:30am–2:30pm; dinner Wed–Sat 5:30–9:30pm.
　　Much praise has been lavished on Regions and chef/owner Mark Ross since the restaurant opened, and hopefully this outstanding new dining establishment will be able to make a go of it. The high-ceilinged, plank-floored room is very open and Spartanly decorated, which allows diners to concentrate on the superb meals. Ross has described his cuisine as "new American eclectic" because his influences come from all over the world.

The menu changes daily and takes up only a single sheet of paper, with perhaps a choice of eight appetizers and eight main dishes. On my recent visit, there was a sparklingly fresh salad of organic greens and lettuces with a shallot-and-grapefruit vinaigrette that shouted summer. The salad of three roasted peppers with capers was also both colorful and flavorful, the capers acting as a piquant counterpoint to the sweetness of the peppers. The grilled black cod with leeks, water chestnuts, tomatillos, and garlic served with Cambazola cheese was a classic example of Ross's eclectic flavor combinations jumping from France to China to Mexico all in the same bite. Desserts, prepared fresh daily by the restaurant's pastry chef, are every bit the equal of the rest of the menu.

RINGSIDE WEST, 2165 W. Burnside St. Tel. 503/223-1513.
　　Cuisine: STEAKS. **Reservations:** Recommended.
$ Prices: Appetizers $3–$8; steaks $11–$20; seafood main dishes $15–$32. AE, MC, V.
　　Open: Dinner only, Mon–Sat 5pm–12:30am, Sun 4–11:30pm.
Stop a native on the street and ask where to get the best steak in town and you will invariably be pointed in the direction of the Ringside. Though boxing is the main theme of the restaurant, the name delivers a two-fisted pun as well, referring to the incomparable onion rings that should be an integral part of any meal here. Have your rings with a side order of one of their perfectly cooked steaks for a real knockout meal.

There is also a Ringside East at 14021 Northeast Glisan Street (tel. 503/255-0750), on Portland's east side, with the same menu. It's open for breakfast daily from 7:30 to 10:30am; for lunch Monday through Friday from 11:30am to 2:30pm; and for dinner daily from 4 to midnight.

MODERATE

ALEXIS RESTAURANT, 215 W. Burnside St. Tel. 503/224-8577.
   Cuisine: GREEK. **Reservations:** Recommended.
$ **Prices:** Appetizers $3.50–$14; main dishes $9–$14. AE, DC, DISC, MC, V.
   Open: Lunch Mon–Fri 11:30am–2pm; dinner Mon–Thurs 5–10pm, Fri and Sat 5–11pm, Sun 4:30–9pm.

   Alexis is a classic Greek taverna, and the crowds keep it packed as much for the great food as for the fun atmosphere. On the weekends there's belly dancing and live music, and if you happen to be in town on March 25, you can help Alexis celebrate Greek Independence Day with a rousing big party.
   The menu has all your Greek favorites, but there is no need to read beyond the appetizer section. Of course, the main dishes are good, but the appetizers are out of this world. The not-to-be-missed list includes saganaki (pan-fried cheese flamed with ouzo), kalamarakia (perfectly fried squid), octopus, and the tart and creamy avgolemono soup. Accompany these with Alexis's own fresh breads (so good they're sold in grocery stores), and wash it all down with a bottle of Domestika wine for a meal beyond compare.

B. MOLOCH/HEATHMAN BAKERY & PUB, 901 SW Salmon St. Tel. 503/227-5700.
   Cuisine: NORTHWEST. **Reservations:** Not accepted.

Ⓕ FROMMER'S SMART TRAVELER: RESTAURANTS

1. Eat your main meal at lunch, when prices are lower. You can eat at some of the city's best restaurants and try Northwest cuisine for substantially less than what it would cost at dinner.
2. Always ask the price of daily specials; they are almost always several dollars more expensive than the highest-priced main dish on the regular menu.
3. Eat early, between 5 and 7pm. Some restaurants offer sunset dinner specials at greatly reduced prices (and you aren't likely to have to wait as long).
4. Make reservations whenever possible. Even at lunchtime, downtown restaurants fill up. If there is someplace where you particularly want to eat, don't risk being disappointed.
5. Pay attention to how much alcohol you drink; even local wines and beers can be expensive.
6. Eat ethnic—there are lots of good inexpensive Asian restaurants all over the city.

$ Prices: Salads $3.75–$7.50; main dishes $6.50–$9. AE, DC, DISC, MC, V.
Open: Mon–Thurs 7am–11pm, Fri 7am–midnight, Sat 8am–midnight, Sun 8am–11pm.

At B. Moloch, corporate climbers and bicycle messengers with spiked green hair rub shoulders, quaff microbrews, and chow down on creative wood-oven pizzas. Get here before the downtown offices let out or you won't get a seat. The atmosphere is bright and noisy amid an industrial decor softened by colorful images of salmon.

Ostensibly, this is the bakery for the Heathman Hotel dining room a block away, and to that end a cavernous wood-burning brick oven was installed. Luckily, someone had the idea to bake a few pizzas in that amazing brick oven, and today those very nouvelle pizzas are the mainstay of the menu here. If you're in the mood for pizza like you'll never get from Mario's back home, try the pie with smoked lamb, feta cheese, spinach, and smoke-dried tomatoes. Anyone wishing to sample the creativity of Northwest chefs can also do so here without spending the small fortune it costs to eat in the hotel's main dining room. Ravioli al forno with smoked salmon, herbs, and cream, or perhaps a smoked-lamb enchilada, will give you a good idea of what Northwest cooking is all about. You have to place your order at the counter here, but a waitress will bring the food to your table.

Though the name B. Moloch is rarely used by people in the know, you might be interested to learn that the restaurant takes its name from the 19th-century French artist who painted the caricatures that hang behind the counter. Next door to the restaurant, on the other side of a wall of glass, is a microbrewery. You can sit in the bar here and watch the brewers at work while sipping one of their beers.

BUSH GARDEN, 900 SW Morrison St. Tel. 503/226-7181.

Cuisine: JAPANESE. **Reservations:** Highly recommended.
$ Prices: Appetizers $4–$8; main dishes $10–$25; lunches $5.25–$11. AE, CB, DC, MC, V.
Open: Lunch Mon–Fri 11:30am–1:45pm; dinner Mon–Sat 5–10pm, Sun 5–9pm.

Japanese businessmen are delighted when their companies send them on assignment to Portland. Why? Because here they can get Japanese food that's as good as that back home, and it costs far less. Groups, and anyone seeking privacy and a special experience, should have their meal in one of the traditional tatami rooms with the shoji rice-paper-screen walls. If you can't sit cross-legged through dinner, ask to be seated in the Western-style dining room, or take a stool at the sushi bar.

The moment you step through the door here, enticing aromas greet you—the outstanding salmon teriyaki, perhaps, or the delicate tempura. If there are two or more of you, you should definitely opt for one of the special dinners. Shabu-shabu is my favorite; you get to do the cooking yourself. For the ultimate Japanese banquet, order the kaiseki dinner, which includes two appetizers, sushi or sashimi, tempura, fish, beef, and dessert.

DAN & LOUIS OYSTER BAR, 208 SW Ankeny St. Tel. 503/227-5906.

Cuisine: SEAFOOD. **Reservations:** Recommended.

$ **Prices:** Appetizers $2.50–$7.50; main dishes $5.75–$11. AE, CB, DC, MC, V.

Open: Sun–Thurs 11am–10pm, Fri–Sat 11am–midnight.

S Dan & Louis has been serving up succulent oysters since 1919. The oysters come from Dan and Louis's own oyster farm on Yaquina Bay, Oregon—they don't come much fresher than this. Half the fun of eating here is enjoying the old-fashioned surroundings. The front counter is stacked high with candies and cigars much as it would have been in the 1920s. The walls are covered with founder Louis Wachsmuth's own collection of old and unusual plates. Beer steins line the shelves, and nautical odds and ends are everywhere.

Louis began his restaurant business serving only two items—oyster stew and oyster cocktails. These two are still on the menu, and as good today as they were 80 years ago. The main courses are simple, no-nonsense seafood dishes, mostly fried, but the prices are great. Popular with families, Dan & Louis serves no alcohol, but you can get alcohol-free beer and wine.

EDDIE LEE'S, 409 SW Second Ave. Tel. 503/228-1874.

Cuisine: NORTHWEST. **Reservations:** For five or more only.

$ **Prices:** Appetizers $4.50–$7.50; main dishes $8.50–$14; lunch $4.50–$9.95. AE, CB, DC, MC, V.

Open: Mon–Thurs 11am–10pm, Fri 11am–11pm, Sat 5–11pm.

★ For trendy meals at down-to-earth prices, try this casual café on the edge of Old Town. Located in two old storefronts, the dining rooms are separated by one of Portland's most unusual shops. Battered and painted hardwood floors, a fake black-marble counter, and black-and-chrome bar stools will have you thinking you've stepped into a 100-year-old diner. A second glance will take in the pale-blue-and-lavender trim, bold red-and-blue director's chairs, and wall stencils way up near the high ceiling. The contemporary art on the walls is for sale, if you happen to see something you like. In summer, there are a few tables out on the sidewalk.

Eddie Lee's version of Northwest cuisine includes such offerings as grilled pork loin medallions with orange, onion, and Gewürztraminer marmalade; egg rolls filled with sun-dried tomatoes, goat cheese, prawns, and vegetables; and rack of lamb rubbed with garlic and cardamon, stuffed with sun-dried tomatoes, and finished with pancetta-apple-mint relish.

HUBER'S, 411 SW Third Ave. Tel. 503/228-5686.

Cuisine: CONTINENTAL. **Reservations:** Recommended.

$ **Prices:** Appetizers $2–$5; main dishes $7–$15.

Open: Lunch Mon–Fri 11am–4pm; dinner Mon–Thurs 5–10pm, Fri–Sat 5–11pm.

Portland's oldest restaurant first opened its doors to the public in 1879, though it didn't move to its present location until 1911. You'll find this very traditional establishment tucked inside the Oregon Pioneer Building. It's easy to miss, since the only sign for Huber's is the name in gold lettering on the building's front door. Down a quiet hallway you'll come to a surprising little room with vaulted stained-glass ceiling, Philippine mahogany paneling, and the original brass cash register. The house specialty has been turkey since the day the first Huber's opened, so there really isn't any question of what to order, even though the menu now features a wide selection of continental and American classics. You can gobble down turkey sandwiches, turkey cordon bleu, turkey Delmonico, turkey nouvelle, or turkey mushroom pie. The menu even has wine recommendations to accompany your different turkey dishes. Lunch prices are lower, with the turkey sandwich the star of the hour.

HUNAN, 515 SW Broadway, Morgan's Alley. Tel. 503/224-8063.

Cuisine: CHINESE. **Reservations:** For five or more only.

$ Prices: Appetizers $2.50–$5.75; main dishes $6–$24; lunch main dishes $4.50–$6. MC, V.

Open: Mon–Thurs 11am–9pm, Fri–Sat 11am–10:30pm, Sun 4:30–9pm. **Parking:** SW 10th Ave. and Washington St., with refund after 6pm.

Located at the end of Morgan's Alley, which is lined with interesting little shops and boutiques, is one of Portland's most reliable Chinese restaurants. Hunan exudes a quiet sophistication. Saltwater and freshwater aquariums bubble and glow in the cool darkness, and ivory statues are displayed in wall niches.

Although the menu lists such appetizing main dishes as champagne chicken and Peking duck, there are two items that should absolutely not be missed. General Tso's chicken is both crispy and chewy at the same time, and the succulent sauce has just the right touch of fire. Lover's eggplant is "dedicated to those of our guests with romantic inclinations as well as to all genuine lovers of eggplant," states the menu. With an introduction like that, how can you pass it by? Beautifully presented and prepared chunks of creamy eggplant are truly an eggplant lover's dream come true.

LAMTHONG TOO, 213 SW Broadway. Tel. 503/223-4214.

Cuisine: THAI. **Reservations:** Recommended for dinner.

$ Prices: Main dishes $6.50–$11; lunch specials $4.75. MC, V.

Open: Lunch Mon–Fri 11am–2:30pm; dinner Mon–Thurs 5–9pm, Fri–Sat 5–10pm.

For years, if you wanted to eat at the best Thai restaurant in Portland, you had to drive out to Beaverton in the city's western suburbs. Today, however, you need go no farther than Broadway, where Lamthong Too serves the same delicious and spicy meals that are so popular at the original. If you make reservations, ask for a table in the Thai-style dining area on the second floor. You'll be seated at a low table, with a pillow to make you comfortable.

My favorite dish is the shrimp with fresh basil leaves and chilis. It has just the right combination of bright and spicy flavors. The chili fish (halibut) is another must, and for sheer drama there is the royal halibut cooked in a herb broth and served over a flame.

NEWPORT BAY RESTAURANT, 0425 SW Montgomery St. Tel. 503/227-3474.

Cuisine: SEAFOOD. **Reservations:** Recommended.

$ Prices: Appetizers $3–$7.50; main dishes $10.50–$30; lunches and light main dishes $4–$9.50. AE, CB, DC, DISC, MC, V.

Open: Mon–Thurs 11am–11pm, Fri–Sat 11am–midnight, Sun 9am–11pm (brunch 9am–3pm).

Though there are Newport Bay restaurants all over Portland, this one has the best location. It's in the middle of the Willamette River. Well, not actually in the middle, kind of to one side. If you feel this building rocking while you dine, it's no surprise—it's floating. And if you happen to have your own boat, you can just tie up to the dock. Located in the marina at Portland's beautiful RiverPlace shopping-and-dining complex, the Newport Bay provides excellent views of the river and the city skyline, especially from the deck. Inside, the atmosphere is cheery and the service is efficient.

Nearly everything on the menu has some sort of seafood in it—even the quiche, salads, and pastas. Main dishes are mostly straightforward and well prepared, nothing too fancy. The short wine list focuses on West Coast wines at reasonable prices. Be sure to save room for the sour-cream-and-raisin pie!

PLAINFIELD'S MAYUR, 852 SW 21st Ave. Tel. 503/223-2095.

Cuisine: INDIAN. **Reservations:** Recommended.

$ Prices: Appetizers $2–$5; main dishes $9–$14. AE, CB, DC, MC, V.

Open: Lunch Mon–Fri 11:30am–1:30pm; dinner daily 5–11pm.

In the words of a friend, "With an Indian restaurant like Mayur's, who needs anything else?" Located in an elegant old Portland home, this is in fact the city's premier Indian restaurant. You can watch the cooks bake breads and succulent tandoori chicken in the only tandoor show kitchen in Oregon. The atmosphere is refined, with bone china and European crystal, and the service is informative and gracious. In addition to the four floors of dining rooms inside, there is a patio out back.

Every dish on the menu is perfectly spiced so that the complex flavors and aromas of Indian cuisine shine through. Be sure to ask them to go easy on the chili peppers if you can't handle spicy food. A tray of condiments accompanies each meal, and consider yourself very lucky if it happens to include the tiny stuffed chili peppers that fire-eaters adore. The dessert list is also an unexpected and pleasant surprise. The hot masala milk, made with their own cardamom liqueur, is ambrosial, and the flan recipe is coveted by a famous food magazine. Save room!

A TOUCH OF CLASS/WESTERN CULINARY INSTITUTE, 1316 SW 13th Ave. Tel. 503/223-2245, or toll free 800/666-0312.

Cuisine: CONTINENTAL. **Reservations:** Imperative.

$ Prices: Five-course lunch $7.95; six- or seven-course dinner $15–$18. MC, V.

Open: Lunch Tues–Fri 11:30am–1pm; dinner Tues–Fri 6–8pm.

⑤ If you happen to be a frugal gourmet whose palate is more sophisticated than your wallet can afford, you'll want to schedule a meal here. The dining room serves five- to seven-course gourmet meals prepared by advanced students at prices even a budget traveler can afford.

Meals are served in a quiet dining room done in pleasing pastels. The decor is modern and unassuming, and the students who wait on you are eager to please. For each course you have a choice among two to five offerings. A sample dinner menu might begin with consommé of Brunoise, followed by pâté of rabbit, a pear sorbet, grilled mahi mahi with citrus lime vin blanc, Chinese salad with smoked salmon, and divine chocolate-mousse cake. Remember, that's all for less than $20! Reservations are strongly recommended, so you don't miss out on this treat. The five-course lunch for only $7.95 is an even better deal.

UNCLE CHEN CHINESE RESTAURANT, 529 SW Third Ave. Tel. 503/248-1199.

Cuisine: CHINESE. **Reservations:** Recommended on weekends.

$ Prices: Appetizers $2.50–$6.75; main dishes $6.50–$16; lunch specials $5. AE, DC, DISC, MC, V.

Open: Mon–Thurs 11am–9:30pm, Fri 11am–10pm, Sat 5–10pm, Sun 5–9:30pm.

It's worth dining at Uncle Chen simply for the fascinating decor. From outside, the building looks like any other Old Town restoration, and the unassuming entrance hall does nothing to dispel that image. However, follow your friendly waiter to a table in the back and you step into a different world. The look here can only be called industrial al fresco. The restaurant has converted an old alleyway into a courtyard dining area with a skylight 10 stories above the tables. Somewhere in the middle hangs a dragon kite. Granite pillars, miniature streetlamps, and an exposed brick wall complete the picture.

Luckily, the menu is also outstanding. You'll find mouthwatering selections from the six culinary regions of China. I encourage you to try one of the special dinners of whole fish. You can have it Hunan style, in spicy bean sauce, or steamed with fermented black beans. You can also order a family dinner for from one to six people. Though not as extravagant as the restaurant's imperial banquet, it is still a substantial repast.

ZEN RESTAURANT, 910 SW Salmon St. Tel. 503/222-3056.

Cuisine: JAPANESE. **Reservations:** Imperative if you want a tatami room.

$ Prices: Appetizers $2.50–$15; main dishes $9–$40. AE, CB, DC, MC, V.

Open: Lunch Mon–Fri 11:30am–2pm; dinner Mon–Sat 5–10pm.

Step through the door here and you'll know you are about to have a dining experience. A rock garden just inside helps guests forget the busy streets outside. For further meditation and contemplation on the Japanese aesthetic, there are ikebana flower arrangements. Step into a tatami room, pull the shoji behind you, and the transformation is complete—you're in Japan.

When in this part of Japan, there's only one meal to order and that's the kaiseki dinner, a Japanese gourmet feast that requires 24 hours' advance notice to prepare. Among the numerous courses offered, you might delight in shrimp wrapped in plum leaves, a delicately flavored clear broth with a few choice vegetables, a bit of sushi, perhaps some succulent noodles, and of course fresh fish, thinly sliced beef, and tempura. Each serving is a work of art, and an evening spent here will soothe your body and soul.

BUDGET

FONG CHONG, 301 NW Fourth Ave. Tel. 503/220-0235.
   Cuisine: CHINESE. **Reservations:** Not taken.
$ Prices: Appetizers $3–$5.50; main dishes $4–$10; dim sum meals, under $10. No credit cards.
   Open: Mon–Thurs 10:30am–9pm, Fri–Sun 10:30am–10pm; dim sum 11am–3pm.

Some of the most popular Chinese restaurants in Portland are in grocery stores, including this one. Don't worry, you won't be eating between the aisles; the restaurant gets its own room. Although most of the food here is above average, the dim sum is the best in the city. Flag down a passing cart and point to the most appetizing-looking little dishes. Be careful or you might end up with a plate of chicken feet. At the end of the meal, your bill is calculated by the number of plates on your table.

HAMBURGER MARY'S, 840 SW Park Ave. Tel. 503/223-0900.

Ⓕ FROMMER'S COOL FOR KIDS
Restaurants

Brasserie Montmartre *(see p. 196)* Though this is more of an adult restaurant, there are paper tablecloths and crayons to keep kids entertained and even a strolling magician most evenings.

Dan & Louis Oyster Bar *(see p. 205)* You'll think you're eating in the hold of an old sailing ship, and all the fascinating stuff on the walls will keep kids entertained.

Hamburger Mary's *(p. 209)* Your kids can play with the Etch-a-Sketch, while they wait for the omelet they've created from the 22 possible ingredients. This place serves one of the best hamburgers in Portland—always a perennial favorite with little ones—at a price that won't bust your budget.

Cuisine: BURGERS. **Reservations:** Not taken.

$ Prices: $4.50–$10. AE, CB, DC, MC, V.

Open: Daily 7am–2am.

As the name implies, this is a place to get a hamburger—one of the best hamburgers in Portland. It's thick and juicy, piled high with crisp lettuce and ripe tomatoes, and served on a whole-wheat bun. You can't miss this little place—a tiny building surrounded by skyscrapers. Step inside and you enter a crowded room where the walls and ceiling are covered with everything from a rusting Sousaphone to an upside-down floor lamp. Grab a table, snag the Etch-a-Sketch, and sink back into childhood fantasies. Stop by in the morning (or whenever you're ready for breakfast) and create your own omelet from the list of 22 possible ingredients.

2. NORTHWEST PORTLAND

EXPENSIVE

L'AUBERGE, 2601 NW Vaughn St. Tel. 503/223-3302.

Cuisine: FRENCH. **Reservations:** Imperative.

$ Prices: Fixed-price dinner—three courses $28, six courses $40. AE, CB, DC, DISC, MC, V.

Open: Dinner only, Mon–Thurs 5pm–midnight, Fri–Sat 5pm–1am, Sun 5:30pm–midnight.

Located at the edge of the industrial district, this little country cottage offers some of the best French cuisine in Portland and has done so for many years. The restaurant is divided into the main dining room and the lounge and deck area, where an à la carte international-bistro menu is available. On Sunday nights the French flavor is forsaken in favor of succulent ribs, and a movie is shown in the bar. A more formal atmosphere reigns in the main dining room, even on Sunday nights. A fireplace and a few antiques create a homey feel, and etched glass between booths lends an air of sophistication. A few works of contemporary art add drama to the setting.

The fixed-price dinners feature meals with a French origin but translated with a Northwest accent. If you happen to be dining downstairs, be sure to stop by the bar first to have a look at the delectable morsels on the dessert tray. Dinners start with bread and pâté, followed by a soup or fish course, sorbet, and salad. There are always four choices of main dishes, such as filet mignon with anchovie sauce or shrimp with leeks in a port-wine-and-ginger sauce. This is all topped off with a choice from that dessert tray.

CAJUN CAFE & BISTRO, 2074 NW Lovejoy St. Tel. 503/227-0227.

Cuisine: CAJUN. **Reservations:** A good idea at lunch, highly recommended for dinner.

$ Prices: Appetizers $2.75–$8; main dishes $14–$20; main dishes at lunch $7–$10. AE, CB, DC, MC, V.

Open: Lunch Mon–Fri 11:30am–2:30pm; dinner Sun–Thurs

5:30–9:30pm, Fri–Sat 5:30–10:30pm; limited menu available all day.

The Cajun Café sits on a busy corner in the fashionable Nob Hill district. Out front, there are a few tables for taking advantage of summer sunshine; inside, the decor is bright even on a dreary winter day. The menu is long and changes daily, and there's a glossary of terms for those unfamiliar with Cajun cooking. From this glossary you learn that andouille is a "fiery smoked pork and potato sausage," and that a pirogue is a "narrow flat-bottomed dugout canoe." Put the two together and you get shrimp-and-andouille creole in an eggplant pirogue. Delicious!

DELPHINA'S, 2112 NW Kearney St. Tel. 503/221-1195.
   Cuisine: ITALIAN. **Reservations:** Highly recommended; required for the Back Kitchen Dinner.
$ Prices: Appetizers and soups $3.50–$7.50; pastas $10–$12; main dishes $13–$18. AE, DC, MC, V.
   Open: Lunch Mon–Fri 11:30am–2:30pm; dinner daily 5–11pm.

Long a Nob Hill mainstay, Delphina's offers excellent Italian food in a casual neighborhood-bistro atmosphere. The tile floors, exposed brick walls, and café curtains on the windows all contribute to the comfortable feeling, while smiling, friendly service makes you feel right at home. Be sure to notice the colander lamps hung from the ceiling.

Northern Italian fare predominates here, but southern Italian and even Pacific Northwest manage to sneak onto the menu. You might want to try the Oregon rabbit, which is prepared a different way each week, or a tenderloin of pork sautéed in a sauce of juniper berries, garlic, white wine, and butter. The latest rage at Delphina's is the Back Kitchen Dinner for parties of eight people. You get to dine in the bustling kitchen, where the chef surprises you with a multicourse menu that your Italian mother-in-law would envy.

ZEFIRO RESTAURANT & BAR, 500 NW 21st Ave. Tel. 503/226-3394.
   Cuisine: MEDITERRANEAN. **Reservations:** Imperative.
$ Prices: Appetizers $4–$7; main dishes $10–$16. AE, MC, V.
   Open: Lunch Mon–Fri 11:30am–2:30pm; dinner Mon–Thurs 6–10pm, Fri 6–11pm, Sat 5:30–11pm.

Trendy both in decor and food preparation, Zefiro caught on with the Nob Hill elite almost immediately after it opened. Unpainted fiberboard walls and tiny black-matte halogen lamps hanging from the ceiling give it a quintessential contemporary urban chic. With two walls of glass fronting onto narrow sidewalks, you may feel a bit as if you were dining in a fishbowl, but no one seems to mind. Wait staff, though dressed in formalwear, provides very casual service.

The menu can only be categorized as Mediterranean, with Italian predominating. However, Moroccan, Mexican, and even Thai influences creep in. This is the sort of place where you have to ask the waiter to define many of the unfamiliar menu terms. Be sure to try the fragrant bowl of warm polenta with marjoram and Mascarpone for an appetizer. The grilled chicken basted with a Moroccan sauce of honey, cumin, and cinnamon and served with couscous and spicy sautéed zucchini makes an unusual blend of the sweet and the spicy. For dessert the fresh-fruit sorbets served with fresh-baked cookies are smooth, flavorful, and refreshing.

MODERATE

CASA-U-BETCHA, 612 NW 21st Ave. Tel. 503/227-3887.
Cuisine: MEXICAN. **Reservations:** Recommended.
$ Prices: Appetizers $2.50–$7; main dishes $6–$14.
Open: Lunch Mon–Fri 11:30am–2:30pm; dinner Sun–Thurs 5–10pm, Fri–Sat 5–11pm.

★ If you like your restaurant to be a work of art, slide into one of the wacky industrial-chic booths at this trendy nouvelle Mexican restaurant. Garishly painted walls, a huge snake sculpture, flashing chile pepper lights, and metal-pipe cacti create a real "scene" at Casa-U-Betcha. Located on an up-and-coming street with fringe art galleries, a repertory movie theater, and a 1950s furniture store, this is Portland's hippest Mexican restaurant. Big baskets of regular and blue corn chips with bowls of red and green salsa wait on every metal-topped table. I find the appetizers menu so fascinating that I usually just make a meal of a couple of these and skip the combo dinners and other Mexican main dishes. My favorite appetizer is the Mexican sushi made with tortillas, smoked salmon, black beans, jicama, guacamole, and wasabi. The soy-ginger-serrano dipping sauce that comes with it is a real knock-out.

BUDGET

ROSE'S RESTAURANT AND DELICATESSEN, 315 NW 23rd Ave. Tel. 503/227-5181. Also at 12329 NE Glisan Street (tel. 503/254-6545) and in the Beaverton Town Square in Beaverton (tel. 503/643-4287).
Cuisine: DELI. **Reservations:** Suggested for dinner.
$ Prices: Main dishes $5–$9; desserts $3–$4. CB, DC, MC, V.
Open: Mon–Thurs 7am–11pm, Fri 7am–midnight, Sat 8am–midnight, Sun 8am–11pm.

Dieters should not step through the door of this famous Portland deli. Immediately inside is a large counter displaying the cakes, sweet rolls, and pastries that have made Rose's famous. It's not that the desserts here are any better than anywhere else (although they are delicious), it's just that the portions are monstrous. A cinnamon roll is roughly 6 inches by 4 inches by 4 inches! Never mind saving room for dessert, save room for the meal. Rose's is also a New York–style kosher deli with a huge selection of main dishes and giant sandwiches.

3. SOUTHEAST PORTLAND

EXPENSIVE

DIGGER O'DELL'S RESTAURANT AND OYSTER BAR, 532 SE Grand Ave. Tel. 503/238-6996.

Cuisine: CAJUN. **Reservations:** Recommended.

$ Prices: Appetizers $3.50–$8.50; main dishes $14–$20. AE, CB, DC, MC, V.

Open: Lunch Mon–Fri 11:15am–4pm; dinner Sun–Thurs 5–10pm, Fri–Sat 5–11pm.

People have been dying to get into this place for years. In fact, when these historic buildings known as the Barber Block were erected in 1890, they housed Barber & Hill, Undertakers & Embalmers. Some 50 years later the buildings housed the Nickelodeon Theatre, a popular vaudeville venue. Today the restaurant's name recalls the building's varied past in its reference to the Irish gravedigger from the 1940s radio show "The Life of Riley."

Beautifully restored, the Barber Block is now home to Portland's first, and still most popular, Cajun restaurant. The interior decor is elegantly Victorian, as befits a building of this age. A sweeping staircase leads up to a mezzanine dining area. Gumbo, jambalaya, blackened fish and steak, shrimp étouffée—all your favorites are here, prepared with fresh Northwest ingredients. Digger's is also an oyster bar, and you'd be remiss if you didn't start your meal with fresh Northwest oysters. Thursday through Saturday nights, there is live music in the lounge.

GENOA, 2832 SE Belmont St. Tel. 503/238-1464.

Cuisine: ITALIAN. **Reservations:** Required.

$ Prices: Fixed-price four-course dinner $32; seven course dinner $40. AE, CB, DC, MC, V.

Open: Dinner only, Mon–Sat 6–9:30pm.

Without a doubt, this is the best Italian restaurant in Portland, and with only 10 tables, it's also one of the smallest dining spots in town. Everything is made fresh in the kitchen, from the breads to the luscious desserts that are temptingly displayed on a maple burl table just inside the front door. This is an ideal setting for a romantic dinner, and service is personal, as only a restaurant of this size can provide.

The fixed-price menu changes every couple of weeks. On my recent visit the evening meal started with an appetizer plate of baby artichokes, focaccia topped with roasted garlic, and chickpeas marinated in olive oil, red-wine vinegar, garlic, black olives, red onions, and herbs. The soup was a satisfying purée of green peas, spinach, onions, and shallots in chicken stock with crème fraîche. The pasta course was tonnarelli alla putanesca (a favorite of mine), which was rich and fiery. Next came a fish course of succulent and crunchy oysters in marjoram-flavored bread crumbs. I passed up the salmon with saffron and orange zest and the pork tenderloin with a sweet-and-sour sauce in favor of scallops of turkey breast with morels, prosciutto, and shallots in a sauce of dry Madeira and cream. For dessert I had an extravagant chocolate hazelnut torte. To top it all off, I savored a few fresh local strawberries.

MODERATE

BREAD & INK CAFE, 3610 SE Hawthorne St. Tel. 503/239-4756.

Cuisine: NORTHWEST. **Reservations:** Recommended.

$ Prices: Appetizers $5–$7.50; main dishes $8–$14; Sun brunch $11.50. MC, V.

Open: Breakfast Mon–Fri 7–11:30am, Sat 8am–2pm; lunch Mon–Fri 11:30am–3pm; dinner Mon–Thurs 5:30–9:30pm, Fri–Sat 5:30–10pm; Sun brunch 9am–2pm.

Bread & Ink has been voted one of the best restaurants in Oregon, but don't expect a stuffy atmosphere here. This is a casual neighborhood café, bright and airy, with pen-and-ink artwork on the walls and fresh flowers on every table.

Every meal here is carefully and imaginatively prepared using fresh Northwest ingredients. The last time I visited, I had a tender chicken breast in a subtle cream sauce with lemon, fresh herbs, and parmesan cheese. Desserts are a mainstay of Bread & Ink's loyal patrons, so don't pass them by. The Yiddish Sunday brunch is one of the most filling brunches in the city.

INDIGINE, 3725 SE Division St. Tel. 503/238-1470.
Cuisine: INDIAN/INTERNATIONAL. **Reservations:** Required.
$ Prices: Appetizers $3.50; main dishes $14–$18; Sat–night Indian feast $25. MC, V.
Open: Dinner only, Tues–Sat 5:30–10pm.

At Indigine you can take your tastebuds dancing through tantalizing flavors the likes of which you may never have encountered before. Step through the door of this brown house with a red roof, red trim, and a riotous little flower and herb garden and you are halfway into the kitchen, which gives you the distinct feel of dining at a friend's house. If only all my friends could cook this well.

The menu at Indigine is eclectic, with Indian, Mexican, French, and American offerings during the week and an extravagant Indian feast on Saturday evenings. In what must be the greatest understatement on any Portland menu, the regular meals are called "Simple Dinners." These begin with freshly baked rolls and a salad basket of definitively fresh vegetables, usually accompanied by a vegetable dip such as herbed guacamole. When the irresistibly tempting appetizer tray comes around, keep in mind that dinner portions here are large enough for two people. During the week you can sample some of Indigine's flavorful Indian cuisine by ordering either the tandoori dinner or the vegetarian sampler. On the other hand, the creamy seafood enchilada perfectly mixes cheeses with shrimp and scallops so fresh you can almost smell the salt air. Before it's too late, stop and save room for one of the luscious desserts, such as ginger cheesecake. If you have never had Indian chai (tea), don't miss this opportunity—it's flavored with cardamom.

4. NORTHEAST PORTLAND

MODERATE

DER RHEINLANDER, 5035 NE Sandy Blvd. Tel. 503/249-0507.

Cuisine: GERMAN. **Reservations:** Suggested.
$ **Prices:** Complete meals $10–$15; early dinners $7–$10. AE, MC, V.
Open: Mon–Sat 4:30–10pm, Sun 3:30–9pm; Sun brunch 10am–2pm.

There's no mistaking this restaurant. It's the only building around with a Black Forest cottage facade and polka music blaring from a loudspeaker out front. For more than 25 years, Der Rheinlander has been known as Portland's most fun-filled restaurant. Let the singing waiters and strolling musicians in lederhosen entertain you while you feast on good old-fashioned German cooking served in belt-loosening portions.

If you can put together a group of six or more people, order the Family Feast. It's served family style, so everyone can have as much as he or she wants. If you don't have a family, try the sampler platter; it has most of the same items. Early-evening dinners cost several dollars less than those served later, and the crowds are waiting at the door at opening time.

5. SPECIALTY DINING

LOCAL FAVORITES

STANICH'S TEN-TIL-ONE TAVERN, 4915 NE Freemont St. Tel. 503/281-2322. Also at 5627 SW Kelly St. Tel. 503/246-5040.
Cuisine: BURGERS. **Reservations:** A necessity at lunch.
$ **Prices:** $2.50–$4. Cash only.
Open: Mon–Sat 11am–11:30pm. (Kelly St., Mon–Thurs 11am–10:30pm, Fri–Sat 11am–11:30pm).

According to Portlanders and the local press, the best burger in town is to be had at Stanich's, a neighborhood tavern that has been serving state governors and a regular lunchtime crowd since 1949. The menu features mostly hamburgers, and Stanich's self-proclaimed "world's greatest hamburger"—a cheeseburger with fried egg, ham, bacon, and all the trimmings—is definitely not for the faint of heart.

HOTEL DINING

ESPLANADE RESTAURANT, RiverPlace Alexis Hotel, 1510 SW Harbor Way. Tel. 503/295-6166.
Cuisine: NORTHWEST. **Reservations:** Essential.
$ **Prices:** Appetizers $5.50–$10; main courses $17–$29. AE, CB, DC, MC, V.
Open: Breakfast Mon–Fri 6:30–10:30am, Sat 6:30–11am, Sun 6:30–10am; lunch Mon–Fri 11:30am–2:30pm; dinner daily 5:30–10pm; brunch Sun 11am–2:30pm.

The Esplanade, surrounded by the quietly sophisticated European-resort atmosphere of the RiverPlace Alexis Hotel, is one of the city's ritziest and finest restaurants. Understated elegance and expansive views of the marina and the city's bridges combine for a stunning setting. Even on the grayest day of Portland's long winter, the pale-yellow walls, colorful contemporary art, and huge flower arrangements will cheer you up.

However, it's the superb cuisine that is truly calculated to brighten your day. The Northwest is sturgeon country, and both the dense meat and the delicate caviar often show up on the menu. Of course, salmon also makes regular appearances, often prepared simply and served with a fragrant butter that lets the flavor of the fish shine through. In summer you can enjoy a salad of wild and gathered greens.

HEATHMAN RESTAURANT AND BAR, The Heathman Hotel, SW Broadway at Salmon St. Tel. 503/241-4100.

Cuisine: NORTHWEST/CONTINENTAL. **Reservations:** Imperative.

$ Prices: Appetizers $5.50–$8.50; main dishes $15–$25. AE, CB, DC, MC, V.

Open: Breakfast Mon–Fri 6:30–11am, Sat 6:30am–noon, Sun 6:30am–3pm; lunch Mon–Fri 11am–2pm, Sat noon–2pm; dinner Sun–Thurs 5–10pm, Fri–Sat 5–11pm.

The Heathman continues to be one of the best restaurants in Portland. The menu changes seasonally, but one thing remains constant: The ingredients are the very freshest of Oregon and Northwest seafoods, meats, wild game, and produce. Small and bright, the restaurant exudes a bistro atmosphere. On the walls are Andy Warhol's Endangered Species—a rhino, zebra, lion, panda, and others—part of the Heathman's extensive collection of classic and contemporary art.

Glancing down the menu, you will detect many different influences—molé broiled pork tenderloin with pumpkin-seed-and-corn salsa, for example, and prawns and scallops sautéed with curry, basil, and baby bok choy—but every item displays a bit of Northwest influence. Curried Dungeness crab cakes with garden salsa and lemon beurre blanc start a meal off brightly, and the salad of herbs and organic greens with raspberry vinaigrette reflects the bounty of this region. Local fruits make their appearance in many of the rich desserts. In the bar, there are Northwest microbrewery beers on tap, while an extensive wine list spotlights Oregon wines.

THE LONDON GRILL, The Benson Hotel, SW Broadway at Oak St. Tel. 503/228-2000.

Cuisine: CONTINENTAL. **Reservations:** Essential.

$ Prices: Appetizers $5.75–$8.25; main dishes $18.50–$22.50; Sun brunch $15.95. AE, CB, DC, MC, V.

Open: Daily 6:30am–11pm; Sunday champagne brunch 9:30am–1pm.

Down in the basement of the luxurious Benson Hotel is one of Portland's top restaurants. Modeled after the original London Grill, which was a favorite with Queen Elizabeth I, it has a dark decor; a vaulted ceiling further enhances the wine-cellar feel of the room. Mahogany paneling reflects the glowing chandeliers, and on cold nights a fire is lit in the fireplace. Service by tuxedoed waiters is impeccable. Breakfast and lunch are both popular with business executives.

The chef emphasizes uncompromising gourmet meals. The ingredients are always fresh and of the highest quality, including many of the finest local fruits and vegetables. Steak Diane, prepared at your table, is always entertaining and delicious. If you have a craving for some imaginative Northwest cuisine, this restaurant should set your taste buds singing. Grilled squab with tangy blood-orange sauce and grilled swordfish with pineapple tomato salsa are two such main dishes. The Sunday champagne brunch is the most elegant in the city.

DINING WITH A VIEW

ALEXANDER'S, Portland Hilton, 921 SW Sixth Ave. Tel. 503/226-1611.
   Cuisine: CONTINENTAL. **Reservations:** Recommended.
$ **Prices:** Appetizers $3.50–$8.50; main dishes $17.50–$38; table d'hôte menu $29. AE, CB, DC, MC, V.
   Open: Dinner only, daily 5:30pm–midnight.

Way up on the 23rd floor of the Hilton is this excellent continental restaurant. Be sure to have a drink in the lounge, which looks out over the densely wooded West Hills. Move on to the dining room and you are treated to a view encompassing Mount Hood, the Willamette River, and downtown Portland. The entrance to the restaurant is past a wall of rough stones, which creates a rustic mountain resort atmosphere. However, lavender tones and flowers on the tables leave no doubt as to the sophisticated ambience at Alexander's.

Fresh seafood is the star on the menu, and you can choose from six fresh fish dishes, prepared either charbroiled, poached, or sautéed with lemon butter. There are also specialties such as salmon in orange sauce or poached with pear sauce. Breast of duck and breast of pheasant both make artful appearances as well. You'll be stopped in your tracks by the dessert tray by the front door. The combinations of chocolate and fresh fruits are gorgeous, and delicious.

ATWATER'S RESTAURANT AND LOUNGE, U.S. Bancorp Tower, 111 SW Fifth Ave. Tel. 503/275-3600.
   Cuisine: NORTHWEST. **Reservations:** Essential.
$ **Prices:** Appetizers $6–$10; main dishes $15–$26; fixed–price meals—$26 three courses, $35 five courses ($47 with wine); Sun brunch $18.50. AE, CB, DC, MC, V.
   Open: Dinner daily 5:30–10:30pm; Sun brunch 10am–3pm.

Atwater's whispers elegance from the moment you step off the elevator on the 30th floor. A rosy light suffuses the hall at sunset, and blond-wood trim fairly glows in the warm light. Oriental carpets on a blond-hardwood floor and large, dramatic flower arrangements on dark-wood tables add splashes of color throughout the restaurant. In the middle of the dining room is a glass-enclosed wine room that would put many wine shops to shame. Far below you are the Willamette River and Portland, and off in the distance stands Mount Hood.

Pacific Northwest cuisine is the specialty here, and it's done to perfection. The combinations of ingredients are unexpected and delectable. Roast breast and sausage of duckling with raspberry port sauce is one such combination. For an appetizer, you should indulge in the cured salmon with sturgeon caviar, asparagus, and a lemon-herb dressing.

RENE'S FIFTH AVENUE, 1300 SW Fifth Ave. Tel. 503/241-0712.
    Cuisine: CONTINENTAL. **Reservations:** Recommended.
$ Prices: $5–$7.50. MC, V.
    Open: Mon–Fri 11:30am–2:30pm.

Comfortable and elegant, this 21st-floor lunch spot is always crowded. Local businesspeople flock here more for the great view than for the food. However, the limited menu does offer daily specials and plenty of seafood. You won't find a view this good at better prices anywhere else in the city.

LIGHT, CASUAL, FAST FOOD

MACHEEZMO MOUSE, 723 SW Salmon St. Tel. 503/228-3491. Also at 811 NW 23rd Ave. (tel. 503/274-0500); 3553 SE Hawthorne Blvd. (tel. 503/232-6588); 1200 NE Broadway (tel. 503/249-0002); and in Pioneer Place (tel. 503/248-0917).
    Cuisine: MEXICAN/HEALTHY. **Reservations:** Not taken.
$ Prices: $3–$5.50. Cash only.
    Open: Salmon St. restaurant, Mon–Sat 11am–9pm, Sun noon–8pm.

Portland has a problem with mice; they seem to be popping up everywhere. Known for both its low-fat, low-salt cooking and its unusual contemporary art, Macheezmo Mouse is a fast-food restaurant for those who care about their health. The menu is primarily Mexican and lists the calorie count for each meal. Most dishes have also been approved by the American Heart Association. This is what fast food should be like.

MAYAS TACQUERIA, 1000 SW Morrison St. Tel. 503/226-1946.
    Cuisine: MEXICAN. **Reservations:** Not taken.
$ Prices: $2.50–$7.50. Cash only.
    Open: Mon–Sat 10:30am–10pm, Sun 11:30am–8pm.

Nothing fancy here, just good home-cooked Mexican food—fast. Watch for the Mayan-style murals on the walls out front. You can watch the cooks prepare your meal just as in any tacqueria in Mexico. The menu above the counter lists the different meals available, and on a separate list you'll find the choice of meats, which includes molé chicken, chile verde pork or chicken, chile colorado beef or chicken, and carne asada.

BREAKFAST/BRUNCH

ATWATER'S RESTAURANT AND LOUNGE, U.S. Bancorp Tower, 111 SW Fifth Ave. Tel. 503/220-3600.

Cuisine: NORTHWEST/CONTINENTAL. **Reservations:** A must.
$ Prices: $18.50. AE, CB, DC, MC, V.
Open: Sun 10am–3pm.

You just can't beat the brunch views from this 30th-floor restaurant. (See "Dining with a View," above, for a full description of the restaurant.)

BIJOU CAFE, 132 SW Third Ave. Tel. 503/222-3187.
Cuisine: INTERNATIONAL/NATURAL. **Reservations:** Not taken.
$ Prices: $3.50–$6. Cash only.
Open: Daily 7am–3pm.

Although open only for breakfast and lunch, the Bijou is still one of the most popular restaurants in Portland, and the lines can be long, especially on weekends. The folks here take both food and health seriously. They'll let you know that the eggs are from Chris's Egg Farm in Hubbard, Oregon, and they'll serve you a bowl of steamed brown rice for breakfast. However, the real hits here are the hash browns and the muffins. Don't leave without trying these two. At lunch, there are plenty of salads, which are made with organic produce whenever possible. Even the meats are natural. If you're concerned about how you eat, drop by the Bijou. Your body will be happy that you did.

BREAD & INK CAFE, 3610 SE Hawthorne Blvd. Tel. 503/ 239-4756.
Cuisine: NORTHWEST. **Reservations:** A necessity.
$ Prices: $11.50. MC, V.
Open: Sun 9am–2pm.

This casual café in southeastern Portland serves up an unbelievably filling four-course Yiddish brunch. (See p. 213 for a description of the restaurant.)

THE LONDON GRILL, The Benson Hotel, SW Broadway at Oak St. Tel. 503/228-2000.
Cuisine: CONTINENTAL. **Reservations:** Essential.
$ Prices: $15.95. AE, CB, DC, MC, V.
Open: Sun 9:30am–1pm.

This is the ritziest and most lavish Sunday brunch in Portland. You'll feel as though you have been admitted to a private club when you cross the marble-floored hotel lobby and descend to the elegantly appointed vaults of the The London Grill. (See p. 216 for a description of the restaurant.)

AFTERNOON TEA

HEATHMAN HOTEL, SW Broadway at Salmon St. Tel. 503/241-4100.
Cuisine: TEA. **Reservations:** Recommended.
$ Prices: $8–$12. AE, CB, DC, DISC, MC, V.
Open: Daily 2–4:30pm.

Once again I must send you back to The Heathman Hotel. (See p. 177 for a description of the hotel.) In the hotel's lobby lounge, tea hostesses in lace aprons serve pâtés, finger sandwiches, scones, pastries, and of course excellent tea (blended especially for the hotel). The service is on Royal Doulton's "Twilight Rose" bone china at marble-topped tables. A pianist plays gentle melodies, and on chilly afternoons a fire crackles in the fireplace. An elegant affair, tea at The Heathman is a welcome respite from shopping or business meetings.

JOHN PALMER HOUSE, 4314 N. Mississippi Ave. Tel. 503/284-5893.

Cuisine: TEA. **Reservations:** Required.

$ Prices: $10. MC, V.

Open: Sat–Sun 2–5pm.

High tea at the Palmer House is a journey back to the Victorian era. This painstakingly restored bed-and-breakfast inn is furnished throughout with period antiques, including a piano that came by ship around Cape Horn. In addition to the elegant and leisurely tea service, guests are given a tour of the home.

LATE NIGHT

GARBANZO's, NW 21st Ave. and Northwest Lovejoy St. Tel. 503/227-4196.

Cuisine: MIDDLE EASTERN. **Reservations:** Not taken.

$ Prices: Salads $1.50–$3.75; sandwiches $3–$3.75; dinners $5.75–$6.75. AE, DISC, MC, V.

Open: Sun–Thurs 11:30am–1:30am, Fri–Sat 11:30am–3am.

Calling itself a falafel bar, this casual little place next door to the Cajun Café & Bistro has become very popular, especially late at night. The menu includes all the usual Middle Eastern offerings, most of which also happen to be American Heart Association approved. You can eat at one of the tiny café tables or get your order to go. They even serve beer and wine.

CHAPTER 17

WHAT TO SEE & DO IN PORTLAND

- **SUGGESTED ITINERARIES**
- **DID YOU KNOW . . . ?**
1. **THE TOP ATTRACTIONS**
- **FROMMER'S FAVORITE PORTLAND EXPERIENCES**
2. **MORE ATTRACTIONS**
3. **COOL FOR KIDS**
4. **SPECIAL-INTEREST SIGHTSEEING**
5. **ORGANIZED TOURS**
6. **SPORTS & RECREATION**

Portland does not have very many museums, and those that it does have are rather small. This isn't to say that there isn't much for the visitor to see or do. Portlanders are active folks and they prefer snow skiing on Mount Hood to museum-going. They prefer gardening over old-homes tours, and consequently there are numerous world-class public gardens and parks within the city. You can easily see all of Portland's tourist attractions in one or two days. No visit to Portland would be complete, however, without venturing out into the Oregon countryside. This is the city's real attraction. Within an hour and a half you can be skiing on Mount Hood or swimming in the chilly waters of the Pacific Ocean. However, for those who prefer more urban and urbane activities, the museums and parks listed below should satisfy.

SUGGESTED ITINERARIES

IF YOU HAVE 1 DAY

Day 1 Start your day at Skidmore Fountain and take a walk around Old Town. If it's a Saturday or Sunday, you can visit the Saturday Market underneath the Burnside Bridge. While in this area, you can also stroll through Chinatown and visit the American Advertising Museum. Walk south through downtown after lunch and visit the Oregon Historical Center and the Oregon Art Institute. Finish your very busy day at the Japanese Gardens and Rose Test Garden in Washington Park.

IF YOU HAVE 2 DAYS

Day 1 Start your first day as outlined above, except for visiting the gardens.

? DID YOU KNOW . . . ?

- Mill Ends Park is the world's smallest dedicated park, measuring 24 inches in diameter.
- Portland is the only city in America with an extinct volcano within its city limits—Mount Tabor.
- Portland has been called the politest U.S. city.
- There are more restaurants per capita in Portland than in any other West Coast city.
- Matt Groenig, creator of the hit television series "The Simpsons," got his start in Portland. Giant wall murals of the Simpsons can be seen on different buildings around town.
- Jean Auel, author of *The Clan of the Cave Bear* and subsequent sequels, is from Portland and studied winter survival techniques on Mount Hood.

Day 2 After visiting the two gardens in the morning, take the miniature train over to the Washington Park Zoo. In the afternoon, visit the Oregon Museum of Science and Industry and the World Forestry Center, both of which are across the street from the zoo.

IF YOU HAVE 3 DAYS

Days 1-2 Follow the two-day strategy as outlined above.

Day 3 On your third day, do the Mount Hood Loop, as described on p. 261.

IF YOU HAVE 5 DAYS OR MORE

Days 1-3 Follow the three-day strategy as outlined above.

Day 4 In the morning, visit the Pittock Mansion and perhaps stroll through Hoyt Arboretum or Forest Park. In the afternoon, visit Fort Vancouver across the Columbia River in Washington State.

Day 5 You might drive to the coast or take a trip through the wine country.

1. THE TOP ATTRACTIONS

AMERICAN ADVERTISING MUSEUM, 9 NW Second Ave. Tel. 226-0000.

✪ I long ago gave up watching television and listening to commercial radio because I have no tolerance for advertising. That this is my favorite Portland museum should tell you something about the exhibits. Not only will you learn about the history of advertising in America, but you'll get to see all your old favorite TV commercials. One exhibit shows the changes in advertising over several centuries, while another displays the all-time best advertising campaigns. Test your familiarity with different logos. There's even a complete series of Burma Shave signs.

Admission: $3 adults, $1.50 senior citizens and ages 6–18, under age 6 free.

FROMMER'S FAVORITE PORTLAND EXPERIENCES

Shopping and Eating at the Saturday Market This large arts-and-crafts market is an outdoor showcase of the best of the Northwest's creative artisans. There are food stalls selling delicious and unusual meals.

Quaffing a Microbrew at the Mission Theater Portland is the microbrewery capital of America, and at this combination movie theater and brew pub you can taste the city's best beers while watching recently released movies. Best of all, the films are free.

Strolling the Grounds of the Japanese Gardens These are the best Japanese gardens in the United States, perhaps the best anywhere outside of Japan. They look particularly stunning in June, when the irises are in bloom, but any time of year they are beautiful and tranquil. There's no better place in the city to relax.

The First Thursday Art Walk On the first Thursday of every month, Portlanders get dressed up and go gallery hopping. There are openings that often include live music, hors d'oeuvres, and wine, as well as plenty of new artworks. The galleries stay open until 9pm, and there are even special shuttle buses to carry people from one gallery district to the next.

Peanut Butter and Jam Sessions At noon on Tuesdays and Thursdays of the summer months, Pioneer Courthouse Square is jammed with people who come to hear local musicians jam. The free concerts last an hour, and over the summer virtually every type of music has its day. An added bonus of the noon hour is the daily weather forecast by the *Weather Machine* sculpture.

Hiking and Skiing on Mount Hood Less than an hour from Portland, Mount Hood offers year-round skiing and hiking. Timberline Lodge, high on the extinct volcano's slopes, was built by the Works Project Administration during the Depression and is a showcase of craftsmanship.

Open: Wed–Fri 11am–5pm, Sat–Sun noon–5pm. **MAX:** Skidmore Fountain Station.

OREGON ART INSTITUTE, 1219 SW Park Ave. Tel. 226-2811.
Although this small museum has a respectable collection of European and American art, it is the Northwest Coast Native American exhibit that requires a special visit. Particularly fascinating are the transformation masks. Worn during ritual dances, the masks are transformed from one face into a completely different

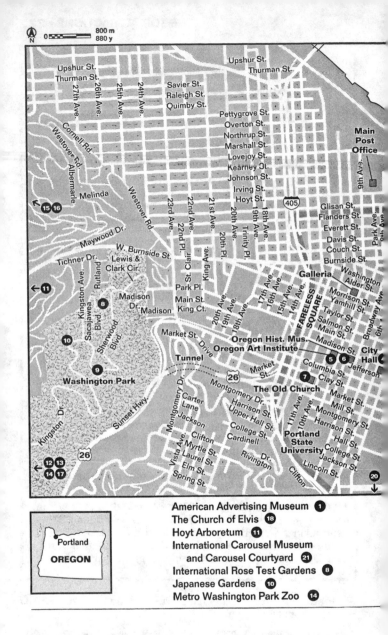

Street and location labels on map:

Upshur St.
Thurman St.
27th Ave.
26th Ave.
25th Ave.
24th Ave.
Savier St.
Raleigh St.
Quimby St.
Cornell Rd.
Westover Rd.
Albermarle
Melinda
23rd Ave.
22nd Ave.
21st Ave.
20th Ave.
22nd Pl.
Clay St.
King
Trinity Pl.
19th Ave.
18th Ave.
Pettygrove St.
Overton St.
Northrup St.
Marshall St.
Lovejoy St.
Kearney St.
Johnson St.
Irving St.
Hoyt St.
405
Glisan St.
Flanders St.
Everett St.
Davis St.
Couch St.
Burnside St.
Main Post Office
9th Ave.
Park Ave.
9th Ave.
Maywood Dr.
Westover Rd.
Tichner Dr.
W. Burnside St.
Lewis & Clark Cir.
Kingston Ave.
Rutland
Sherwood Blvd.
Sacajawea Blvd.
Madison Dr.
Madison
Park Pl.
Main St.
King Ct.
Market St.
Market St. Drive
Washington Park
Kingston Dr.
Sunset Hwy.
Tunnel
26
Montgomery Dr.
Carter Lane
Jackson
Clifton
Myrtle St.
Vista Ave.
Laurel St.
Elm St.
Spring St.
Montgomery Dr.
Harrison St.
Upper Hall St.
College St.
Cardinell
Dr. Rivington
Clifton
17th Ave.
16th Ave.
15th Ave.
14th Ave.
13th Ave.
18th Ave.
9th Ave.
11th Ave.
10th Ave.
Galleria
Washington St.
Alder St.
FARELESS SQUARE
Morrison St.
Yamhill St.
Taylor St.
Salmon St.
Main St.
Madison St.
Columbia St.
Jefferson
Clay St.
Market St.
Mill St.
Montgomery St.
Harrison St.
Hall St.
College St.
Jackson St.
Lincoln St.
Broadway
6th Ave.
City Hall
Oregon Hist. Mus.
Oregon Art Institute
The Old Church
Portland State University
5 6
7
20
15 16
11
8
10
9
12 13
14 17

800 m
880 y
0
N

American Advertising Museum 1
The Church of Elvis 18
Hoyt Arboretum 11
International Carousel Museum and Carousel Courtyard 21
International Rose Test Gardens 8
Japanese Gardens 10
Metro Washington Park Zoo 14

Portland
OREGON

visage by pulling several strings. A totem pole and many other woodcarvings show the amazing creative imagination of the Northwest tribes. There are also exhibits of pre-Columbian art, Asian antiquities, primitive African art from Cameroon, and a large hall for temporary exhibits. If you happen to be in town on the first Thursday of any month, you can save the admission by

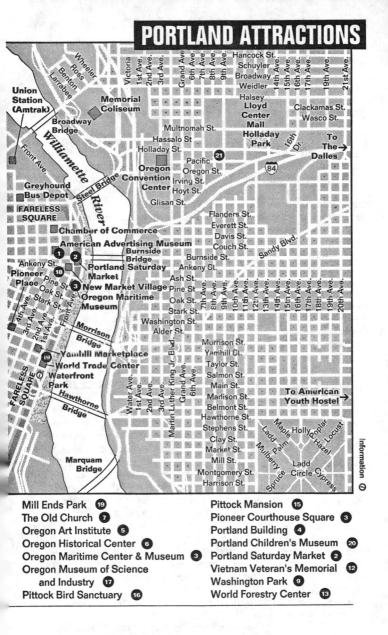

PORTLAND ATTRACTIONS

coming between 5 and 9pm; this free admission is part of the First
Thursday program of art-gallery openings throughout Portland.
On this night galleries stay open late and throw opening-night
parties. Chic Portlanders crowd the sidewalks on a sophisticated
gallery crawl. On Wednesday nights outside of the summer months,
the Museum After Hours program presents live music.

Admission: $3 adults, $1.50 ages 12–18; 50¢ ages 6–12; under age 6 free. Free 5–9pm on first Thurs of each month.

Open: Tues–Sat 11am–5pm, Sun 1–5pm; first Thurs of each month 11am–9pm. **Bus:** 57.

OREGON HISTORICAL CENTER, 1230 SW Park Ave. Tel. 222-1741.

The Oregon Territory was a land of promise and plenty. Thousands of hardy individuals set out along the Oregon Trail, crossing a vast and rugged country to reach the fertile valleys of Oregon's rivers. Others came by ship around the Horn. Today the state of Oregon is still luring immigrants with its bountiful natural resources, and those who wish to learn about the people who discovered Oregon before them should visit this well-designed museum. Oregon history from before the arrival of the first white men to well into this century is chronicled in an educational and fascinating exhibit. The displays incorporate parts of old buildings; objects such as snow skis, dolls, and bicycles; fashions; Native American artifacts; nautical and surveying instruments; even a covered wagon. Museum docents, with roots stretching back to the days of the Oregon Trail, are often on hand to answer questions. There is also a research library that includes many journals from early pioneers.

Admission: Free.
Open: Mon–Sat 10am–4:45pm. **Bus:** 57.

OREGON MUSEUM OF SCIENCE AND INDUSTRY (OMSI), 4015 SW Canyon Rd. Tel. 222-2828).

Although this museum is aimed primarily at children, adults will also find it fascinating, and sometimes downright thought-provoking. The constantly changing exhibits here are always interactive, with lots of fun hands-on learning being done by visitors of all ages. Since the major purpose of the museum is to educate, there are always interesting classes being held. There are summer camps for kids, including a very popular space camp where they train to be astronauts, actually getting a chance to use some of the same equipment that real astronauts train on. There is a computer center where you can learn to use a computer or hone your existing skills. Physics and chemistry labs, with trained specialists supervising, are available for conducting experiments. For the toddler set, there's the Discovery Space, which introduces science to children as young as 2 years old. In the evenings, there are laser shows and night-sky programs in the planetarium.

Admission: $5.25 adults, $4.25 senior citizens, $3.50 ages 3–17, under age 3 free.
Open: Sat–Thurs 9am–5:30pm, Fri 9am–7pm. **Closed:** Christmas Day. **Bus:** 63.

PITTOCK MANSION, 3229 NW Pittock Dr. Tel. 823-4469.

At nearly the highest point in the West Hills, 1,000 feet above sea level, stands the most impressive mansion in Portland. Once slated to be torn down to make way for new housing, this grand château built by the founder of Portland's *Oregonian* newspaper has been fully restored and is open to the public. Built in 1914 in a French Renaissance style, the mansion featured many innovations, including a built-in vacuum system and amazing multiple showerheads in the baths. Today it is furnished with 18th- and 19th-century antiques, much as it might have been at the time the Pittocks occupied the building. Lunch and afternoon tea are available in the Gate Lodge, the former caretaker's cottage.

Admission: $3.50 adults, $3 senior citizens, $1.50 ages 6–18.

Open: Daily 1–5pm. **Closed:** Nov 28–30, most major holidays, and the first three weeks of Jan. **Bus:** 20 to Burnside and Barnes. Half-mile walk.

PORTLAND SATURDAY MARKET, underneath the Burnside Bridge between SW First Ave. and SW Ankeny St. Tel. 222-6072.

The Saturday Market (held on both Saturday and Sunday) is arguably Portland's single most important and best-loved event. For years the Northwest has attracted artists and craftspeople, and every Saturday and Sunday nearly 300 of them can be found selling their exquisite creations here. In addition to the dozens of craftspeople's stalls, you'll find flowers, fresh produce, ethnic and unusual foods, and lots of free entertainment. This is the single best place to shop for one-of-a-kind gifts in Portland. The atmosphere is always cheerful and the crowds are always colorful. At the heart of the Skidmore District, the Saturday Market makes an excellent starting or finishing point for a walk around Portland's most historic neighborhood. Don't miss this unique market. On Sunday, on-street parking is free.

Admission: Free.

Open: Mar–Christmas, Sat 10am–5pm and Sun 11am–4:30pm. **MAX:** Skidmore Fountain Station.

WORLD FORESTRY CENTER, 4033 SW Canyon Rd. Tel. 228-1367.

Although with each passing year Oregon depends less and less on the timber industry, the World Forestry Center is still busy educating visitors about the importance of our forest resources. Step inside the huge wooden main hall and you come face to bark with a very large and very lifelike tree. Press a button at its base and it will tell you the story of how trees live and grow. In other rooms you can see exhibits on the logging industry, forests of the world, and a collection of woods from every type of tree grown in America. In the summer, there is a vintage carousel on the grounds, and one ride is free with admission.

Admission: $3 adults, $2 senior citizens and ages 2–18, under age 2 free.

Open: Daily 9am–5pm. **Closed:** Christmas Day. **Bus:** 63.

2. MORE ATTRACTIONS

CHURCHES

THE CHURCH OF ELVIS, 219 Ankeny St.

⭐ Two blocks from the Saturday Market on narrow little Ankeny Street is Portland's most bizarre attraction: the first 24-hour video psychic and church of Elvis. A window full of kitschy contraptions bearing the visage of the "King" never fails to stop people in their tracks as they stroll past. What is it? Well, for a quarter, you can find out. Care to have Elvis hear your confession? No problem. The "King" will absolve you of your sins, unless, of course, you have committed the unforgivable one of believing that Elvis is dead. Great fun if you are a fan of Elvis, tabloids, or the bizarre.

Admission: 25¢.
Open: 24 hours. **MAX:** Skidmore Fountain Station.

THE OLD CHURCH, 1422 SW 11th Ave. Tel. 222-2031.

Built in 1883, this wooden Carpenter Gothic church is a Portland landmark. It incorporates a grand traditional design, but is constructed with spare ornamentation. An active church until 1967, the deteriorating building was to be torn down; however, preservationists stepped in to save it. Today it's a community facility, and every Wednesday there's a free lunchtime concert performed on the church's original pipe organ.

Admission: Free.
Open: Tues–Fri 11am–3pm. **Bus:** 57, 59, 88, or 89.

MUSEUMS

OREGON MARITIME CENTER & MUSEUM, 113 SW Front Ave. Tel. 224-7724.

Portland is a busy port city, and not too long ago the ships were anchoring right out in front of where this museum now stands. Today urban beautification in the form of Waterfront Park has replaced the dreary docks that used to line this stretch of the Willamette River. To learn about Portland's shipping history, and to see handmade models of famous vessels, drop by this little museum. Often there is even someone building a model ship just inside the front door.

Admission: $2 for adults, $1.25 for senior citizens and students, under age 8 free.
Open: Fri–Sun 11am–4pm. **MAX:** To Portland Saturday Market Stop.

OUTDOOR ART/PLAZAS/ ARCHITECTURAL HIGHLIGHTS

OREGON CONVENTION CENTER, 777 NE Martin Luther King Jr. Blvd. Tel. 235-7575.

As you approach downtown Portland from the direction of the airport, it is impossible to miss this unusual architectural bauble on the city skyline. Christened "Twin Peaks" even before it opened in the summer of 1990, the center is worth a visit even if you don't happen to be in town for a convention. Its "twin peaks" are two tapering glass towers that channel light into the center of this huge complex. Outside the main entrance are two Asian temple bells. Inside are paintings on a scale to match the building, a dragon boat hanging from the ceiling, and a brass pendulum swinging slowly through the hours. Small plaques on the outside wall of the main lobby spotlight telling quotes about life in Oregon.

Admission: Free for self-guided tours.
Open: Daily. MAX: To Convention Center.

PIONEER COURTHOUSE SQUARE, bounded by Broadway, Sixth Ave., Yamhill St., and Morrison St.

Today it is the heart of downtown Portland and acts as an outdoor stage for everything from flower displays to concerts to protest rallies. But not too many years ago this beautiful brick-paved square with its tumbling waterfall fountain and free-standing columns was nothing but a parking lot—created on the rubble that remained after the city's grande dame Portland Hotel, an architectural gem of a Queen Anne–style château, was bulldozed in 1951. Today the square is Portland's favorite gathering spot, especially at noon, when the *Weather Machine,* a mechanical sculpture, forecasts the upcoming 24 hours. Amid a fanfare of music and flashing lights, the *Weather Machine* sends up clouds of mist and then raises either a sun (clear weather), a dragon (stormy weather), or a blue heron (clouds and drizzle).

Max: To Pioneer Courthouse Square stop. **Bus:** Any downtown bus that goes to the Transit Mall.

PORTLANDIA AND THE PORTLAND BUILDING, 1120 SW Fifth Ave.

Portlandia is the symbol of the city, and this hammered bronze statue of her is the second-largest such statue in the country. The largest, of course, is New York City's Statue of Liberty. The massive kneeling figure holds a trident in one hand and with the other reaches toward the street. Strangely enough, this classically designed figure reminiscent of a Greek goddess perches above the entrance to Portland's most controversial building: The Portland Building, considered the first postmodern structure in the country. Today anyone familiar with the bizarre constructions of Los Angeles architect Frank Gearhy would find it difficult to understand how such an innocuous and attractive building could have ever raised such a fuss, but it did.

PARKS & GARDENS

FOREST PARK, bounded by W. Burnside St., Newberry Rd., St. Helens Rd., and Skyline Rd. Tel. 823-4492.

With 4,800 acres of wilderness, this is the largest forested city park in the United States. There are 50 miles of trails and old fire roads for hiking and jogging. More than 100 species of birds call these forests home, making this park a birdwatcher's paradise.

Admission: Free.
Open: Daily dawn to dusk. **Bus:** 15, 17, 20, or 63.

INTERNATIONAL ROSE TEST GARDEN, 400 SW Kingston Ave., Washington Park. Tel. 248-4302.

Portland is the City of Roses, and this garden is the reason why. Acres and acres of roses blossom well into December. This is the largest rose test garden in the country, boasting more than 400 varieties. Since 1907 the city has been holding an annual Rose Festival to highlight its fragrant flowers.

Admission: Free.
Open: Daily dawn to dusk. **Bus:** 63.

JAPANESE GARDEN SOCIETY OF OREGON, off Kingston Ave. in Washington Park. Tel. 223-4070.

⭐ I have always loved Japanese gardens and have visited them all over the world. Outside of those in Japan, this is still my favorite. What makes it so special is not only the design, plantings, and tranquility, but the view. From the Japanese-style wooden house in the center of the garden, on a clear day you have a view over Portland to Mount Hood. This perfectly shaped volcanic peak is so reminiscent of Mount Fuji that it seems almost as if it were placed there just for the sake of this garden.

Admission: $3.50 adults, $2 students and senior citizens, under age 6 free. **Bus:** 63.

Open: Apr 1–Sept 30, daily 10am–6pm; Oct 1–Mar 31, daily 10am–4pm. **Closed:** Thanksgiving, Christmas, and New Year's Day. **Bus:** 63.

METRO WASHINGTON PARK ZOO, 4001 SW Caynon Rd., Washington Park. Tel. 226-1561.

⭐ This zoo has been successfully breeding elephants for many years and has the largest breeding herd of elephants in captivity. The Africa exhibit, which displays zebras, rhinos, giraffes, and a few other animals, is the most lifelike habitat I have ever seen in a zoo—and it's giving the elephants a lot of competition. In June 1991, the zoo added a new rain-forest exhibit to this already impressive African section. Equally impressive is the Alaskan-tundra exhibit, with grizzly bears, wolves, and musk oxen. Throughout the Cascade Exhibit, the trees and shrubbery are labeled. There's an outdoor pond with birds, and you'll see otters and beavers. This is also where you'll find the trout on view.

For the younger set, there's a children's petting zoo filled with farm animals and a center where many of the zoo's new babies are kept. Be sure to check in the flyer you get at the front gate to find out what special programs are being held on the day of your visit.

The Washington Park and Zoo Railway travels between the zoo and the International Rose Test Garden and the Japanese Gardens. Tickets for the miniature railway are $2.50 for adults, $1.75 for senior citizens and children 3 to 11. In the summer, there are jazz concerts on Wednesday nights and bluegrass on Thursday nights from 6:30 to 8:30pm. Concerts are free with zoo admission.

Admission: $4.75 adults, $3 senior citizens, $2.50 ages 3–11, under age 2 free; free second Tues of each month from 3pm to closing.

Open: May–Oct, daily 9:30am–6pm; Oct–May, daily 9:30am–4pm. **Bus:** 63.

MILL ENDS PARK, SW Taylor St. and SW Front Ave.

★ Pay attention as you cross the median strip on Front Avenue or you might walk right past this famous Portland park. The smallest public park in the world, it contains a whopping 452.16 square inches of land. It was the whimsical creation of Dick Fagen, a local journalist who used to gaze down from his office at a hole left after a telephone pole was removed from the middle of Front Avenue. He dubbed the park Mill Ends (the name of his column) and peopled it with leprechauns. On St. Patrick's Day of 1976, it was officially designated a Portland city park. Despite the diminutive size of the park, it has been the site of several weddings

3. COOL FOR KIDS

The **Oregon Museum of Science and Industry** (p. 226) is primarily geared for kids, with lots of hands-on exhibits, classes, an astronaut-training program, and laser shows in its planetarium. At the **World Forestry Center** (p. 227), there is a carousel operating during the summer months. The **Metro Washington Park Zoo** (p. 230) is one of the best in the country, and is particularly well known for its elephant-breeding program. From inside the zoo, it's possible to take a small train through Washington Park to the Rose Gardens.

In addition to these attractions, discussed above, there are three other attractions in Portland of particular interest to kids:

PORTLAND CHILDREN'S MUSEUM, 3037 SW Second Ave. Tel. 248-4587.

Although this museum is small, it's a lot of fun. Visitors can shop in a kid-size grocery store or climb into a real saddle in a western corral. On the second floor a miniature version of Portland's own MAX light-rail system goes round and round in circles, making more noise than the real thing. There's a tiny firehouse where kids can try on real firemen's clothes, as well as a tiny African native hut. Listening to seashells, banging on drums, blowing bubbles—there's plenty to entertain kids at this big little museum.

Admission: $3 adults, $2.50 children, under 6 months free.
Open: Tues–Sat 9am–5pm, Sun 11am–5pm. **Closed:** National holidays. **Bus:** 1, 12, 40, 41, 43, 45, or 55.

INTERNATIONAL CAROUSEL MUSEUM AND CAROUSEL COURTYARD, 710 NE Holladay (between Seventh Ave. and Ninth Ave.). Tel. 235-2252 or 230-0400.

With a colorful carousel in the courtyard out front, the Carousel Museum is a nostalgic treat of oldsters and a mesmerizing delight for youngsters. Inside the museum you'll find American and European carved carousel animals, as well as organs and memorabilia; there are also special exhibits on specific woodcarvers. However, it's the carousel out front that is most likely to interest children.

Admission: $1 adults, under age 6 free; carousel ride $1.
Open: Museum, daily 11am–4pm; carousel, daily 11am–5pm.
MAX: to Seventh Ave. stop.

OAKS PARK, east end of the Sellwood Bridge. Tel. 233-5777.

What would summer be without the screams of happy thrillseekers risking their lives on a roller coaster? Pretty boring, right? Just ask the kids. They'll tell you that the real Portland excitement is at Oaks Park. Covering more than 44 acres, this amusement park first opened in 1905 to coincide with the Lewis & Clark Exposition. John Phillip Sousa used to play his famous marches in the park, and his bandstand, now restored, is still here. The largest roller-skating rink in the Northwest is also here.

Admission: Free (all activities are on individual tickets).
Open: Mar–Sept, Mar–Memorial Day, Fri 7–10pm, Sat 12–9pm, Sun 12–6pm; June–Labor Day, Tues–Fri 1–10pm, Sat noon–10pm, Sun noon–8pm. Labor Day–End of Sept, Fri 7–10pm, Sat 12–9pm, Sun 12–6pm.

---

4. SPECIAL-INTEREST SIGHTSEEING

FOR THE TRAIN & TROLLEY BUFF

WILLAMETTE SHORE TROLLEY, 333 S. State St., Lake Oswego. Tel. 222-2226.

If you like to reminisce about the good old days of rail travel or long to ride an old-fashioned trolley but don't want to go to San Francisco to do so, book a trip on this historic trolley. The 1931 trolley car rides the rail along the scenic banks of the Willamette River between downtown Portland and the prestigious suburb of Lake Oswego. The journey takes 45 minutes in each direction and you can either stay on and return immediately or get off and do a bit of exploring before returning. Cherry wood and brass and lots of little details make this old trolley a real gem. Plans are under way to extend the tracks to the RiverPlace shopping area at the south end of Waterfront Park. For most of the year the trolley runs only on weekends, but in the summer it runs Tuesday through Sunday.

Fare: $7 adults, $5 senior citizens and children.

5. ORGANIZED TOURS

BUS TOURS

Gray Line (tel. 285-9845) offers quite a few half-day and full-day tours. One tour visits the International Rose Test Garden and the World Forestry Center, another stops at the Japanese Gardens and the Cascades exhibit at the Metro Washington Park Zoo. Both of these tours are priced at $13 for adults and $6.50 for children. You can combine the two trips for $22 for adults and $11 for children. However, the trip I most highly recommend is the full-day Mount Hood loop ($26 for adults, $13 for children). By taking this tour rather than driving it yourself, you can enjoy the scenery instead of keeping your eyes on the road. There's also a Columbia Gorge excursion that includes a ride on a sternwheeler, and a tour of the northern Oregon coast—both of these are priced at $26 for adults and $13 for children.

RIVER CRUISES

For those wishing to get out on the mighty Columbia River or the less thrilling but equally important Willamette River, there are quite a few possibilities. A century ago it was paddlewheelers similar to those used on the Mississippi River that helped open up the Oregon Territory to settlers. Today paddlewheelers are once again cruising the rivers.

The sternwheeler **Columbia Gorge** (tel. 223-3928) cruises the Columbia River between mid-June and September and the Willamette River between October and mid-June. The trip up the Columbia River, with its towering cliffs, is a spectacular and memorable excursion. This trip includes stops at the Cascade Locks and Bonneville Dam. There are lunch, brunch, dinner, and dance cruises (call for information and reservations). The basic 2-hour day trips are priced at $9.95 for adults and $5.95 for children. Ticket prices range all the way up to $55 for the annual 5-hour cruise back down the Columbia River to Portland at the end of the summer season.

The **Crusader Princess,** operated by Rose City Riverboat Cruises and Charters (tel. 289-6665), is a modern catamaran power yacht. It cruises the Willamette River on a regular basis from mid-April through October. There are dinner, moonlight, Sunday brunch, Portland Harbor, and Willamette River tours, with ticket prices ranging from $9 to $30 for adults.

CARRIAGE TOURS

Another way to see Portland is by horse-drawn carriage. These tours are operated by the **John Palmer House,** a bed-and-breakfast inn (tel. 284-5893), and are best combined with a stay at this magnificently restored Victorian painted lady. A quick 10-minute ride along the waterfront is $10, and a full hour's tour is $50. These prices are per carriage, which will hold four adults. June through August, carriage rides are given daily from 6 to 10pm. In April, May, September, and October, they are given on Friday and Saturday from 6 to 10pm and on Sunday from noon to 6pm.

6. SPORTS & RECREATION

SPECTATOR SPORTS

AUTO RACING

The **Portland International Raceway,** 1940 N. Victory Blvd. (tel. 285-6635), operated by the Portland Bureau of Parks and Recreation, is home to road races, drag races, motocross and other motorcycle races, go-kart races, and even vintage-car races. February to October are the busiest months here. Admission is $5 to $72.

BASEBALL

The **Portland Beavers Baseball Club** plays professional baseball at the Civic Stadium, SW 20th Ave. and Morrison St. (tel. 2-BEAVER). The box office is open Monday through Saturday from 9am to 5pm. Admission is $4.50 to $6.50 for adults, $2 for ages 14 and under.

BASKETBALL

The **Portland Trail Blazers** pound the boards at Memorial Coliseum, 1401 N. Wheeler St. (tel. 231-8000), between October and April. Call for current schedule and ticket information. Admission is $9.50 to $38.50.

GREYHOUND RACING

The race season at the **Multnomah Kennel Club,** NE 223rd Ave., Fairview (tel. 243-2706 or 667-7700), runs from May to September. Post time is 7:30pm Tuesday through Saturday, with a Saturday matinee at 1pm. In July and August, there are also Sunday matinees.

IMPRESSIONS

While the people of Portland are not mercurial or exciteable—and by Californians or people "east of the mountains" are even accused of being lymphatic, if not somnolent—they are much given . . . to recreation and public amusements.
—HARVEY SCOTT, EDITOR OF THE *OREGONIAN,* 1890

You must be 18 to bet on the greyhounds, and if you've never bet on dog races before, they'll gladly give you a quick course. To reach the track, take I-84 east to the 181st Street exit south and then turn left on Glisan Street. It's also easy to reach the park by public transit. Take the MAX light-rail system to the Gresham City Hall or Central Station and transfer to bus no. 82, which goes directly to the racetrack. Admission is $1.25 to $3.50.

HORSE RACING

Portland Meadows, 1001 N. Schmeer Rd. (tel. 285-9144), is the place to go if you want to catch a little horse-racing action. The race season runs from October to April, with post time at 7:30pm on Friday and 1pm on Saturday and Sunday. By car, take I-5 north to the Delta Park exit. Admission is $2.50 to $6.

ICE HOCKEY

The **Portland Winter Hawks,** a semipro hockey team, carve up the ice at Memorial Coliseum, 1401 N. Wheeler St. (tel. 238-6366), from October to March. Call for schedule and ticket information.

MARATHONS

The **Portland Marathon** is held in September. For further information, call 626-2348.

RECREATION

Although Portland has its share of spectator sports, this is an active health- and fitness-minded city. You'll find that the opportunities for working up a sweat are numerous and varied.

BEACHES

The nearest ocean beach to Portland is **Cannon Beach,** about 90 miles to the west. See Section 2 of Chapter 21 for more information.

BICYCLING

You'll notice a lot of bicyclists on the streets of Portland. If you want to get rolling with everyone else, head over to the **Agape Cycle & Sports,** 2610 SE Clinton St. (tel. 230-0317), where you can rent bikes for $15 to $25 per day. Once you have your bike, you can head for **Waterfront Park,** where there's a 2-mile bike path. The **Terwilliger Path** starts at the south end of Portland State University and travels for 10 miles up into the hills to Tryon Creek State Park. The views from the top are breathtaking. Stop by a bookstore to pick up a copy of the "From Here to There by Bike" map.

FISHING

If you hadn't guessed it from the menus in all the restaurants, this is salmon, steelhead, sturgeon, and trout country. You can find out about licenses and seasons from the **Oregon Department of Fish and Wildlife,** P.O. Box 59, Portland, OR 97207 (tel. 503/229-5403). If you prefer to have a guide take you where the big ones are always biting, contact **Northwest River Outfitters,** 12845 SW Tarpon Dr., Beaverton, OR 97005 (tel. 503/646-3953). They provide the tackle, the boat, and more than 20 years' experience fishing the waters of Oregon. A day of fishing will cost you around $100.

GOLF

If you're a golfer, don't forget to bring your clubs along on a trip to Portland. There are plenty of public courses around the area, and greens fees are only $12 for 18 holes on a weekday and $14 on weekends and holidays. Public golf courses operated by the Portland Bureau of Parks and Recreation include **Eastmoreland Golf Course,** 2425 SE Bybee Blvd. (tel. 775-2900); **Heron Lakes Golf Course,** 3500 N. Victory Blvd. (tel. 289-1818); **Rose City Golf Course,** 2200 NE 71st Ave. (tel. 253-4744); and **Progress Downs Golf Course,** 8200 SW Scholls Ferry Rd., Beaverton (tel. 646-5166).

HIKING

The hiking opportunities in the Portland area are almost unlimited. If you head over to Mount Hood National Forest, you can get on the **Pacific Crest Trail** and hike all the way to Mexico. There are also plenty of other shorter hikes in this region. For details, contact the **U.S. Forest Service,** Zig Zag, OR 97049 (tel. 666-0771).

If you are interested in a more strenuous mountain experience, Mount Hood offers plenty of mountain- and rock-climbing opportunities. **Timberline Mountain Guides,** P.O. Box 112, Timberline Lodge, OR 97028 (tel. 272-3717), leads summit climbs from April to August, with ski descents during these same months. They also offer climbing courses between mid-April and September. If you're an experienced mountain climber, you can rent equipment here also. You can also buy or rent camping and climbing equipment from **REI Co-op,** 1798 Jantzen Beach Center (tel. 283-1300), or at 7410 SW Bridgeport Rd., Tualatin (tel. 624-8600). This huge outdoor recreation-supply store also sells books on hiking in the area.

For shorter hikes, you don't even have to leave the city. Bordered by West Burnside Street on the south, Newberry Road on the north, St. Helens Road on the east, and Skyline Road on the west, **Forest Park** is the largest city park in the country. You'll find more than 50 miles of trails through this urban wilderness.

SAILING

If you're not content to stroll the banks of the Willamette River and long to be out on the water yourself, visit the **Sailing Center,** located at the foot of Southeast Marion Street (tel. 233-1218). They'll put you in a 14-foot dinghy and set you afloat. Rental rate is $45 for 5 hours.

Serious **sailboarding** enthusiasts already know about the

sailboarding mecca at the town of **Hood River** on the Columbia River. The winds come howling down the gorge with enough force to send sailboards airborne.

SKIING

Skiing is probably Portland's favorite sports activity after jogging. This is because the city has several ski resorts within about an hour's drive. One of them even boasts skiing all summer. To help you get to the slopes, there is the **Mount Hood Express** (tel. 250-4379 in Portland, or 800/468-1543 in the Mount Hood area). This van service from the Portland area to the ski resorts of Mount Hood costs from $62 for one person and $2 for each additional passenger— that's up to $72 for six people—from the airport to Timberline Lodge. They have airport pickups that can whisk you directly from the baggage area to the slopes in less than an hour.

Timberline Ski Area, Timberline, OR 97028 (tel. 231-7979 in Portland, or toll free 800/547-1406), high on the slopes of Mount Hood, offers skiing all the way through to Labor Day. Six chair lifts carry skiers to miles of tree-lined runs. After dark, three lifts continue running for those diehards who just can't get enough of the slopes. In addition to the excellent skiing here, there is the stunning **Timberline Lodge,** which was built during the Depression by the WPA (See Section 1 of Chapter 21 for details.) The ski area is open November to September, daily from 9am to 10pm in winter and from 7am to 1:30pm in summer. Lift rates in winter, day or night, are $22 for adults, $14 for children (lift tickets for shorter hours are cheaper); in summer, $20 for all ages.

Mount Hood Meadows (tel. 337-2222 or 246-7547 in Portland; 227-7669 for snow report) is the largest ski resort on Mount Hood, with more than 2,000 skiable acres. There are nine chair lifts that can carry 14,400 skiers per hour. With 2,777 vertical feet and a wide variety of terrains, Mount Hood Meadows is ideal for everyone from beginner to expert. In the day lodge, you can sit and watch the action on the slopes through a 120-foot-long wall of glass. When you're ready to hit the slopes yourself, there are rentals and 200 instructors to help you improve your form. The resort even offers direct bus service to and from Portland (tel. 287-5438). Lift tickets are $27 for adults and $17 for children 11 and under (tickets for night skiing and shorter hours are less expensive). The ski area is open from mid-November to mid-May: Monday and Tuesday from 9am to 4:30pm, Wednesday through Saturday from 9am to 10pm, and on Sunday from 9am to 7pm.

Multorpor SkiBowl (tel. 272-3206) is the closest ski area to Portland and offers 61 slopes to challenge skiers of all levels of ability. There are four double-chair lifts and five surface tows. With 1,500 vertical feet, SkiBowl has more expert slopes than any other ski area on the mountain. This is the largest lighted ski area in the United States. In summer there's an Alpine Slide for exhilarating runs down warm grassy slopes. Multorpor SkiBowl is open from Thanksgiving to April: on Monday from 4 to 10pm, Tuesday through Thursday from 9am to 10pm, on Friday from 9am to

11pm, on Saturday from 8am to 11pm, and on Sunday from 8am to 10pm. Lift rates are $19 for adults for day skiing, $13 at night; children aged 11 and under are charged $13 for day skiing, $10 at night.

TENNIS

The Portland Bureau of Parks and Recreation operates dozens of tennis courts, both indoor and out, all over the city. Outdoor courts are generally free and available on a first-come, first-served basis. My personal favorites are those in Washington Park just behind the Rose Garden. Some of these courts can be reserved by contacting the **Portland Tennis Center,** 324 NE 12th Ave. (tel. 823-3189). Rates are $2 per hour. If the weather isn't cooperating, head for the Portland Tennis Center itself. They have indoor courts and charge $4.25 per person per hour for singles matches and $3.25 per person per hour for doubles. The hours here are 7:30am to 10pm.

WHITE-WATER RAFTING

The mountains of Oregon produce some of the best white-water rafting in the country. The Deschutes River and Clackamas River offer plenty of opportunities to shoot the rapids from early spring to early fall. **River Drifters,** 13570 NW Lakeview Dr., Portland, OR 97229 (tel. 645-6264), leads trips on both of these rivers for $55 (with lunch included). **Carrol White-Water Rafting,** P.O. Box 130, Maupin, OR 97037 (tel. 395-2404), and **Ewings' Whitewater,** P.O. Box 427, Maupin, OR 97037 (tel. 395-2697), offer similar trips. A 4-hour trip will cost between $50 and $60. Longer trips are also possible.

CHAPTER 18

STROLLING AROUND PORTLAND

Portland's compactness makes it an ideal city to explore on foot. In fact, the local government is doing all it can to convince Portland's citizens to give up their cars when they come downtown. There's no better way to get a feel for Portland than to stroll through the Skidmore Historic District and down along the Waterfront Park. If it happens to be a weekend, you'll also get to visit the Saturday Market. No matter where you walk in Portland, you're never far from a public work of art. Keep your eyes peeled.

WALKING TOUR — Old Town

Start: Skidmore Fountain.
Finish: Skidmore Fountain.
Time: Allow approximately 1½ hours, not including museum and shopping stops.
Best Times: Saturday and Sunday, when the Saturday Market is open.
Worst Times: After dark, when this neighborhood is not as safe as in the daylight.

Although Portland was founded in 1843, most of the buildings in Old Town date from the 1880s. A fire in 1872 razed much of the town, which afterward was rebuilt with new vigor. Ornate pilasters, pediments, and cornices grace these brick buildings, one of the largest collections of such structures in the country. However, their most notable features are their cast-iron facades.

Begin your exploration of this 20-block historic neighborhood at the corner of Southwest First Avenue and Ankeny Street at the:

1. **Skidmore Fountain,** the heart of Old Town. Erected in 1888, the fountain was intended to provide refreshment for "horses, men, and dogs," and that it did for many years. Today, however, the bronze-and-granite fountain is purely decorative. Across Southwest First Avenue is the:
2. **New Market Block,** which was constructed in 1872 to house the unlikely combination of a produce market and a theater.

The New Market Block now houses popular shops and restaurants, as do many of the restored historic buildings in this area. The freestanding wall of archways extending out from the New Market Building was salvaged from another Old Town structure that didn't survive the urban renewal craze of the 1960s. Two blocks south is the:

3. **Failing Building** (235 SW First Ave.). Built in 1886, this attractive building integrates French and Italian influences. Turn left on Southwest Oak Street and left again on Southwest Front Avenue and you'll pass by the:

4. **Smith's Block,** some of the most beautifully restored buildings in Old Town. At one time this whole district was filled with elegant structures such as these. The cast-iron filigree appears both solid and airy at the same time. The:

5. **Oregon Maritime Center & Museum** (113 SW Front Ave.) is dedicated to Oregon's shipping history (see p. 228). If it's a Saturday or Sunday between April and Christmas, you will no doubt have noticed the crowds under the bridge ahead of you. This is Portland's:

6. **Saturday Market,** where you'll find the best of Northwest crafts being sold by their makers.

REFUELING STOP The Saturday Market makes an excellent refueling stop in this neighborhood. In **7. the market's food court** you can get all manner of delicious, healthful, and fun foods. Stalls sell everything from "dragon toast" to overstuffed fajitas to pad thai to barbecued ribs. There are always entertainers performing in this area also, so you can enjoy a bit of music while you eat.

At the MAX tram stop, cross First Avenue and turn right. Just as you leave the shadow of the Burnside Bridge, you will be walking along the covered sidewalk of the:

8. **Norton House.** Though this is not the original covered sidewalk, it is characteristic of Portland buildings 100 years ago. Continue to the next corner and turn left on Northwest Couch Street (pronounced Kooch). At the next corner, on your left, is the:

9. **Blagen Block,** another excellent example of the ornate cast-iron facades that appeared on nearly all the buildings in this area at one time. Note the cast-iron figures of women wearing spiked crowns. They are reminiscent of the Statue of Liberty, which had been erected two years before this building opened in 1888. Continue up Northwest Couch Street to the corner of Northwest Second Avenue. Just around the corner to your left on the opposite side of the street is the:

10. **American Advertising Museum** (9 NW Second Ave.). This is the only museum in the United States dedicated to the history of advertising (see p. 222). Back in the late 1800s this was the very popular Erickson's Saloon, with a 684-foot-long bar, card rooms, and a brothel. If you return to Northwest Couch Street and continue to the corner of Northwest Third Avenue, you will see on the northwest corner the:

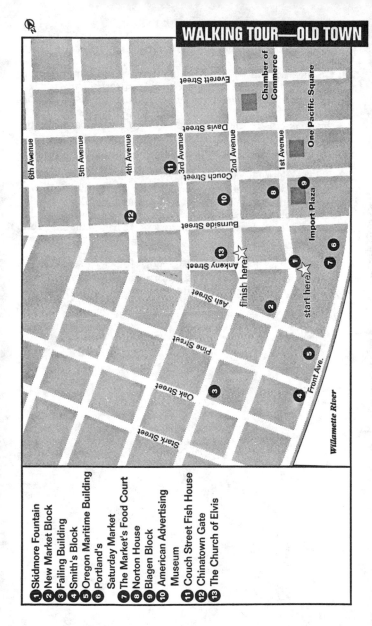

WALKING TOUR—OLD TOWN

Everett Street

Chamber of Commerce

One Pacific Square

Davis Street

6th Avenue
5th Avenue
4th Avenue
3rd Avenue
2nd Avenue
1st Avenue

Couch Street

⑪

⑩

⑧   ⑨

⑫

Import Plaza

Burnside Street

⑬ ☆ finish here

Ankeny Street

① ☆ start here

②

Ash Street

Pine Street

⑤

Front Ave.

Oak Street

③

④

Stark Street

Willamette River

11. Couch Street Fish House, an excellent example of how Portland has used innovative methods to renovate Old Town. This excellent and highly recommended restaurant incorporates two historic buildings into its design. One building houses the restaurant itself, the inside of which is very modern. The other building is merely an ornate brick facade behind which you'll find the restaurant's parking lot. Continue up Northwest Couch

Street to Fourth Avenue and turn left. Directly ahead of you is the:

12. **Chinatown Gate.** Since you are already in Chinatown, you will have to cross to the opposite side of the brightly painted three-tiered gateway to appreciate its Asian ornateness, including two huge flanking bronze Chinese lions. After passing through this gate, cross Burnside Street and turn left on narrow, little Ankeny Street. In two blocks you will see on your left the:

13. **The Church of Elvis** (219 Ankeny St.). This bizarre little altar to kitsch is the world's only 24-hour coin-operated video psychic and church of Elvis (see "Churches" in Section 2 of Chapter 17 for details). For a quarter you can have one of the interactive videos in the window hear your confession. For $1 you can be married by the King himself. It's all very tongue-in-cheek and great fun. From here it's only a block and a half to the Skidmore Fountain.

A Warning: Although much of Old Town has been restored, there are still parts that are a bit seedy. This, unfortunately, happens to be the mission district for the city, and homeless people congregate in the area. It can be very unappealing after dark, so I suggest that you plan to finish the tour before sunset.

CHAPTER 19

PORTLAND SHOPPING

1. THE SHOPPING SCENE

2. SHOPPING A TO Z

Perhaps the single most important fact about shopping in Portland, and all of Oregon for that matter, is that there is no sales tax. The price on the tag is the price you pay. If you come from a state with a high sales tax, you might want to save your shopping for your visit to Portland.

1. THE SHOPPING SCENE

Over the past few years Portland has managed to preserve and restore a good deal of its historic architecture, and many of these late 19th-century and early 20th-century buildings have been turned into unusual and very attractive shopping centers. New Market Village (50 SW Second Ave.), Morgan's Alley (515 SW Broadway), and Skidmore Fountain Square (28 SW First Ave.) are all outstanding examples of how Portland has preserved its historic buildings and kept its downtown area filled with happy shoppers. Yamhill Market (SW First Ave. and Yamhill St.), although it is a new building, was constructed to fit in with the classic architecture of the neighborhood surrounding it.

Portland's most "happening" area for shopping is the Nob Hill district of northwestern Portland. Northwest 23rd Avenue beginning at West Burnside Street is the heart of Nob Hill. Along this stretch of road, and on adjoining streets, you'll find antiques stores, boutiques, card shops, design studios, ethnic restaurants, florists, galleries, home furnishings stores, interior decorators, pubs, and all the other necessities of a bohemian neighborhood gone upscale.

Hours Most small stores in Portland are open Monday through Saturday from 9 or 10am to 5 or 6pm. Shopping malls are usually open Monday through Friday from 9 or 10am to 9pm, on Saturday from 9 or 10am to 6pm, and on Sunday from noon until 5pm. Most art galleries and antiques stores are closed on Monday. Department stores stay open on Friday night until 9pm.

2. SHOPPING A TO Z

ANTIQUES

OLD SELLWOOD ANTIQUE ROW, at east end of Sellwood Bridge on SE 13th St.

With its old Victorian homes and turn-of-the-century architecture, Sellwood is Portland's main antiques district. You'll find 13 blocks with more than 30 antiques dealers and restaurants.

ART GALLERIES

If you're in the market for art, try to arrange your visit to coincide with the first Thursday of a month. On these days galleries in downtown Portland schedule coordinated gallery openings in the evenings. Stroll from one gallery to the next, meeting artists and perhaps buying an original work of art. As an added bonus, the **Oregon Art Institute,** 1219 SW Park Ave. (tel. 226-2811), offers free admission from 5 to 9:30pm on these nights.

An art-gallery guide listing more than 50 Portland galleries is available from the **Portland/Oregon Visitors Association,** Three World Trade Center, 26 SW Salmon St., Portland, OR 97204-3299 (tel. 222-2223).

QUINTANA GALLERIES-OLD TOWN (Native American Art), 139 NW Second Ave. Tel. 223-1729.

Virtually a small museum of contemporary Native American arts, this Old Town store sells baskets and Navajo rugs by various tribes. Their jewelry selection is outstanding, though prices are not cheap.

Quintana's grew so big that it had to split off its Northwest Coastal Indian and Inuit art offerings, as well as Edward S. Curtis photogravures. These can now be found at the downtown gallery, 818 SW First Ave. (tel. 228-6855). Masks, soapstone carvings, prints, and contemporary paintings and sculptures fill the smaller gallery.

RAINDANCE GALLERY, 1115 Northwest Glisan St. Tel. 224-4020.

Located in the Pearl District, a former shipping center that now houses galleries and living lofts, Raindance features works by established Northwest artists. There are several rooms full of ceramics, paintings, sculptures, jewelry, and hand-blown glass from the Pilchuck School in Washington State.

BOOKS

POWELL'S "CITY OF BOOKS," 1005 W. Burnside St. Tel. 228-4651.

This is one of the largest bookstores on the West Coast selling new and used books, and no visit to Portland would be complete without a stop here. You'll find nearly a million volumes in this massive store. To help you locate subjects, there's a handy map of the store available at the front door. Just so you don't starve to death while wandering the aisles, they also have a coffee shop. You should actually try to make this one of your first stops in town so you can pick up a copy of their excellent free map of downtown Portland. Open: Mon–Sat 9am–11pm, Sun 9am–9pm.

If you are looking for a technical book, try **Powell's Technical Books,** 32 NW 11th St. (tel. 228-3906), a block away.

POWELL'S TRAVEL STORE, 701 SW Sixth Ave. Tel. 228-1108.

Literally in the middle of Pioneer Courthouse Square and down below street level, this travel bookstore has plenty of books on Portland, Oregon, and the Northwest, as well as every other part of the world. They often have slide presentations in the evenings here. Ask at the checkout counter if there will be programs during your stay in town. Open: Mon–Sat 9am–9pm, Sun 11am–6pm.

CRAFTS

For the largest selection of local crafts, visit the Saturday Market (see below for details). This entertaining outdoor market is a showcase for the high-quality crafts that are created in this part of the country.

CONTEMPORARY CRAFTS GALLERY, 3934 SW Corbett Ave. Tel. 223-2654.

In business since 1937, this is the nation's oldest nonprofit art gallery showing exclusively artwork in clay, glass, fiber, metal, and wood. It's located in a residential neighborhood between downtown and the John's Landing neighborhood, and has a spectacular tree-shaded porch overlooking the Willamette River. The bulk of the gallery is taken up by glass and ceramic pieces, with several cabinets full of designer jewelry.

HOFFMAN GALLERY, 8245 SW Barnes Rd. Tel. 297-5544.

The Hoffman Gallery is located on the campus of the Oregon School of Arts and Crafts, which has been one of the nation's foremost crafts education centers since 1906. The gallery shows not only works by its own graduates but also works by fine craftspeople from all over the United States. The adjacent gift shop has an outstanding selection of handcrafted items.

THE REAL MOTHER GOOSE, 901 SW Yamhill St. Tel. 223-9510.

⭐ This is Portland's premier crafts shop. They showcase only the very finest contemporary American crafts, including imaginative ceramics, colorful artglass, intricate jewelry, exquisite wooden furniture, handmade fashions, and sculptural works. Hundreds of craftspeople and artists from all over the United States are represented here, and even if you're not buying, you should stop by to see the best of American craftsmanship.

Other locations include Washington Square; Tigard (tel. 620-2243); and the Portland Airport, Main Terminal (tel. 284-9929).

DEPARTMENT STORES

MEIER & FRANK, 621 SW Fifth Ave. Tel. 223-0512.

Meier & Frank is a Portland institution. They have been doing business here for more than 100 years. Their flagship store on Pioneer Courthouse Square was built in 1898 and, with 10 stories, was at one time the tallest store in the Northwest. Today those 10 stories of

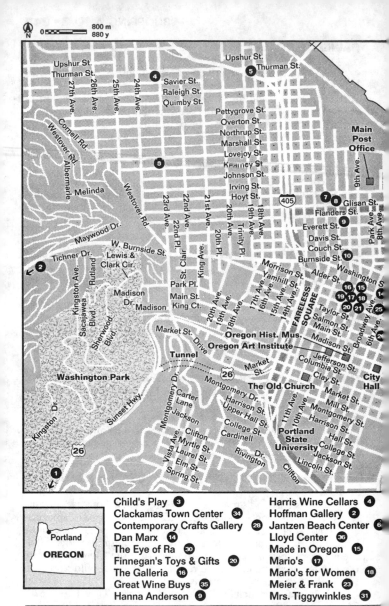

consumer goods still attract crowds of shoppers. The store is open daily, with Monday and Friday usually the late nights. Other locations include 1100 Lloyd Center (tel. 281-4797), and 9300 Southwest Washington Square Road in Tigard (tel. 620-3311).

NORDSTROM, 701 SW Broadway. Tel. 224-6666.

Directly across the street from Pioneer Courthouse Square and a block away from Meier & Frank, Nordstrom is spearheading a

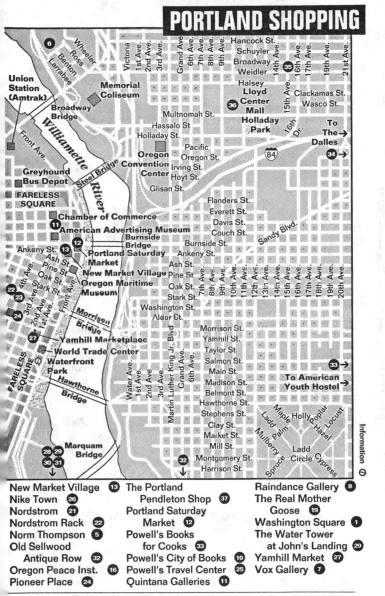

PORTLAND SHOPPING

retailing revolution that's sweeping the nation. Nordstrom is **a** top-of-the-line department store that originated in the Northwest and takes great pride in its personal service and friendliness. This pride is well founded—the store has devoutly loyal customers who would never dream of shopping anywhere else. Although Nordstrom's legendary service is primarily aimed at repeat customers, visitors should not let that dissuade them from doing their shopping here.

DISCOUNT STORES

NORDSTROM RACK, 401 SW Morrison St. Tel. 299-1815.

⭐ Nordstrom is the premier Northwest department store and this is their merchandise clearance store. You'll find discontinued lines, end-of-the-season overstock, and much more packed into a crowded underground shop. Before heading to the main store, be sure to stop by the Rack. You might make your shopping dollars go a lot further.

FASHIONS

NIKE TOWN, 930 SW Sixth Ave. Tel. 221-6453.

⭐ This super-glitzy, ultra-contempo showcase for Nike products blasted onto the Portland shopping scene with all the subtlety of a Super Bowl celebration. Matte black decor, George Segal–style plaster statues of athletes, and videos everywhere give Nike Town the feel of a sports museum or disco. A true shopping experience. Open: Mon–Thurs 10am–8:10pm, Fri 10am–9:23pm, Sat 10am–7:01pm, Sun 11:34–6:16pm.

NORDSTROM, 701 SW Broadway. Tel. 224-6666.

For fashions for the whole family, I must once again send you to this incomparable department store. Their personal service is second to none, and they have a wide selection of fashions at competitive prices. They also offer wardrobe consultations and an alteration service.

NORM THOMPSON, 1805 NW Thurman St. Tel. 221-0764.

Known throughout the rest of the country from its mail-order catalogs, Norm Thompson is a mainstay of the well-to-do in Portland. Classic styling for men and women is the name of the game here.

THE PORTLAND PENDLETON SHOP, SW Fourth Ave. (between Salmon and Taylor). Tel. 242-0037.

Pendleton wool is as much a part of life in the Northwest as forests and salmon. This company's fine wool fashions for men and women define the country-club look in the Northwest and in many other parts of the country. Pleated skirts and tweed jackets are de rigueur here, as are the colorful blankets that have helped keep generations of Northwesterners warm through long chilly winters.

CHILDREN'S

MRS. TIGGYWINKLES, 5331 SW Macadam Ave. Tel. 227-7084.

Located in the Water Tower at John's Landing shopping center, Mrs. Tiggywinkles sells handmade (and appropriately expensive) children's clothing, dolls, and toys. That special little munchkin in your life will look absolutely adorable in one of the unique outfits available here.

MEN'S

MARIO'S, 921 SW Morrison St. Tel. 227-3477.
Located inside the Galleria, Mario's sells self-consciously stylish European men's fashions straight off the pages of *GQ* and *M*. Prices are as high as you would expect. If you long to be European, but your birth certificate says otherwise, here you can at least adopt the look.

WOMEN'S

THE EYE OF RA, 5331 SW Macadam Ave. Tel. 224-4292.
Women with sophisticated tastes in ethnic fashions will want to visit this pricey shop in The Water Tower at John's Landing shopping center. Silks and rayons predominate, and there is plenty of ethnic jewelry by creative designers to accompany any ensemble you might put together here.

MARIO'S FOR WOMEN, 811 SW Morrison St. Tel. 241-8111.
Flip through the pages of a European edition of *Vogue* magazine and you'll get an idea of the fashions you can find at the women's version of fashionable Mario's. Up-to-the-minute and back-to-the-future European fashions fill the racks.

FOOD

The Made in Oregon shops have the best selection of local food products such as hazelnuts, marionberry and raspberry jams, and smoked salmon. See the "Gifts/Souvenirs" section, below, for details.

GIFTS/SOUVENIRS

For unique handmade souvenirs of your trip to Portland, your best bet is the Saturday Market (see "Markets," below, for details).

MADE IN OREGON, 921 SW Morrison St. (in the Galleria). Tel. 241-3630.
Though the prices are a bit high, this is your one-stop shop for all manner of made-in-Oregon gifts, food products, and clothing. Every product they sell here was either grown, caught, or made in Oregon. This is the place to go for salmon, filberts, jams and jellies, Pendleton woolens, and Oregon wines. If you forgot to pick up a

salmon or any of their other popular products while you were in town, give them a call at their toll-free number (tel. 800/828-9673).

Other branches can be found in the Portland Airport's Main Terminal (tel. 282-7827); in Lloyd Center, SE Multnomah St. and SE Broadway (tel. 282-7636); and at Washington Square, off Oregon Hwy. 217 in Tigard (tel. 620-4670), All branches are open daily, though hours vary from store to store.

JEWELRY

DAN MARX, 511 SW Broadway. Tel. 228-5090.

For almost as long as Portland has existed, Dan Marx has been selling its better-off citizens fine jewelry. Everything sparkles and shines inside this store, and the helpful staff will be happy to educate you on the fine points of buying precious stones.

MALLS/SHOPPING CENTERS

GALLERIA, 921 SW Morrison St. Tel. 228-2748.

Located in the heart of downtown Portland, the Galleria is a three-story atrium building with more than 50 specialty shops, including a Made in Oregon store where you can stock up on Oregon-made gifts. Before being restored and turned into its present incarnation, this building was one of Portland's earliest department stores. Parking validation available at adjacent parking garage.

JANTZEN BEACH CENTER, 1405 Jantzen Beach Center. Tel. 289-5555.

This large shopping mall is located on the site of a former amusement park, and the old carousel is still in operation. There are three major department stores and more than 100 other shops. You'll also find the R.E.I. co-op recreational-equipment store here. This mall has long been popular with residents of Washington State, who come to shop where there is no sales tax.

LLOYD CENTER, bounded by SE Multnomah St., SE Broadway, SE 16th Ave., and SE Ninth Ave. Tel. 282-2511.

Lloyd Center was the largest shopping mall on the West Coast when it opened in 1960. In the summer of 1991 an extensive renovation was completed to bring it up to current standards. There are now more than 165 shops here, including a Nordstrom and a Meier & Frank. A food court, ice-skating rink, and eight-screen cinema complete the mall's facilities.

NEW MARKET VILLAGE, 50 SW Second Ave. Tel. 228-2392.

Housed in a brick building built in 1872, this small shopping center is listed in the National Register of Historic Places. You'll find it directly across the street from the Skidmore Fountain and the Saturday Market. A long row of freestanding archways salvaged from a demolished building creates a courtyard on one side of the New Market Village building. Also on this side are several open-air restaurants.

PIONEER PLACE, 700 SW Fifth Ave. Tel. 228-5800.

⭐ Located only a block from Pioneer Courthouse Square, Portland's newest downtown shopping center is also its most upscale. Anchored by a Saks Fifth Avenue, Pioneer Place is where the elite shop when looking for high fashions and expensive gifts. You'll also find Portland's branch of the Nature Company and the city's only Godiva *chocolatier* here.

WASHINGTON SQUARE, off Oregon Hwy. 217 in Tigard. Tel. 639-8860.

This is the only shopping mall in the Northwest with six major department stores, plus more than 130 shops and eating establishments. It's the main shopping center for Portland's western suburbs. Lots of free parking.

THE WATER TOWER AT JOHN'S LANDING, 5331 SW Macadam Ave. Tel. 228-9431.

As you're driving south from downtown Portland on Macadam Avenue, you can't miss the old wooden water tower for which this unusual shopping mall is named. Standing high above the roof of the mall, it was once used as a storage tank for fire-fighting water. The building, originally a furniture factory, was converted to a shopping and office complex in 1973. Hardwood floors, huge overhead beams, and a tree-shaded courtyard paved with Belgian cobblestones from Portland's first paved streets give this place plenty of character. There are about 40 specialty shops here.

YAMHILL MARKET, 110 SW Yamhill St. Tel. 224-6705.

Built to resemble the old buildings of the nearby Skidmore District, Yamhill Market blends in well with its downtown surroundings. The multilevel shopping center is filled with large and small specialty shops. Upstairs there's a food court serving everything from deli fare to South American cuisine. In the summer, there are live music performances on the roof, and a piano in the food court is for the use of market patrons.

MARKETS

PORTLAND SATURDAY MARKET, underneath the Burnside Bridge (between SW First Ave. and SW Ankeny St.). Tel. 222-6072.

⭐ The Saturday Market (which is held on both Saturday and Sunday) is arguably Portland's single most important and best-loved event. For years the Northwest has attracted artists and craftspeople, and every Saturday and Sunday nearly 300 of them can be found selling their exquisite creations here. In addition to the dozens of craftspeople's stalls, you'll find flowers, fresh produce, ethnic and unusual foods, and lots of free entertainment. This is the single best place to shop for one-of-a-kind gifts in Portland. The atmosphere is always cheerful and the crowds are always colorful. At the heart of the Skidmore District, the Saturday Market makes an excellent starting or finishing point for a walk around Portland's most historic neighborhood. Don't miss this unique market. On Sunday, on-street parking is free. Open: March to Christmas, Sat 10am–5pm, Sun 11am–4:30pm. MAX: Skidmore Fountain station.

TOYS

FINNEGAN'S TOYS & GIFTS, 922 SW Yamhill St. Tel. 221-0306.

We all harbor a bit of child within ourselves, and this is the sort of place that has that child kicking and screaming in the aisles if you don't buy that silly little toy you never got when you were young. Kids love this place too. It's the largest toy store in downtown Portland. Open: Mon–Sat 10am–6pm, Sun noon–5pm.

WINES

An excellent selection of Oregon wines can be found at any Made in Oregon shop. They're located in the Lloyd Center shopping mall, the Galleria, Washington Square, and Portland Airport. See the "Gifts/Souvenirs" section, above, for details.

There are quite a number of wineries within easy driving distance of Portland where you can taste and buy wines. See Section 3 of Chapter 21 for details.

GREAT WINE BUYS, 1515 NE Broadway. Tel. 287-BUYS.

Enophiles who have developed a taste for Oregon wines will want to stop in here and stock up before heading home. This is one of the best wine shops in Portland. Open: Mon–Thurs 10am–5:30pm, Fri 10am–8pm, Sat 10:30am–5pm, Sun noon–5pm.

HARRIS WINE CELLARS LTD, 2300 NW Thurman St. Tel. 223-2222.

Located at the northern and less fashionable end of Northwest 23rd Avenue, Harris Wine Cellars caters to serious wine connoisseurs, and has been doing so for many years. It isn't glamorous, but the folks here know their wines. Open: Daily 10am–6pm.

CHAPTER 20

PORTLAND NIGHTS

1. THE PERFORMING ARTS
- **MAJOR CONCERT & PERFORMANCE HALLS**
2. THE CLUB & MUSIC SCENE
3. THE BAR SCENE
4. MORE ENTERTAINMENT

Portland has become the Northwest's second cultural center. Its symphony, ballet, and opera are all well regarded, and the many theater companies offer classic and contemporary plays. If you are a jazz fan, you'll feel right at home—there's always a lot of live jazz being played around town. In summer, festivals move the city's cultural activities outdoors.

To find out what's going on during your visit, pick up a copy of **Willamette Week,** Portland's weekly arts-and-entertainment newspaper. You can also check the Friday and Sunday editions of **The Oregonian,** the city's daily newspaper.

Many of the theaters and performance halls in Portland offer discounts for students and senior citizens. You can often save money by buying your ticket on the day of a performance or within a half hour of curtain time.

Anyone who wants can pick up half-price day-of-show tickets to theater performances at **PDX TIX,** 921 SW Morrison St. (tel. 241-4903). This phone number is for information only, since they don't take telephone reservations. The small ticket counter is located inside the Galleria shopping center and is open Thursday through Saturday from noon to 6pm, or Sunday from noon to 5pm.

1. THE PERFORMING ARTS

MAJOR PERFORMING ARTS COMPANIES
OPERA & CLASSICAL MUSIC

OREGON SYMPHONY ORCHESTRA, Arlene Schnitzer Concert Hall, SW Broadway and SW Main St. Tel. 228-1353.

Founded in 1896, this is the oldest symphony orchestra on the West Coast. Under the expert baton of conductor James DePreist, it has achieved national recognition and status. Four series are held each season, including classical, pops, Sunday matinees, and children's concerts. The season runs from September to June.

MAJOR CONCERT & PERFORMANCE HALLS

Intermediate Theatre. Tel. 248-4496.
New Rose Theatre. Tel. 222-2487.
Portland Civic Auditorium. Tel. 248-4496.
Portland Civic Theatre. Tel. 226-3048.
Portland Repertory Theater. Tel. 224-4491.
Arlene Schnitzer Concert Hall. Tel. 248-4496.
Dolores Winningstad Theatre. Tel. 248-4496.

Prices: $12.50–$35. Sun matinees are the least expensive. Senior citizens and students may purchase half-price tickets 1 hour before a classical concert.

PORTLAND OPERA, 1516 SW Alder St. Tel. 241-1802.

The Portland Opera, which performs at the Portland Civic Auditorium, offers four different productions each season, ranging from traditional grand opera to light opera to world premieres. Performances are usually held in September, November, March, and May.

Prices: $19–$75. Senior citizens and students may attend dress rehearsals for a nominal charge.

THEATER COMPANIES

OREGON SHAKESPEARE FESTIVAL PORTLAND, 1111 SW Broadway. Tel. 274-6588.

The immensely popular Oregon Shakespeare Festival, which takes place every summer in Ashland, way down near the California state line, became so popular a few years back that they brought the whole program to Portland for the winter season. The season, which runs from November to April, sees five productions of classic and modern plays.

Prices: $8–$25. Student and senior-citizen rush tickets available 1 hour before a show for $8.

DANCE COMPANIES

OREGON BALLET THEATRE, 1119 SW Park Ave. Tel. 227-6867.

This company was formed in late 1989 from two popular Portland ballet companies, and is now much stronger than either of its two predecessors ever were. Programs range from traditional ballets such as *The Nutcracker* and *Romeo and Juliet* to new works. Performances are given in the Civic Auditorium, and each year's season includes a guest performance by a visiting nationally acclaimed company.

Prices: $8–$50.

MAJOR CONCERT HALLS & ALL-PURPOSE AUDITORIUMS

The **Portland Center for the Performing Arts,** SW Broadway and SW Main St. (tel. 248-4496), has helped spur a renaissance along Southwest Broadway, once the busy heart of Portland's dining and entertainment district. Four theaters fall under the one long name.

ARLENE SCHNITZER CONCERT HALL, SW Broadway and SW Main St. Tel. 248-4496.

Formerly a 1920s movie palace, the Schnitz, as it is known locally, still displays the original Portland theater sign and marquee out front. Inside, you'll be thrilled by the immaculate restoration of this stately old theater. It is home to the Oregon Symphony Orchestra, and also hosts popular music bands, lecturers, a travel-film series, and many other special performances.

Tours: Wed 11am, and Sat 11am, noon, and 1pm; free.
Prices: $4.50–$40

NEW THEATRE BUILDING, SW Broadway and SW Main St. Tel. 248-4496.

Across the street from the Schnitz is the beautiful New Theatre Building, which houses two smaller theaters—the **Intermediate** and the **Winningstad.** A brilliant contrast to the art deco Schnitz, this building is a sparkling glass jewelbox. The Intermediate Theatre is home of the Oregon Shakespeare Festival Portland, while the two theaters together host stage productions by local and visiting companies.

Tours: Wed 11am, and Sat 11am, noon, and 1pm; free.
Prices: $6–$25. Student and senior-citizen discounts sometimes available.

PORTLAND CIVIC AUDITORIUM, SW Third Ave. and SW Clay St. Tel. 248-4496.

The Civic Auditorium is a few blocks from the three theaters mentioned just above. It was constructed shortly after World War I and completely remodeled in the 1960s. Touring Broadway musicals perform in this large hall. This is also the home of both the Oregon Ballet Theatre and the Portland Opera.

Prices: $13–$74.

THEATERS

NEW ROSE THEATRE, 904 SW Main St. Tel. 222-2487.

Performances at the New Rose Theatre are sometimes uneven, but usually have their strong points. The productions range from old standards to lesser-known plays. The theater is adjacent to the Oregon Art Institute.

Prices: $10–$15.

PORTLAND CIVIC THEATRE, 1530 SW Yamhill St. Tel. 226-3048.

Portland's oldest theater company has had a rough time of it over the past few years, but seems to be staying afloat despite all the competition in town. There are year-round performances of Broadway musicals, children's theater, and comedies held Thursday through Sunday nights. If you happen to be in town during the Christmas season, try to catch the annual performance of *Peter Pan*. It's a timeless hit with children and adults.

Prices: $12–$14.

PORTLAND REPERTORY THEATER, World Trade Center, 25 SW Salmon St. Tel. 224-4491.

✪ Portland's oldest Equity theater offers consistently excellent productions, which have such a reputation that it is almost impossible to get individual tickets to performances. The Rep does reliable plays, nothing too avant-garde and no classics (who can compete with the Oregon Shakespeare Festival Portland?).

Prices: $20–$22. Half-price rush tickets are available a half hour before performances.

2. THE CLUB & MUSIC SCENE

NIGHTCLUBS & CABARETS

DARCELLE XV, 208 NW Third Ave. Tel. 222-5338.

This campy Portland institution with a transvestite show has been a huge hit with the natives for years. Darcelle, a one-time transvestite beauty-contest winner, is so much a part of the Portland scene that he shows up on floats in official city parades.

Showtimes: Tues 8:30pm, Wed–Sat 8:30 and 10:30pm.
Admission: $8. Reservations required Fri–Sat.

COMEDY CLUBS

THE LAST LAUGH, 426 NW Sixth Ave. Tel. 295-2478.

This is Portland's grandest and most popular comedy club, where local and nationally known comedians perform. You'll think you're in Las Vegas when you see the interior of this place. Dinner and drinks are available.

Open: Nightly 6pm to 12:30am.
Showtimes: Sun–Thurs 8pm; Fri–Sat 8 and 10:30pm.
Admission: Sun–Thurs $6; Fri–Sat $9.

FOLK & ROCK

KEY LARGO, 31 NW First Ave. Tel. 224-3147.

One of Portland's most popular nightclubs, Key Largo has been packing in music fans for a decade. A tropical atmosphere prevails at this spacious club and Cajun food is served. Rock, reggae, blues, and jazz performers all find their way to the stage here, with local R&B bands a mainstay. The occasional nationally known act shows up here. Open nightly.

Admission: $3–$5 (higher for national acts).

ROSELAND THEATER, 8 NW Sixth Ave. Tel. 227-0071.

⭐ Formerly called Starry Night, the Roseland Theater is only a couple of blocks from Key Largo. The same diversity of popular musical styles prevails. A couple of heavy-metal nights each week attract a rougher crowd than you're likely to find at Key Largo, but other nights you might encounter the likes of Marshal Crenshaw or the Divinyls. Open nightly.

Admission: $5–$15.

SATYRICON, 125 NW Sixth Ave. Tel. 243-2380.

A block away from the Roseland Theater, Satyricon leans heavily toward heavy metal, post-punk trash, and neo-psychedelia. Though most of the bands playing here are locals, the occasional national act also shows up. The crowds are young and rowdy. Open nightly.

Admission: $3–$5 (higher for national acts). No cover charge until 11pm on weeknights.

THE DAKOTA CAFE, 239 SW Broadway. Tel. 241-4151.

Portland's largest nightclub is extremely popular with the college kids and young downtown professionals. There's live music five or more nights per week, with blues, jazz, and swing alternating with R&B and rock. Thursdays and Saturdays are $1 nights, with $1 drinks, dancing to a DJ, and no cover before 9pm. There is also a full restaurant menu. Open nightly.

Admission: $3–$5.

JAZZ & BLUES

Portland is well known as a jazzed-up town. You'll find that lots of restaurants and bars feature live or recorded jazz nightly. Because of this reputation, you're likely to encounter jazz greats performing here at any time of year. In the summer, there are numerous jazz festivals and special jazz concert series in the area. Below are some of the more popular jazz clubs.

BRASSERIE MONTMARTRE, 626 SW Park Ave. Tel. 224-5552.

There's live jazz music nightly after 9pm at this French restaurant. Both the food and the music are popular with a primarily middle-aged clientele that likes to get dressed up when they go out on the town. Dress the part and expect a line at the door at any hour of the day or night. This is the place to see and be seen if you're part of the Portland social scene. Open: Nightly 8pm–1am.

Admission: Free.

PARCHMAN FARM, 1204 SE Clay St. Tel. 235-7831.

If you're into jazz, Parchman Farm is where you hang out in Portland. This club features a music library of more than 1,000 jazz albums, and there's live music Monday through Saturday starting at 9pm. A quiet, casual spot in which to dine and listen to great jazz, Parchman Farm attracts the sort of audience that gets up onstage and starts jamming with the evening's main act. The place also serves "American-style Italian food with a nouvelle flair."

Admission: Free most nights.

THE HOBBIT, 4420 SE 39th Ave. Tel. 771-0742.

The Hobbit has been at the forefront of the Portland jazz scene for years. There's live music six nights a week featuring local and national acts, and every Sunday afternoon from 3:30 to 7pm there's a jam session that attracts local jazz musicians.
Admission: $3–$15.

DANCE CLUBS/DISCOS

MAXI'S LOUNGE, Red Lion/Lloyd Center, 1000 NE Multnomah St. Tel. 281-6111.

For an evening of dancing to live or recorded Top 40 music, head for this or any of the other Red Lions in the Portland area. They all offer elegant settings for dancing the night away, though this lounge is the most spectacular. A long corridor of quilted dusty-rose velvet trimmed with red neon leads to a dark and sparkling disco with glowing etched-glass pillars, two dance floors, and lots of comfortable seating and live music nightly.

Brickstone's, Red Lion/Columbia River, 1401 N. Hayden Island Dr. (tel. 283-2111), attracts a similar upscale crowd.
Admission: Free.

A GAY DISCO

EMBERS, 110 NW Broadway. Tel. 222-3082.

Though this is still primarily a gay disco, straights have discovered its great dance music and have started making the scene as well. Lots of flashing lights and sweaty bodies until the early morning. On Saturday nights, there are drag shows.
Admission: Thurs–Sat $2.

---

3. THE BAR SCENE

PUBS

If you are a beer connoisseur, you'll probably find yourself with little time out from your brew tasting to see any other of Portland's sights. This is the heart of the Northwest microbrewery explosion and has more microbreweries than any other city in the United States. They're brewing beers up here the likes of which you won't taste anywhere else this side of the Atlantic. Although many of these beers—as well as ales, stouts, and bitters—are available in restaurants, you owe it to yourself to go directly to the source. At any of these pubs, you can pick up a guide and map to Portland's microbreweries and brew pubs.

BRIDGEPORT BREWERY & BREW PUB, 1313 NW Marshall St. Tel. 241-7179.

Portland's oldest microbrewery was founded in 1984, and is housed in the city's oldest industrial building. Windows behind the bar let you watch the brewers. It has four to seven of its brews on tap on any given night, and live music on weekends.

HILLSDALE BREWERY & PUBLIC HOUSE, 1505 SW Sunset Blvd. Tel. 246-3938.

★ This was the cornerstone of the McMenamin brothers' microbrewery empire, which now includes more than 20 pubs in the greater Portland metropolitan area. The McMenamins pride themselves in crafting flavorful and unusual ales with bizarre names like Terminator stout and Purple Haze.

Some of their other pubs include the Cornelius Pass Roadhouse, Sunset Hwy. and Cornelius Pass Rd., Hillsboro (tel. 640-6174), in an old farmhouse; the Blue Moon Tavern, 432 NW 21st St. (tel. 223-3184), on a newly fashionable street in northwest Portland; and The Ram's Head, 2282 NW Hoyt St. (tel. 221-0098), between 21st and 22nd avenues.

SPECIALTY BARS
A BAR WITH A VIEW

ATWATER'S, 111 SW Fifth Ave. Tel. 275-3600.

Up on the 30th floor of the pale-pink US BanCorp building is one of Portland's most expensive restaurants and certainly the one with the best view. However, if you'd just like to sit back and sip a martini while gazing out at the city lights below, they have a splendid little bar. Perfect for a romantic nightcap.

A SINGLES BAR

SHANGHAI LOUNGE, 0309 SW Montgomery St. Tel. 220-1865.

Located in the same upscale waterfront shopping and dining complex that houses the Alexis Hotel, the Shanghai Lounge is where Portland's working girls and working boys from the downtown office towers meet and mingle. There's live music several nights a week and recorded Top 40 dance tunes the rest.

A SPORTS BAR

CHAMPIONS, 1401 SW Front Ave. (at the Portland Marriott). Tel. 274-2470.

Portland's premier sports bar boasts "good food, good times, and good sports." If sports are your forte, this is the bar for you. However, there is also a small dance floor here, with dancing to the DJ's Top 40 tunes nightly.

4. MORE ENTERTAINMENT

MOVIES

CINEMA 21, 616 NW 21st Ave. Tel. 223-4515.

Located on the edge of Nob Hill, Portland's most fashionable neighborhood, Cinema 21 is a reliable foreign-film house. This is also where you can catch animation festivals and the occasional revival of an obscure classic.

Admission: $2–$5.

NORTHWEST FILM & VIDEO CENTER, 1219 SW Park Ave. Tel. 221-1156.

Affiliated with the Oregon Art Institute, this repertory cinema schedules an eclectic blend of classics, foreign films, daring avant-garde films, documentaries, animation, even old B-movies. There's no telling what might turn up on any given night.

Admission: $3.50–$8.

BAGDAD THEATER & PUB, 3702 SE Hawthorne Blvd. Tel. 230-0895.

This is the McMenamin brothers' latest Portland establishment. In a reversal of recent cinematic trends, the ever-inspired brothers restored a classic Arabian Nights movie palace to its original size after it had been split up into a multiplex theater. They now show second-run films and pull more than 20 microbrew drafts at the bar. There's good pizza by the slice to go with your brew.

Admission: $1.

MISSION THEATER & PUB, 1624 NW Glisan St. Tel. 223-4031.

This was the McMenamin brothers' first theater pub. Movies are recent releases that have played the main theaters already but not yet made it onto video. Because they don't charge admission, they can't advertise what they're showing, so you'll have to call to find out.

Admission: Free.

CHAPTER 21

EASY EXCURSIONS FROM PORTLAND

1. THE MOUNT HOOD LOOP

2. THE OREGON COAST

3. A WINERY TOUR

Portland likes to boast about how close it is to both the mountains and the ocean, and no visit would be complete without a trip or two out into the countryside. In an hour and a half you can be swimming in the Pacific Ocean or skiing in the Cascade Mountains. In fact, you'll even have this choice in the middle of summer, when there is still snow skiing on Mount Hood. A drive through the Columbia River Gorge is an absolute must. If wine is your interest, you can spend a day visiting wineries and driving through the rolling farmland that enticed early pioneers to travel the Oregon Trail.

1. THE MOUNT HOOD LOOP

If you have time for only one excursion from Portland, I strongly urge you to do the Mount Hood Loop. This is a long trip, so start your day as early as possible.

To begin your trip, take I-84 east out of Portland. Sixteen miles from downtown, take the second Troutdale exit onto the **Columbia River Scenic Highway** (U.S. 30), which was opened in 1915. The highway is an engineering marvel, but it is dwarfed by the spectacular vistas that present themselves whenever the scenic road emerges from the dark forest. To learn more about the road and how it was built, stop at the **Vista House,** 733 feet above the river on **Crown Point.** There are informative displays, including old photos and a spectacular view of the gorge, including **Beacon Rock,** an 800-foot-tall monolith on the far side of the river.

Between Troutdale and Ainsworth State Park, 22 miles east, the road passes nine **waterfalls** and six state parks. Latourelle, Shepperds Dell, Bridal Veil, Wahkeena, Horsetail, Oneonta, Multnomah—the names of the falls evoke the Native American and pioneer heritage of this region. Of all the falls, **Multnomah** is the most famous. At 620 feet from the lip to the pool, it's the tallest waterfall in Oregon. An arched bridge stands directly in front of the falls and is a favorite of photographers.

The next stop on your tour should be the **Bonneville Lock and Dam.** One of the dam's most important features, and the attraction drawing thousands of visitors each year, is the fish ladders. These ladders allow anadromous fish (fish that are spawned in fresh water, mature in salt water, and return to fresh water to spawn) to migrate upstream. Underwater windows allow visitors to see fish as they pass through the ladders. Visit the adjacent fish hatchery to see how trout, salmon, and sturgeon are raised before they are released into the river.

Not far past the dam is the **Bridge of the Gods,** which connects Oregon to Washington at the site where an old tribal legend says a natural bridge once stood. Because of the unusual formation of rocks in the river at this site, as well as the frequent volcanic activity here in the past, geologists tend to believe the legend.

Just beyond the Bridge of the Gods are the **Cascade Locks.** These navigational locks were built to allow river traffic to avoid the treacherous passage through the cascades here. In earlier years many boats were portaged around the cascades instead of attempting the dangerous trip. When the locks were opened in 1896, they made traveling between The Dalles and Portland much easier. But the completion of the Columbia River Scenic Highway in 1915 made the trip even easier by land. With the construction of the Bonneville Dam, the cascades were flooded and the locks became superfluous. There are two small museums here at the locks, one of which also holds the ticket office for the sternwheeler **Columbia Gorge** (tel. 223-3928), which makes regular trips on the river all summer.

HOOD RIVER
WHAT TO SEE & DO

Anyone who sailboards has heard of Hood River. This section of the Columbia River is one of the most popular sailboarding spots in the world because of the strong winds that come rushing down the gorge. Almost every other car in this once-sleepy little town has a sailboard on the roof. If you want to try this thrilling sport yourself, stop by **Sailboards Hood River,** Fourth St. and State St. (tel. 503/386-5363). They offer sales, rentals, and lessons for beginners and advanced sailors. In the winter (and summer for that matter) they rent and sell skis and snowboards.

If you are staying overnight on the Loop, you might want to consider getting out of your car and riding the rails. The **Mount Hood Railroad,** 110 Railroad Ave. (tel. 503/386-3556), operates its Fruit Blossom Special from mid-April to early December. The cars that carry you up the Hood River are vintage Pullman coaches, and the Mount Hood Railroad Depot is a National Historic Site. The morning excursion, departing at 10am, lasts 4 hours and costs $17 for adults, $15 for senior citizens, and $10 for children 2 to 11. The afternoon trip, departing at 3pm, lasts 2 hours and costs $10 for adults, $8 for senior citizens, and $6 for children 2 to 11. In summer the train runs daily except Monday, and in late spring and early fall it runs Wednesday through Sunday, changing to weekends only in the colder months.

WHERE TO STAY

When the scenic highway was opened, it made an immediate hit, and the builder of what is now The Benson Hotel in Portland decided that there should be a hotel in the gorge for motorists. He chose a beautiful spot above a 208-foot-high waterfall that overlooks the Columbia River. Opened in 1921, the **Columbia Gorge Hotel,** 4000 W. Cliff Dr., Hood River, OR 97031 (tel. 503/386-5566, or toll free 800/826-4027; fax 503/386-3359), was an immediate success, attracting the likes of Rudolf Valentino and Clara Bow. The hotel underwent a full renovation in 1989 to re-create its jazz-age grandeur. The pale-yellow facade and red-tile roof of the hotel blend attractively with the rich greens of the surrounding forests, and a 10-acre formal garden is perfect for quiet walks.

All 46 rooms are different, and many of them have canopy or brass beds. If you arrive here between 8am and 2pm Monday through Friday, or between 8am and 2:30pm on a Saturday or Sunday, you can indulge in the most famous breakfast in Oregon. The "Farm Breakfast" is not for those on a diet, those who are in a hurry, or those who are short on cash. It costs a hefty $23 for all you can eat and more, but that price does not include champagne. The best way to enjoy breakfast is to book yourself into the hotel the night before, in which case the breakfast is complimentary. Double-room rates are $175. American Express, Carte Blanche, Diners Club, Discover, MasterCard, and VISA are accepted.

RESORTS SOUTH OF HOOD RIVER & RETURN

From Hood River, turn south on Oregon Hwy. 35, passing through thousands of acres of apple and pear **orchards.** Every fall, roadside stands in this area sell fresh fruit, butters, and juices. The orchards are especially beautiful in the spring, when the trees are in bloom. No matter what time of year, you will have the snow-covered peak of Mount Hood in view as you drive through the orchards, making them all the more spectacular.

About 10 miles off Oregon Hwy. 35, just south of Parkdale, is the **Cooper Spur Ski Area,** a day-use area. (In summer, there is camping hereabouts at Cloud Cap Saddle Campground and Tilly Jane Campground.) **Mount Hood Meadows** (tel. 503/246-7547 or 246-1722), the largest ski area on Mount Hood with seven double-chair lifts and a triple-chair lift, can transport 12,500 skiers per hour to the nearly 3,000 acres of ski slopes.

Beyond Mount Hood Meadows, you reach **Barlow Pass.** At 4,157 feet, it's the highest point on the Loop. This is where the Pacific Crest Trail crosses the highway on its 2,000-mile journey between Canada and Mexico.

Just after U.S. 26 enters Oregon Hwy. 35 from the south, turn right on the road to **Timberline Lodge,** Timberline Lodge, OR 97028 (tel. 503/231-5400, or toll free 800/547-1406 between 9am and 4pm Monday through Saturday for reservations only; tel. 503/231-7979 for information; fax 503/272-3710), which offers skiing almost year round. This historic ski resort was constructed during the Great Depression as a WPA program. It was conceived as a showcase for the talents of local artisans and craftsmen, and it is constructed almost entirely of local materials. From the moment you walk up the wide stone steps and into the stone-walled downstairs lobby of this grand, old-world-style mountain lodge, you know you're in a very special hotel. The work of skilled woodcarvers and blacksmiths is evident everywhere. Aged wood, both indoors and out, fairly glows; wide-plank floors echo in the cavernous hall of the main lobby; massive doors with giant wrought-iron knockers swing slowly open on their handmade hinges; fires crackle in the stone fireplaces of the lower lobby. A permanent display room for visitors in the lower lobby is part of an exhibit about the hotel and its construction. There are also regularly scheduled tours.

This is the sort of place skiers and romantics dream about. Each of the 59 rustic rooms is decorated with either original hand-loomed rugs and blankets or recent reproductions of the originals. Wood paneling and watercolors of wildflowers add warmth and color. Room rates range from $52, single or double (with a bath down the hall), to $135, single or double (for a fireplace room). There are two bars—the Ram's Head on a mezzanine above the main lobby and the Blue Ox down in the stone-walled basement. The Cascade Dining Room is a formal restaurant featuring salmon, steak, lamb, seafood, even squab, in the $15 to $21 range. American Express, Discover, MasterCard, and Visa accepted.

Back down on U.S. 26 heading west toward Portland, there is another popular ski area, the **Multorpor SkiBowl** (tel. 503/243-3937). It's also open in the summer, with an Alpine Slide and go-kart racing. The SkiBowl, the closest ski area to Portland, is located near the town of Government Camp, which has many small lodges and restaurants that cater primarily to winter skiers.

However, not too much farther down the highway is an all-season resort. **The Resort at the Mountain,** 68010 E. Fairway Ave., Welches, OR 97067 (tel. 503/622-3101, or toll free 800/669-7666; fax 503/622-5227), offers 27 holes of golf, swimming, hiking, tennis, mountain biking, nearby skiing, and conference facilities for up to 1,000 people. The grounds are landscaped to blend into the Northwest landscape, and the rooms are in low-rise buildings scattered across the property. There are both an indoor and an outdoor pool, a sauna, fitness room, golf shop, restaurant, lounge, coffee shop, and snack shop. A huge fireplace in the lobby crackles with enormous fires in the winter. In the Augusta Lounge there's live entertainment and dancing on the weekends.

The rooms are all quite large and come with coffee makers, patios or balconies, lots of closet space (even special coat closets where you can store your skis). Before you head for your room, be sure to ask for a map of the resort—it's so large that it's easy to get lost. Rooms run $99 to $125 for doubles, and $130 to $178 for suites.

Even if you aren't staying at the resort, you can play a round of golf. Greens fees range from $15 to $30. For more information, phone toll free 800/669-GOLF.

Between Government Camp and The Resort at the Mountain, watch for the marker beside the road showing where the end of the **Oregon Trail toll road** around Mount Hood was located. There is a reconstruction of the gate that once stood on this spot, and you can still see the trail itself.

It's a lot easier to cover those last 40 miles to Portland now than it was 150 years ago. Just stay on Oregon Hwy. 26 all the way back to town or follow the signs for I-84.

2. THE OREGON COAST

With so much water around Portland, it is often difficult to believe that it's 90 miles to the coast. Still, the miles go by quickly, and before too long you are thrilled by the spectacular vistas, crashing surf, and long quiet beaches. Since there are more than 400 miles of coastline in Oregon, I'll concentrate on the section that's most accessible to Portland.

The quickest route from Portland to the Oregon coast is on U.S. Hwy. 26, also called Sunset Highway. From downtown to the beach takes less than 2 hours. Just before reaching the junction with U.S. Hwy. 101, watch for a sign marking the **world's largest Sitka spruce tree.** This giant is located in a small park just off the highway. Trees of this size were once common throughout the Coast Range, but almost all have now been cut down. The fight to preserve the remaining big trees is a bitter one that has the citizens of Oregon divided.

At the junction with U.S. Hwy. 101, turn north and watch for the turnoff for **Ecola Beach State Park.** Located just north of the town of Cannon Beach, this park provides some of the most spectacular views on the coast. Just offshore stands **Haystack Rock,** a massive rock island 235 feet tall, that is the most photographed rock on the coast. And stretching out to the south is Cannon Beach. There are stands of old-growth spruce, hemlock, and Douglas fir in the park, and a number of trails offer a chance to walk through this lush forest. The trail down to the beach is steep, but you can still get a good view of sea lions basking in the sun even if you don't go all the way down.

Cannon Beach, known as the Provincetown or Carmel of the Northwest depending on which coast you are more familiar with, is named for the cannon and capstan of the USS *Shark,* which washed ashore here after the ship sank in 1849. Haystack Rock, only a few feet out from the beach, is popular with beachcombers and tidepool explorers. In town, there are many art galleries and interesting shops, even a popular little theater (the Coaster Theater), which stages performances all year. Every summer the **Cannon Beach Sandcastle Contest** attracts sand sculptors and thousands of appreciative viewers. Any time of year, you'll find the winds here ideal for kite flying.

Heading south out of Cannon Beach will bring you to the rugged and remote **Oswald West State Park,** named for the governor who enacted legislation to preserve all beaches as public property. The beach is in a cove that can only be reached by walking a few hundred yards through dense rain forest; once you are there, all you will hear is the crashing of the surf. The beach is strewn with huge driftwood logs that give it a wild look. High bluffs rise up at both ends of the cove and it is possible to hike to the top of them. There are plenty of picnic tables and a campground for tent campers only.

Hwy. 101 continues south from Oswald West State Park and climbs up over **Neahkahnie Mountain.** Legend has it that at the base of this oceanside mountain, the survivors of a wrecked Spanish galleon buried a fortune in gold. Keep your eyes open for elk, which frequently graze on the meadows here at the top of Neahkahnie Mountain.

Just below this windswept mountain is the quiet resort village of **Manzanita.** Tucked under the fir, spruce, and hemlock trees are the summer homes of some of Portland's wealthier residents. There is also a long stretch of sandy beach at the foot of the village.

Tillamook Bay is one of the largest bays on the Oregon coast and at its north end is the small town of Garibaldi, which is a popular sportfishing spot. If you aren't an angler, you can still go for a cruise either around the bay or to look for whales.

Just before reaching the busy town of **Tillamook,** you will come to the **Tillamook Cheese Factory.** This region is one of Oregon's main dairy-farming regions, and much of the milk is turned into cheddar cheese and butter. The first cheese factory opened here in 1894. Today you can watch the sophisticated cheese-making process through large windows. The cheese-factory store is a busy place, but the lines move quickly and you can be on your way to the next picnic area with an assortment of tasty cheeses.

From Tillamook the **Three Capes Scenic Route** leads to Cape Meares, Cape Lookout, and Cape Kiwanda, all three of which provide stunning vistas of rocky cliffs, misty mountains, and booming surf. As the name implies, this is a very scenic stretch of road, and there are plenty of places to stop and enjoy the views and the beaches.

Cape Meares State Park perches high atop the cape, with the Cape Meares lighthouse just a short walk from the parking lot. This lighthouse, 200 feet above the water, was built in 1890. Today it has been replaced by an automated light a few feet away. Be sure to visit the **octopus tree** here in the park. This Sitka spruce has been twisted and sculpted by harsh weather.

As you come down from the cape, you will come to the village of **Oceanside,** which clings to the steep mountainsides of a small cove. There are one tavern and one restaurant in town, and that's the way folks here like it. After seeing the overdevelopment in other coastal towns, I'm sure you'll understand why.

South of Oceanside the road runs along a flat stretch of beach before reaching **Cape Lookout State Park.** Cape Lookout, a steep forested ridge jutting out into the Pacific, is an excellent place for whale watching in the spring. A trail leads from either the main (lower) parking area or the parking area at the top of the ridge out to the end of the point. From the upper parking lot it is a 5-mile round trip to the point.

At Sandlake Junction, about 14 miles south of Oceanside, turn left and you will return to U.S. Hwy. 101. Head north to Tillamook, where Oregon Hwy. 6 heads east toward Portland. This road is subject to landslides and is sometimes closed so be sure to ask in Tillamook before heading east. Oregon Hwy. 6 joins U.S. Hwy. 26 about 25 miles west of Portland. Allow about 2½ hours to get back.

3. A WINERY TOUR

In recent years Oregon wines have been winning many awards for their outstanding quality. This isn't surprising when you realize that Oregon is on the same latitude as France's wine-growing regions. The climate is also very similar — cool, wet winters and springs and long, dry summers with warm days and cool nights. These are ideal conditions for growing wine grapes, and local vineyards are making the most of a good situation.

A "Discover Oregon Wineries" brochure describing more than 50 Oregon wineries is available from the **Oregon Winegrowers' Association,** 1200 NW Front Ave., Suite 400, Portland, OR 97209 (tel. 503/228-8403). Almost all of these wineries are within an hour or two of Portland, and consequently a day of driving from one winery to another makes for a pleasant outing. I suggest picking four or five that sound interesting to you and then mapping out the best routes between them. A trip through wine country is a chance to see the fertile valleys that lured pioneers down the Oregon Trail. For more information about the Oregon wine scene, including a calendar of winery events, pick up a copy of **Oregon Wine,** a monthly newspaper, in any local wine shop, or contact the **Oregon Wine Press,** 644 SE 20th Ave., Portland, OR 97214 (tel. 503/232-7607). With summer festivals a big part of the Oregon winery scene, you can enjoy picnics while listening to live jazz bands at many vineyards.

The trip outlined below is one of the easiest, and my favorite. Start the tour by heading west from Portland on U.S. 26 (Sunset Highway) to Oregon Hwy. 217 (Beaverton–Tigard Highway). Take the Scholls Ferry Road exit heading west. After 4½ miles, turn left on Vandermost Road and you'll arrive at **Ponzi Vineyards** (tel. 503/628-1227), producers of award-winning Pinot Noirs, Chardonnays, and white Rieslings. It's open on Saturday and Sunday from noon to 5pm; closed in January.

Continue on Oregon Hwy. 210 (Scholls Ferry Road) to Oregon Hwy. 219 toward Hillsboro to reach **Oak Knoll Winery** (tel.

503/648-8198), which is at the end of Burkhalter Road. They have been bottling wines for more than 20 years here—Chardonnay, Pinot Noir, Gewürztraminer, Cabernet Sauvignon, and Riesling. Visits are Wednesday through Sunday from noon to 5pm.

In Forest Grove, due west of Hillsboro on Oregon Hwy. 8, there are three vineyards. **Laurel Ridge Winery** is at 255 David Hill Rd. (tel. 503/842-7744), west of Forest Grove on Oregon Hwy. 8. There was wine produced on this site as far back as the 1800s; today the vineyard is planted with Pinot Noir, Gewürztraminer, Semillon, Sylvaner, and Riesling. They also produce sparkling wines by the *méthode champenoise*. The vineyard is open daily from noon to 5pm; closed in January. **Shafer Vineyard Cellars,** just off Oregon Hwy. 8 west of town (tel. 503/357-6604), is situated on rolling hillsides planted with Chardonnay, white Riesling, Pinot Noir Blanc, Pinot Noir, Gewürztraminer, and Sauvignon Blanc. In July and August, there are jazz concerts here on Sunday. Visits are June to September, daily from noon to 5pm; October to May, on Saturday and Sunday from noon to 5pm. **Tualatin Vineyards,** on Seavey Road, off Clapshaw Hill Road, which leaves Oregon Hwy. 8 just beyond Gales Creek (tel. 503/357-5005), has a large tasting room and picnic tables overlooking the Tualatin Valley. They produce Chardonnay, white Riesling, Gewürztraminer, and Pinot Noir. The vineyards are open Monday through Friday from 10am to 4pm, on Saturday and Sunday from noon to 5pm; closed January and holidays.

From here take Seavey Road to Clapshaw Hill Road, continuing east when the two roads come together. Turn left on Thatcher Road and then right on Greenville Road. Take a left again at the intersection with Oregon Hwy. 47. Turn east on Oregon Hwy. 6, which soon merges with U.S. Hwy. 26 heading into Portland, which is a little more than 20 miles away.

INDEX

GENERAL INFORMATION

SIGHTS & ATTRACTIONS

SEATTLE

EXCURSION AREAS

PORTLAND

NOTE: An asterisk (*) indicates an Author's Favorite

EXCURSION AREAS

ACCOMMODATIONS

SEATTLE

KEY TO ABBREVIATIONS: *B* = Budget; *B&B* = Bed and Breakfast; *E* = Expensive; *M* = Moderate; *VE* = Very Expensive; * = an Author's Favorite; $ = Super-Special Value

RESTAURANTS BY CUISINE

SEATTLE

AMERICAN/CONTINENTAL
Café Sophie (M), 75–6
Canlis (E), 80–1
The Georgian Room (E), 89
Merchants Café (M), 76–7, 79
The Palm Court (E), 89–90
13 Coins Restaurant (E), 92
Top of the Hilton (E), 91
Western Coffee Shop (B$), 80

CAJUN
Franglor's Cajun and Creole Café (B$), 79

CHINESE
Linyen (M$), 76

EASTERN EUROPEAN
Labuznik (E), 72

FRENCH
Campagne (E), 86
La Rive Gauche (E$), 74
Le Gourmand (E*$), 84
Le Tastevin (E), 81–2
Maximilien in the Market (E$), 72

INDONESIAN/MALAYSIAN
Wild Ginger (M*), 78

INTERNATIONAL
Café Sophie (M*), 75–6
Cutter's Bayhouse (E), 92

ITALIAN
Il Bistro (E), 67–70
The Pink Door (M*), 77
Prego (E), 90

JAPANESE
Kamon on Lake Union (E), 81
Takara (M), 77

MEXICAN
Macheezmo Mouse (B$), 91
Tlaquepaque (M), 77–8

NATURAL
Gravity Bar (B*), 79, 80

NORTHWEST
Café Alexis (E), 86–7
Café Sport (E*), 70
Chez Shea (E), 70
Dahlia Lounge (E*), 70–1
The Emerald Suite & Space Needle Restaurant (E), 90
Fuller's (E*), 87–8
The Georgian Room (E*), 88–9
The Hunt Club (E), 89
The Palm Court (E), 89–90
Peter's on the Park (E), 82
Rain City Grill (E), 82–3
Raison d'Etre (E), 74
Rover's (E*), 83

PIZZA
Pizzeria Pagliacci (B), 84

SEAFOOD
Elliott's (E), 71
Emmet Watson's Oyster Bar (B), 78–9
Hiram's at the Locks (E), 84–5
Ivar's Acres of Clams (M), 76
Ivar's Captain's Table (M), 82
Ivar's Salmon House (M), 79, 86
McCormick & Schmick's (E), 72–3
McCormick's Fish House & Bar (E), 73
Ray's Boathouse (E), 85
Triples (E), 85–6

STEAKS
FX McRory's Steak, Chop & Oyster House (E), 71–2
Metropolitan Grill (E), 73–4

THAI
Siam on Broadway (M), 83–4

VIETNAMESE
Café Hue (M*$), 74–5

KEY TO ABBREVIATIONS: B = Budget; E = Expensive; M = Moderate; VE = Very Expensive; * = an Author's Favorite; $ = Super-Special Value

PORTLAND

FROMMER'S CITY GUIDES

(Pocket-size guides to sightseeing and tourist accommodations and facilities in all price ranges)

☐ Amsterdam/Holland	$8.95	☐ Minneapolis/St. Paul	$8.95
☐ Athens	$8.95	☐ Montréal/Québec City	$8.95
☐ Atlanta	$8.95	☐ New Orleans	$8.95
☐ Atlantic City/Cape May	$8.95	☐ New York	$12.00
☐ Bangkok	$12.00	☐ Orlando	$12.00
☐ Barcelona	$12.00	☐ Paris	$8.95
☐ Belgium	$7.95	☐ Philadelphia	$11.00
☐ Berlin	$10.00	☐ Rio	$8.95
☐ Boston	$8.95	☐ Rome	$8.95
☐ Cancún/Cozumel/Yucatán	$8.95	☐ Salt Lake City	$8.95
☐ Chicago	$9.95	☐ San Diego	$8.95
☐ Denver/Boulder/Colorado Springs	$8.95	☐ San Francisco	$12.00
☐ Dublin/Ireland	$10.00	☐ Santa Fe/Taos/Albuquerque	$10.95
☐ Hawaii	$12.00	☐ Seattle/Portland	$12.00
☐ Hong Kong	$7.95	☐ St. Louis/Kansas City	$9.95
☐ Las Vegas	$8.95	☐ Sydney	$8.95
☐ Lisbon/Madrid/Costa del Sol	$8.95	☐ Tampa/St. Petersburg	$8.95
☐ London	$12.00	☐ Tokyo	$8.95
☐ Los Angeles	$8.95	☐ Toronto	$8.95
☐ Mexico City/Acapulco	$8.95	☐ Vancouver/Victoria	$7.95
☐ Miami	$8.95	☐ Washington, D.C.	$12.00

FROMMER'S $-A-DAY® GUIDES

(Guides to low-cost tourist accommodations and facilities)

☐ Australia on $40 a Day	$13.95	☐ Israel on $40 a Day	$13.95
☐ Costa Rica, Guatemala & Belize		☐ Mexico on $45 a Day	$18.00
on $35 a Day	$15.95	☐ New York on $65 a Day	$15.00
☐ Eastern Europe on $25 a Day	$16.95	☐ New Zealand on $45 a Day	$16.00
☐ England on $50 a Day	$17.00	☐ Scotland & Wales on $40 a Day	$18.00
☐ Europe on $45 a Day	$19.00	☐ South America on $40 a Day	$15.95
☐ Greece on $35 a Day	$14.95	☐ Spain on $50 a Day	$15.95
☐ Hawaii on $70 a Day	$18.00	☐ Turkey on $40 a Day	$22.00
☐ India on $40 a Day	$20.00	☐ Washington, D.C., on $45 a Day	$17.00
☐ Ireland on $40 a Day	$17.00		

FROMMER'S CITY $-A-DAY GUIDES

☐ Berlin on $40 a Day	$12.00	☐ Madrid on $50 a Day (avail. Jan '92)	$13.00
☐ Copenhagen on $50 a Day	$12.00	☐ Paris on $45 a Day	$12.00
☐ London on $45 a Day	$12.00	☐ Stockholm on $50 a Day (avail. Dec. '91)	$13.00

FROMMER'S FAMILY GUIDES

☐ California with Kids	$16.95	☐ San Francisco with Kids	$17.00
☐ Los Angeles with Kids	$17.00	☐ Washington, D.C., with Kids (avail. Jan	
☐ New York City with Kids (avail. Jan '92)	$18.00	'92)	$17.00

SPECIAL EDITIONS

☐ Beat the High Cost of Travel	$6.95	☐ Marilyn Wood's Wonderful Weekends	
☐ Bed & Breakfast—N. America	$14.95	(CT, DE, MA, NH, NJ, NY, PA, RI, VT)	$11.95
☐ Caribbean Hideaways	$16.00	☐ Motorist's Phrase Book (Fr/Ger/Sp)	$4.95
☐ Honeymoon Destinations (US, Mex &		☐ The New World of Travel (annual by	
Carib)	$14.95	Arthur Frommer for savvy travelers)	$16.95

(TURN PAGE FOR ADDITONAL BOOKS AND ORDER FORM)

0891492

| ☐ Paris Rendez-Vous . . . .$10.95 | ☐ Travel Diary and Record Book. . . . .$5.95 |
| ☐ Swap and Go (Home Exchanging) . . . . .$10.95 | ☐ Where to Stay USA (from $3 to $30 a night). . . . .$13.95 |

FROMMER'S TOURING GUIDES

(Color illustrated guides that include walking tours, cultural and historic sites, and practical information)

☐ Amsterdam. $10.95	☐ New York $10.95
☐ Australia $12.95	☐ Paris $8.95
☐ Brazil $10.95	☐ Rome. $10.95
☐ Egypt. $8.95	☐ Scotland. $9.95
☐ Florence $8.95	☐ Thailand $12.95
☐ Hong Kong $10.95	☐ Turkey $10.95
☐ London $12.95	☐ Venice $8.95

GAULT MILLAU

(The only guides that distinguish the truly superlative from the merely overrated)

☐ The Best of Chicago $15.95	☐ The Best of Los Angeles $16.95
☐ The Best of Florida $17.00	☐ The Best of New England $15.95
☐ The Best of France $16.95	☐ The Best of New Orleans. $16.95
☐ The Best of Germany $18.00	☐ The Best of New York $16.95
☐ The Best of Hawaii $16.95	☐ The Best of Paris $16.95
☐ The Best of Hong Kong $16.95	☐ The Best of San Francisco $16.95
☐ The Best of Italy. $16.95	☐ The Best of Thailand. $17.95
☐ The Best of London $16.95	☐ The Best of Toronto $17.00
☐ The Best of Washington, D.C. $16.95	

THE REAL GUIDES

(Opinionated, politically aware guides for youthful budget-minded travelers)

☐ Amsterdam $9.95	☐ Mexico. $11.95
☐ Berlin. $11.95	☐ Morocco $12.95
☐ Brazil $13.95	☐ New York $9.95
☐ California & the West Coast $11.95	☐ Paris $9.95
☐ Czechoslovakia $13.95	☐ Peru. $12.95
☐ France $12.95	☐ Poland $13.95
☐ Germany $13.95	☐ Portugal. $10.95
☐ Greece $13.95	☐ San Francisco $11.95
☐ Guatemala $13.95	☐ Scandinavia $14.95
☐ Hong Kong $11.95	☐ Spain $12.95
☐ Hungary $12.95	☐ Turkey $12.95
☐ Ireland $12.95	☐ Venice $11.95
☐ Italy. $13.95	☐ Women Travel $12.95
☐ Kenya. $12.95	☐ Yugoslavia $12.95

ORDER NOW!

In U.S. include $2 shipping UPS for 1st book; $1 ea. add'l book. Outside U.S. $3 and $1, respectively.

Allow four to six weeks for delivery in U.S., longer outside U.S. We discourage rush order service, but orders arriving with shipping fees plus a $15 surcharge will be handled as rush orders.

Enclosed is my check or money order for $_____

NAME_____

ADDRESS_____

CITY_____ STATE_____ ZIP_____

0891492